CUBA AND AFRICA, 1959–1994

CUBA AND AFRICA, 1959–1994

WRITING AN ALTERNATIVE ATLANTIC HISTORY

EDITED BY
GIULIA BONACCI, ADRIEN DELMAS AND KALI ARGYRIADIS

WITS UNIVERSITY PRESS

Published in South Africa by:
Wits University Press
1 Jan Smuts Avenue
Johannesburg 2001

www.witspress.co.za

First published 2020

http://dx.doi.org.10.18772/22020116338

978-1-77614-633-8 (Paperback)
978-1-77614-637-6 (Hardback)
978-1-77614-634-5 (Web PDF)
978-1-77614-635-2 (EPUB)
978-1-77614-636-9 (Mobi)

This book was published with the support of the Fondation Maison des Sciences de l'Homme (FMSH) and the French Institute of South Africa-Research (IFAS-Recherche, Johannesburg). Under the authority of the French ministry of foreign affairs and the French National Centre for Scientific Research (CNRS), IFAS promotes research in the humanities and social sciences about southern Africa and within this framework supports scientific cooperation.

Project manager: Simon Chislett
Copyeditor: Russell Martin
Proofreader: Inga Norenius
Indexer: Sanet le Roux
Cover design: Hybrid Creative
Typeset in 10 point Minion Pro

CONTENTS

FIGURES AND TABLE

FOREWORD

Shamil Jeppie
University of Cape Town

In the early 2000s I had the fortune to travel regularly to wonderful places, like Timbuktu, for instance, on the banks of the Niger River in the north of the Republic of Mali. As it was rather isolated at this time, without any road connecting it to a large city and with only irregular flights in and out of the place, many of the locals knew in no time who had newly arrived in town. At that time, it was relatively safe to travel overland in those parts. Adventurous tourists arrived for a quick visit and ticked it off their wish lists. Whenever a fresh load of travellers arrived, kids would rush to the hotels to take the newcomers around. After sunset we would go for long strolls around the dimly lit town.

Since I was a fairly regular visitor to the town, my friends had to find new attractions to show me. On two separate occasions they took me and my fellow travellers to meet two recently arrived people – not tourists but residents – a man and a woman. They were from Cuba and were medical doctors serving at the local hospital, where they had a scheduled two-year stay. I had often wondered what the state hospital close to the Sankoré mosque might look like on the inside, but I never ventured there. The two doctors from the Caribbean island, however, knew all about it. Apart from Spanish the doctors probably spoke some French, but that was not going to take them very far with their patients. They would have had translators with them but they also picked up a smattering of the local Songhai language, at least so it seemed from the banter they were engaged in at the makeshift restaurant where we met. As the ancient radio on the counter played wonderful Malian music non-stop in the background, the doctors appeared totally at home speaking Spanish-accented French and Songhai – peppered with well-known Arabic phrases – with the locals in the rather ramshackle eating-drinking-meeting place.

They were only two of the far larger number of Cuban doctors in Mali and, indeed, in many other parts of the continent. Cuban relations with African countries did not rest on short-term economic interest or longer-term political gain. For traditional international relations experts, Cuban foreign policy was, and remains, hard to explain in terms of the standard rubrics they use. Instead, there was always a deep and genuine interest in the idea of Pan-African solidarity rooted in Cuba's own history of colonial domination, slavery and resistance. Right into the early 2000s South Africa did not even have an embassy in Bamako and there were more Cuban embassies across the continent than South African ones.

I had, of course, known that Cuban doctors served all over the continent. Even in South Africa, which had numerous medical schools and highly developed, albeit uneven, medical infrastructure, unlike the thinly stretched and basic set-up in Mali, Cuban doctors were brought in to serve in rural communities. And students from South Africa have gone to study on the island, with the first medical graduates now back in the country. But I was enormously impressed that I could meet Cuban medics even in the fabled 'furthest place' called Timbuktu.

As a young South African coming to political consciousness in the 1980s, one could not but have a high regard for Cuban assistance to the liberation struggles on the continent and especially in southern Africa. I still clearly recall the celebrations at political rallies when speakers would mention the apartheid military's defeat at Cuito Cuanavale in 1988 as signalling a turning point for the apartheid state. Our sense of global strategic affairs was heightened by such discussions of the impact of military matters further north in the subcontinent and the involvement of Cuba under the revolutionary leadership of Fidel Castro in all of this. Cuban engagement in the civil war in Angola can easily form the beginning and end of any discussion on Cuba and Africa, but more than a decade before its 1975 entry into the conflict Cuba had supported liberation struggles on the continent. In 1959 the country achieved its own liberation after a long insurgency against a decrepit military dictatorship; and barely two years later it started sending civilian, humanitarian missions to the continent. In a highly tense and costly Cold War context, Cuba's commitment to Africa was without peer. It did not begin with military intervention, even in Angola, but in supportive roles, particularly medical missions, as the chapters in this volume show. The military dimension has been closely studied, particularly its decisive role in southern Africa between 1975 and 1990. This collection goes far beyond that, however, and therefore provides a refreshing and expansive opening of vistas on the Cuba–Africa relationship.

If anti-racism and non-racialism defined the struggle against apartheid locally in the 1980s, then the ethos of anti-imperialism and internationalism shaped our perspective of struggles on a global scale. The small island of Cuba, which was blockaded by the most powerful military in the world, demonstrated in practice what anti-imperialism and internationalism meant. Under Fidel Castro it selflessly supported, in word and deed, unlike any other country – certainly of its size – the forces of liberation in Africa. President Nelson Mandela's 1991 visit to Havana was one of his first trips after his release from prison and an appropriate salute to the Cuban role in Africa.

Of course, there was and is much more to Cuba than solidarity. There were multiple, intertwined strands of connection and involvement embracing elites and ordinary citizens such as the artists and musicians who crossed the Atlantic.

Reading the chapters in this volume introduced me to, and deepened for me, insights into a range of issues and perspectives on Cuba and Africa that I would not otherwise have had. It gives us a big screen in full high-quality colour – the continental context – and at the same time a micro-level view against which I see those two Cuban doctors in that dimly lit, warm Timbuktu night.

ACKNOWLEDGEMENTS

An edited collection is always a collective work, and *Cuba and Africa, 1959–1994* is by no means an exception. Discussion of the papers was launched in May 2016, on the occasion of a conference we organised over two days at the Institute for Humanities in Africa (HUMA) at the University of Cape Town, South Africa. We want to take the opportunity to thank all the colleagues who contributed to the wealth of those two days, including those whose chapters are published here of course, as well as Jean Albergel, Yonas Ashine, Emma Gobin, Nahayeilli B. Juárez Huet, Agustin Laó Montes, José Luis Martin Romero, Marzia Milazzo and Karo Moret Miranda. In addition to our warm host, Prof. Shamil Jeppie, we were supported by a number of institutions, including the French Institute of South Africa (IFAS), the Institute of Research for Development (IRD, France), the Research Unit Migrations and Society (URMIS, UMR205), the Fondation Maison des Sciences de l'Homme (FMSH), the French Centre for Ethiopian Studies (CFEE, Addis Ababa), the University of Havana, and the Instituto Cubano de Antropología (Cuban Institute of Anthropology, ICAN, Havana). A year later, in 2017, a workshop co-organised by FMSH and by URMIS, UMR205 was hosted by the French Ministry of Research in Paris. This represented a unique occasion to discuss the book project with Pablo Rodríguez Ruiz, Laëtitia Atlani-Duault, Jean-Pierre Dozon, Bernard Grau and Nelson Vallejo-Gomez. Last but not least, we are grateful to our commissioning editor Roshan Cader, to Wits University Press and to the anonymous reviewers who have supported this project with a keen eye and a sense of purpose.

ACRONYMS AND ABBREVIATIONS

ACYC	Asociación cultural Yoruba de Cuba / Yoruba Cultural Association of Cuba
AFSCME	American Federation of State, County and Municipal Employees (USA)
ALN	Armée de libération nationale / National Liberation Army (Algeria)
ANC	African National Congress (Republic of South Africa)
APL	Armée populaire de libération / People's Army of Liberation (Congo-Kinshasa)
CATC	Confédération africaine des travailleurs croyants / African Confederation of Believing Workers (Congo-Brazzaville)
CEAO	Centro de Estudos Afro-Orientais / Centre for Afro-Oriental Studies (Brazil)
CFN	Conjunto folklórico nacional de Cuba / National Folklore Ensemble of Cuba
CGTA	Confédération générale des travailleurs africains / General Confederation of African Workers (Congo-Brazzaville)
CIA	Central Intelligence Agency (USA)
CID-FAR	Centro de información de la defensa de las Fuerzas Armadas Revolucionarias / Centre of Information for the Armed Revolutionary Forces (Cuba)
CNL	Conseil national de libération / National Council of Liberation (Congo-Kinshasa)
CPSU	Communist Party of the Soviet Union
CSR	Conseil suprême de la révolution / Supreme Council of the Revolution (Congo-Kinshasa)
DGI	Dirección general de inteligencia / Cuban Intelligence Agency
EGREM	Empresa de grabaciones y ediciones musicales / Musical Recording and Publishing Company (Cuba)
ENTV	Établissement national de télévision / National Public Television (Algeria)
FAPLA	Forças armadas populares de libertação de Angola / People's Armed Forces of Liberation of Angola

FESTAC	Deuxième festival mondial des arts nègres / Second World Black and African Festival of Arts and Culture (1977, Lagos, Nigeria)
FFS	Front des forces socialistes / Socialist Forces Front (Algeria)
FIS	Front islamique du salut / Islamic Salvation Front (Algeria)
FLEC	Front de libération de l'enclave de Cabinda / Front for the Liberation of the Enclave of Cabinda
FLN	Front de libération nationale / National Liberation Front (Algeria)
FNLA	Frente Nacional para a libertação de Angola / National Front for the Liberation of Angola
FRELIMO	Frente de libertação de Moçambique / Mozambique Liberation Front
GICI/GII	Gabinete de intercambio e cooperação internacional / Gabinete de intercambio internacional / Department for International Cooperation of the Ministry of Education (Angola)
GPRA	Gouvernement provisoire de la république d'Algérie / Provisional Government of the Algerian Republic
ICAN	Instituto Cubano de antropología / Cuban Institute of Anthropology
ICAP	Instituto Cubano de amistad con los pueblos / Cuban Institute of Friendship with Peoples
IEF	Instituto de etnología y folklore / Institute of Ethnology and Folklore (Cuba)
IRIC	Institut des relations internationales du Cameroun / International Relations Institute of Cameroon
JMNR	Jeunesse du mouvement national de la révolution / Youth of the National Movement of the Revolution (Congo-Brazzaville)
MDA	Mouvement pour la démocratie en Algérie / Movement for Democracy in Algeria
MED	Ministério da educação / Ministry of Education (Angola)
MINREX	Ministerio de relaciones exteriores / Ministry of Foreign Affairs (Cuba)
MLS	Mouvement de libération de la Saguia el-Hamra et du Rio de Oro / Liberation Movement of Saguia el-Hamra and of Rio de Oro (Western Sahara)
MNC–L	Mouvement national congolais – Patrice Lumumba / National Congolese Movement – Patrice Lumumba (Congo-Kinshasa)
MNR	Mouvement national de la révolution / National Movement of the Revolution (Congo-Brazzaville)
MNRG	Mouvement national de la révolution gabonaise / National Movement of the Gabonese Revolution
MPLA	Movimento popular de libertação de angola / Popular Movement for the Liberation of Angola
OAU	Organisation of African Unity

OSPAAAL	Organización de solidaridad con los pueblos de Africa, Asia y América Latina / Organisation of Solidarity with the Peoples of Asia, Africa and Latin America
PAGS	Parti de l'avant-garde socialiste / Socialist Vanguard Party (Algeria)
PAIGC	Partido Africano para a independência da Guiné e Cabo Verde / African Party for the Independence of Guinea and Cape Verde
PCC	Partido comunista de Cuba / Communist Party of Cuba
PUN	Partido único nacional / United National Party (Equatorial Guinea)
PUNT	Partido único nacional de los trabajadores / United National Workers' Party (Equatorial Guinea)
RCA	Radio Corporation of America (USA)
RPA	República popular de Angola / People's Republic of Angola
SEGESA	Sociedad de electricidad de Guinea Ecuatorial / National Electricity Company of Equatorial Guinea
SIECSA	Sociedad mercantil servicios de ingeniería eléctrica / Power Engineering Services (Cuba)
SWAPO	South West Africa People's Organisation (Namibia)
TNC	Teatro nacional de Cuba / National Theatre of Cuba
UCT	University of Cape Town (Republic of South Africa)
UDEAC	Union douanière et économique de l'Afrique centrale / Customs and Economic Union of Central Africa
UGTA	Union générale des travailleurs algériens / General Union of Algerian Workers
UN	United Nations
UNEAC	Unión nacional de escritores y artistas de Cuba / National Union of Writers and Artists of Cuba
UNESCO	United Nations Educational, Scientific and Cultural Organization
UNITA	União nacional para a independência total de Angola / National Union for the Total Independence of Angola
UPC	Union des populations du Cameroun / Union of the Peoples of Cameroon
US / USA	United States of America
USSR	Union of Soviet Socialist Republics
ZANU	Zimbabwe African National Union

TIMELINE OF HISTORICAL EVENTS

1503	First mention of the introduction of a slave of African origin into Cuba
1804	Independence of Haiti
1847	Independence of Liberia
1868	Start of the Ten Years' War in Cuba
1873	Last known landing of a slave ship in Cuba
1886	Abolition of slavery in Cuba
1895	Start of the last Cuban War of Independence
1898	US protectorate and military occupation of Cuba (until 1902)
1900	First Pan-African Conference in London
1902	Foundation of the Republic of Cuba
1920	First Congress of the Peoples of the East, in Baku
1922	Foundation of the Union of Soviet Socialist Republics (USSR)
1937	Foundation by Fernando Ortiz in Cuba of the Sociedad de Estudios Afrocubanos and the Asociación Nacional contra las Discriminaciones Racistas
1953	Attack on Moncada Barracks that launched the revolution in Cuba
1955	Bandung Conference
1956	Nationalisation of Suez Canal
	Independence of Tunisia and Morocco
1957	Independence of Ghana
1958	Independence of Guinea
	All-African Peoples' Conference in Accra
1959	Victory of the Cuban Revolution
1960	Sharpeville massacre in South Africa
	Castro visit to the UN in New York
	Independence of Cameroon, Senegal, Togo, Madagascar, Congo, Somalia, Benin, Niger, Burkina Faso, Ivory Coast, Chad, Central Africa, Mali, Nigeria, Mauritania and the Republic of Congo

1961	Break of diplomatic relations between Cuba and the US
	Bay of Pigs failed invasion
	Beginning of Angolan War for Independence
	Recognition of the Provisional Government of the Algerian Republic by Cuba, delivery of weapons to the National Liberation Army (ALN)
	Independence of Sierra Leone and Tanzania
	Assassination of Patrice Lumumba
	Foundation of the Instituto de Etnología y Folklore in Cuba
1962	First US total embargo on Cuba
	Cuban Missile Crisis
	Visit of Algerian President Ben Bella to Cuba
	Cuban American pilots in Congo-Léopoldville
	Foundation of the Victoria de Girón School of Medicine in Havana
	Foundation of the Conjunto Folklórico Nacional (CFN) in Cuba
	Independence of Rwanda, Burundi, Algeria and Uganda
1963	Castro visit to the Soviet Union
	First Cuban medical mission in Algeria
	Cuban mission in Congo-Brazzaville
	Che Guevara in Algiers
	The Sand War between Algeria and Morocco; 'Operation Dignity': contingent of 686 officers and soldiers, 22 tanks and artillery sent by Cuba to defend Algeria from Moroccan invasion
1964	Mali–Cuba cultural convention
	First tour of the CFN in Africa; ethnographic mission of León Argeliers in Mali, Ghana and Nigeria for the Instituto de Etnología y Folklore (IEF)
	Cuban mission in Guinea-Bissau
1965	Guevara speech in Algiers on the occasion of the Afro-Asian solidarity conference
	Launch of a revolutionary movement in eastern Congo by Guevara; contact made by Jorge Risquet with the Popular Movement for the Liberation of Angola (MPLA)
	General Mobutu launched coup in Congo
1966	First Tricontinental conference of solidarity between the peoples of Africa, Asia and Latin America in Havana
	Cuban military support for Guinea-Bissau war of independence
	World Festival of Black Arts in Dakar

1967	Resumption of diplomatic relations between Algeria and Cuba
	Che Guevara captured and executed by the Bolivian army
1968	Prague Spring, Czechoslovakia
	Independence of Equatorial Guinea
1969	Pan-African Festival in Algiers
1972	Castro's first African tour, to Conakry and Algeria
	Diplomatic relations between Cuba and Equatorial Guinea
1973	Independence of Guinea-Bissau
1974	Carnation Revolution in Portugal
1975	Angolan Independence Day set for 11 November 1975
	South African troops occupied southern Angola; launch of Operation Carlota in Angola by Cuba
1976	UN Security Council condemnation of South Africa's role in Angola but no mention of Cuba's intervention
	Soweto uprising in South Africa
	Signing of the Economic, Scientific and Technical Cooperation Framework Agreement (Cuba–Angola)
1977	Cuban military support for Ethiopia in the Ogaden War against Somalia
	Second World Black and African Festival of Arts and Culture (FESTAC) in Lagos
1978	UN Security Council Resolution 435, demanding South African withdrawal from Namibia and free elections
1980	Independence of Zimbabwe; launch of South Africa's Total Onslaught against the Front Line States
1981	Ronald Reagan elected US president; linking Cuban withdrawal from Angola to the Namibian peace process proposed by Chester Crocker
	Operation Protea by South Africa in Angola
1984	Soviet military aid to Cuba and the MPLA
	Start of Cuban ethnographic fieldwork in Angola
1986	Creation of an Anti-Apartheid Committee in Cuba
1987	Visit of the Ife Ooni in Cuba
1988	Battle of Cuito Cuanavale; final Cuban–South African clashes of the Angolan War
	New York Peace Accords signed by Angola, South Africa and Cuba, providing for the implementation of UN Resolution 435, and the withdrawal of all Cuban and South African forces from Angola and Namibia

1989	First Namibian free elections
	Berlin Wall came down
1990	Independence of Namibia
	Nelson Mandela released from prison; visit to Algiers
	Period of transition in South Africa and dismantling of apartheid
1991	Last Cuban troopship left Angola
	Mandela's official visit to Cuba
	Beginning of the Algerian civil war
	Beginning of the Cuban economic crisis or *período especial*
1994	First free elections in South Africa

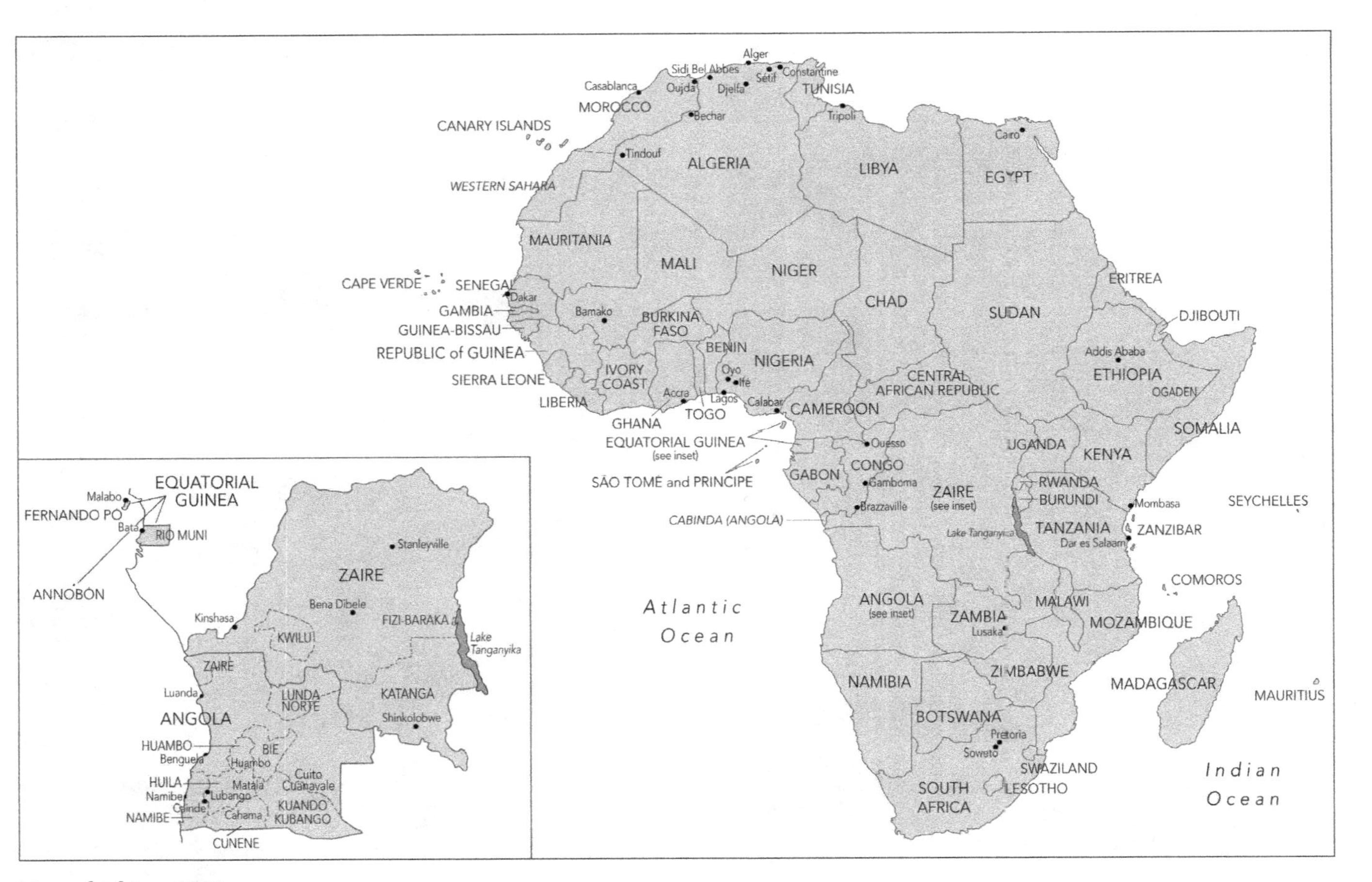

Map of Africa, 1994

INTRODUCTION

Reconfiguring the Cuba–Africa Encounter

Kali Argyriadis, Giulia Bonacci and Adrien Delmas

The relations between Cuba and Africa took shape rapidly after the Cuban Revolution of 1959, at a time when the struggles for African independence were at their height. In a world marked by the Cold War, these relations set the stage for new forms of international solidarity that still remain misunderstood.[1] Admittedly, the Cuban presence in Africa was but one of several theatres of Cuban internationalism, from Latin America to Asia, of which the Tricontinental conference and the creation of the Organisation of Solidarity with the Peoples of Asia, Africa and Latin America (OSPAAAL), in January 1966, represented the high points. But the intensity and especially the consequences of Cuban engagement on the African continent make these features distinctive. Following the 1959 revolution, there was an immediate rapprochement with African revolutionary and independence movements, and succeeding years opened a new era in the centuries-old history of Atlantic relations. Cuba's engagement in Africa was conducted in the name of 'principles, convictions and blood', as Fidel Castro, its principal instigator, pronounced in 1975,[2] and took so many different forms – political, military, social, educational, economic, medical, humanitarian, cultural, linguistic, and so on – that it seems presumptuous to attempt a complete account. Without making any claim to exhaustiveness, this book seeks to outline this half-century between Cuba and Africa and to suggest an initial overall view.

Nelson Mandela's homage to Cuba, delivered at Matanzas, Cuba, in 1991, the year after his release from an apartheid prison, reminds us of the strength of a link that for decades nourished imaginations all over the continent:

> We have long wanted to visit your country and express the many feelings that we have about the Cuban revolution, about the role of Cuba in Africa, southern Africa, and the world. The Cuban people hold a special place in the hearts of the people of Africa. The Cuban internationalists have contributed to African independence, freedom, and justice, unparalleled for its principled and selfless character.[3]

In the words of South Africa's first black president, Cuba participated, more than any other nation, in the decades of struggle for African independence and the definitive ousting of colonialism on the continent. The outlines of this involvement in the anti-imperialist armed struggle are well known.[4] In December 1961, a Cuban ship arrived in Casablanca, Morocco, to supply weapons to the Algerian National Liberation Front (FLN), which was fighting against the French colonial occupation. It departed carrying wounded and orphans from the war of independence. Two years later, some 700 Cuban soldiers arrived to fight alongside the FLN, this time against Morocco's attempted incursion into Algerian territory. In 1965, Congo-Brazzaville asked for armed Cuban support, while a group led by Ernesto 'Che' Guevara tried, in vain, to launch a revolutionary movement in eastern Congo. Cuban military assistance in the war of independence in Guinea-Bissau, from 1966 to 1974, was more effective, as was the commitment to support Ethiopian forces against Somalia in the Ogaden war of 1977–8. But these episodes represent no more than an initial, one-off wave of support for wars of independence and international conflicts on the continent. The second wave was on a completely different scale, and saw tens of thousands of Cuban soldiers mobilised in support of Angolan independence and in the civil war between the various Angolan liberation movements, all of them supported externally. Between 1975 and 1990, the Cuban intervention decisively affected the outcome of the largest conflict on African soil since the Second World War. It irreparably swung the balance of power in southern Africa, one of the consequences of which was that the apartheid regime, against which Cuban troops were fighting in Angola, came to an end in 1990.[5] In the light of this, Nelson Mandela's homage acquires its full meaning.

The story of Cuban military intervention in Africa has been the subject of many studies.[6] Without pretending to write a new account, but also without losing sight of it, we wish to complete the picture and to shift its focus, first of all by examining all the non-military efforts that accompanied, and formed part of, the engagement between Cuba and Africa. In this respect, the official title of Jorge Risquet, effectively in charge of the war effort from 1975, is significant: 'responsible for civil cooperation'. 'Cooperation' included various domains: humanitarian and medical, scientific and educational, cultural and artistic efforts, which accompanied, and even preceded, Cuban soldiers right from the start. In considering the many non-military sides of Cuba's African commitment, one quickly observes that the direct connections that emerged between the island and the continent go beyond single theatres of conflict and political spaces, while at the same time being closely linked to them. These non-military aspects also draw on the origins of a particular Cuban history, of whose importance it is worth reminding ourselves: a history marked by the struggle against all forms of slavery, but also by a frustrated independence from the colonial power, for which the revolution of 1959 represented, from an internal point of view, the true humanist, anti-colonial and anti-imperialist achievement. It is a history that bursts open, and then telescopes, in an entirely original way, the East–West polarity characteristic of the post-war period and gives form to the relationships that today we call 'South–South'. The Cold War, the intense global struggle for ideological supremacy between the capitalist forces led by the United States and the communist forces led by the Soviet Union, altered the global power balance. Nevertheless, on 'the periphery', particularly in Africa, nationalist movements, local struggles and the domestic dynamics of decolonisation had a considerable influence on the reconfiguration of these power relations.[7]

We have also tried to shift the history of Cuban engagement in Africa, and to observe it not only from the summits of political or military hierarchies, but also from the point of view of those who took part in it on a day-to-day basis, with profound impacts on their lives and the lives of their families. Because if this is a history played out in the diplomatic arenas of a world immersed in a Cold War, from the United Nations to the Kremlin, it is also the story of tens of thousands of individuals who crossed the Atlantic, from one side to the other, as doctors, scientists, soldiers, students, religious leaders or artists. The story of their trajectories, and of those they came into contact with, whether the Cubans who departed for Africa or the Africans who travelled to Cuba – in short, the history of the circulation of people, ideas and representations – we can approach only at the local level. This approach, which we think is instructive, opens the way to engage in a decentred analysis of the major and intimately linked historical questions of the nineteenth and twentieth centuries – colonialism and racialism.

OF OLD TIES BETWEEN CUBA AND AFRICA

Before we tackle our subject, it is useful to recall that the links between Cuba and a considerable part of the African continent are old, and, like the plantation societies of the Americas, are tied to the history of trade and slavery. At the time of the 1959 revolution, this history was still fresh in the memory. The abolition of slavery in Cuba was only declared in 1886, and the last known disembarkation of a slave ship took place in 1873.[8] Many Cuban citizens of African descent knew the origins of their parents and grandparents well and practised localised forms of their religions,[9] and the oldest could recall their past as slaves.[10] Some spoke the languages of their forefathers;[11] for example, the great singer and composer Arsenio Rodríguez (see Charlotte Grabli's chapter) learned Kikongo from his grandfather. This memory was also the memory of struggle: the revolts of runaway slaves that punctuated four centuries of colonial oppression,[12] anti-slavery rebellions, as well as the memory of inter-ethnic or transnational solidarity and, sometimes, the memory of a return to the continent. We must review certain elements of this history in order to understand things that sometimes arise suddenly, in ordinary moments, as in the accounts, experiences and speeches cited in this book.

In 1812, José Antonio Aponte, an artisan cabinetmaker, former officer in the 'black and mulatto battalions',[13] a free man of colour, was executed in Havana after being named as the ringleader of a rebellion planned against the colonial authorities on the Caribbean island. In his personal effects, the police found a library consisting of a dozen works, as well as a manuscript written in his own hand, the *libro de pinturas*, made up of 72 plates of images and texts. This work was probably destroyed, and we know of its contents today thanks only to the description given by Aponte during his five-day interrogation. Apart from showing the influence of the Haitian Revolution on the abolitionist and pro-independence tendencies of the period, the *libro de pinturas* is remarkable for its vision of a universal history centred on Africa, and in particular on Ethiopia.[14] In their way, these lost plates of Aponte from the beginning of the nineteenth century reflect all the complexity of the relationships that united the Caribbean island and the African continent. They provide a glimpse of the multiple 're-creations' of an original Africa by its descendants on the other side of the Atlantic.

The links between them and their continent of origin were never completely broken. The Atlantic slave trade, which arose at the beginning of the sixteenth century,[15] accelerated considerably following the Haitian Revolution (1791–1804).[16] A substantial part of the Cuban population of African descent was well organised.[17] Under the Spanish crown, slaves had the right to join together, according to their place of origin, in mutual aid associations called *cabildos de nacíon*, an institution established in the fourteenth century on the Iberian peninsula.[18] They could also redeem themselves and buy back their family members, even on credit, so much so that in Havana in 1820, nearly 20 per cent of the population consisted of 'free people of colour'.[19] The objective of the authorities was to maintain African inter-ethnic rivalries in the Americas by means of the *cabildos* in such a way as to prevent any unitary protest movement.[20] In Cuba, this objective was not achieved; quite the contrary, and in the nineteenth century the *cabildos* embraced the spouses, adopted children, godchildren, fellow voyagers (*caravelas*), close friends, both free and slave, *congos*, *mandingas*, *carabalí*, *lucumí*, *iyesá*, *mina*, *gangá*, *makuá* or *arará*.[21] They included as many 'blacks' as 'mulattos', and sometimes even Spanish and Chinese indentured labourers, prisoners of a debt they could not repay that made them, in fact, neo-slaves.[22] Many cultural and religious practices of African origin were transmitted within the *cabildos*,[23] and gradually a new structure of kinship was constructed, abandoning in part the logic of lineage in order to privilege various modes of 'kinship by affinity'.[24] Many *cabildos* also played an important role in anti-slavery and anti-colonial uprisings. The Spanish government realised the threat they represented, and subjected these institutions to severe repression, including forced evangelisation and confiscation of their property, before finally banning them in 1888 and preventing them from transforming themselves into mutual aid and assistance societies or remaining in the informal sector.[25]

At the home of José Antonio Aponte, who was linked to the *cabildo* Changó Teddún (devoted to the divinity Changó, native to the town of Oyo in present-day Nigeria), the police found ritual objects, arms and the *libro de pinturas*, in which portraits of the Haitian heroes Jean-Jacques Dessalines, Toussaint Louverture and Henri Christophe were placed side by side with representations of biblical Ethiopia. And if Aponte seems to have been a descendant of a Lucumí slave, his comrades, imprisoned and beheaded with him, were themselves linked to some of the other *cabildos* and thus, perhaps, to Masonic lodges, which played an important role in the Haitian Revolution. By extending this analysis, one might identify the traditions of social organisation that lay at the origin of the Pan-African idea, which spread throughout the Americas in this period, or even the premises of the internationalism of the oppressed so dear to Che Guevara. In any case, this was how Cuban historians of the 1960s chose to portray this 'proto-martyr',[26] and it is in this way that the preamble to the constitution of the Republic of Cuba, enacted under the revolution, expresses the continuity of successive struggles and acts of resistance carried out by the victims of colonialism and imperialism:

> WE, CUBAN CITIZENS,
> heirs and continuators of the creative work and the traditions of struggle, firmness, heroism and sacrifice fostered by our ancestors;
> by the Indians who preferred extermination to submission;
> by the slaves who rebelled against their masters;
> . . .
> by those who, en masse, accomplished heroic internationalist missions;[27]

Apart from the comradeship shown between fellow oppressed on the island, other forms of solidarity would sometimes have spread their wings, quite explicitly, in the transatlantic world. The traffic between Cuba and Africa was not only in an east–west direction. In the second half of the nineteenth century, Spanish possessions in Africa, particularly the island of Fernando Po, today part of Equatorial Guinea, were also used by the crown as sites of colonisation, where Cubans 'of colour' and freed slaves regarded as more resistant to the climate and to tropical diseases would be sent. Then, between 1866 and 1897, they served as places of detention and deportation for prisoners of all skin colours – including a considerable number of members of the male secret society Abakuá, which originated in Calabar – some of whom would later return to Cuba.[28] Finally, after the treaty banning the slave trade, signed by Britain in 1807, and by Spain in 1817, captives from slave ships intercepted by British vessels off the Cuban coast were typically brought ashore on the island and subjected to forced labour for ten years, under the terms of which they acquired the status of 'emancipated'.[29] Many thousands of them, as well as 'free people of colour', were thus able to apply and to obtain from the British crown, after years of privation and bargaining with the Cuban authorities, the right to embark with their families for the coast of Africa (essentially Lagos, via Jamaica and Britain). Some of them kept in touch by letter with family members who stayed in Cuba, or who returned to the island.[30]

Today, thanks to a number of studies,[31] we understand the importance of the role of these 'returnees', creoles and yellows (*amaros*), political deportees, freed captives and slaves emancipated or redeemed by themselves, peasants from the southern United States or from Jamaica, in the founding and construction of the national identity of African states. The birth of Sierra Leone and Liberia, driven by Britain and the United States from the early nineteenth century, served as an intellectual reservoir for the training of West African nationalism; the urban and cosmopolitan cultures of Ghana, Benin,

Nigeria and Kenya were influenced by the arrival of 'Brazilians' and 'free Africans' in the mid-nineteenth century; this was also the case in Ethiopia, which welcomed returnees from the end of the nineteenth century. Research on the circulation between Africa and its diasporas has also opened up an exciting field, that of the 'return of the boomerang of slavery', to use the term coined by the Trinidadian Pan-Africanist George Padmore, or another post-slavery history, which brings to light extraordinary individual stories and the strength of the links – real, affective, filial, political, cultural and not only imaginary – that unite people of the same lineage or ethnicity from one part of the Atlantic world to another.[32]

OVERCOMING RACIALISM?

Starting from the 'War of Ten Years' (1868–79), the whole history of the Cuban independence struggle is marked by the massive participation of slaves and 'free people of colour' in the pro-independence forces, and by their promotion to officer rank. The revolutionary historiography takes up this theme abundantly, which is presented as a founding element in the emergence of a Cuban national consciousness that would, ideally, at this moment in history, transcend racial divisions. This was also what Fidel Castro recalled, in the speech cited earlier, delivered on 22 December 1975, soon after the launch of Operation Carlota in Angola:

> The imperialists mean to forbid us from helping our Angolan brothers. But we must say to the Yankees not to forget that we are not simply a Latin American country, but also a Latino-African country. The blood of Africa flows copiously in our veins. And from Africa, as slaves, came many of our ancestors to this land. And how they fought, these slaves, and how they fought in the liberation army of our country. We are the brothers of the Africans, and for Africans we are prepared to struggle![33]

Though less well known outside Latin America, the truly internationalist engagement of those who thought and wrote about independence should also be emphasised. This intellectual and militant filiation, obvious for the revolutionary government of the 1960s, has not always been understood by its European and African interlocutors or by its critics, who have often restricted their analyses to the field of the history of socialist movements and the context of the Cold War. But in the late nineteenth century, at the time when the European great powers were sharing out the 'African cake', the last Spanish colonies became the cradle of a pioneering transnational anti-imperialist movement. In an extension of the ideals of Simón Bolívar, who 'from 1813 saw the relationship between the liberation of the American colonies and the emancipation of the Afro-Asiatic colonies',[34] the mulatto general Antonio Maceo and the founder of the Cuban Revolutionary Party (1892), José Martí, envisaged the goals of liberation within the context of solidarity with the rest of the Antilles, which were themselves struggling to achieve their independence or safeguard their sovereignty in the face of an increasingly encroaching North American neighbour. A project for an Antillean confederation, including, initially, Haiti, the Dominican Republic, Puerto Rico and Cuba, was even elaborated, at the urging of the Puerto Rican Ramón Emeterio Betances, and with the support of other eminent political figures, such as the Puerto Rican Eugenio María de Hostos, the Dominican Gregorio Luperón and the Haitian Anténor Firmin. Humanist, 'anti-racist by its content, multiracial by its expression',[35] this project advocated both the elimination of social inequality and access to health care and education for all. To paraphrase the celebrated words of José Martí, a radical critic of the very notion of race,[36] beyond 'our America' the homeland for which the *mambises*[37] – the soldiers of the liberation army – eventually struggled was humanity itself.

This development was in many respects a prefigurement, as it was not until the end of the Second World War that the notion of race was decisively discredited, this time by the participation of scientific and intellectual elites in UNESCO. It was, however, cut short in 1898 by American military intervention in Cuba and the annexation of Puerto Rico. For the American occupier, the Cubans – all the Cubans – even if they looked like whites, had 'negroid'[38] traits. The Platt Amendment, ratified in 1901, enshrined the island's economic dependence and the United States' right of military intervention; article V required the Cuban authorities to 'sanitise' the island and its inhabitants, particularly to protect the ports and population of the southern United States from epidemics and infections. On the island, the black and mulatto veterans of the revolutionary army suffered denigration and exclusion from power, while a policy of de-Africanisation and the whitening of the population was put in place by means of a system of subsidised immigration from Europe and the Canary Islands.[39] The corollary of this strategy was a hunt for African 'sorcerers', accused of perpetrating ritual crimes on white children: they were pursued, incarcerated, deprived of their ritual objects and instruments, and sometimes even executed or lynched.[40] The first half of the twentieth century in Cuba was thus marked by ferocious segregation,[41] and Africa became, even for its descendants, the paradigm of a shameful barbarity from which it suited the most educated people, including those 'of colour', to distinguish themselves absolutely.

In this context, direct links with the continent became quite tenuous, limited to intrafamilial or spiritual transmission, that is, carried out within the framework of initiatory linkages of *santería*, Ifá or *palo-monte*, which, themselves, did not always have a relation to the ethnic origins of the practitioners. However, from the 1920s, in reaction to North American interference on the island, there developed an Afro-'recentred' imaginary of Cubanism in literary and artistic circles, influenced by both African art and the cultural movement of the Harlem Renaissance. Its adherents were interested particularly in the stories, songs and costumes of African descendants in Cuba, and presented them as an integral part of the national culture.[42] A crucial role was played by the lawyer and anthropologist Fernando Ortiz, who eventually became involved in a patriotic and anti-racist struggle.[43]

The movement consolidated itself after the dictatorship of Gerardo Machado (1925–33), and the revolutionary struggles of the early 1930s, and in 1937 Fernando Ortiz, together with the poet Nicolás Guillén, founded the Sociedad de Estudios Afrocubanos (Society of Afro-Cuban Studies). The Society encouraged its informants, musicians and dancers to appear on the stage of prestigious national theatres. At the same time, it declared its opposition to the fact that the same informants were contributing to the popularisation of what the Society saw as an inauthentic and commercialised version of the 'Afro-Cuban' repertoire, and to its massive diffusion in the market via records, cinema and tourist shows.[44] These years also saw the flowering of a renewed movement demanding an end to segregation, led by black and mulatto journalists and essayists who refused to be labelled and folklorised under the 'Afro-Cuban' heading.[45] This initiative continued during the 1940s and 1950s, and attempted to combine, not without contradictions or ambiguity,[46] the struggle against racial discrimination, the affirmation of a Cuban identity (including a part assumed to be of African cultural origin), the fight for sovereignty, the construction of a cohesive nation rejecting racial divisions, and the idea of social progress. For Cuban intellectuals of this period, the debate turned entirely towards the Americas and Europe; they still largely misunderstood the ideas and texts of their contemporary African peers.

This brief historical summary allows us to understand that, for its subjects, the Cuban Revolution of 1959 represented both a radical break and a continuity. It was a major break because the direct internationalist engagement of its leaders, after bitter failures in Caribbean countries,[47] quickly turned, without any precedent, to the African continent, which at the time was at the height of its anti-colonial and independence struggle. Although these engagements were also pursued in Latin America, and even once in Asia, it is really towards Africa, where it met with relative success, that the Cuban revolutionary government massively concentrated its efforts during the three decades that followed its arrival in power. As a result certain authors have analysed, for example in the light of the Cuban engagement in Angola, the evolving construction of a Cuban identity embracing a more Afrocentric vision.[48] There was also continuity in that from the late nineteenth century the independence project had contained the idea of an anti-colonial internationalism,[49] and the Africanness of Cuban identity had been thought through by the generation preceding the revolutionaries. Moreover, this generation was immediately given responsibility for setting up institutions for research and artistic diffusion valorising this African contribution, in both its aesthetic and resistance dimensions.[50] Finally, it was the logical extension of a familial and religious heritage, anchored in the memories and practices of a section of the Cuban population, that became the common heritage of almost everyone, thanks to the institutions produced by those of working-class background and the people who filled them, and in spite of a growing materialist ethos from the end of the 1960s and a resurgence of racism in the 1990s.[51]

In other words, if we can discern in the matrix of slavery and in the history of the relations between Cuba and Africa elements that shed light on the specificity of the Cuban engagement in Africa after 1959, it is right to consider, above all, the long history of the shared struggles, on the island, against all forms of enslavement. For this we need to go beyond the divisions imposed by class, race, even nationality, and beyond, too, the constant reconstruction of the links of mutual aid and of transethnic and religious filiation. We hope that the exchanges described in this book will provide readers less familiar with Cuban history with insight into certain implicit dimensions of what took place, from the Cuban point of view.

THE 'HISTORY OF PEOPLE WITHOUT HISTORY'

The goal of this book is not to explore the place of Africa in the construction of pre-revolutionary Cuban identity, though this is never far from our concerns. Indeed, our goal is to understand what played out later on – the reopening of direct relations between the island and the continent after the 1959 revolution. The contributions brought together in this book speak to the accelerated rapprochement between Cuba and Africa from 1960, which was fed largely by the history and debates outlined above, and which contributed in part to a reformulation of the knowledge and representations of Cuba on the continent. But, above all, these encounters played a direct and irreversible role within the movements for independence and sovereignty, and against colonialism and segregation, throughout the African continent. How, then, do we propose an overall view of the connections formed over five decades?

The first paradox that confronts us is this: if the literature on the Cuban engagement in Africa since 1959 continues to be enriched by increasingly in-depth, specialised and well-documented studies, these find their place only marginally in the histories of contemporary Africa.[52] In themselves, neither the presence of Che Guevara in the Congo in 1965 nor the participation of thirty thousand Cuban soldiers in the Angolan conflict allows for an appreciation of the depth, complexity and richness of the links created. From this observation comes the desire to contribute to a historiography of Africa that can account for the multiplicity of relations with Cuba: what, for example, are the links between Cuba and Mali, between Cuba and Tanzania, between Cuba and Ethiopia? In the Horn of Africa, references to the Cuban engagement are rare, even though the last great deployment of Cuban troops between 1977 and 1978 allowed the military dictatorship of Mengistu Haile Mariam to remain in power. Likewise, there are other dimensions of these exchanges that require study, beyond the military field, particularly those concerning culture, language, family life, music and religious practice. Here lies the central claim of this work: these fields offer material to reread the Cuban engagement in Africa, to grasp the formation of relationships and solidarities on levels other than international geopolitics and military history.

The chapters presented here suggest a methodological and thematic shift in the relations between Cuba and Africa in the twentieth century. We would like to offer both a global and continental perspective, and a national and local perspective.[53] Only a constant movement between these different scales or dimensions in which the actors operated, whether as doctors or musicians, permits an account of their experiences between two continents.[54] Thus, while keeping in mind the importance of the political, military and medical engagement of the Cuban government in Africa, we have chosen to let ourselves be surprised, and to attempt to grasp that which lies next to the better-known or usual accounts: 'the history of people without history', so dear to Cuban historians of the 1960s,[55] or 'history from below', through which historiography has been profoundly renewed.[56] A history presented in broad terms, composed of the living memories of a multitude of eyewitnesses, requires that we place ourselves at the level of the individuals who made it. The last Cuban soldiers to leave the African continent embarked in 1991, but many citizens of the Caribbean island stayed behind or returned. Moreover, these circulations operated in two directions, since tens of thousands of Africans studied and worked in Cuba, to say nothing of those who studied in Moscow or Leningrad, and rubbed shoulders with many Cuban students they met there.[57] Here lies the second goal of this work: to gain an 'intimate' point of view of these meetings, to counterpoise the political and diplomatic agendas with the experiences of individuals thrown into this civil cooperation.

Because it takes place over a wide area, and because there is a strong memory of Cuba's revolutionary and anti-imperialist engagement in Africa, this history is not easy to grasp. The presence of Cuban men and women all over the continent, even when this might have brought about the heroic history of independence, does not seem to have left much trace, in the sense of material traces, or vestiges. Thus, the book would like to begin to sketch the contours of an archive of Cuba in Africa.[58] A military cemetery, a monument, a museum, Freedom Park in Pretoria, 'Cuban' evenings in Zanzibar or Addis Ababa, an association of friendship of peoples or an outpost of OSPAAAL, some photographs of Ben Bella beside Che Guevara sold by strolling vendors in Algiers – all these lend weight to the observation that in Africa, unlike in Cuba, this history is not often part of the public record. Nor does it enter easily into the national histories of African states, and, with a few exceptions, it is quite simply not part of the well-established framework of academic history.

THE MANY CUBAN ENGAGEMENTS IN AFRICA

The chapters presented in this volume contribute to an understanding of the full range of experiences, at once singular, unprecedented and quotidian, of those who participated in the engagements between Cuba and Africa. Various academic disciplines are employed, and sources and texts in a number of languages and scholarly traditions are used: English, French, German, Portuguese, Spanish, as well as Yoruba and Kikongo. To grasp the importance of this engagement between Cuba and Africa, we also need to consider not only the diversity and overlapping of subjects involved, but the extent of its geographical spread. No corner of the continent was unaffected by this cooperation.

Many of the contributions propose 'to see Cuba from Africa' by zooming in on national cases, and begin by analysing the bilateral political dimensions, state to state, of who presided over and organised these connections. Emmanuel Alcaraz, for example, examines Cuba's participation in the 'anti-imperialist congress' – to use Amílcar Cabral's expression – that Algiers became immediately following independence and that brought together liberation movements from all over Africa and beyond. This first encounter with Algeria, between 1962 and 1965, seems to have set in train an engagement that would eventually extend to the four corners of the continent in the decades to come.[59] Delmas Tsafack turns to the case of Equatorial Guinea, where bilateral relations, launched in 1969, allowed Equatorial Guinea to distance itself from Spain and to pave the way for the growth of the education and health sectors, an essential stage of development for this tiny West African country. Héloïse Kiriakou and Bernardo J.C. André compare Congo-Brazzaville and Angola. They show that, far from Cuba imposing a politico-social agenda on African states, which military advantage and legitimacy would lead us to believe happened, the newly independent African governments retained a degree of autonomy and agency by engaging in political negotiations to determine the form and extent of Cuban assistance.[60]

Military and civil cooperation offered a temporal and political framework in which other relationships were deployed. These are often less visible but exciting in what they reveal about the extent of the relations between Cuba and Africa, rich in social, religious, cultural and familial circulation. If Che Guevara's sojourn in eastern Congo in 1965 is well known, the history that followed in his wake is not: 17 young Congolese guerrillas departed for Havana with Che Guevara. Michel Luntumbue brings to light their trajectories, as well as those of other Congolese, associated with the leadership of the National Council of Liberation (CNL), who followed them; he thus questions the existence and outlines of a Cuban-Congolese or 'Afro-Cuban' culture. Similarly, Pablo Rodríguez Ruiz and Kali Argyriadis look into the profiles and itineraries of another type of expert who wove links between Cuba and Africa from the 1960s, namely, researchers in the human and social sciences. Rodríguez Ruiz provides direct testimony of his experience as an ethnologist in wartime Angola, working on post-conflict reconstruction at a moment of crisis in Cuban anthropology, which was at the time being reshaped according to the Soviet model. For her part, Argyriadis returns to the role played by many important figures from the Cuban intellectual world (folklorists, historians and writers called upon to carry out diplomatic work in Nigeria during the first three decades of the revolution) in the later process of re-Africanisation of Cuban religious practices of Yoruba origin.

Music is one of the best-known bridges linking Cuba and Africa. Charlotte Grabli and Elina Djebbari explore this dimension in Mali and Congo-Kinshasa. Here again, they give body and life to the symmetrical circulations of Cuban, Malian and Congolese music and musicians, to their singular journeys, and to the transformations that they prompted, on both sides of the Atlantic, highlighting certain little-known meanderings in the transnational routes followed by the 'national' history of musical genres.

Each of these themes – military, medical, scientific or cultural – certainly deserves a complete study in its own right. But each of these points of entry shows that they cannot be considered in isolation. Music is (also) part of diplomacy, military aid (also) part of anthropological views, and religion (also) part of commercial agreements.

By focusing only on one dimension, do we not lose sight of the coherence of this engagement? Above all, do we not fail to grasp the real significance of an encounter, sometimes quite other than the political intentions that provoked it? The contribution of Christine Hatzky is particularly illuminating in this respect. In coming to grips with the Cuban military effort in the course of fifteen years in Angola, she shows the extent to which the agenda of civil cooperation, carried out by doctors and teachers, technicians and architects, came to complement the politico-military agenda. As a consequence, the image of a conflict perceived as peripheral to the ideological and political confrontation of the two Cold War blocs was transformed, probably more accurately, into one of social and political cooperation between two nations trying to exit from their postcolonial situation. In fact, this medical and humanitarian cooperation is probably the major area that has given Cuba international governmental and popular recognition. These exchanges and stable relations, in the aftermath of the revolutions in Cuba and many African countries, perhaps suggest another kind of practice of the often-debased notions of 'cooperation' and 'development'.

Through the various case studies developed in this collection, we aim to present an overall view, both transnational and continental, of the internationalism that made Cuba so famous. This also had the distinctive feature, in Africa, of interacting with the dynamics of Pan-Africanism, in its many dimensions. Pan-Africanism, the political ideology first produced in the Caribbean and then appropriated by Africa from the start of the twentieth century, is structured around intellectual and political figures from Africa and the Americas, notably the Jamaican Marcus Garvey, the Trinidadian George Padmore, the American W.E.B. Du Bois, the South African Pixley ka Isaka Seme, the Ghanaian Kwame Nkrumah or the Tanzanian Julius Nyerere.[61] Opposed ideological positions (communism vs capitalism, racialism vs continentalism, the unitary state vs federalism) ran through it, and it was shaped by different local and transnational cultural practices (social, religious and musical in particular).[62] Initially a movement for the defence of the interests of black populations, whether in Africa or the Americas, Pan-Africanism was an ideological resource that fed the anti-colonial struggles and political and cultural nationalism throughout the Atlantic world. Given rhythm by significant encounters (political summits, congresses and cultural festivals), it acquired institutionalised form in the Organisation of African Unity (OAU), founded in 1963 in Addis Ababa by the independent African states. The first declared aim of the OAU was the liberation of the whole of Africa, in particular those countries still under colonial rule, including South Africa.[63] It was a cause clearly shared with Cuban internationalism, and to achieve it an international solidarity was developed between people subjected to dominant racist, colonial and capitalist ideologies and laws.

TOWARD ANOTHER ATLANTIC HISTORY

The racial question, which is foundational to our contemporary world, and in particular the question of the equality of races (a structuring element of Pan-Africanism), was first imposed by the West on Africa. But through its part in eradicating the two matrices of the racialisation of Africa in the nineteenth and twentieth centuries – slavery and colonisation – the Cuban ideal took the exact opposite course.[64] In fact, the struggle against racism arose internally for revolutionary Cuba and then was almost immediately projected outwards to the African continent.[65] While Atlantic history is well known for its racialisation of individuals, representations, science, institutions and societies, it also seems to have given birth to another ideal, anti-racial in kind. Cuba thus played a decisive role in the process leading to the fall of the apartheid regime in South Africa, a Pan-African cause par excellence.[66] João Felipe Gonçalves, in his chapter, examines Nelson Mandela's visit to Miami in 1990, and the virulent presence on that occasion of Cuban Americans, for whom their conflicted relationship with Cuba saturated the event. He also explores other forms of mobilisation in the political and cultural fields and their relation with Africa, showing how, in the context of practices of racial categorisation specific to the United States, this relationship is as much a mirror, through which they construct their Afro-Cubanness, as a battlefield on which they fight with their island compatriots. On the island, as the chapter by Rodríguez Ruiz shows, the engagement of internationalists in Africa seems to have contributed to the evolution of representations of the continent. By disrupting prejudices that still associated Africans with 'barbarians', cohabitation and collaboration made of them allies, friends and potential comrades.

And it is perhaps on the periphery of these exchanges, outside the political, military, commercial or medical fields, in Miami as in Havana, that the deepest links were forged: the filiation of *santería*, completely liberated from biology because based on initiation, inserts each novice into a transnational network of ritual kinship that today, as Argyriadis and Gonçalves remind us, largely extends beyond national borders. Through a chain of alliances and rivalries, this network links a large proportion of Cubans of all skin colours to Nigerian practitioners who claim adherence to 'Yoruba religion' – as well as to all the others, American or European. The religious practices called 'Afro-Cuban', diffused among the whole population (on the island or outside, following migratory waves) during the years of Cuban engagement in Africa, have come to form an integral part of the definition of a national cultural identity that assumes, among other things, an African origin.

This Cuban engagement in Africa invites us to leave behind the North–South perspective so paradigmatic in the analysis of the political and ideological patterns of decolonisation, and to adopt a South–South perspective, which we argue is central to the formation of our contemporary world.[67] In view of the contributions that make up this work, we must plead for a history of the Cuban engagement in Africa as seen from Africa.[68] It is no longer possible to think of the Atlantic, of cultural circulations, or of the social practices of international solidarity without giving Africa its proper place, without considering the destinies and trajectories of Africans, without analysing local, national and regional contexts on the continent. Here, perhaps, is one of the major ambitions of this book: to participate in an Atlantic perspective that is firmly anchored in Africa. It is this anchoring that allows us to shift our gaze in an attempt to perceive this vast and more complex interface, this zone of contact between Cuba and Africa which, while having given form to an original kind of cooperation through the second half of the twentieth century, perhaps prefigures the terms of South–South relations at the dawn of the twenty-first century.

NOTES

1. On the links between the Cold War and African struggles for independence, see for example Jeremi Suri, 'The Cold War, Decolonization, and Global Social Awakenings: Historical Intersections,' *Cold War History* 6, no. 33 (2006): 353–63.
2. Speech of 22 December 1975. See Mary-Alice Waters, *Cuba and Angola: Fighting for Africa's Freedom and Our Own* (New York: Pathfinder, 2013), 31.
3. Waters, *Cuba and Angola*, 49.
4. Piero Gleijeses, *Conflicting Missions: Havana, Washington, and Africa, 1959–1976* (Chapel Hill, NC: University of North Carolina Press, 2003), and *Visions of Freedom: Havana, Washington, Pretoria, and the Struggle for Southern Africa 1976–1991* (Chapel Hill, NC: University of North Carolina Press, 2013). See also Christine Hatzky, *Cubans in Angola, South–South Cooperation and Transfer of Knowledge, 1976–1991* (Madison: University of Wisconsin Press, 2015).
5. Adrien Delmas, 'Cuba and Apartheid,' in *A Global History of Anti-Apartheid: 'Forward to Freedom' in South Africa*, ed. Anna Konieczna and Rob Skinner (Cham: Palgrave Macmillan, 2019), 133–50.
6. See Edward George, *The Cuban Intervention in Angola, 1965–1991: From Che Guevara to Cuito Cuanavale* (London: Routledge, 2005); as well as Horace Campbell, *The Siege of Cuito Cuanavale* (Uppsala: Scandinavian Institute of African Studies, 1990); Gleijeses, *Conflicting Missions*, 2002, and *Visions of Freedom*, 2013.
7. Kenneth Kalu, 'Africa and the Cold War,' in *The Palgrave Handbook of African Colonial and Postcolonial History*, ed. Martin S. Shanguhyia and Toyin Falola (New York: Palgrave Macmillan, 2018), 661–80.

8 Juan Pérez de la Riva, 'Síntesis cronológica alrededor de la esclavitud en Cuba,' *Actas del Folklore* 5 (May 1961).

9 Rómulo Lachateñeré, 'La influencia Bantú-Yoruba en los cultos afrocubanos,' *Estudios Afrocubanos* IV (1940): 27–38; Fernando Ortiz, *La africanía de la música folklórica afrocubana* (Havana: Ministerio de Educación, 1950); Lydia Cabrera, *El monte: Igbo, finda, ewe orisha, vititi nfinda* (Havana: C.R., 1954).

10 Miguel Barnet, *Biografia de un cimarron* (Havana: Instituto de Etnología y Folklore, Academia de Ciencias de Cuba, 1966).

11 William R. Bascom, 'The Yoruba in Cuba,' *Nigeria Magazine* 37 (1951); Lydia Cabrera, *Anagó, vocabulario lucumí* (Havana: C.R., 1957).

12 José Luciano Franco Ferrán, *Los palenques de los negros cimarrones* (Havana: Departamento de Orientación Revolucionaria del Comité Central del PCC, 1973).

13 Special army units composed exclusively, under the Spanish crown, of free blacks and mulattos.

14 That is to say, on biblical and historical Ethiopia of which the author had knowledge through illustrated pages showing Ethiopian priests visiting the Pope, and on which he had then compiled information. See, for example, Franco Ferrán and José Luciano, *La conspiración de Aponte* (Havana: Consejo Nacional de Cultura, 1963); Jorge Pavez Ojeda, 'The "Painting" of Black History: The Afro-Cuban codex of José Antonio Aponte (Havana, Cuba, 1812),' in *Written Culture in a Colonial Context, Africa and the Americas, 1500–1900*, ed. Adrien Delmas and Nigel Penn (Leiden: Brill, 2012), 271–303.

15 The first reference to the presence of African slaves (imported from Spain) in Cuba dates from 1503. Banned in 1820, the trade was carried on clandestinely for more than fifty years. Between 1790 and 1840 nearly 550 000 slaves were brought to the island, compared with some 60 000 over the entire previous period. See Pérez de la Riva, 'Síntesis cronológica.'

16 In becoming the world's leading exporter of sugar at the beginning of the nineteenth century, Cuba had a continuous need for slave labour. See Manuel Moreno Fraginals, *El ingenio: Complejo económico-social cubano del azúcar* (Havana: Editorial de Ciencias Sociales, 1978).

17 Rodolfo Sarracino, *Los que volvieron a Africa* (Havana: Editorial de Ciencias Sociales, 1988), 14.

18 Fernando Ortiz, 'Los cabildos,' *Revista Bimestre Cubana* 16 (1921): 5–39.

19 Pérez de la Riva, 'Síntesis cronológica.'

20 Rafael Leovigildo López Valdés, *Componentes africanos en el etnos cubano* (Havana: Editorial de Ciencias Sociales, 1985), 190.

21 Generic names given in Cuba to the African ethnic groups represented, according to their declaration of membership or of the African port of embarkation from where they were brought. For example, *congos reales* referred to slaves from the kingdom of Kongo, *mina* to those brought from the port of Mina, *carabalí* to slaves originating from the Calabar region, *lucumí* to speakers of Yoruba dialects, and *iyesá* to the population of the same name from the Oshogbo region of present-day Nigeria.

22 On the conditions of life of the first workers 'recruited' in the nineteenth century, see Antonio Bachiller y Morales, *Los negros* (Barcelona: Gorgas y Compañía, 1887), who from 1861 took a position against this disguised form of slavery; see also Moreno Fraginals, *El ingenio*, 296–309. On the other hand, it was not uncommon that 'free people of colour' owned slaves, sometimes of the same ethnic origin as themselves; see

Pedro Deschamps Chapeaux, *El negro en la economía habanera del siglo XIX* (Havana: UNEAC, 1971).

23 Giving birth to such cultural practices as *santería*, the cult of Ifá, *palo-monte*, the secret men's society Abakuá and the *arará* cult, and strongly influencing the Cuban variants of *voudou*, Catholicism and spiritualism.

24 María del Carmen Barcia Zequeira, *La otra familia: Parientes, redes y descendencia de los esclavos en Cuba* (Havana: Casa de las Américas, 2003), 113–36.

25 María del Carmen Barcia Zequeira, *Del cabildo de nación a la casa de santo* (Havana: Fundación Fernando Ortiz, 2012).

26 For a critique describing this interpretation of the role of Aponte, see Stephan Palmié, *Wizards and Scientists: Explorations in Afro-Cuban Modernity and Tradition* (London: Duke University Press, 2002), 79–158.

27 *Constitución de la República de Cuba* (Havana: Politica, 1992): 1–2.

28 José Luciano Franco Ferrán, 'Antecedentes de las relaciones entre los pueblos de Guinea y Cuba,' *Revista de la Biblioteca Nacional José Martí* XVIII, no. 2 (1976): 5–10; Isabela de Arazandi, 'El legado cubano en África: Ñáñigos deportados a Fernando Poo: Memoria viva y archivo escrito,' *Afro-Hispanic Review* 31, no. 1 (2012): 29–60; Ivor Miller, *Voice of the Leopard: African Secret Societies and Cuba* (Jackson: University Press of Mississippi, 2009), 127.

29 In spite of these measures, Cuba would serve as a place of transit for contraband blacks, and tried to pass these captives off as slaves bought on the island in order to resell them there or in other slave-owning countries, as was the case with the ship *Amistad*; see John W. Blassingame, *Slave Testimony: Two Centuries of Letters, Speeches, Interviews, and Autobiographies* (Baton Rouge: Louisiana State University Press, 1977), 30–46; and Sarracino, *Los que volvieron*, 31–44.

30 Sarracino, *Los que volvieron*.

31 One thinks in particular, of Pierre Verger, 'Influence du Brésil au Golfe de Bénin,' *Les Afro-Américains: Mémoires de l'IFAN* 27 (1953): 11–101; *Flux et reflux de la traite des nègres entre le Golfe de Bénin et Bahia de Todos os Santos du XVIIème au XIXème siècle* (Paris: Mouton & Co, 1968); and Kwesi Kwa Praah, ed., *Back to Africa: Afro-Brazilian Returnees and Their Communities* (Cape Town: CASAS, 2009); for Cuba, see Juan Pérez de la Riva, 'Documentos para la historia de las gentes sin historia,' *Revista de la Biblioteca Nacional José Martí* VI, no. 1 (1964): 27–52; and Sarracino, *Los que volvieron*; for Nigeria, see John Peel, *Religious Encounter and the Making of the Yoruba* (Bloomington: Indiana University Press, 2000); for Kenya, see Joseph Harris, *Repatriates and Refugees in a Colonial Society: The Case of Kenya* (Washington, DC: Howard University Press, 1987); for Ethiopia, see Giulia Bonacci, *Exodus! Heirs and Pioneers, Rastafari Return to Ethiopia* (Kingston: UWIP, 2015); for West Africa, see Nemata Blyden, *West Indians in West Africa: A Diaspora in Reverse* (Rochester: University of Rochester Press, 2000); for Liberia, see Claude A. Clegg, *The Price of Liberty: African Americans and the Making of Liberia* (Chapel Hill, NC: University of North Carolina Press, 2004).

32 Pérez de la Riva, 'Síntesis cronológica.'

33 The speech (in Spanish) is available at http://www.cuba.cu/gobierno/discursos/1975/esp/c221275e.html, accessed 4 January 2019.

34 Rodolfo Sarracino, *José Martí, nuestra América y el equilibrio internacional* (Havana: Centro de Estudios Martianos, 2015), 110.

[35] Paul Estrade, 'Remarques sur le caractère tardif, et avancé, de la prise de conscience nationale dans les Antilles espagnoles,' *Cahiers du Monde Hispanique et Luso-Brésilien* 38 (1982): 108.

[36] For the immense oeuvre of José Martí, one can consult the 27-volume critical edition (*Obras completas*), published by the Centro de Estudios Martianos, http://www.josemarti.cu/obras-edicion-critica/, accessed 4 January 2019; or Paul Estrade, *José Martí (1853–1895): Les fondements de la démocratie en Amérique latine* (Paris: Les Indes Savantes, 2017 [1987]).

[37] The name given to combatants of the liberation army, both in Cuba and the Dominican Republic.

[38] Aline Helg, *Our Rightful Share: The Afro-Cuban Struggle for Equality, 1886–1912* (Chapel Hill, NC: University of North Carolina Press, 1995), 93. In this respect, we recall that during his official visit to the United Nations in September 1960, Fidel Castro could not stay in Manhattan hotels, which refused him on the pretext that he was a person 'of colour'. He then chose to stay at the Hotel Theresa in Harlem, where he had discussions with Malcolm X and expressed his wish to support Patrice Lumumba; see Ralph D. Matthews, 'Going Upstairs: Malcolm X Greets Fidel,' *New York Citizen-Call* (September 1960): 1.

[39] In attempting to organise themselves in 1908 within the Partido Independiente de Color (which also campaigned, it must be emphasised, in favour of the rights of workers and peasants of all skin colours and for access to education and medical care for all), they were massacred in their thousands in 1912 after having started an uprising in the east of the island to protest against the banning of their party, which was declared racist and unconstitutional; see Helg, *Our Rightful Share*.

[40] Juan Pérez de la Riva, 'Cuba y la migración antillana, 1900–1931,' *Anuario de Estudios Cubanos* 2 (1979): 3–75; Ernesto Chávez Alvarez, *El crimen de la niña Cecilia: La brujería en Cuba como fenómeno social (1902–1925)* (Havana: Editorial de Ciencias Sociales, 1991).

[41] Alejandro de la Fuente, *A Nation for All: Race, Inequality and Politics in Twentieth-Century Cuba* (Chapel Hill, NC: University of North Carolina Press, 2001). This racism, particularly virulent towards Haitians and Jamaicans and their descendants, was still very much alive in the early 1960s, to such an extent that the main writers who stood up to denounce it, such as Walterio Carbonell or Carlos Moore, were rapidly ostracised; this was a time of national cohesion, including, paradoxically, the framework of Cuban engagement in Africa, for which it was necessary to form a united front and avoid being reminded of internal contradictions. See Walterio Carbonell, *Crítica: Como surgió la cultural nacional* (Havana: Ediciones Yaka, 1961) or Carlos Moore, 'Le peuple noir a-t-il sa place dans la révolution cubaine?', *Présence Africaine* 52 (1964): 177–230.

[42] Niurka Núñez González, María del Rosario Díaz Rodríguez, and Jhon Picard Byron, 'Vers une ethnologie nationale: Folklore, science et politique dans l'œuvre de Jean Price-mars et de Fernando Ortiz,' in *Cuba–Haïti: Engager l'anthropologie. Anthologie critique et histoire comparée (1884–1959)*, ed. Kali Argyriadis, Emma Gobin, Maud Laëthier, Niurka Núñez González and Jhon Picard Byron (Montreal: CIDIHCA, 2020), 279–311.

[43] Fernando Ortiz, 'Por la integración cubana de blancos y negros,' speech delivered at Club Atenas, 12 December 1942, reproduced in *Ultra* XIII, no. 77 (1943): 69–76; Fernando Ortiz, *El engaño de las razas* (Havana: Páginas, 1946).

[44] Without assessing, of course, its future impact on African music; see in this respect the chapters of Grabli and Djebbari in this volume.

[45] Forming links with the intellectuals of the Harlem Renaissance, they refused to create a purely Afro-Cuban movement and the ghettoisation that would have resulted, but underlined 'the contribution of Afro-Cuban culture to our national civilisation'; see Gustavo Urrutia, 'Sensemayá,' *Diario de la Marina* (November 1935): 2.

[46] Tomás Fernández Robaina, *El negro en Cuba, 1902–1958* (Havana: Editorial de Ciencias Sociales, 1994); Alejandro de la Fuente, 'Antídotos de Wall Street: Raza y racismo en las relaciones entre Cuba y los Estados Unidos,' in *Culturas encontradas: Cuba y los Estados Unidos*, ed. Rafael Hernandez and John H. Coatsworth (Havana: CIDCC Juan Marinello and Harvard University, David Rockefeller Center for Latin American Studies, 2001), 243–61.

[47] Let us recall that Fidel Castro, who had already participated in an abortive invasion of the Dominican Republic in 1947, alongside future president Juan Bosch, backed the landing in the Dominican Republic in 1959 of Cuban-trained Dominican combatants, which were massacred by the forces of Rafael Trujillo (with whom Fulgencio Batista had found refuge). In August 1959 as well, a small group of Cuban-Haitian combatants, among them the writer Jacques-Stephen Alexis, landed secretly in Haiti. They were massacred by the troops of François Duvalier; see René Depestre, *Bonsoir tendresse: Autobiographie* (Paris: Odile Jacob, 2018), 91, 165–67.

[48] Christabelle Peters, *Cuban Identity and the Angolan Experience* (New York: Palgrave Macmillan, 2012).

[49] Paul Estrade, 'La Révolution Cubaine (1959–1992): Une histoire sommaire de ses origines, son déroulement, ses accomplissements,' *Les Langues Néo-Latines* 39 (December 2006): 59–103.

[50] Argeliers León, 'La expresión del pueblo en el Teatro Nacional Cubano,' *Actas del Folklore* 1 (January 1961): 5–7; 'Creación del Instituto de Etnología y Folklore,' *Actas del Folklore* 1 (October–December 1961): 33–35.

[51] Niurka Núñez González, Pablo Rodríguez Ruiz, María Pérez Álvarez, and Odalys Buscarón Ochoa, *Las relaciones raciales en Cuba: Estudios contemporáneos* (Havana: Fundación Fernando Ortiz, 2011). See as well the chapter by Argyriadis in this volume.

[52] Elikia M'Bokolo, *Afrique noire: Histoire et civilisations*, 2 vols. (Paris: Hatier, 2004); John Parker and Richard Rathbone, *African History: A Very Short Introduction* (Oxford: Oxford University Press, 2007); Frederick Cooper, *L'Afrique depuis 1940* (Paris: Payot, 2008), 140–41; Martin Shanguhyia and Toyin Falola, eds, *The Palgrave Handbook of African Colonial and Postcolonial History* (Basingstoke: Palgrave Macmillan, 2018).

[53] On the rapprochement between global history and micro-history, see Romain Bertrand, *Le long remords de la conquête* (Paris: Seuil, 2015), 25.

[54] Jacques Revel, ed., *Jeux d'échelles: La micro-analyse à l'expérience* (Paris: Seuil, 1996).

[55] Pérez de la Riva, 'Documentos para la historia de las gentes sin historia,' 27–52.

[56] Simona Cerutti, 'Who Is Below? E.P. Thompson, historien des sociétés modernes: Une relecture,' *Annales: Histoire, Sciences Sociales* 4 (2015): 931–56.

[57] See Patrice Yengo and Monique de Saint Martin, eds, 'Élites de retour de l'Est,' special issue, *Cahiers d'Études Africaines* 226 (2017).

[58] On the question of the archive in Africa, see Carolyn Hamilton et al., *Refiguring the Archive* (Dordrecht and Boston: Kluwer Academic, 2002).

[59] On socialism in Africa, see for example Louis-Vincent Thomas, *Le socialisme et l'Afrique* (Paris: Le Livre Africain, 1966); M. de Saint-Martin, G. Scarfò Ghellab, and K. Mellakh, eds, *Etudier à l'Est: Expériences de diplômés africains* (Paris: Karthala, FMSH, 2015).

[60] See Jean-François Bayart, *L'État en Afrique: La politique du ventre* (Paris: Fayard, 1990); Alexander Kees, *Ethnicity and the Colonial State: Finding and Representing Group Identifications in a Coastal West African and Global Perspective (1850–1960)* (Leiden: Brill, 2016); Paul Nugent, *Africa since Independence: A Comparative History* (Houndmills: Palgrave Macmillan, 2004); Crawford Young, *The Postcolonial State in Africa: Fifty Years of Independence, 1960–2010* (Madison: University of Wisconsin Press, 2012); and Cooper, *L'Afrique depuis 1940*.

[61] H. Adi and M. Sherwood, *Pan-African History: Political Figures from Africa and the Diaspora since 1787* (London and New York: Routledge, 2003).

[62] P. Olisanwuche Esedebe, *Pan-Africanism: The Idea and the Movement, 1776–1991* (Washington, DC: Howard University Press, 1994); Hakim Adi, *Pan-Africanism: A History* (London: Bloomsbury, 2018).

[63] Amzat Boukari Yabara, *Africa unite! Une histoire du panafricanisme* (Paris: La Découverte, 2014), 192–94.

[64] As did, in his time, the Haitian Anténor Firmin, author of the response to the Comte de Gobineau, *De l'égalité des races humaines: Anthropologie positive* (Paris: Librairie Cotillon et F. Pichon, 1885).

[65] De la Fuente, *A Nation for All*.

[66] Adrien Delmas, 'Cuba and Apartheid.'

[67] Luiz Felipe de Alencastro, *The South Atlantic, Past and Present* (Dartmouth: Tagus Press, 2015).

[68] This reversal which underscores a view *from* Africa is being applied to various social and cultural fields, see for example Thomas Fouquet, 'Construire la *blackness* depuis l'Afrique, un renversement heuristique,' *Politique Africaine* 4 (2014): 5–19.

REFERENCES

Adi, Hakim. *Pan-Africanism: A History*. London: Bloomsbury, 2018.

Adi, Hakim and M. Sherwood. *Pan-African History: Political Figures from Africa and the Diaspora since 1787*. London and New York: Routledge, 2003.

Arazandi, Isabela de. 'El legado cubano en Africa: Ñáñigos deportados a Fernando Poo: Memoria viva y archivo escrito.' *Afro-Hispanic Review* 31, no. 1 (2012): 29–60.

Argyriadis, Kali, E. Gobin, M. Laëthier, N. Núñez González and J. P. Byron, eds. *Cuba–Haïti: Engager l'anthropologie. Anthologie critique et histoire comparée (1884–1959)*. Montreal: CIDIHCA, 2020.

Bachiller y Morales, Antonio. *Los negros*. Barcelona: Gorgas y compañía, 1887.

Barcia Zequeira, María del Carmen. *Del cabildo de nación a la casa de santo*. Havana: Fundación Fernando Ortiz, 2012.

Barcia Zequeira, María del Carmen. *La otra familia: Parientes, redes y descendencia de los esclavos en Cuba*. Havana: Casa de las Américas, 2003.

Barnet, Miguel. *Biografia de un cimarron*. Havana: Instituto de Etnología y Folklore, Academia de Ciencias de Cuba, 1966.

Bascom, William R. 'The Yoruba in Cuba.' *Nigeria Magazine* 37 (1951): 14–20.

Bayart, Jean-François. *L'État en Afrique: La politique du ventre*. Paris: Fayard, 1990.

Bertrand, Romain. *Le long remords de la conquête*. Paris: Seuil, 2015.

Blassingame, John W. *Slave Testimony: Two Centuries of Letters, Speeches, Interviews, and Autobiographies*. Baton Rouge: Louisiana State University Press, 1977.

Blyden, Nemata. *West Indians in West Africa: A Diaspora in Reverse*. Rochester: University of Rochester Press, 2000.

Bonacci, Giulia. *Exodus! Heirs and Pioneers, Rastafari Return to Ethiopia*. Kingston: UWIP, 2015.

Boukari-Yabara, Amzat. *Africa unite! Une histoire du panafricanisme*. Paris: La Découverte, 2014.

Cabrera, Lydia. *Anagó, vocabulario lucumí*. Havana: C.R., 1957.

Cabrera, Lydia. *El monte: Igbo, finda, ewe orisha, vititi nfinda*. Havana: C.R., 1954.

Campbell, Horace. *The Siege of Cuito Cuanavale*. Uppsala: Scandinavian Institute of African Studies, 1990.

Carbonell, Walterio. *Crítica: Como surgió la cultural nacional*. Havana: Ediciones Yaka, 1961.

Cerutti, Simona. 'Who Is Below? E.P. Thompson, historien des sociétés modernes: Une relecture.' *Annales: Histoire, Sciences Sociales* 4 (2015): 931–56.

Chávez Alvarez, Ernesto. *El crimen de la niña Cecilia: La brujería en Cuba como fenómeno social (1902–1925)*. Havana: Editorial de Ciencias Sociales, 1991.

Clegg, Claude A. *The Price of Liberty: African Americans and the Making of Liberia*. Chapel Hill, NC: University of North Carolina Press, 2004.

Cooper, Frederick. *L'Afrique depuis 1940*. Paris: Payot, 2008.

De Alencastro, Luiz Felipe. *The South Atlantic, Past and Present*. Dartmouth: Tagus Press, 2015.

De la Fuente, Alejandro. *A Nation for All: Race, Inequality and Politics in Twentieth-Century Cuba*. Chapel Hill, NC: University of North Carolina Press, 2001.

De la Fuente, Alejandro. 'Antídotos de Wall Street: Raza y racismo en las relaciones entre Cuba y los Estados Unidos.' In *Culturas encontradas: Cuba y los Estados Unidos*, edited by Rafael Hernandez and John H. Coatsworth, 243–61. Havana: CIDCC Juan Marinello and Harvard University, David Rockefeller Center for Latin American Studies, 2001.

Delmas, Adrien, and Nigel Penn, eds. *Written Culture in a Colonial Context: Africa and the Americas, 1500–1900*. Leiden: Brill, 2012.

Delmas, Adrien. 'Cuba and Apartheid.' In *A Global History of Anti-Apartheid: 'Forward to Freedom' in South Africa*, edited by Anna Konieczna and Rob Skinner, 133–50. Cham: Palgrave Macmillan, 2019.

Depestre, René. *Bonsoir tendresse: Autobiographie*. Paris: Odile Jacob, 2018.

De Saint-Martin, Monique, G. Scarfò Ghellab, and K. Mellakh, eds. *Etudier à l'Est: Expériences de diplômés africains*. Paris: Karthala, FMSH, 2015.

Deschamps Chapeaux, Pedro. *El negro en la economía habanera del siglo XIX*. Havana: UNEAC, 1971.

Esedebe, P. Olisanwuche. *Pan-Africanism: The Idea and the Movement, 1776–1991*. Washington, DC: Howard University Press, 1994.

Estrade, Paul. *José Martí (1853–1895): Les fondements de la démocratie en Amérique latine*. Paris: Les Indes Savantes, 2017 [1987].

Estrade, Paul. 'La Révolution Cubaine (1959–1992): Une histoire sommaire de ses origines, son déroulement, ses accomplissements.' *Les Langues Néo-Latines* 39 (December 2006): 59–103.

Estrade, Paul. 'Remarques sur le caractère tardif, et avancé, de la prise de conscience nationale dans les Antilles espagnoles.' *Cahiers du Monde Hispanique et Luso-Brésilien* 38 (1982): 89–117.

Fernández Robaina, *Tomás. El negro en Cuba, 1902–1958*. Havana: Editorial de Ciencias Sociales, 1994.

Firmin, Anténor. *De l'égalité des races humaines: Anthropologie positive*. Paris: Librairie Cotillon et F. Pichon, 1885.

Fouquet, Thomas. 'Construire la *blackness* depuis l'Afrique, un renversement heuristique.' *Politique Africaine* 4 (2014): 5–19.

Franco Ferrán, José Luciano. *La conspiración de Aponte*. Havana: Consejo Nacional de Cultura, 1963.

Franco Ferrán, José Luciano. *Los palenques de los negros cimarrones*. Havana: Departamento de Orientación Revolucionaria del Comité Central del PCC, 1973.

Franco Ferrán, José Luciano. 'Antecedentes de las relaciones entre los pueblos de Guinea y Cuba.' *Revista de la Biblioteca Nacional José Martí* XVIII, no. 2 (1976): 5–10.

George, Edward. *The Cuban Intervention in Angola, 1965–1991: From Che Guevara to Cuito Cuanavale*. London: Routledge, 2005.

Gleijeses, Piero. *Conflicting Missions: Havana, Washington, and Africa, 1959–1976*. Chapel Hill, NC: University of North Carolina Press, 2003.

Gleijeses, Piero. *Visions of Freedom: Havana, Washington, Pretoria, and the Struggle for Southern Africa 1976–1991*. Chapel Hill, NC: University of North Carolina Press, 2013.

Hamilton, Carolyn, Verne Harris, Michèle Pickover, Graeme Reid, Razia Saleh and Jane Taylor, eds. *Refiguring the Archive*. Dordrecht and Boston: Kluwer Academic, 2002.

Harris, Joseph. *Repatriates and Refugees in a Colonial Society: The Case of Kenya*. Washington, DC: Howard University Press, 1987.

Hatzky, Christine. *Cubans in Angola, South–South Cooperation and Transfer of Knowledge, 1976–1991*. Madison: University of Wisconsin Press, 2015.

Helg, Aline. *Our Rightful Share: The Afro-Cuban Struggle for Equality, 1886–1912*. Chapel Hill, NC: University of North Carolina Press, 1995.

Kalu, Kenneth. 'Africa and the Cold War.' In *The Palgrave Handbook of African Colonial and Postcolonial History*, edited by M. S. Shanguhyia and T. Falola, 661–80. New York: Palgrave Macmillan, 2018.

Kees, Alexander. *Ethnicity and the Colonial State: Finding and Representing Group Identifications in a Coastal West African and Global Perspective (1850–1960)*. Leiden: Brill, 2016.

Lachateñeré, Rómulo. 'La influencia Bantú-Yoruba en los cultos afrocubanos.' *Estudios Afrocubanos* IV (1940): 27–38.

León, Argeliers. 'Creación del Instituto de Etnología y Folklore.' *Actas del Folklore* 1 (October–December 1961): 33–35.

León, Argeliers. 'La expresión del pueblo en el Teatro Nacional Cubano.' *Actas del Folklore* 1 (January 1961): 5–7.

López Valdés, Rafael Leovigildo. *Componentes africanos en el etnos cubano*. Havana: Editorial de Ciencias Sociales, 1985.

Martí, José. *Obras completas*. Havana: Centro de Estudios Martianos, Tercera Edición, 28 vols., 2010–2018.

Matthews, Ralph D. 'Going Upstairs: Malcolm X Greets Fidel.' *New York Citizen-Call* (September 1960): 1.

M'Bokolo, Elikia. *Afrique noire: Histoire et civilisations*. Paris: Hatier, 2004.

Miller, Ivor. *Voice of the Leopard: African Secret Societies and Cuba*. Jackson: University Press of Mississippi, 2009.

Moore, Carlos. 'Le peuple noir a-t-il sa place dans la révolution cubaine?' *Présence Africaine* 52 (1964): 177–230.
Moreno Fraginals, Manuel. *El ingenio: Complejo económico-social cubano del azúcar*. Havana: Editorial de Ciencias Sociales, 1978.
Nugent, Paul. *Africa since Independence: A Comparative History*. Houndmills: Palgrave Macmillan, 2004.
Núñez González, Niurka, María del Rosario Díaz Rodríguez and Jhon Picard Byron. 'Vers une ethnologie nationale: Folklore, science et politique dans l'œuvre de Jean Price-Mars et de Fernando Ortiz.' In *Cuba–Haïti: Engager l'anthropologie. Anthologie critique et histoire comparée (1884–1959)*, edited by Kali Argyriadis, Emma Gobin, Maud Laëthier, Niurka Núñez González and Jhon Picard Byron, 279–311. Montreal: CIDIHCA, 2020.
Núñez González, Niurka, Pablo Rodríguez Ruiz, María Pérez Álvarez and Odalys Buscarón Ochoa. *Las relaciones raciales en Cuba: Estudios contemporáneos*. Havana: Fundación Fernando Ortiz, 2011.
Ortiz, Fernando. *El engaño de las razas*. Havana: Páginas, 1946.
Ortiz, Fernando. *La africanía de la música folklórica afrocubana*. Havana: Ministerio de Educación, 1950.
Ortiz, Fernando. 'Los cabildos.' *Revista Bimestre Cubana* 16 (1921): 5–39.
Ortiz, Fernando. 'Por la integración cubana de blancos y negros.' *Ultra* XIII, no. 77 (1943): 69–76.
Palmié, Stephan. *Wizards and Scientists: Explorations in Afro-Cuban Modernity and Tradition*. London: Duke University Press, 2002.
Parker, John and Richard Rathbone. *African History: A Very Short Introduction*. Oxford: Oxford University Press, 2007.
Pavez Ojeda, Jorge. 'The "Painting" of Black History: The Afro-Cuban Codex of José Antonio Aponte (Havana, Cuba, 1812).' In *Written Culture in a Colonial Context: Africa and the Americas, 1500–1900*, edited by Adrien Delmas and Nigel Penn, 271–303. Leiden: Brill, 2012.
Peel, John. *Religious Encounter and the Making of the Yoruba*. Bloomington: Indiana University Press, 2000.
Pérez de la Riva, Juan. 'Cuba y la migración antillana, 1900–1931.' *Anuario de Estudios Cubanos* 2 (1979): 3–75.
Pérez de la Riva, Juan. 'Documentos para la historia de las gentes sin historia.' *Revista de la Biblioteca Nacional José Martí* VI, no. 1 (1964): 27–52.
Pérez de la Riva, Juan. 'Síntesis cronológica alrededor de la esclavitud en Cuba.' *Actas del Folklore* 5 (May 1961).
Peters, Christabelle. *Cuban Identity and the Angolan Experience*. New York: Palgrave Macmillan, 2012.
Praah, Kwesi Kwaa, ed. *Back to Africa: Afro-Brazilian Returnees and Their Communities*. Cape Town: CASAS, 2009.
Revel, Jacques, ed. *Jeux d'échelles: La micro-analyse à l'expérience*. Paris: Seuil, 1996.
Sarracino, Rodolfo. *José Martí, nuestra América y el equilibrio internacional*. Havana: Centro de Estudios Martianos, 2015.
Sarracino, Rodolfo. *Los que volvieron a Africa*. Havana: Editorial de Ciencias Sociales, 1988.
Shanguhyia, Martin and Toyin Falola, eds. *The Palgrave Handbook of African Colonial and Postcolonial History*. Basingstoke: Palgrave Macmillan, 2018.
Suri, Jeremi. 'The Cold War, Decolonization, and Global Social Awakenings: Historical Intersections.' *Cold War History* 6, no. 3 (2006): 353–63.

Thomas, Louis-Vincent. *Le socialisme et l'Afrique*. Paris: Le Livre Africain, 1966.
Urrutia, Gustavo. 'Sensemayá.' *Diario de la Marina* (November 1935).
Verger, Pierre. *Flux et reflux de la traite des nègres entre le Golfe de Bénin et Bahia de Todos os Santos du XVIIème au XIXème siècle*. Paris: Mouton & Co, 1968.
Verger, Pierre. 'Influence du Brésil au Golfe de Bénin.' *Les Afro-Américains: Mémoires de l'IFAN* 27 (1953): 11–101.
Waters, Mary-Alice. *Cuba and Angola: Fighting for Africa's Freedom and Our Own*. New York: Pathfinder, 2013.
Yengo, Patrice and Monique de Saint Martin, eds. 'Élites de retour de l'Est', special issue, *Cahiers d'Études Africaines* 226 (2017).
Young, Crawford. *The Postcolonial State in Africa: Fifty Years of Independence, 1960–2010*. Madison: University of Wisconsin Press, 2012.

PART I

POLITICS AND SOLIDARITY

CHAPTER

1

Cubans in Algiers: The political uses of memory

Emmanuel Alcaraz

Algeria and Cuba first established friendly relations in the context of the Algerian War of Independence (1954–62). On 27 June 1961, Cuba was the first country in the western hemisphere to recognise the Provisional Government of the Algerian Republic (GPRA) in exile in Tunisia, Egypt and Morocco.[1] In October of the same year, the Cuban government sent an emissary, Jorge Ricardo Masetti (1929–64),[2] who was a friend of Castro,[3] with a message of support for the GPRA. Then in December, in a decisive show of support, the Cuban ship *Bahía de Nipe* delivered weapons to the National Liberation Army (ALN), the armed wing of the National Liberation Front (FLN),[4] before returning to Cuba with 78 wounded Algerian fighters and 20 orphaned children. The weapons were transported to Oujda in Morocco, headquarters of the ALN General Staff, under the command of Colonel Houari Boumediene.

This strong signal of support has remained in the Algerian collective memory,[5] both official and public.[6] Nor have the Cuban people forgotten the support of President Ahmed Ben Bella at the time of the 1962 missile crisis. Following an official visit to the United States, the Algerian president visited Cuba two days after US U-2 spy planes produced evidence of Soviet missile launch sites on the island.[7] On that occasion, he proclaimed: 'We will never forget all you did for our refugees in Tunisia and Morocco. Comrade Fidel Castro, the National Liberation Front of Algeria awards you the *mujâhid* medal of honour, as a token of our gratitude.'[8]

Ben Bella also supported Cuban demands for the return of the US naval base at Guantánamo Bay and celebrated the first anniversary of the Bay of Pigs victory over an American-led invading force. This political act is still commemorated in the official Cuba media. Fidel Castro subsequently made statements praising the courage of the Algerian people in supporting Cuba when the United States declared an embargo in February 1962. Whenever a Cuban leader visits Algeria or an Algerian official visits Cuba, Ben Bella's gesture is remembered in official speeches and in the media, as well as in *Granma*, the official organ of the Cuban Communist Party.

Any discussion of Cuban–Algerian relations must include the issue of the Tricontinental Movement, whose three key figures were the Algerian Ben Bella, the Moroccan Mehdi Ben Barka (an opponent of King Hassan II) and the Argentinian Che Guevara.[9] All three were instrumental in setting up the Tricontinental conference of solidarity between the peoples of Africa, Asia and Latin America, held at the Habana Libre Hotel in Havana in January 1966. The aim of the conference, which was attended by representatives of liberation movements from around the globe, with China and the USSR limited to observer status, was to create an anti-imperialist platform.[10]

But already before then, Che Guevara had paid two visits to Algiers in 1963 and 1965 to further the goals of the Tricontinental Movement, visits that were instrumental in creating the myth of Algiers as the world capital of revolutionaries.[11] At that time, Ben Bella's Algeria welcomed political activists fighting against dictatorships in southern Europe or governments controlled by Latin American oligarchies, as well as sub-Saharan anti-colonial activists and those fighting the apartheid system in South Africa. To support these movements, Che Guevara came to Algiers on 5 July 1963, Algerian Youth Day, which celebrates the country's independence in 1962, and again in February 1965 on the occasion of the Afro-Asian solidarity conference, as part of a grand tour of the African continent. It was in Algiers that he made his famous speech criticising the Soviet Union for giving insufficient support to Third World revolutionary movements. He also attempted to shift away from the official Cuban position, although at that time Fidel Castro had not yet fully aligned his country with Soviet foreign policy; he was to do this later, in 1968, when he supported the Warsaw Pact intervention in Czechoslovakia to crush the Prague Spring.

Ben Bella's presidency (from 1962 to 1965, when he was overthrown in a coup by Boumediene), represents the golden age of Algerian–Cuban relations. These had several dimensions: a political dimension, through support for Third World revolutionary activists; a military dimension, through Cuban military intervention in Algeria in 1963; and a medical and technical dimension, through cooperation with Algeria in these fields. From 1962 to 1965, thanks to Algerian support, the Cubans were able to strengthen their revolutionary networks in Africa and, to a lesser extent, in Latin America and Asia. Algeria and Cuba did not share the same state ideology, even if both regimes were seeking a specific path to socialism. However, the Algerian and Cuban leadership did have common policy orientations: the fight against colonialism and imperialism, and condemnation of the exploitation of the countries of the South by those of the North.

ALGIERS, AN AFRO-CUBAN *LIEU DE MEMOIRE*?

If Algiers is a *lieu de mémoire*[12] – a site vested with historical significance in the popular collective memory – of the anti-imperialist struggle at the time of Ben Bella, it is as the site of actual events that have been memorialised. Real historical events took place that contributed to the making of the myth of Algiers as 'the Mecca of revolutionaries' under the Ben Bella presidency. This was a term coined by the Cape Verdean activist Amílcar Cabral (1924–73) during an interview with journalists in Algiers, when he said: 'Catholics have Rome, Muslims have Mecca, Jews have Jerusalem, and revolutionaries have Algiers.'

Havana became the capital of Third World revolutionary activists after 1965 in part because the Cuban leadership was able to benefit from anti-imperialist and anti-colonial networks set up in Algiers between 1962 and 1965. Previously, it was Cairo that had held this status. The Cuban leadership had first developed relations with the Nasser regime and with the more Marxist-leaning regime of General Qasim in Iraq. However, Egypt's network of influence involved fewer sub-Saharan activists than that of Algiers. The Algerian regime, on the other hand, had gained from the FLN's highly active diplomacy in sub-Saharan Africa during the Algerian War. According to Régis Debray,[13] who discussed the matter with Guevara himself and with Jorge Papito Serguera, a commander in the Cuban Revolution and Cuban ambassador to Algeria at the time, the expansion of the Cuban revolutionary network in sub-Saharan Africa was mainly due to the Algerian FLN, which had extensive diplomatic and activist connections in the region after independence.[14]

Crucial in the establishment of this network of influence was the role of Frantz Fanon, the Martinique-born psychiatrist who practised in Blida in colonial Algeria. As a key FLN leader in charge of diplomatic relations with sub-Saharan Africa,[15] Fanon had supported the idea of an African revolution.[16] He was the first to refer to the African dimension of the Algerian Revolution, which he saw as a model for other revolutions on the continent. In June 1961, this idea was taken up by the FLN and enunciated in the Tripoli Programme,[17] which stated that the FLN should support all national liberation struggles on the African continent. Fanon also had considerable influence on the Cuban Revolution. It was Guevara himself who introduced Fanon's works to Cuba. As a doctor, Fanon offered a clinical analysis of the cultural alienation experienced by the colonised as a result of colonialism. Fanon's works were published in Spanish between 1965 and 1968 with the support of the Cuban cultural institution, Casa de las Américas. Even though the Cuban Revolution had, with few exceptions, been led by a white creole elite of Spanish origin,[18] Fanon exerted a powerful influence on Cuban intellectuals during the 1960s.[19] Forgotten for a time (probably due to the Cuban Revolution's alignment with the USSR), then rediscovered by Cubans in the 1990s after the fall of the Eastern bloc, Fanon advocated a revolution led by Third World peasants rather than by the workers, the latter being more in line with the Soviet Marxist-Leninist credo. Fanon had a similar impact on many activists, such as Amílcar Cabral in Guinea-Bissau and Steve Biko in South Africa. Biko himself was influenced by the theory that associated the black liberation movement with socialism via the concept of 'black consciousness', as set out in Fanon's book *Black Skin, White Masks* (1952), one of the first works to theorise the 'black condition'.[20] Fanon gave the Algerian Revolution great prestige by ensuring that African people the length of the continent became aware of the event.

Among the key South African activists from the African National Congress (ANC) who received support from the ALN, mention must of course be made of Nelson Mandela, Oliver Tambo, who was in charge of the ANC's diplomatic mission, and Robert Resha. In the wake of the Sharpeville massacre in 1960,[21] the ANC sought assistance from the FLN in organising the armed struggle through its military wing, Umkhonto we Sizwe (Spear of the Nation), which confined its activities, initially, to acts of sabotage that did not target civilians. The South African activists were first housed in FLN bases in Morocco. During his FLN training in the early 1960s, Mandela learned to link armed struggle with political struggle by appealing to international public opinion, thanks to his discussions with Dr Chawki Mostefaï, GPRA ambassador to Morocco at the time.

During the Algerian War, the diplomatic struggle had been vital for the FLN in order to obtain support from the nations of the 'South' at the United Nations and to gain international recognition for the GPRA. This policy continued after Algerian independence. In the 1964 Charter of Algiers, the Algerian Republic guaranteed asylum for freedom fighters.[22] According to Gérard Chaliand,[23] editor of an Algerian periodical entitled *Révolution Africaine*, the majority of the activists in Algiers were African – around 3000 between 1963 and 1964. Activists seeking independence for Portuguese colonies (Angola, Mozambique, Guinea-Bissau and Cape Verde), in particular, were taken in by the Algerian regime. And it was the liberation movements of these African countries that were given the greatest assistance by Cuba in terms of military and medical cooperation, which continued once their countries gained independence at the time of the Cold War between the Eastern and Western blocs in the 1970s. Among the organisations present in Algiers were the PAIGC (African Party for the Independence of Guinea and Cape Verde), led by Cabral and established in the capital since 1963; FRELIMO (the Mozambique Liberation Front) present since 1964; and the MPLA (Popular Movement for the Liberation of Angola).[24] Agostinho Neto had set up an MPLA office in Algiers in 1963.[25] According to Mario Pinto de Andrade, 250 fighters of this organisation received military training in Algeria.[26] Also represented in Algiers were delegates from SWAPO (South West Africa People's Organisation) from Namibia, which was colonised by South Africa, and ZANU (Zimbabwe African National Union), present since 1963.[27] Nor should the MLS (Liberation Movement of Saguia el-Hamra and of Rio de Oro [Western Sahara]), which struggled against Spanish colonialism in the Western Sahara, be forgotten.

For the Cuban leadership, apart from the opportunity to strengthen their international network of revolutionary activists, the relations established in Algiers enabled them to emerge from the diplomatic isolation caused by the 1962 Cuban Missile Crisis and the US embargo. Cuban leaders could meet African activists in several sites in Algiers. The Algerian government accommodated the activists in villas and provided offices for them. The ANC office was in Rue Larbi Ben M'Hidi, one of the main urban thoroughfares in Algiers, with Robert Resha (1920–74), a member of the ANC's National Executive Committee, as its representative. He was followed in 1963 by Johnny Makhathini, who later became the ANC's representative at the United Nations. All these activists received financial support and were entitled to Algerian passports.

Another important meeting place for the activists was the Cuban embassy in Algiers, which also housed the Prensa Latina news agency, whose representative was Gabriel Molina. They attended the receptions of the Algerian government and were invited to the villas of the Algerian leaders, which became important venues for political meetings. The Algerian leadership was able to act as an intermediary between the Cuban officials and sub-Saharan activists. For example, the third secretary at the Cuban embassy, Dario Urra, met Cabral for the first time in January 1963 at the private residence of Captain Nourredine Bakhti, an official of the Algerian Ministry of National Defence.[28] During a reception in 1963, Alphonse

Massamba-Débat (1921–77),[29] an opponent of Fulbert Youlou, president of Congo-Brazzaville, was able to meet with the Cuban ambassador, Jorge Serguera, thanks to Ben Bella.[30]

On the Algerian side, the main decision-makers in this network were the presidency, with Ben Bella, the Ministry of National Defence and Military Security, the latter two institutions being controlled by Boumediene. The Cubans' primary contact was Slimane Hoffman, a high-ranking military officer and member of the Oujda Group within the FLN,[31] formed around Boumediene.[32] This revolutionary network was therefore under the influence of the Algerian People's National Army (ANP) and partly outside Ben Bella's control, as his close adviser, Mohammed Harbi, has confirmed.[33] According to Harbi, secrecy was the rule when it came to Algerian–Cuban relations, except for the propaganda aimed at international public opinion. Even the Algerian president's Foreign Affairs Office had limited access to information about the relations. The main venue for propaganda in this 'Mecca of revolutionaries' was the Villa Boumaaraf, used by the Algerian regime for meetings and press conferences. To escape Algerian scrutiny, the Cuban embassy was favoured, alternating with the offices of Prensa Latina where, according to Gérard Chaliand,[34] several officers from the DGI (Cuban Intelligence Agency) worked.

Despite the importance of this revolutionary network, the relations between Algeria and Cuba (and with the sub-Saharan activists) should not be idealised. Each side needed the other in order to gain legitimacy in the international arena, and, to this end, they succeeded in overcoming ideological differences. Even though both Algeria and Cuba subscribed to a Third World ideology, they followed different approaches, each seeking its own specific path to socialism. While Cuba was not fully aligned with the USSR, the Cubans were aware that the Algerians were not communists but left-wing nationalists influenced by Nasserism and Arab nationalism. The Algerian regime organised large grassroots rallies in Algiers with revolutionary slogans that reflected the national liberation struggle. It was drawn not only to the African continent but also to the Middle East, through its support for the Palestinian cause.[35] At the same time, many of the sub-Saharan activists in Algiers did not subscribe to the Marxist-Leninist doctrines – Nelson Mandela for one – even though the ANC and SACTU (South African Congress of Trade Unions) had many communist members.

Mohammed Harbi confirms that the Cubans were aware of the ideological distance that separated them from the Algerians. Harbi met Che Guevara in 1963. During this meeting, Guevara expressed criticism of the self-management approach that characterised Algeria's road to socialism, which, for him, was simply a form of capitalism that did nothing to change the nature of the relations of production.

Aware of these differences, the communist activist Henri Curiel left Algiers for Paris to set up his organisation Solidarité, which aimed to support Third World national liberation movements.[36] When the Algerian Communist Party was banned in 1964, the newspaper *Alger Républicain* was probably only tolerated because of Cuban support.[37] Its editor, Henri Alleg, had published in it a series of articles favourable to the Cuban Revolution: 'Victorieuse Cuba'.[38]

Despite these ideological differences with the Algerian authorities, the Cubans succeeded in collaborating with the Ben Bella regime from 1962 to 1965. Initially, the Cuban Revolution was a socialist revolution carried out without the support of a communist party and, in its first phase, Cuban socialism was a spontaneous movement that rejected any ideological alignment.[39]

CUBAN MEDICAL MISSIONS TO ALGERIA

In 1963, Fidel Castro decided to send Cuban doctors to help Algeria rebuild the newly independent country after eight years of war. Initially, this was an act of solidarity as, according to information given to Fidel Castro by Cuban ambassador Jorge Serguera, at the end of 1962 Algeria had only 700 doctors for a population of 11 million.[40] Most European doctors had left the country. Health care in Cuba was not first-class, but it was better than in Algeria. For a population of 7 million, Cuba had 3000 doctors. On 17 October 1962, Fidel Castro had set up the Victoria de Girón School of Medicine to develop medical infrastructure in Cuba and also to send Cuban doctors to all Third World countries.[41] The first medical mission to Algeria, and more broadly to the African continent, was based on the principle of volunteering and ran from May 1963 to June 1964.[42] A team of 56 doctors was established, with 45 men and 11 women.[43] It was a case of one Third World country assisting another, free of charge. The Cuban health minister, José Ramón Machado Ventura, came to Algeria to launch the mission, which was headed by Dr Gerald Simón Escalona. The Cuban medical team was split into several groups. The largest was placed at the disposal of the Algerian army, while the others were sent mainly to remote regions: the isolated Aurès-Nemencha region in the east of the country; the regions of Setif and Constantine, also in eastern Algeria; and the region of Sidi Bel Abbes in the west of the country.[44]

The Cuban doctors faced a language barrier: they spoke no Arabic and had to use Algerian interpreters. At times, the teams' work was also hindered by local mentalities – the Algerian men did not want their wives to be treated by male doctors – and the staff were insufficient in number. The pace of work was intense, with up to

200 operations per day. The teams had to deal with all the ills of the Third World: poverty, malnutrition, and diseases such as tuberculosis, diphtheria, tetanus and trachoma. With regard to the last-mentioned, the Cuban team was highly qualified in ophthalmology. One difference between this and subsequent medical missions to sub-Saharan Africa was that the doctors in this first team were not accompanied by Cuban military advisers.

Later, in the 1980s, Cuban doctors were identified by journalists in the Polisario Front's military camps in the Algerian town of Tindouf.[45] And, according to Gérard Chaliand, Cuban doctors accompanied Cuban military advisers to Congo-Brazzaville in 1964, to support the socialist experiment being conducted by the Massamba-Débat regime. According to Chaliand, who met Cabral in Algiers and travelled with him to Guinea-Bissau,[46] there were two Cuban doctors in the PAIGC underground, who treated both soldiers and civilians. After 1965, medical cooperation in Algeria was briefly interrupted until the resumption of diplomatic relations between Algeria and Cuba in 1967.

The medical missions to Algeria and sub-Saharan Africa were a source of prestige that enhanced Cuban political influence in Third World countries. They also enabled Cuba to obtain sociological and anthropological data that would allow it to exert greater influence on civilian populations, in preparation for possible military intervention during the Cold War, to support left-wing regimes (see the chapter by Rodríguez Ruiz in this volume).

CUBAN MILITARY INTERVENTION DURING THE SAND WAR

The first Cuban military mission to the African continent also took place in Algeria. The country did not have a modern army although the ANP was heir to the ALN, which had fought the French colonial army for eight years. In fact, the Algerian army was made up of disparate elements that needed to be unified, ranging from a mainly rural internal resistance force to externally based troops with modern equipment, stationed in Morocco and Tunisia, with little combat experience apart from the Battle of the Frontiers in 1958. The army's equipment came mainly from FLN allies during the war: the countries of Eastern Europe, the USSR and China. The army command was also disparate, and beset by tensions between the group of deserters from the French army and officers trained in military academies in the Middle East.[47] Moreover, under the Ben Bella regime, a rebellion had broken out in 1963 in the Kabylie region, supported by a majority of the Kabyle resistance fighters under the command of Colonel Mohand Ould Hadj and of Hocine Aït Ahmed, who founded the FFS (Socialist Forces Front) in the same year. At that time, the Moroccan army was better organised than its Algerian counterpart.

When Algeria was attacked by Morocco, a NATO ally, during the Sand War (October 1963 to February 1964), a conflict over Saharan borders that had been poorly demarcated by the former colonial power, Fidel Castro decided to send Cuban troops to help the Algerians. This operation was code-named Dignity.[48] The Cuban and Algerian versions of this event are similar. The Cuban combat force included 120 soldiers, aircraft, tanks and artillery, and was led by Commander Efigenio Ameijeiras. On 23 May 1963, two Cuban ships landed in Oran, and the Cuban units set up a base in a former French Foreign Legion camp in Sidi Bel Abbes. They were accompanied by a medical unit. The Cuban soldiers were incorporated into the Algerian military strategy. The Moroccans crossed the border and occupied Tindouf: the Algerian plan was for Algerian and Cuban units to attack the Moroccans near Aricha, cross the Atlas Mountains and march on Casablanca.

However, the Cubans did not fight, as the Moroccans chose to negotiate. Half of the Cuban soldiers remained in camps in Algeria, where they briefly worked as military advisers. To thank the Cubans, the Algerians invited them to a military parade in Algiers on 2 April 1964, organised to celebrate the fifth anniversary of the Cuban Revolution.

From 1962 to 1965, Algiers became the headquarters and base for Cuban military interventions in sub-Saharan Africa. Sub-Saharan African militants could, of course, travel directly to Cuba to undergo military training, without going through Algiers. For example, the Zanzibar Nationalist Party opened an office in Havana in 1961. Several hundred sub-Saharan students were given military training in Havana from 1962 to 1965 without going through Algiers. The first groups, which came from South Africa, Kenya, Angola, Tanganyika and Zanzibar, learned guerrilla tactics. However, with the notable exception of East Africa, where Algeria played no role in the rebellions on either the military or medical front, in most cases the Cubans had agreements with the Algerians for the sub-Saharan *guerrilleros* to be trained in Algeria, which did not accept Cuban military advisers in the name of protecting its sovereignty.

A *LIEU DE MÉMOIRE* FORGOTTEN AND REDISCOVERED

After the coup d'état by Boumediene in 1965, referred to in Algeria as a 'revolutionary correction', Algiers was no longer the capital of Third World revolutionary movements, although sub-Saharan activists continued to be taken in. It was Havana that took over the role. Castro admired Ben Bella for his idealism and generosity and was mistrustful of the Algerian putsch.[49] In retaliation, the office of the Cuban news agency Prensa Latina in Algiers was closed and the Cuban ambassador recalled. All the socialist countries expressed their disapproval, boycotting the Ninth World Youth Festival in Algiers, which had to be cancelled. Under Boumediene, Algiers could no longer serve as a beacon for Third World revolutionary movements. His regime had opted for a policy of balanced relations with both the Eastern and Western blocs, and had signed agreements with US multinationals in the oil and natural gas sector for the transfer of operating rights.[50]

In the official memory of the Boumediene regime, from 1965 until the triumphal welcome given to Fidel Castro in Algeria in May 1972, and despite the normalisation of Algerian–Cuban relations in 1967, there is little celebration of Algerian–Cuban friendship; few traces are to be found in the official Algerian media. The image of Che Guevara is also preferred to that of Fidel Castro. One of the main avenues on the sea front in Algiers was named after Che six months after his death in Bolivia in October 1967. This act of remembrance was carried out by Boumediene himself on 24 April 1968 and broadcast on Algerian television.[51] On 5 July 1967, several representatives from sub-Saharan national liberation movements attended a ceremony celebrating International Youth Day and the struggle against colonialism, at which the figure of Che was invoked.

The situation changed somewhat after Boumediene's nationalisation of the oil and natural gas industry in 1971. Abdelaziz Bouteflika, minister of foreign affairs and later president, paid a visit to Havana that year.[52] Castro declared that 'Algeria is the pillar of the revolution in the Arab world', but excluded the African world. Boumediene had become a left-wing nationalist in the Non-Aligned Movement by choosing, on the domestic front, to collectivise the agricultural sector and to 'industrialise industry', an economic policy advocated by Gérard Destanne de Bernis, a French economist from the University of Grenoble. In terms of foreign policy, he called for a new international order on the occasion of the Non-Aligned Movement Summit in Algiers in 1973, attended by Fidel Castro.[53] Nevertheless, the Cuban and Algerian regimes were moving in different directions. Castro abandoned the guiding principle of his pre-1968 foreign policy, 'neither Moscow nor Peking',[54] and adopted a Soviet vision of the world. Cuban involvement in Africa no longer meant the same as it had in the 1960s. Cuba was gradually becoming the military arm of the USSR on the African continent, especially after the Carnation Revolution in Portugal in April 1974, a prelude to the decolonisation of Portuguese colonies in sub-Saharan Africa,[55] and the resumption of the Cold War between the Eastern and Western blocs in the wake of the Helsinki Conference in 1974–5. Indeed, when

South African troops, backed by the United States, occupied southern Angola in August 1975, Cuban troops intervened to support the Marxist-Leninist MPLA.

For Boumediene, all-out interventionism was no longer the priority: instead, he favoured development. From an ideological standpoint, his policy statements were confined to condemning exploitation of the countries of the South by the countries of the North. The PAGS (Socialist Vanguard Party), successor to the Algerian Communist Party, was still banned although it retained unofficial influence within the sole Algerian trade union, UGTA (General Union of Algerian Workers), which supported Boumediene's industrial and 'socialist villages' policies. In people's minds, however, Boumediene remained associated with Algiers' heyday as 'the Mecca of revolutionaries', a period during which he played a crucial role as vice-president of the Council and minister of national defence. In the Algerian official memory, he could therefore be shown to be one of the prime movers of this golden age of Algerian Third World diplomacy, which aimed to offer a haven for all the revolutionary activists of the countries of the South in Algiers, with priority given to those from the African continent. Photographs of Boumediene and Fidel Castro from 1972 could be sold by street vendors on the pavements of Algiers' main thoroughfares, at the cost of falsifying history by making it appear as though Algiers was still 'the Mecca of revolutionaries' in the 1970s. While the policy of support for sub-Saharan liberation movements continued, under the strict control of Military Security, which was responsible for ensuring that their presence did not harm Algerian national interests, its scope was more limited than under the Ben Bella presidency. Boumediene did, nevertheless, together with Cuba, provide substantial support for the Polisario Front, which was fighting for the Sahrawi people's right to self-determination.

In the 1970s Ben Bella, who lived under house arrest at the Château Holden in Douera, a suburb of Algiers, was subject to a *damnatio memoriae*, an erasure from public memory, to the benefit of Boumediene, who was acclaimed in the official history. This *a posteriori* reconstruction of history lasted for many years in Algeria, even after Ben Bella's release in 1980, ending only in the 2000s with his full rehabilitation by the Algerian regime when he no longer presented any political danger because of his advanced age.

From 1979 to 1992, under the presidency of Chadli Bendjedid, it was photos of Boumediene with Che Guevara and Fidel Castro that were put on public display in the new museums at Riadh El Feth in Algiers, Algeria's central memorial complex: the National Museum of Moudjahid, inaugurated in 1982, and the Museum of the Armed Forces, opened to the public in 1984. It was only in the 2000s that photographs of Ben Bella taken with Guevara in 1963 reappeared among the informal street vendors on Algiers' main thoroughfares. It is interesting to note that Che Guevara and Fidel Castro are part of Algeria's revolutionary mythology, alongside the pantheon of war heroes from the Algerian War of Independence, in a country where the blood of the martyrs, the Algerian fighters who died for the independence of their nation, remains until today a major source of legitimacy for the exercise of power. Even if they did not live through the Algerian War, in order to have any claim to govern Algerian leaders must present themselves as heirs of the martyrs (the *chuhadâ*) and the *mujâhidîn*, those who fought in the Holy War – to use the official terminology – to drive out the colonial power.

On the death of Fidel Castro in 2016, the Algerian National Archives organised an exhibition on his links with Algeria, as a propaganda exercise for the Algerian regime. Fidel was shown with the rehabilitated Ben Bella and with Boumediene, as well as with President Chadli Bendjedid during his visit to Havana in 1985. President Bouteflika's speech on the occasion of Raúl Castro's 2009 visit to Algeria was also on display, evidence of Algerian support for the current Cuban regime. Invoking Fidel Castro, who enjoys great popularity in Algeria and in Africa as a whole, is a way of imparting a 'sacred impetus' to the declining revolutionary legitimacy of the Algerian regime, whose social foundations are diminishing as time passes, especially among the younger generations. To invoke the golden age of Algerian diplomacy, with no distinction between the Ben Bella and Boumediene years prior to the 1980s, which were marked by the rise of political Islam, and the 'Black Decade' of the 1990s, dominated by terrorism, attests to a strategy intended to legitimise a regime struggling to find its 'second wind'.

The documentary *Alger, Mecque de la révolution*, directed by Mohamed Ben Salama in 2016, follows the same line, reactivating this revolutionary mythology without making a clear distinction between the Ben Bella and the Boumediene years. Unlike Ben Bella, Boumediene supported foreign revolutionary movements only if Algeria's best interests were not threatened. The Black Panthers, for example, were asked to leave Algiers so as not to damage Algerian–American relations. In fact, under Boumediene, an unofficial diplomatic policy of rapprochement with the United States was set in motion, led by Boumediene's henchman, the businessman Messaoud Zeghar, who was tasked with convincing the Americans that the nationalisation of Algerian oil and natural gas was in line with their interests.[56] Furthermore, under Boumediene, who sought to present himself as the champion of Arab nationalism in the 1970s, Algerian diplomacy shifted more towards the Middle East than towards Africa. Despite this, Algeria has continued to the present day to back the Polisario Front in Western Sahara by providing financial and military aid, a logistics base on its territory, and diplomatic support in the form of condemnation of 'Moroccan colonialism' in that part of the world, to adopt the terminology used by the Algerians.

RENEWING TIES BETWEEN CUBA AND AFRICA

While the figures of Che Guevara and Fidel Castro (after his 1972 tour) enjoyed great popularity in Algeria, and boosted the resurgence of the myth of 'Algiers, the Mecca of revolutionaries', by evoking the country's anti-imperialist Cuban–African networks, it was Nelson Mandela's visit to Algiers in 1990 that gave a new significance to transatlantic relations. In his capacity as vice-president of the ANC after his release from prison in February 1990, Mandela undertook a world tour to thank the countries that had supported the anti-apartheid struggle in South Africa and to call for the lifting of economic sanctions against his country. Wearing a scarf with the Algerian colours, Mandela met young Algerians at the Olympic Stadium, brandishing Palestinian flags, pennants, Sahrawi banners and portraits of Boumediene and Che Guevara.[57]

In his speech, Mandela paid tribute to Ahmed Ben Bella, Boumediene, Fidel Castro and Che Guevara. Mandela's visit occurred in the context of a democratic opening in Algeria. After the brutal suppression of the October 1988 riots, the political situation in Algeria made new memorial narratives possible, including the partial rehabilitation of Ben Bella. While the Algerian regime allowed Mandela to meet young Algerians at a mass rally, its aim was to organise a kind of gathering of enlightened young people against popular mobilisation by the FIS (Islamic Salvation Front), which embodied the political Islam of the time. On his return from exile in Switzerland in 1990, Ben Bella was even allowed to set up a political party in Algeria, the Movement for Democracy in Algeria (MDA), and to tour the whole country, addressing young Algerians who were excluded from a share in oil revenues, but also expressing views characterised by an Arab-Muslim ideology. This democratisation process was stifled in Algeria after the electoral process was suspended in 1991 and the Algerian army seized power, demanding the resignation of President Chadli Bendjedid in January 1992.

Nelson Mandela subsequently made an official visit to Cuba[58] on 26 July 1991, when he paid tribute to Fidel Castro for his medical and military support to the African continent. It was on this occasion that he made his famous speech describing the decisive Battle of Cuito Cuanavale in January 1988 as a 'turning point in the struggle to free the continent from the scourge of apartheid', marking the end of thirteen years of military intervention in Angola by the apartheid regime.

According to Mandela, this led to the independence of Namibia and played a major role in the end of the apartheid regime, a point that is, however, debated among historians.[59] By including both Algeria and Cuba in his tour, Mandela symbolically renewed Cuban ties with the African continent. Similarly, after his election as president in 1994, Mandela's first state visits were to sub-Saharan African countries, Algeria, and Cuba, although the Algerian context was quite different then because of the civil war of the 1990s. At an international level, as a president crowned with the success of his victory over apartheid, Mandela symbolically retraced the steps of the African militants who had travelled to Algiers and Havana.

THE CUBAN MODEL OF MISSIONS TO AFRICA

The Cuban missions to Algeria in 1963 influenced many subsequent Cuban missions to sub-Saharan Africa and Latin America in the 1960s and 1970s. Thanks to these, Cuba, a small country under embargo, was able to exert influence in the Third World. The cooperation and technical assistance Cuba offered to the Algerians was not only medical or military but also financial and technical. It is therefore also the place of these missions in Algerian and Cuban memory that should be made explicit, as well as the extent of their legacy in Algeria.

In terms of memorialisation of the past, the memory of the first medical mission is still alive in Algeria today. Medical cooperation has indeed continued, and its *lieux de mémoire*[60] are the four eye hospitals where Cuban doctors work. They are everyday sites of memory, the most effective in terms of their social impact and of memory education, addressing a fundamental human need. At the entrance to each hospital, photographs of the Cuban medical missions to Algeria since 1963 tell their story to the public. Documentaries are also regularly broadcast by Algerian public television, reporting on Algerian–Cuban medical cooperation from 1963 to the present day. These Cuban hospitals were nationalised by the Algerian state in 2009, but Cuban teams continue to work there. The memory of these medical missions legitimises the cooperation programmes between the two countries, which continue to operate in the fields of vaccination, obstetrics (in Djelfa and Bechar), and urology (in Bechar).

In Cuba itself, the Cuban medical missions to Algeria are remembered on the occasion of anniversaries. Documentaries are shown on television; conferences are organised in the medical faculties. Those who participated in the missions are honoured in order to encourage new volunteers to do the same. The slogan 'The best go to Algeria' is still part of the collective memory, alluding to the memory of the first medical mission to the African continent. In this way, by glorifying the revolutionary elite, whose skills and courage are renowned, the regime itself acquires legitimacy and a share of the reflected glory. The health minister in 1963 at the time of the first mission to Algeria, José Ramón Machado Ventura, was recently still second secretary of the Communist Party of Cuba and first vice-president of the Cuban Council of State and Council of Ministers.

As for the memory of the Cuban military mission to Algeria, it is regularly mentioned in the press and in documentaries broadcast by the Algerian state television company EPTV (formerly RTA and ENTV) and is also commemorated by the official media in Cuba. However, no memorial exists in Cuba or Algeria honouring Algerian–Cuban friendship in either its military or medical forms. Algerian museums show only photographs of the highest-ranking leaders: Boumediene, Castro, Che Guevara and, since the 2000s, Ben Bella. For its part, the Cuban regime addresses the issue of internationalism in its official memory with reference to José Martí (1853–95), whereas the Algerian memory focuses more on bilateral cooperation. At the Museum of the Revolution in Havana, no mention is made of either the missions to Algeria or, more broadly, the missions to the larger African continent. As far as relations between Cuba and Africa are concerned, reference is made only to the slave revolts that led up to the 1898 War of Independence, and to the 1959 Cuban Revolution. A common Algerian–Cuban memory emerges, however, from the official press and media, evoking a sense of sacrifice and a culture of martyrdom and duty to the national community, despite differences in the two nations' religious roots.[61]

The memory of the history of Algerian–Cuban relations between 1962 and 1965 constitutes the founding myth of the Cuban internationalist network in Africa. The goal of this commitment was the struggle against colonialism, apartheid and imperialism as well as condemnation of the exploitation of the countries of the South by the countries of the North. Thanks to the network set up in Algeria, numerous Cuban missions in the 1960s followed the example set: Congo-Brazzaville in 1963, Guinea-Bissau in 1964, Congo-Kinshasa in 1965. As Cuba was not aligned with the USSR at the time, these initiatives should be analysed as a model of South–South diplomacy. The leaders of the two nations of Cuba and Algeria were capable of autonomous political choices, and during the Cold War it was therefore public actors who defended these values. Today, the same values are upheld by private actors who are against globalisation (trade unions, voluntary associations, fair trade advocates) and operate outside state control through social forums that offer an alternative to global neoliberalism, in keeping with the new transnational paradigm that prevails in the age of globalisation.[62]

NOTES

1 Algerian National Archives, GPRA archives (1958–1962), File 10/3/22, Memos to the Ministry of Foreign Affairs from Lakhdar Brahimi, Algerian representative in Cuba.

2 Author of a war journal on the Cuban guerrilla movement, *Los que luchan y los que lloran* (1958), Masetti was an Argentine revolutionary and journalist who helped found the Cuban news agency Prensa Latina. He received support from Algeria after independence to organise a revolutionary movement in northern Argentina, where he died in 1964.

3 Piero Gleijeses, *Conflicting Missions: Havana, Washington and Africa 1959–1976* (Chapel Hill, NC: University of North Carolina Press, 2002), 31.

4 Gilbert Meynier, *Histoire intérieure du FLN (1954–1962)* (Paris: Fayard, 2002), 589.

5 In the meaning given to this concept by Roger Bastide: 'a system of interrelations between individual memories'; see Roger Bastide, 'Mémoire collective et sociologie du bricolage,' *L'Année Sociologique* 21 (1970): 65–108.

6 Official memory designates a political use of the past in the form of the beliefs imposed by a political regime in order to gain legitimacy. This concept is relevant to both Cuba and Algeria, and despite the abolition of the one-party system in 1989 in Algeria, memory continues to be monitored.

7 Robert Merle, *Ahmed Ben Bella* (Paris: Gallimard, 1965), 207–21; Irwin Wall, *Les Etats Unis et la guerre d'Algérie* (Paris: Soleb, 2013). During this visit, despite Senator Kennedy's support for the Algerian people's struggle for independence in his 1957 speech, Ben Bella criticised segregation in the United States and met Martin Luther King. He told the American press that Algeria had opted for non-alignment. In reality, relations between the United States and Algeria had deteriorated because of American criticism of Ben Bella's seizure of power and policy of nationalisation. For the Americans, this was proof of the Ben Bella regime's socialist leanings.

8 Speech by Ahmed Ben Bella (17 October 1962) in *Revolución* (30 October 1962): 7.

9 René Gallissot and Jacques Kergoat, eds, *Medhi Ben Barka: De l'indépendance marocaine à la Tricontinentale* (Paris: Karthala, 1997), 128.

10 Roger Faligot, *La Tricontinentale* (Paris: La Découverte, 2013).

11 Pierre Kalfon, *Che: Ernesto Guevara, une légende du siècle* (Paris: Seuil, 2013), 366, 400, 409.

12 A *lieu de mémoire* is 'any significant entity, whether material or non-material in nature, which by dint of human will or the work of time has become a symbolic element of the memorial heritage of any community'. See Pierre Nora, *Realms of Memory: Rethinking the French Past* (New York: Columbia University Press, 1996), xvii.

13 Interview with Régis Debray, Paris, April 2016. All interviews quoted in this chapter were conducted by the author, who was granted permission to quote and name the interviewees. Régis Debray is a former companion of Che Guevara. Debray was arrested in Bolivia and imprisoned from 1967 to 1971. He is now an academic, specialising in philosophy and 'mediology'.

14 Guy Pervillé, 'Le panafricanisme du FLN,' in *L'Afrique noire française: L'heure des indépendances*, ed. C.R. Ageron and M. Michel (Paris: CNRS Editions, 1992), 513–22. See also Guy Pervillé, *Histoire iconoclaste de la guerre d'Algérie et de ses mémoires* (Paris: Vendémiaire, 2018).

15 David Macey, *Frantz Fanon, une vie* (Algiers: Chihab Editions, 2013); René Gallissot, ed., *Algérie: Engagements sociaux et question nationale: De la colonisation à l'indépendance de 1830 à 1962: Dictionnaire biographique du mouvement ouvrier: Maghreb* (Algiers: Barzakh, 2007), 270–8.

16 Saïd Bouamama, *Figures de la révolution africaine* (Paris: Editions Zones, 2014).
17 *Qu'est-ce que le programme de Tripoli?* (Algiers: Direction de la documentation et des publications, 1961).
18 Carlos Moore, *Pichón: Race and Revolution in Castro's Cuba: A Memoir* (Chicago: Chicago Review Press, 2008).
19 Roberto Zurbano Torres, 'Un fantasma en el Caribe? Muerte y resurrección de Frantz Fanon en cuarenta años de lecturas cubanas,' 2015, accessed 8 January 2018.
20 Robert Blackey, 'Fanon and Cabral: A Contrast in Theories of Revolution for Africa,' *Journal of Modern African Studies* 12, no. 2 (1974): 191–209.
21 The FLN newspaper *El Moudjahid* ran the following headline in Issue 62, 31 March 1960: 'Alger–Le Cap: L'axe du colonialisme: Des massacres de Philippeville aux massacres de Sharpeville' (From Algiers to the Cape: The Colonial Axis: From the Philippeville Massacres to the Sharpeville Massacres).
22 Jean Leca and Jean-Claude Vatin, *L'Algérie politique: Institutions et régime* (Paris: Presses de Sciences Po, 1975).
23 Interview with Gérard Chaliand, Paris, April 2016.
24 Scott Thomas, *The Diplomacy of Liberation: The Foreign Relations of the ANC since 1960* (London: Tauris Academic Studies, 1996), 42.
25 Fernando Andresen Guimaraes, *The Origins of the Angolan Civil War: Foreign Intervention and Domestic Political Conflict* (London: Palgrave Macmillan, 2001), 61.
26 Michel Laban, *Mario Pinto de Andrade, una entrevista* (Lisbon: Sa da Costa, 1997).
27 Southern Rhodesia was a colony until Ian Smith's Declaration of Independence in 1965.
28 Jeffrey James Byrne, *Mecca of Revolution: Algeria, Decolonization and the Third World Order* (Oxford: Oxford University Press, 2016), 197.
29 Byrne, *Mecca of Revolution*, 246–7.
30 Byrne, *Mecca of Revolution*, 249. On Congo-Brazzaville, see Kiriakou and André in this volume.
31 Oujda was one of the FLN's external bases in Morocco during the Algerian War. The Oujda Group was made up of FLN officials close to Boumediene.
32 Hugh Roberts, *The Battlefield: Algeria, 1988–2002: Studies in a Broken Polity* (London and New York: Verso, 2003), 52.
33 Interview with Mohammed Harbi, Paris, April 2016.
34 Interview with Gérard Chaliand, Paris, April 2016.
35 Jeffrey James Byrne, in *Mecca of Revolution*, does not take Arab-Muslim ideology sufficiently into account as an explanation for the Ben Bella regime's political choices, unlike Robert Malley, *The Call from Algeria: Third Worldism, Revolution and the Turn to Islam* (Berkeley: University of California Press, 1996), or James McDougall, '"Soi-même" comme un "autre" : Les histoires coloniales d'Ahmed Tawfiq Al Madani (1899–1983),' *Revue des Mondes Musulmans et de la Méditerranée*, 95–98 (April 2002): 95–110.
36 René Gallissot, *Henri Curiel: Le mythe mesuré à l'histoire* (Paris: Riveneuve, 2009).
37 Interview with Henri Alleg, Palaiseau, December 2011.
38 Henri Alleg, *Victorieuse Cuba: De la guérilla au socialisme* (Paris: Éditions de Minuit, 1963); Henri Alleg, *Mémoire algérienne* (Alger: Casbah Editions, 2005), 365.
39 Louis A. Perez, *Cuba: Between Reform and Revolution* (Oxford: Oxford University Press, 2014), 268.
40 Kamel Kateb, *Européens, 'indigènes' et juifs en Algérie (1830–1962)* (Paris: INED/PUF, 2001).
41 Gisela García, *La misión internacionalista de Cuba en Argelia (1963–1964)* (Havana: Dirección Política de las FAR, 1990).

[42] Jaime Saruski, 'Los médicos cubanos en Argelia,' *Revolución*, Havana, 16 December 1963; Gabriel Molina, 'La asistencia médica de Cuba a Argelia,' *Revolución*, Havana, 23 June 1964.
[43] Washington Rosell Puig, *Recuerdos de aquel primer viaje* (Havana: ENSAP, 1998); Washington Rosell Puig, 'Antecedentes de la primera misión internacionalista cubana en el campo de la docencia médica,' *Educación Médica Superior* 20, no. 1 (2006).
[44] National Archives of Algeria, Algerian Ministry of Health, 1962–1965, File 1550, Box 120.
[45] *Le Monde*, 21 March 1983.
[46] Interview with Gérard Chaliand, Paris, April 2016.
[47] Abderrezak Bouhara, *Les viviers de la libération* (Algiers: Casbah Editions, 2001), 232.
[48] Cuban Archives, Flavio Bravo, Deputy Commander of the Cuban Forces in Algeria, to Raúl Castro, Algiers, 21 October 1963, Centro de Información de la Defensa de las Fuerzas Armadas Revolucionarias (CID-FAR), Havana, digitalarchive.wilsoncenter.org/document/112126.
[49] Gleijeses, *Conflicting Missions*, 53.
[50] Nicole Grimaud, *La politique extérieure de l'Algérie: 1962–1978* (Paris: Karthala, 1984), 71.
[51] ENTV's Audio-Visual Archives (Algerian National Public Television), Television News, 24 April 1968.
[52] *Le Monde*, 9 May 1972.
[53] Alcaraz, Emmanuel, *Les lieux de mémoire de la guerre d'indépendance algérienne* (Paris: Karthala, 2017), 351–61.
[54] *Le Monde*, 12 April 1967.
[55] Angola gained its independence on 11 November 1975.
[56] Seddik S. Larkeche, *Si Zeghar, l'iconoclaste algérien: La véritable histoire de Rachid Casa* (Lyons: Ena Editions, 2014).
[57] Interview with Aïcha Mecheri, Tunis, July 2016. Aïcha Mecheri is a lawyer and member of the Algiers bar, who was present at the Olympic Stadium during Nelson Mandela's visit on 17 May 1990.
[58] Mandela also visited the United States, including Miami: regarding the reception he was given by the Cuban community in exile, see the chapter by Gonçalves in this volume.
[59] Gleijeses, *Conflicting Missions*.
[60] Pierre Nora, *Les lieux de mémoire*, 3 vols. (Paris: Gallimard, 1997); John E. Bodnar, *Remaking America: Public Memory, Commemoration and Patriotism in the Twentieth Century* (Princeton: Princeton University Press, 1992); Patrick Garcia, 'Les lieux de mémoire: Une poétique de la mémoire?' *Espace Temps* 74–75 (2000): 122–42; Emmanuel Alcaraz, *Les lieux de mémoire de la guerre d'indépendance algérienne* (Paris: Karthala, 2017).
[61] Louis A. Perez, *To Die in Cuba: Suicide and Society* (Chapel Hill, NC: University of North Carolina Press, 2007); Emmanuel Alcaraz, 'Le devenir des restes des *mujâhidîn* de 1962 à nos jours,' in *Le Funéraire: Mémoires, protocoles, monuments*, ed. G. Delaplace and F. Valentin (Paris: De Boccard, 2015), 137–47.
[62] James Rosenau, *Turbulence in World Politics: A Theory of Change and Continuity* (Princeton: Princeton University Press, 1990).

PRIMARY SOURCES

Alleg, Henri. *Mémoire algérienne*. Alger: Casbah Editions, 2005.
Alleg, Henri. *Victorieuse Cuba: De la guérilla au socialisme*. Paris: Éditions de Minuit, 1963.

Ben Salama, Mohamed. *Alger, la Mecque des révolutionnaires (1962–1974)*. EPTV/Arte, 2016 (Benjamin Stora was historical adviser for the documentary).
Centro de Información de la Defensa de las Fuerzas Armadas Revolucionarias (CID-FAR), Havana, wilsoncenter.org.
García, Gisela. *La misión internacionalista de Cuba en Argelia (1963–1964)*. Havana: Dirección Política de las FAR, 1990.
Granma, Havana, 1965–1968.
Masetti, Jorge Ricardo. *Los que luchan y los que lloran y otros escritos ineditos*. Buenos Aires: Nuestra America, 2006.
National Archives of Algeria, Algiers.
Qu'est-ce que le programme de Tripoli? Algiers: Direction de la documentation et des publications, 1961.
Revolución. Havana, 1963–1964.
Révolution Africaine. Algiers, 1962–1997.
Rosell Puig, Washington. Antecedentes de la primera misión internacionalista cubana en el campo de la docencia médica. Havana: Escuela Nacional de Salud Pública, 2006.
Rosell Puig, Washington. *Recuerdos de aquel primer viaje*. Havana: Escuela Nacional de Salud Pública, 1998.

INTERVIEWS WITH AUTHOR

Alleg, Henri. Palaiseau, December 2011.
Chaliand, Gérard. Paris, April 2016.
Debray, Régis. Paris, April 2016.
Harbi, Mohammed. Paris, April 2016.
Mecheri, Aïcha, Tunis, July 2016.

BIBLIOGRAPHY

Alcaraz, Emmanuel. 'Le devenir des restes des *mujâhidîn* de 1962 à nos jours.' In *Le Funéraire: Mémoires, protocoles, monuments*, edited by G. Delaplace and F. Valentin, 131–47. Paris: De Boccard, 2015.
Alcaraz, Emmanuel. *Les lieux de mémoire de la guerre d'indépendance algérienne*. Paris: Karthala, 2017.
Andrade, Mario de. 'Amilcar Cabral: Profil d'un révolutionnaire africain.' *Présence Africaine* 185–186 (2012): 81–94.
Bain, Mervyn J. 'Havana and Moscow (1959–2009): The Enduring Relationship?' *Cuban Studies* 41 (2010): 85–104.
Bastide, Roger. 'Mémoire collective et sociologie du bricolage.' *L'Année Sociologique* 21 (1970): 65–108.
Blackey, Robert. 'Fanon and Cabral: A Contrast in Theories of Revolution for Africa.' *Journal of Modern African Studies* 12, no. 2 (1974): 191–209.
Bodnar, John E. *Remaking America: Public Memory, Commemoration and Patriotism in the Twentieth Century*. Princeton: Princeton University Press, 1992.

Bouamama, Saïd. *Figures de la révolution africaine*. Paris: Editions Zones, 2014.
Bouhara, Abderrezak. *Les viviers de la libération*. Algiers: Casbah Editions, 2001.
Bravo, Douglas. *Avec Douglas Bravo dans les maquis vénézuéliens*. Paris: Maspero, 1968.
Byrne, Jeffrey James. *Mecca of Revolution: Algeria, Decolonization and the Third World Order*. Oxford: Oxford University Press, 2016.
Campbell, Horace. *The Siege of Cuito Canavale*. Current African Issues 10. Uppsala: Scandinavian Institute of African Studies, 1990.
Chaliand, Gérard. *L'Algérie est-elle socialiste?* Paris: Maspero, 1964.
Chaliand, Gérard. *Les luttes armées en Afrique*. Paris: Maspero, 1969.
Chaliand, Gérard. *Mémoires, vol. I, La pointe du couteau*. Paris: Robert Laffont, 2011.
Chaliand, Gérard. *Un itinéraire combattant*. Paris: Karthala, 1997.
Connelly, James Matthew. *A Diplomatic Revolution: Algeria's Fight for Independence and the Origins of the Post-Cold War Era*. Oxford: Oxford University Press, 2002.
Faligot, Roger. *La Tricontinentale*. Paris: La Découverte, 2013.
Fanon, Frantz. *Pour la révolution africaine: Ecrits politiques*. Paris: La Découverte, 2006.
Feinsilver, Julius M. 'Fifty Years of Cuba's Medical Diplomacy: From Idealism to Pragmatism.' *Cuban Studies* 41 (2010): 85–104.
Gallissot, René, ed. *Algérie: Engagements sociaux et question nationale: De la colonisation à l'indépendance de 1830 à 1962: Dictionnaire biographique du mouvement ouvrier: Maghreb*. Algiers: Barzakh, 2007.
Gallissot, René. *Henri Curiel: Le mythe mesuré à l'histoire*. Paris: Riveneuve, 2009.
Gallissot, René and Jacques Kergoat, eds. *Medhi Ben Barka: De l'indépendance marocaine à la Tricontinentale*. Paris: Karthala, 1997.
Garcia, Patrick. 'Les lieux de mémoire: Une poétique de la mémoire?' *Espace Temps* 74–75 (2000): 122–42.
Gleijeses, Piero. *Conflicting Missions: Havana, Washington and Africa 1959–1976*. Chapel Hill, NC: University of North Carolina Press, 2002.
Gleijeses, Piero. 'Cuba's First Venture in Africa: Algeria, 1961–1965.' *Journal of Latin American Studies* 28, no. 1 (1996): 159–95.
Gleijeses, Piero. *Visions of Freedom: Havana, Washington, Pretoria, and the Struggle for Southern Africa, 1976–1991*. Chapel Hill, NC: University of North Carolina Press, 2013.
Grimaud, Nicole. *La politique extérieure de L'Algérie: 1962–1978*. Paris: Karthala, 1984.
Guimaraes, Fernando Andresen. *The Origins of the Angolan Civil War: Foreign Intervention and Domestic Political Conflict*. London: Palgrave Macmillan, 2001.
Harbi, Mohammed. 'Frantz Fanon et le messianisme paysan.' *Tumultes* 31 (2008): 11–15.
Kalfon, Pierre. *Che: Ernesto Guevara, une légende du siècle*. Paris: Seuil, 2013.
Kateb, Kamel. *Européens, 'indigènes' et juifs en Algérie (1830–1962)*. Paris: INED/PUF, 2001.
Krull, Catherine. *Cuba in a Global Context: International Relations, Internationalism and Transnationalism*. Gainesville: University Press of Florida, 2014.
Laban, Michel. *Mario Pinto de Andrade, una entrevista*. Lisbon: Sa da Costa, 1997.
Larkeche, Seddik S. *Si Zeghar, l'iconoclaste algérien: La véritable histoire de Rachid Casa*. Lyons: Ena Editions, 2014.
Leca, Jean and Jean-Claude Vatin. *L'Algérie politique: Institutions et régime*. Paris: Presses de Sciences Po, 1975.
Lentin, Albert-Paul. 'La reconstrucción del FLN y la lucha por el socialismo en Argelia.' *Cuba Socialista* 42 (1965): 63–73.
Macey, David. *Frantz Fanon, une vie*. Algiers: Chihab Editions, 2013.

Malley, Robert. *The Call from Algeria: Third Worldism, Revolution and the Turn to Islam*. Berkeley: University of California Press, 1996.
McDougall, James. *A History of Algeria*. Cambridge: Cambridge University Press, 2017.
McDougall, James. '"Soi-même" comme un "autre": Les histoires coloniales d'Ahmed Tawfîq Al Madanî (1899–1983).' *Revue des Mondes Musulmans et de la Méditerranée* 95–98 (April 2002): 95–110.
Merle, Robert. *Ahmed Ben Bella*. Paris: Gallimard, 1965.
Meynier, Gilbert. *Histoire intérieure du FLN (1954–1962)*. Paris: Fayard, 2002.
Michel, Johann. *Gouverner les mémoires*. Paris: PUF, 1994.
Moore, Carlos. *Pichón: Race and Revolution in Castro's Cuba: A Memoir*. Chicago: Chicago Review Press, 2008.
Nora, Pierre. *Les lieux de mémoire*, 3 vols. Paris: Gallimard, 1997.
Nora, Pierre. *Realms of Memory: Rethinking the French Past*. New York: Columbia University Press, 1996.
Perez, Louis A. *Cuba: Between Reform and Revolution*. Oxford: Oxford University Press, 2014.
Perez, Louis A. *To Die in Cuba: Suicide and Society*. Chapel Hill, NC: University of North Carolina Press, 2007.
Pérez Cabrera, Ramón. *La historia cubana en Africa*, 3rd edn. Havana: Centro Nacional de Derecho de Autor, 2013.
Pervillé, Guy. *Histoire iconoclaste de la guerre d'Algérie et de ses mémoires*. Paris: Vendémiaire, 2018.
Pervillé, Guy. 'Le panafricanisme du FLN.' In *L'Afrique noire française: L'heure des indépendances*, edited by C.R. Ageron and M. Michel, 513–22. Paris: CNRS Editions, 1992.
Roberts, Hugh. *The Battlefield: Algeria, 1988–2002: Studies in a Broken Polity*. London and New York: Verso, 2003.
Rosenau, James. *Turbulence in World Politics: A Theory of Change and Continuity*. Princeton: Princeton University Press, 1990.
Rouquié, Alain. *Amérique latine: Introduction à l'Extrême-Occident*. Paris: Le Seuil, 1998.
Thomas, Scott. *The Diplomacy of Liberation: The Foreign Relations of the ANC since 1960*. London: Tauris Academic Studies, 1996.
Valdés, Nelson P. 'Revolutionary Solidarity in Angola.' In *Cuba in the World*, edited by C. Blasier and C. Mesa-Lago, 87–117. Pittsburgh: University of Pittsburgh Press, 1979.
Wall, Irwin. *Les Etats Unis et la guerre d'Algérie*. Paris: Soleb, 2013.
Zurbano Torres, Roberto. 'Un fantasma en el Caribe? Muerte y resurrección de Frantz Fanon en cuarenta años de lecturas cubanas.' 2015. Accessed 8 January 2018. http://www.afrocubaweb.com/fantasma.html.

CHAPTER

2

Cuban Policy and African Politics: Congo-Brazzaville and Angola, 1963–1977

Héloïse Kiriakou and Bernardo J.C. André

When Fidel Castro came to power in 1959, one of his goals was to develop a new foreign policy based on cooperation and mutual aid in accordance with the principles formulated by the Non-Aligned Movement, which emerged during the Bandung Conference in 1955.[1] Che Guevara, then minister of foreign affairs, was responsible for implementing this Cuban 'internationalism' in Africa. In 1964, he travelled around the continent (to Egypt, Algeria, Ghana, Guinea, Mali, Benin and Congo-Brazzaville) to meet several African leaders and set up a network of mutual assistance. Its objectives were to provide military support to liberation movements and to strengthen specific political regimes. Cuban diplomacy was conducted in official agreement with the Organisation of African Unity (OAU), which had also taken a number of measures to support liberation movements since its creation in 1963.

Since the 1960s, the history of Cuban internationalism has been the subject of several books and articles in newspapers (such as *Le Monde Diplomatique*) and academic journals (such as *Présence Africaine* and *Politique Étrangère*).[2] Most authors have written about this topic in the wider context of the historiography of international relations. Firstly, they analysed the Cuban intervention as an episode of the Cold War (intrinsically linked to this external context).[3] They also tended to present it as the result of the Soviet Union's intervention in Africa.[4] Secondly, the majority of authors stressed the extent, sometimes great indeed, of the Cuban military deployment and its considerable impact on the political history of African countries.[5] For example, Edward George highlights the impact of Cuban interventions (such as Operation Carlota) on the political evolution of Angola, as well as their impact on the balance of power during the Cold War.[6] Such studies mainly promoted the view held by the Cuban government, which was omnipresent in those countries' diplomatic archives, sometimes giving the impression that they were the only actors involved in these operations.

However, recent research illustrates the influence of local contexts and interpersonal relations between African policy frameworks and the Cuban government on the evolution of this internationalism. In her book *Cubans in Angola: South–South Cooperation and Transfer of Knowledge* (2015), historian Christine Hatzky explains how the decision to massively expand civil cooperation in Angola from 1977 – on top of military cooperation – was connected to the context of the civil war and the need to help the Popular Movement for the Liberation of Angola (MPLA) to consolidate its grasp on the country.[7]

In the wake of these approaches, we aim to analyse Cuban internationalism on the basis of its implementation in both Congo-Brazzaville and Angola in this chapter, in order to show how it evolved and how it took shape differently in these two African countries between 1963 and 1977. More precisely, we study the complexity of the political actors' strategies and the way the Cuban government's and African politicians' interests led to the construction of a 'real'[8] internationalism in Central Africa (in continuity with the one they had developed earlier in Algeria).

This four-hand comparative study demonstrates how the Cuban government tested its internationalism in Congo-Brazzaville from 1965 to evaluate its effectiveness, and how it was spread in Angola from 1974, using the same methods and often the same Cuban volunteers until 1977. In Congo-Brazzaville, Cuba helped the regime of Alphonse Massamba-Débat to consolidate new socialist institutions (for instance, through the creation of a militia to thwart the influence of the army). Cuba also set up a rear base in Brazzaville to support liberation movements in Central Africa (especially the MPLA, the UPC (Union of the Peoples of Cameroon) and the CNL (National Council of Liberation) of Congo-Kinshasa led by Pierre Mulele). Eventually, Cuba gave help to Alphonse Massamba-Débat during what turned out to be a successful coup by Marien Ngouabi in 1968, by providing him with military support.[9]

As for Angola, the Cuban government unwaveringly supported Agostinho Neto, the president of the MPLA, during the war against Portugal. It continued to do so once the country had acquired independence, during the conflicts with

South Africa and other liberation movements, namely UNITA (National Union for the Total Independence of Angola) and FNLA (National Front for the Liberation of Angola). Eventually, the Cuban government also intervened militarily to help Agostinho Neto when MPLA internal conflicts escalated (for example, in the conflicts with Daniel Chipenda, the chief of the army on the east front in 1969–74, and later with Nito Alves, the leader of the urban militias of Luanda, who attempted a coup in May 1977).[10] This important cooperation was extended until the 1990s and had a significant impact on Angola's domestic policy.

THE FORMATION OF CIVIL DEFENCE: THE ENTRY POINT IN CONGO-BRAZZAVILLE

In Congo-Brazzaville, the political situation had been extremely unstable since the insurrection of August 1963, which resulted in the resignation of President Fulbert Youlou. Indeed, the two trade union organisations – CATC (African Confederation of Believing Workers) and CGTA (General Confederation of African Workers) – which organised the general strike on 13 August 1963 to protest against the establishment of a single party, were overtaken by the scale of the movement. Demonstrators, exasperated by the stubbornness of President Fulbert Youlou who did not want to withdraw his single-party project, demanded his resignation and the end of the corrupt clientelist system he had sponsored since independence in 1960. Thus, on 15 August 1963, the Congo found itself with no government and no one thinking about its future. In this context, trade unionists appointed Alphonse Massamba-Débat (former president of the Assembly and then in conflict with Youlou) to lead the transitional government. Massamba-Débat set up a tight-knit government of 'technicians', made up of experienced technocrats and young graduates, in order to answer civil society's expectations and establish a fairer political system.

On the one hand, the supporters of the former president became increasingly militant and collaborated with regular army officers to plot several coups in neighbouring Zaire. On the other hand, students trained in France, who had acquired militant experience in trade unions and progressive parties, returned to the Congo to take part in the revolution and put pressure on the government to accelerate reforms. For example, Ambroise Noumazalaye and Claude-Ernest Ndalla Graille arrived in Brazzaville at the end of August 1963 after a visit to the USSR to gather support from the CPSU (Communist Party of the Soviet Union) for funding a revolutionary newspaper, *Dipanda* ('independence' in Lingala). In June 1964, Massamba-Débat decided to create a single party, the MNR (National Movement of the Revolution), whose aim was to bring together all the political movements. Under the influence of prime minister Pascal Lissouba during the Constituent Congress, delegates unanimously adopted 'scientific socialism' as the official doctrine of the new party. They granted the constituent groups that made up the party, mainly the JMNR (Youth of the National Movement of the Revolution),[11] the power to apply socialist measures locally.

At this point, the government decided to sign cooperation agreements with socialist countries such as the USSR, China and Cuba. While Che Guevara spent a few days in Brazzaville at the beginning of January 1965 during his African tour, Cuba and Congo signed their first cooperation agreement. This included targeted military assistance to bring together the various militias formed since the insurrection of August 1963 and to create an armed force loyal to the new regime (which was somewhat in opposition to the views of the army). Cuban instructors, in agreement with President Massamba-Débat, decided to significantly increase the power of the Civil Defence Corps since its creation in July 1965, a few days after army officers were once again involved in an attempted coup. Civil Defence thus found itself with massively increased power and influence.

Civil Defence was divided into seven camps spread throughout the city of Brazzaville.[12] Each camp was led by a commanding officer and a political commissar. Camps were organised on a military basis and Cuban instructors provided them with a programme of daily activities (ideological training and military exercises). Most of the Cuban instructors were accommodated in Madibou (south of Brazzaville, on a property owned by former president Fulbert Youlou, which was seized after the revolution) where they organised military training for some Civil Defence militiamen. Cuban instructors were also involved in the establishment of the Institute of Ideological Formation, located in the south of Brazzaville on an old farm requisitioned after the revolution. This was an official party institute involved in the full-time training of all Congolese activists (and militants of the liberation movements in exile in Brazzaville). It included ideological training in socialist theories, often assisted by African intellectuals like UPC Cameroonians René Jacques Woungly-Massaga and Castor Osendé Afana,[13] and courses on the history of revolutions, focusing to a large extent on the revolutions in the USSR and Cuba. Beyond military techniques and ideological training, Cuban influence was also apparent in clothing and food. Militiamen wore the Cuban army's olive-green uniform and ate canned *puerco* (boxes of pork directly imported from Cuba). The motto of the Civil Defence was also the same as that of the Cuban Revolution, 'Homeland or death, we shall conquer' (*la patrie ou la mort, nous vaincrons*).

Figure 2.1: Civil Defence militiamen at a meeting of President Massamba-Débat in the 'square of freedom' in Brazzaville (1966). Source: National Museum of Congo in Brazzaville.

Figure 2.2: Official parade of the Civil Defence in Brazzaville (1966). The man with his arms crossed in the foreground is Ange Diawara, head of Civil Defence. Source: National Museum of Congo in Brazzaville.

In 1968 the Cuban government intervened in an internal conflict between President Massamba-Débat and Commander Marien Ngouabi. The two men had been in conflict since 1966 with Ngouabi criticising Massamba-Débat's exercise of power, especially his decision to reduce the power of the military. In July 1968, after a difficult year for Massamba-Débat, Ngouabi succeeded in gathering around him all the disgruntled members of the regime, notably the group of army officers to which he belonged, Civil Defence cadres and some officials from the party. In this way, he found himself in a position of authority to negotiate President Massamba-Débat's resignation and the establishment of a transitional government. Yet, on or about 30 August 1968, some Civil Defence junior officers who had remained loyal to Massamba-Débat decided to take action against Ngouabi as a way of protest against his institutional coup.[14] For a few days, they took refuge in Camp Météo, located in the neighbourhood of Bacongo, which they renamed Camp Biafra, in reference to the civil war in Nigeria (1967–70). The mutineers of the Civil Defence were only fifty in number and mostly made up of the same ethnic group as that to which Massamba-Débat belonged.[15] According to several witnesses, several Cuban instructors were also involved. They took part in the fight and helped the mutineers escape through the back of the camp when the situation became critical. According to Colonel da Costa, who oversaw intelligence service and who was close to Massamba-Débat, the Cuban ambassador also offered the president the chance to escape to Havana.[16]

In Congo, the Cuban embassy thus provided support to the Massamba-Débat regime, although it was covert. The main intention of the Cubans was to develop a rear base for all the liberation movements of the region in order to make Brazzaville the front line of their internationalist policy in Central Africa.

CUBAN SUPPORT TO ANGOLA'S MPLA IN BRAZZAVILLE

Between 1965 and 1975, Congo-Brazzaville became the rear base of all liberation movements in the region. At that time, these movements included the UPC of Cameroon, the CNL of Congo-Kinshasa, the MPLA of Angola, the FLEC (Front for the Liberation of the Enclave of Cabinda) and the MNRG (National Movement of the Gabonese Revolution). All these were supported by the Cuban embassy and the Congolese government, to varying degrees.

As for the UPC, the Cuban embassy provided it with instructors and helped it to open a front in northern Congo, on the border with Cameroon. According to the French intelligence services in Congo (who were very concerned by the UPC's action because the French government had waged a war against the movement from 1955 to 1962 in Cameroon and had maintained a strong military presence on the ground), Cuba assisted UPC militants in Brazzaville to develop a column of 70 fighters called 'Ruben Um Nyobè' (in reference to the political leader of the UPC, assassinated in 1958).[17] Cuban officers also supported them in the north, around Ouesso, to establish an effective operational base on the border between the two countries. To promote the success of this deployment, the Cuban ambassador himself went to support the guerrillas in Ouesso. The establishment of this rear base enabled the UPC to conduct targeted raids against the Cameroonian government and thus to continue the armed struggle, although it was a difficult time for the movement.

The CNL of Pierre Mulele was one of the first movements to benefit from Cuba's practical support since Che Guevara wanted to organise military intervention in Congo by relying on the various Lumumbist movements that had been fighting against Moïse Tshombe since 1961.[18] Pierre Mulele had been minister of education in Patrice Lumumba's government and in 1963 he founded a *maquis* (underground military camp), based on the Maoist model, in the Kwilu region of the province of Bandundu.[19] The Congolese government made available to the Cuban instructors and CNL activists an underground military camp in Gamboma, some 300 kilometres from Brazzaville, near the border with Congo and the Kwilu region.[20] Gamboma camp was only in operation for a relatively short time (about two years intermittently) because Moïse Tshombe and Joseph-Désiré Mobutu regularly threatened to attack the government of Brazzaville if they continued to help the Lumumbists from 1965 onwards.

Unlike the CNL, the MPLA received more official support from the Cuban and Congolese governments. The MPLA came to settle in Brazzaville in November 1963 after they were expelled from Léopoldville by Tshombe's government and especially after refusing to make an alliance with the FNLA of Roberto Holden, thereby rejecting the OAU's recommendations, which wanted a single organisation to be recognised for Angola. The MPLA delegation in Brazzaville was made up of a few activists, their families and some officials. The leaders in Congo were Lucio Lara, head of organisation and management, and Mario de Andrade, former MPLA president and head of its foreign affairs department. Agostinho Neto and other leaders such as Daniel Chipenda regularly travelled to Brazzaville. The MPLA received very little practical assistance. For this reason, they promptly asked the Cuban embassy for its help. During his stopover in Brazzaville, Guevara met the leaders of the MPLA to sign the first cooperation agreement between the two parties.[21]

Congo-Brazzaville thus became the MPLA's main ideological and military training centre, at least until the effective opening of a rear base in Zambia in

Figure 2.3: MPLA headquarters in the 'Angola Libre' district in Brazzaville, which are still visible today. © Photographs by Héloïse Kiriakou, September 2013.

1973. The Cuban government used its cooperation with Massamba-Débat's government to send several instructors, goods and equipment in large quantities to the MPLA. The Congolese government also made available to the MPLA a plot of several hectares, called 'Angola Libre', in the district of Makelekele in the south of Brazzaville, where it could house most of its activists. Angola Libre was located on the site of the former airport, which held some modern facilities: a helicopter pad, guerrilla barracks, training camps and a radio station. The control tower, which is still visible today, served as the MPLA's headquarters. MPLA also had offices in Moungali (in the north of Brazzaville) and premises at Mpila (a neighbourhood located west of the city, near the harbour) used for the printing of propaganda newspapers (such as *Vitória ou Morte*). The MPLA also took advantage of its presence in Congo to organise a set of effective operational bases on the border with the Portuguese enclave of Cabinda. Cuban teachers taught MPLA guerrillas at the Angola Libre camp, yet they also allowed them to receive specialised training within the Civil Defence units. With the help of the Cuban instructors, MPLA activists developed and tested guerrilla strategies based on mobile and flexible units and a network of military bases on the Congolese side of the border, to which they could quickly withdraw. They would extend these techniques a few years later in Zambia and Angola. Thanks to the support of Cuban instructors, MPLA guerrillas were always able to maintain their presence in the battlefield. Their victories over the Portuguese military greatly helped strengthen the influence of Cuban instructors

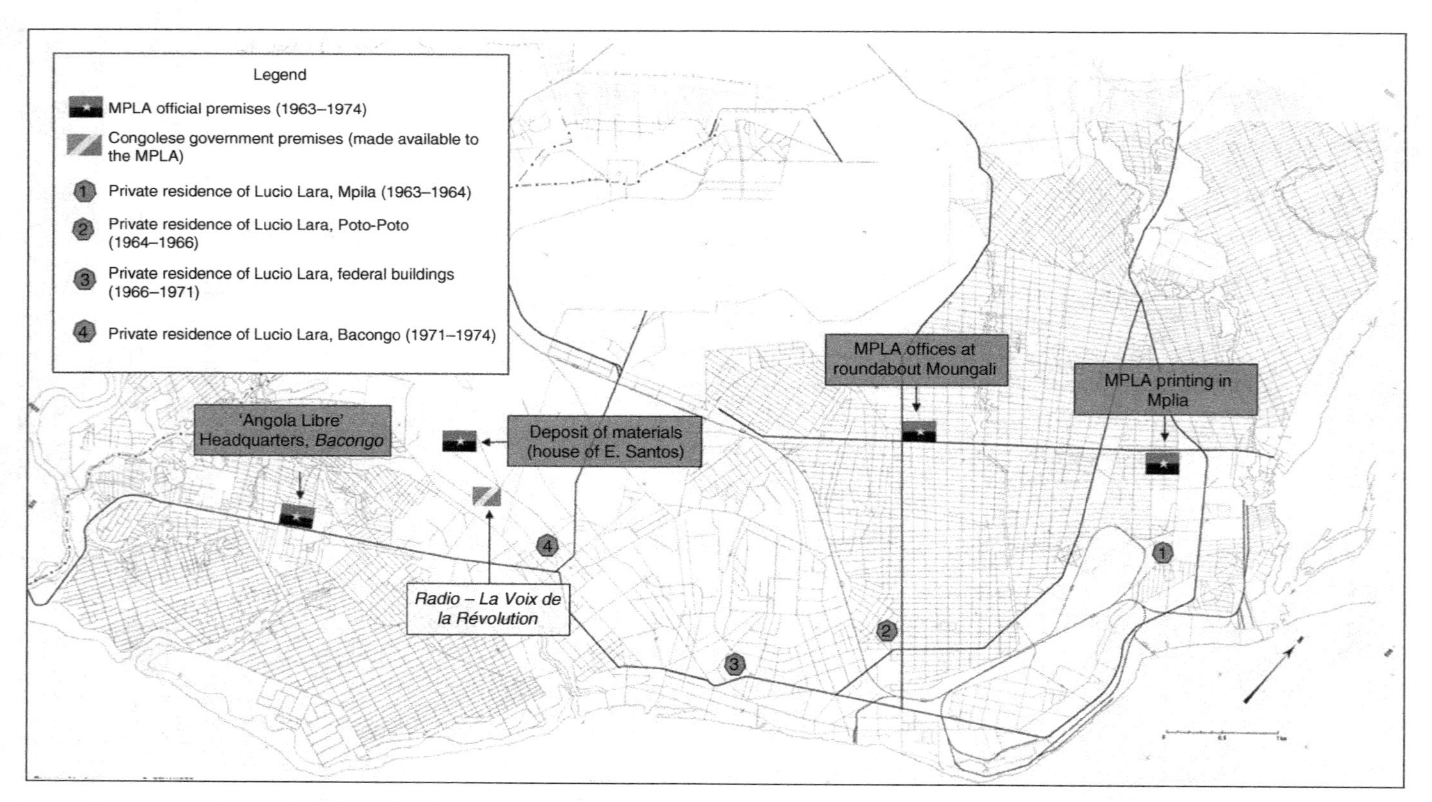

Figure 2.4: Location of the MPLA facilities in Brazzaville (1963–74). Map by Héloïse Kiriakou from a plan of the French military services (GR 10 T 646, note of 7 April 1969).

and ensure the MPLA's legitimacy internationally. The MPLA was recognised by the OAU in 1965.

Between 1965 and 1974, therefore, Congo-Brazzaville became a vast battlefield in the north for the UPC, in the centre for the CNL, and in the south for the MPLA. The Congolese experience provided the liberation movements with a number of lessons. For one thing, the concentration of revolutionaries from all over Central Africa in Brazzaville, supervised by the Cuban government, allowed for the effective transmission of knowledge and expertise, and the militants developed a unique revolutionary culture. For the Congo itself, the presence of the Cubans and African guerrillas provided a tremendous opportunity to consolidate the Massamba-Débat regime, to give the country a prominent place in Central Africa, and to make Brazzaville the showcase of socialist solidarity. As for Cuba, this experience allowed the Cuban government to test its internationalist approaches and policies in the Congolese field, before extending them to Angola on a larger scale, particularly to help the MPLA to take power at the time of independence.

THE CONTINUOUS SUPPORT OF CUBA FOR THE MPLA UNTIL INDEPENDENCE

Until the Carnation Revolution in Portugal in 1974, struggles between the Angolan liberation movements were rare and almost non-existent. These movements were based in areas that were far apart and they organised resistance separately against Portuguese colonialism in their own disparate ways. When the Portuguese government decided to grant independence, the struggle for power began. At that time, the OAU played an important role. It chose to recognise particular movements and legitimated three of them: the FNLA, UNITA and the MPLA. The OAU then organised a meeting between them in Mombasa, on 5 January 1975. The objective of this meeting was to establish a common agenda in order to negotiate with the Portuguese government. After that, they met with the Portuguese government in Alvor, on 15 January 1975, to sign the official agreements for independence. These provided for the establishment of a transitional period until Independence Day, on 11 November 1975, with an equitable sharing of power between the three movements. They also provided for the creation of a combined army composed of 48 000 men (24 000 Portuguese soldiers and 8000 men from each liberation movement) to support the Portuguese disengagement.[22]

In practice, the joint military force never became a reality. Neto signed with the Cuban government a cooperation agreement that anticipated the strengthening of their military presence; the FNLA did the same with the pro-American regime of Mobutu in Zaire. Cuban instructors in Angola oversaw the integration of FAPLA fighters (the People's Armed Forces of Liberation of Angola, created a few months before and formed by Cuban instructors) into the contingent of 8000 men, and the Cuban government sent 250 additional instructors. Neto asked the Cuban government to open 16 military camps in areas either still controlled by the Portuguese military or claimed by UNITA.[23] In this way, they could spread the MPLA's presence throughout the country's southern part, in order to appear as the most legitimate movement at the time of independence, scheduled for November. This strategy generated conflicts over the control of the major cities, especially between the MPLA and FNLA in Luanda in May 1975. The resistance of FNLA soldiers prompted Neto to ask Fidel Castro to intervene. In October 1975, Castro launched Operation Carlota to protect Luanda and help the MPLA win power one month after independence.[24]

The complexity of the independence process in Angola and the increased opposition between the three liberation movements forced the Cuban government to step up its commitment. Yet the decision to launch Operation Carlota also illustrates the existence of a strong friendship between MPLA officials, especially Agostinho Neto, and the Cuban government. Castro did not want to sacrifice ten years of struggle alongside the MPLA because of identity clashes between the founding elites of the three nationalist organisations. In October 1975, South Africa's military involvement cemented the Cuban decision to fully intervene.

Since August 1975, South Africa had been looking for a justification to attack Angola. The South African army was sent to Luambo to consolidate its position in the south of the country. Witnessing Cuban intervention in the north, and with the support of the United States, South Africa decided to invade Angola. This marked the beginning of Operation Savannah, renamed Operation Zulu (October 1975 to 27 March 1976). Despite divisions within the South African government, the goal was to fight the MPLA and the Cuban government and to conquer the capital of Luanda before independence in November 1975.[25] Yet the South African military was defeated by Cuban troops 500 kilometres from Luanda, forcing them to retreat so as to avoid a frontal confrontation. Thus, Operation Carlota was a triple victory, over the FNLA, the Zaire army and the South African army.

However, the threat represented by South Africa did not decrease. Neto and Castro decided to maintain the 12 000 Cuban soldiers who had fought during Operation Carlota in Angola, in the event of a further attack by South Africa.[26] In 1979, Neto implemented conscription for compulsory military service in Angola for males, officially for two years. He also strengthened training agreements with Fidel

Castro. As early as 1976, South Africa broke off the peace process with Angola and again embarked on an aggressive policy. The South African government accused the MPLA of supporting SWAPO (South West Africa People's Organisation) militants who fought against South Africa in Namibia, while the OAU officially authorised the MPLA to assist SWAPO.[27] Contingents of the South African army attacked several SWAPO infrastructures and FAPLA military bases in southern Angola. As a result, the MPLA no longer had access to various regions of the country. For South Africa, it was a way to further strengthen UNITA in the south and destabilise the country.

South Africa's aggressive policy forced the Cuban government to maintain a sizeable military contingent in Angola in order to guarantee the security of the MPLA. Yet, as with Congo-Brazzaville, the Cuban government also maintained its military presence in the field in order to organise SWAPO's rear base in the south of the country. The Cuban military trained and armed the SWAPO guerrillas against South Africa, while continuing to participate in the conflict in Angola. Indeed, the Cuban government's ambition was to deploy their internationalism throughout the region and to contribute to the collapse of the apartheid regime.

A PERSONIFIED COOPERATION?

In order to sustain this policy on a long-term basis, the Cuban government was also sometimes forced to intervene in the internal conflicts of the parties they supported. In Angola, they had always supported Agostinho Neto in the conflicts which had for long raged within the MPLA. The longevity of the armed struggle and the fact that the MPLA's bases were geographically dispersed led to the development of ideological oppositions within the party. Yet the deterioration of the movement was mainly due to conflicts within its leadership. At various moments, several founding members of the politburo disputed Neto's control over the party, and especially his authoritarian and individualistic style of exercising power.[28] The Carnation Revolution in Portugal, which took place in April 1974, further accentuated these conflicts as the independence of Angola approached. The MPLA politburo was divided into three main movements: the 'Active Revolt' of Pinto de Andrade (a brother of Mario de Andrade) and other leaders also based in Brazzaville; the 'Eastern Revolt' of Daniel Chipenda (commander-in-chief of the army on the east front), based in Angola; and the Agostinho Neto faction, more dispersed but mainly based in Zambia.[29] Daniel Chipenda, like other members of 'Active Revolt', called for a reform of the party institutions in order to create a more equitable share of power.

The seriousness of the conflict led the OAU to intervene in order to force the different tendencies to organise a congress.[30] The OAU even suspended its aid to the movement until the conflict was resolved. Neto, feeling that the MPLA's collapse was close, organised a congress in Lusaka, Zambia, from 12 to 19 August 1974.[31] The objective was to elect a new politburo, the last election having been held in 1962 in Léopoldville. Yet, delegates soon appeared to favour Daniel Chipenda,[32] a choice which did not please Neto, who left the congress before its end. Chipenda was eventually elected president of the MPLA. Neto disputed the legitimacy of this election and organised a second congress a few months later. This took place in Angola, and he was re-elected president with a new executive. It was during this congress that he promoted a new generation of leaders like José Eduardo dos Santos (later president of Angola) and Nito Alves, who were responsible for the youth organisation[33] and the R1 (First Military Region) of MPLA.[34]

Cuba did not take part in those congresses, but recognised the results of the second congress and the victory of Agostinho Neto. The OAU, however, refused to acknowledge the validity of the results and urged the various factions to find a solution. The decision of the Cuban government to favour Neto was mainly due to their limited knowledge of Chipenda. He was a soldier who built his entire career in the field in eastern Angola and had no prior relation with Cuba. If Neto feared the 'Active Revolt' so much it was because Lucio Lara and Mario de Andrade were very close to the Cuban government's representatives. Yet they eventually accepted Neto's victory after the second congress. One of the reasons behind the creation of FAPLA was to counter the weight of Chipenda, who controlled the main contingents of the MPLA in the east. Chipenda decided to continue to fight Neto by force and became the ally of Roberto Holden of the FNLA. For ideological and political reasons, the Cuban government chose to support Neto, and in this way played an active role in the conflicts within the MPLA.

A few years later, in 1977, the Cuban government intervened again in an internal conflict of the MPLA to help Agostinho Neto. Nito Alves, a member of the Central Committee and then Angola's minister of internal administration, proposed a more radical political programme than the president of the MPLA.[35] He was the leader of Luanda's urban militias and was fighting for a popular revolution. His aim was to provide the neighbourhood committees with more autonomy, as well as to decentralise power, but these steps were contrary to Neto's vision. Neto considered that the revolution had to be centralised and led by a strong single party in charge of organising the actions of local committees. Following this meeting, several members of the Central Committee joined Alves. His confrontation with Neto then reached new heights. Several assemblies were organised, while Nito Alves published his *13 teses*[36] (13 theses) to explain his ideological position. On 23 May 1977, Alves was expelled from the party. Other members of the party as well as the 9th Brigade of FAPLA sided with him.[37]

The intervention of the Cuban government illustrates once again the strength of the friendship between President Neto and Fidel Castro. They had a common political vision and a similar way of exercising power, which left no room for less centralised management models like Alves's. Yet the intervention also reveals the desire of the Cuban regime to secure the success and sustainability of its internationalism on the world scene. Angola was the showcase of its internationalism in Africa, first applied in Congo, and Fidel Castro was ready to sacrifice much to prove it.

CONCLUSION

The examples of Congo-Brazzaville and Angola allow us to shed light on the similarities in the relations that Cuba established with these two countries. Indeed, the Cuban government developed a model, know-how, and military expertise to carry out their internationalist missions in Africa. They firstly experimented with their strategy in Brazzaville before implementing it on a larger scale in Angola.

Initially, Cuban internationalism in Africa was a targeted process of cooperation involving the formation of militias, which then evolved into a more broad-ranging cooperation with the liberation movements that took power. Unlike the two big superpowers of the US and USSR, or France and England, Cuba was able to exert a presence in the field, and do so for a long time. Indeed, right up to the 1990s, the Cuban government wielded considerable influence on Angola's internal political life and helped shape the political and institutional structures of the Angolan state. Its impact is still visible today.

NOTES

1. On the construction of Cuban internationalism, see Fidel Castro, *Cuba's Internationalist Foreign Policy 1975–1980* (New York: Pathfinder, 1981); Fidel Castro, *The Declarations of Havana* (London: Verso, 2007); Fidel Castro and Michael Taber, *Fidel Castro Speeches: Cuba's Internationalist Foreign Policy 1975–1980* (New York: Pathfinder Press, 1981).
2. *Le Monde Diplomatique* devoted many articles (such as 'La vocation latino-africaine de Cuba', January 1979, available in the journal's online archive); *Présence Africaine* also published an issue on Angola: *Présence Africaine* 1962–3 (XLII).
3. Roger Faligot, *La Tricontinentale* (Paris: La Découverte, 2013), 7–12; Sergio Diaz-Briquets, *Cuban Internationalism in Sub-Saharan Africa* (Pittsburgh: Duquesne University Press, 1989);

Piero Gleijeses, *Conflicting Missions: Havana, Washington, and Africa, 1959–1976* (Chapel Hill, NC: University of North Carolina Press, 2002).

4 Daniel R. Kempton, *Soviet Strategy toward Southern Africa: The National Liberation Movement Connection* (London: Praeger, 1989); Arthur Klinghoffer, *The Angolan War: A Study of Soviet Policy in the Third World* (Boulder: Westview Press, 1990); Vladimir Shubin, *The Hot Cold War: The USSR in Southern Africa* (London: Pluto Press, 2008).

5 Herbert Ekwe-Ekwe, *Conflict and Intervention in Africa: Nigeria, Angola, Zaïre* (Basingstoke: Macmillan, 1990); Carlos Antonio Carrasco, 'L'intervention étrangère dans la guerre angolaise', PhD diss., INALCO, Paris, 1996; Antoine Rozès, 'Angola: Guerre civile et interventions extérieures, 1975–1988', PhD diss., University of Nantes, 1996.

6 Edward George, *The Cuban Intervention in Angola, 1965–1991: From Che Guevara to Cuito Cuanavale* (London and New York: Frank Cass, 2005).

7 Christine Hatzky, *Cubans in Angola: South–South Cooperation and Transfer of Knowledge, 1976–1991: Africa and the Diaspora* (Madison: University of Wisconsin Press, 2015). See also Hatzky's chapter in this volume.

8 For current historiographical research about 'real' socialism, see Larissa Zakharova, 'Le quotidien du communisme: Pratiques et objets', *Annales: Histoire, Sciences Sociales* 2 (2013): 305–14; Sheila Fitzpatrick, *Le stalinisme au quotidien: La Russie soviétique dans les années trente* (Paris: Flammarion, 2002); Anne E. Gorsuch, *Youth in Revolutionary Russia: Enthusiasts, Bohemians, Delinquents* (Bloomington: Indiana University Press, 2000); Nadège Ragaru and Antonela Capelle-Pogăcean, eds, *Vie quotidienne et pouvoir sous le communisme* (Paris: Karthala, 2010).

9 Concerning the sources related to Congo-Brazzaville, we mainly used the Archives of the Historical Service of Defence (SHD) in France (series GR 10 T 645 to 651); the Archives of the Ministry of Foreign Affairs in Congo and the National Archives of Congo (series PR 1 to 83). We also used print sources, including newspapers (*Dipanda*, *Etumba*) and oral sources with political actors of that era or former Civil Defence militiamen.

10 Regarding the sources related to Angola, we used the Archives of the Foreign Ministry of Portugal (series 944 MAE) and the PIDE (International and State Defence Police of Portugal) Archives (PIDE/DSG series, DOL Angola, P1.1100030), as well as the Archives of the Mario Soares Foundation (MPLA file, series 04339.00200 to 35).

11 Pierre Bonnafé, 'Une classe d'âge politique: La JMNR et la République du Congo-Brazzaville', *Cahiers d'Études Africaines* 8, no. 31 (1968): 327–68.

12 José Maboungou, *Sur le sentier d'un enfant de la Défense Civile* (Paris: Paari, Collection le griot bantu, 2016), 87. Concerning Civil Defence activities, Héloïse Kiriakou also interviewed Jean-Saturnin Malonga, Benoit Moundele Ngolo, Benjamin Ndalla, Maxime Ndebeka, Camille Bongou, Gabriel N'Zambila and Bernard Malamou in Brazzaville between 2010 and 2016.

13 René Jacques Woungly-Massaga, *La révolution au Congo: Contribution à l'étude des problèmes politiques d'Afrique centrale* (Paris: Maspero, 1974).

14 For the chronological details of this event, see Rémy Bazenguissa-Ganga, *Les voies du politique au Congo: Essai de sociologie historique* (Paris: Karthala, 1997), 130–41; Maboungou, *Sur le sentier d'un enfant de la Défense Civile*, 121–34.

15 The manipulation of ethnic differences had been part of the strategy of Congolese politicians since the colonial period, but the socialist regime and the establishment of a single party had made it possible to blunt these unhealthy processes. However, the political crisis of 1968 was conducive to the return of these identity strategies because

Marien Ngouabi was originally from the north of the country and Massamba-Débat from the south. Some of his supporters used this to legitimise their power grab.

16 This event was recounted by Sika Dacosta during six interviews with Héloïse Kiriakou held in Brazzaville between August 2013 and September 2014. He was deputy director of the security and intelligence service (a department headed by Michel Mbindi). Sika Dacosta is the adopted son of Massamba-Débat and is very attached to the memory of his father.

17 Report of the military attaché of the French embassy in Brazzaville, 16 January 1968: Carton GR 10 T 636, Service Historique de la Défense (France).

18 Ludo Martens, *Pierre Mulele ou la seconde vie de Patrice Lumumba* (Berchem: EPO, 1985), 216. See the chapter by Michel Luntumbue in this volume.

19 On the maquis of Pierre Mulele, see Théophile Bula-Bula, *Pierre Mulele et le maquis du Kwilu en RD Congo: Témoignage d'un survivant du maquis* (Paris: L'Harmattan, 2010).

20 Note of 23 July 1965, box PR 9, National Archives of Congo-Brazzaville.

21 Lucio Lara, *Imagens de um percurso* (Luanda: Tchiweka Édition ATD, 2009), 64.

22 Articles 7 and 8 of the Alvor Agreements provide that 'the Angolan liberation movements must establish themselves in the areas they now control [15 January 1975]. The Portuguese State shall gradually transfer to the organs of Angolan sovereignty all the powers which it holds and exercises in Angola. In addition, it is planned to create a mixed army, during the gradual withdrawal of the Portuguese army (the final withdrawal is expected on 29 February 1976).'

23 'Raúl Díaz Argíelles to the Cuban Armed Forces Minister [Raúl Castro],' 11 August 1975, History and Public Policy Program Digital Archive, accessed January 2017, https://digitalarchive.wilsoncenter.org/document/112128.

24 Gabriel García Márquez, *Operación Carlota: Los Cubanos en Angola, el Che Guevara en Africa, la batalla contra el Reich sudafricano* (Lima: Mosca Azul & Horizonte, 1977).

25 African Union Commission Archives: CM/Res.453–472(XXVI), Council of Ministers, Addis Ababa, 23 February – 1 March 1976, accessed January 2017, http://archive.au.int/collect/auassemb/import/English/OAU_PUB_18_E.pdf.

26 'Military Agreement between Cuba and Angola,' 14 September 1978, History and Public Policy Program Digital Archive, accessed January 2017, https://digitalarchive.wilsoncenter.org/document/117939.

27 The MPLA was an active partner of the Liberation Movement Support Committee of the OAU.

28 Jean-Michel Mabeko-Tali, 'Le Congo et la question angolaise de 1963 à 1976: Les méandres d'une solidarité,' Master's thesis, University of Bordeaux III – CEAN, 1987, 354.

29 Archives of Mario Soares Foundation. Several documents refer to the splits within the MPLA from 1974, in particular a note of 19 December 1974 which explains the 'Active Revolt' to the militants. In the list of signatories, there is Mario de Andrade's name. The leaflets were in French because they were based in Brazzaville. They organised several meetings of the 'Active Revolt' in Brazzaville between February and May 1974.

30 Mario de Andrade, 'The Thorny Question of Unity in the MPLA,' 1974, available in the Casa Comum archives online (box 04339.002.003).

31 MPLA, *First Congress of M.P.L.A., Luanda, 4–10 December 1977* (London: Mozambique, Angola and Guinea Information Centre, 1979).

32 Press conference by Daniel Chipenda after his victory at the congress (1974), which can be consulted in the Casa Comum archives (box 04307006008).

[33] MPLA Central Committee, *1979–1989: 10 anos ao serviço da revolução* (Luanda: Ed. Vanguarda, and Paris: Berger-Levrault International, 1990).

[34] A note from 1974 entitled, 'MPLA – 1° Congresso – Intervenção Cdte Nito Alves' (available in the online Casa Comum archives).

[35] Centre de Informação e Documentação Amilcar Cabral (CIDAC), *Politica agricola e participação camponesa na Republica Popular de Angola* (Lisbon: CIDAC, 1980), 12–16. Also see the article of *Le Monde*, 30 May 1977.

[36] Newspaper article entitled '27 de Maio: Treze teses em minha defesa,' *Folha* 8, 13 February 1977; republished in Dalila Cabrita Mateus and Álvaro Mateus, *Purga em Angola: O 27 de Maio de 1977* (Porto: ASA, 2007).

[37] Mateus and Mateus, *Purga em Angola.*

REFERENCES

Alves, Nito. 'As teses em minha defesa,' Luanda, 13 February 1977. In *Purga em Angola: O 27 de Maio de 1977*, edited by Dalila Cabrita Mateus and Álvaro Mateus, 64–8. Porto: ASA, 2007.

Bazenguissa-Ganga, Rémy. *Les voies du politique au Congo: Essai de sociologie historique.* Paris: Karthala,1997.

Bernault, Florence. *Démocraties ambiguës en Afrique centrale: Congo-Brazzaville, Gabon, 1940–1965.* Paris: Karthala, 1996.

Bonnafé, Pierre. 'Une classe d'âge politique: La JMNR et la République du Congo-Brazzaville.' *Cahiers d'Études Africaines* 8, no. 31 (1968): 327–68.

Bula-Bula, Théophile. *Pierre Mulele et le maquis du Kwilu en RD Congo: Témoignage d'un survivant du maquis.* Paris: L'Harmattan, 2010.

Carrasco, Carlos Antonio. 'L'intervention étrangère dans la guerre angolaise.' PhD diss., INALCO University, 1996.

Castro, Fidel. *Cuba's Internationalist Foreign Policy 1975–1980.* New York: Pathfinder, 1981.

Castro, Fidel. *The Declarations of Havana.* London: Verso, 2007.

Castro, Fidel and Michael Taber. *Fidel Castro Speeches: Cuba's Internationalist Foreign Policy 1975–1980.* New York: Pathfinder Press, 1981.

Centre de Informação e Documentação Amilcar Cabral (CIDAC). *Politica agricola e participação camponesa na Republica Popular de Angola.* Lisbon: CIDAC, 1980.

Diaz-Briquets, Sergio. *Cuban Internationalism in Sub-Saharan Africa.* Pittsburgh: Duquesne University Press, 1989.

Ekwe-Ekwe, Herbert. *Conflict and Intervention in Africa: Nigeria, Angola, Zaïre.* Basingstoke: Macmillan, 1990.

Faligot, Roger. *La Tricontinentale.* Paris: La Découverte, 2013.

Fitzpatrick, Sheila. *Le stalinisme au quotidien: La Russie soviétique dans les années trente.* Paris: Flammarion, 2002.

García Márquez, Gabriel. *Operación Carlota: Los Cubanos en Angola, el Che Guevara en Africa, la batalla contra el reich sudafricano.* Lima: Mosca Azul & Horizonte, 1977.

George, Edward. *The Cuban Intervention in Angola, 1965–1991: From Che Guevara to Cuito Cuanavale.* London and New York: Frank Cass, 2005.

Gleijeses, Piero. *Conflicting Missions: Havana, Washington, and Africa, 1959–1976.* Chapel Hill, NC: University of North Carolina Press, 2002.

Gorsuch, Anne E. *Youth in Revolutionary Russia: Enthusiasts, Bohemians, Delinquents*. Bloomington: Indiana University Press, 2000.

Hatzky, Christine. *Cubans in Angola: South–South Cooperation and Transfer of Knowledge, 1976–1991: Africa and the Diaspora*. Madison: University of Wisconsin Press, 2015.

Kempton, Daniel R. *Soviet Strategy toward Southern Africa: The National Liberation Movement Connection*. London: Praeger, 1989.

Klinghoffer, Arthur. *The Angolan War: A Study of Soviet Policy in the Third World*. Boulder: Westview Press, 1990.

Lara, Lucio. *Imagens de um percurso*. Luanda: Tchiweka Édition ATD, 2009.

Mabeko-Tali, Jean-Michel. 'Dissidences et pouvoir d'état: Le MPLA face a lui-meme.' PhD diss., University of Lille, 1996.

Mabeko-Tali, Jean-Michel. 'Le Congo et la question angolaise de 1963 à 1976: Les méandres d'une solidarité.' Master's thesis, University of Bordeaux III – CEAN, 1987.

Maboungou, José. *Sur le sentier d'un enfant de la Défense Civile*. Paris: Paari, Collection le griot bantu, 2016.

Martens, Ludo. *Pierre Mulele ou la seconde vie de Patrice Lumumba*. Berchem: EPO, 1985.

Mateus, Dalila Cabrita and Álvaro Mateus. *Purga em Angola: O 27 de Maio de 1977*. Porto: ASA, 2007.

Messiant, Christine. *L'Angola post colonial, et sociologie politique d'une oléocratie*. Paris: Karthala, 2009.

MPLA. *First Congress of M.P.L.A., Luanda, 4–10 December 1977*. London: Mozambique, Angola and Guinea Information Centre, 1979.

MPLA Central Committee. *1979–1989: 10 anos ao serviço da revolução*. Luanda: Ed. Vanguarda, and Paris: Berger-Levrault International, 1990.

Ragaru, Nadège and Antonela Capelle-Pogăcean, eds. *Vie quotidienne et pouvoir sous le communisme*. Paris: Karthala, 2010.

Rozès, Antoine. 'Angola: Guerre civile et interventions extérieures, 1975–1988.' PhD diss., University of Nantes, 1996.

Shubin, Vladimir. *The Hot Cold War: The USSR in Southern Africa*. London: Pluto Press, 2008.

Woungly-Massaga, René Jacques. *La révolution au Congo: Contribution à l'étude des problèmes politiques d'Afrique centrale*. Paris: Maspero,1974.

Zakharova, Larissa. 'Le quotidien du communisme: Pratiques et objets.' *Annales: Histoire, Sciences Sociales* 2 (2013): 305–14.

CHAPTER

3

Motivation and Legacies of the Cuban Presence in Equatorial Guinea from 1969 to the Present

Delmas Tsafack

Cuba's domestic dynamics as well as its foreign policy and activities on a global scale have defied conventional wisdom on opportunities open to poor countries, or to countries relegated to the global periphery of the world order. The Cuban Revolution of 1959 must hence be placed in its correct historical context if we are to understand the foreign policy that the Cuban state leadership has adopted since 1959, and its central focus on Africa in order to develop a proletarian internationalist foreign policy. Cuba's policy toward Africa in particular, an economically marginalised continent facing a number of domestic constraints, and its general development of an internationalist foreign policy aimed at assisting governments in the Third World, form a challenge to those assumptions.[1]

Between 1975 and 1988 there were in total over 70 000 Cuban aid workers and skilled professionals such as physicians, nurses, agricultural specialists and other professionals providing their services in Africa.[2] Moreover, over 40 000 Africans have studied in Cuba, with all expenses paid by the government of Cuba.[3] According to these estimates, it is evident that Cuba has played a significant role in recent African history, the extent of which is still to be fully assessed.[4]

From the end of the Cold War in the early 1990s, Cuba's aid to Africa took the form of development assistance, and numerous scholarships were offered to

African students in order to pursue their education in Cuba.[5] The new international order had serious implications for Cuba's social and economic development, but the overall aims and policy towards states and people in the global South remained largely the same and programmes of assistance continued despite economic difficulties.[6] Cuban military programmes accompanied those of technical and medical assistance, with volunteers assisting in the field of health care, education and construction in Angola, Cape Verde, Mozambique, Guinea-Bissau, Guinea, Ethiopia, São Tomé and Príncipe, Tanzania, Congo-Brazzaville, Benin, Burkina Faso, Algeria and Equatorial Guinea.[7]

The history of Cuba in Africa largely remains to be written.[8] In the historiography of the African liberation struggles or in foreign policy analysis, Cuba's foreign policy towards African states is often absent, simplified or overlooked as a mere proxy affair, and in effect marginalised. In fact, very little has been written about Cuba's involvement in Africa, besides work on Cuba's role in Angola from 1959 until 1988. Here one can mention Piero Gleijeses,[9] Edgard Dosman,[10] Hedelberto López Blanch,[11] William LeoGrande[12] and Isaac Saney,[13] whose writings form some of the few in-depth analyses and historical accounts of Cuba's involvement in Africa throughout the Cold War and after. Most academic textbooks on African politics and recent African history, intended for students of international relations and foreign policy analysis, barely mention Cuba or its relations with African countries.[14] In this chapter, this omission will be rectified by a close examination of Equatorial Guinea.

AN ISOLATED CUBAN GOVERNMENT IN SEARCH OF PARTNERS IN AFRICA

After the Cuban Revolution of 1959, the revolutionary government spent its first decade struggling to survive. American hegemony ended in Cuba, and the country found itself isolated. The US shifted to a strategy of reasserting hegemony over Cuba, which was characterised by a combination of coercive measures such as economic sanctions, subversive propaganda, psychological warfare, covert operations, armed interventions, political subversion and military coercion.[15] As part of the restrictions, sanctions and interventions against Cuba imposed by the US government, it is important to understand the dynamics of the blockade against Cuba, which was instituted in 1962.[16] As Carlos Alzugaray states, '[it was] not a simple "embargo", as the U.S. Government claims, … demonstrated by the fact that it is much more than a refusal to trade with Cuba'.[17]

With the economic and diplomatic isolation imposed by the US, Cuba struggled to enlarge its sphere of bilateral relations. In Africa, it quickly developed close ties with Ghana and Algeria.[18] Che Guevara, Cuba's foreign minister, visited Algeria where he met Ben Bella of the FLN (National Liberation Front) before travelling to Mali, Congo, Guinea, Ghana, Benin and Egypt.[19] Subsequently, Cuba multiplied its interventions in African countries to assist friendly African political parties and governments. The 1970s saw a great expansion of Cuban influence in Africa and the Third World, heralded by Fidel Castro's tour of the continent in 1972.[20] Just after his trip, approximately one hundred Cuban advisers were dispatched to Sierra Leone and Equatorial Guinea.[21]

THE CUBAN PRESENCE IN AFRICA AND THE COLD WAR

Cuba's presence in Africa in general, and in Equatorial Guinea in particular, can thus be explained by the constraints of the context in which Cuba found itself after the revolution, being marginalised in the global capitalist system, politically and economically, as well as culturally and epistemologically. Its presence in Africa can also be explained by the context of the Cold War. During the first decade after independence, Cuba's foreign policy was focused entirely on the Caribbean and American region. Isolated in the western hemisphere and by the Organization of American States during the 1960s, Cuba expanded its diplomatic and economic relations to other areas of the world.

Cuba's role in shaping international affairs during the Cold War does not represent a typical case of Third World foreign policy.[22] Few Third World states were able to project their influence or shape historical developments beyond their own regions, and yet Cuba was a noteworthy exception.[23] In mainstream traditions of international relations theory, states and actors within the global South are usually cast as subordinate players within the 'high politics', the security and military concerns, of the superpowers.[24] Richard Saull, on the other hand, analyses the Cold War as a globalised social conflict between states and social forces, in which the Third World played a central role in shaping historical developments and in impacting on the actions and decisions of the two superpowers. In Saull's view, the global South was central to the dialectical developments of the Cold War, as well as to developments leading to its demise.[25]

This reconceptualisation of the Cold War is essential to understanding Cuba's foreign policy towards Africa and the Third World, and to explaining its motivations, aims and consequences at a local, regional, national and global scale.

The form of the state in Cuba as well as its foreign policy constituted a challenge to the world order, yet they also revealed the agency open to Third World countries to chart their own course beyond the push and pull of the Western capitalist system.[26]

CUBA AS AN ANSWER TO EQUATORIAL GUINEA'S PROBLEMS WITH SPAIN

On 12 October 1968, the Independence Day of Equatorial Guinea, Spain sent Iribane Fraga, its new minister of foreign affairs, to attend the ceremony in Malabo and appointed as its ambassador Juan Duran Loriga. Spanish–Guinean relationships were based on a statement of intent signed on 22 June 1968, two months before the proclamation of independence. In it Spain recognised the sovereignty of Equatorial Guinea, assured the country of its assistance in preserving its independence, and guaranteed the convertibility of the Equatorial Guinean currency to cover expenses related to the transition period.[27] Spain's main aim was to preserve its influence in the Gulf of Guinea. According to Max Liniger-Goumaz,[28] Spain imagined an independent Equatorial Guinea organised around Madrid's interests.

Spanish troops were stationed in Equatorial Guinea after independence. This foreign military assistance, while it protected the small African state against aggression and discouraged any attempt at annexation by its neighbours, exposed at the same time its fragility.[29] The use of foreign troops seemed to be a necessity because the new state did not have a viable military and security force.

Despite the agreement signed in 1968 between the two countries, the relationship between the young state and its former colonial power came to be marked by a series of incidents that cooled relations between them. Francisco Macías Nguema, the first president of Equatorial Guinea, described Spanish colonisation as having left 'a devastated and burned country exploited of all the wealth that God and nature have assigned to us, stolen by the colonialists'.[30] Constant disputes between the two governments led Spain to suspend its aid to Equatorial Guinea, nor did it keep its promises to fund the former colony's budget. One of the reasons for the suspension of aid had to do with the struggle that existed between the two branches of Spanish capitalism: transnational capitalism represented by García Trevijano,[31] a supporter of Macías Nguema, and national capitalism operating within Equatorial Guinea, represented by the powerful minister Luis Carrero Blanco,[32] a supporter of Bonifacio Ondo Edú-Aguong,[33] who was an opponent of Nguema's. Max Liniger-Goumaz attributes the breakdown in relations between Equatorial Guinea and Spain to the failure of Carrero Blanco's candidacy in the first presidential election in 1968.[34] Following a series of anti-Spanish speeches by Macías Nguema a few months after independence, demonstrations took place in Rio Muni, the continental part of Equatorial Guinea, in February 1969. In March 1969, the anti-Spanish protests prompted the departure of nearly 800 Spanish nationals, and the closure of large agripastoral businesses owned by relatives of Carrero Blanco. Carrero Blanco encouraged the departure of the Spanish and the closure of these companies in order to 'punish Garcia Trevijano's candidate'.[35]

The Spanish refusal to fund Equatorial Guinea's budget created a series of crises between the two countries. Equatorial Guinea abolished the payment of bonuses to expatriate Spanish civil servants working in the country. In turn, Spanish companies refused to finance domestic trade in Malabo, and the incident in which Spanish flags were taken down caused the massive departure of Spaniards.[36] Furthermore, there was a coup attempt in March 1969 by Ndongo Miyone, minister of foreign affairs in the first government, which was suspected of being supported by Spain.[37]

The diplomatic and political troubles in Equatorial Guinea plunged the country into economic crisis. Macías Nguema then instituted a dictatorial regime. Political opponents were accused of being abetted by Spain, and there was a witch hunt against intellectuals and politicians. Fearing a coup d'état, Macías Nguema decreed a state of emergency and created an apparatus of repression and propaganda.[38] The country became unsettled and slid into a chronic economic depression. In 1971, Nguema abolished all political parties that had fought for independence and created the PUN (United National Party), later transformed into PUNT (United National Workers' Party) in 1973. He became president for life, styled himself the 'only miracle of Equatorial Guinea', and led the 'most nepotistic Government of the time in Africa'.[39] Already compromised by its small population, the scarcity of labour and the smallness of the territory, the Equatorial Guinean economy was seriously affected by the consequences of the deterioration of political relations with Spain.

Upon independence, Equatorial Guinea had created its own currency, the Guinean peseta, whose convertibility was guaranteed by the Spanish peseta. The discord with Spain led Equatorial Guinea to require Spain to pay for its goods in US dollars. The existence of a parallel market eroded the Equatorial Guinean peseta.[40] Following the deterioration of relations, the former colony created a new currency, the ekwele, and abandoned the system of parity with the Spanish peseta.[41] In the end, it was the reduction in Equatorial Guinea's exports, and the erosion of the ekwele by the black market, that forced Equatorial Guinea to seek the support of the Soviet Union and its satellites such as Cuba.

In December 1972, just a few years after independence, Equatorial Guinea established diplomatic relations with Cuba. The latter sent 'important aid in scientific, technical, economic domains and ensured the training of managers, which allowed it to establish ties of friendship, solidarity and bilateral cooperation, in the areas of health, education, construction, fishing, basic industry, radio and television, the environment, energy and mining, transport and agriculture.'[42]

Equatorial Guinea benefited from this new relationship.[43] The cooperation between the two countries was economic, political and military in nature.

According to Paul Gerard Nsah-Voundy, the alliance with Havana (and with Moscow) was a 'diplomatic gesture' that was meant to bring about much-needed economic aid. Indeed, during the Cold War economic aid was a weapon wielded by both East and West to secure the allegiance of underdeveloped countries. In this struggle between 'dollar and rouble', Equatorial Guinea received help simultaneously from Cuba and the USSR, an aid package 'determined by political motives in the form of loans and military protection'.[44] Because it was then unable to participate in the international trading market, the country started an economic relationship with Cuba based on barter.

From a political point of view, the position of the government, 'facing the double imperative of consolidating national sovereignty and control of its internal power base',[45] was strengthened by its alliance with Cuba. Equatorial Guinea proclaimed itself a 'revolutionary and popular government'. By adopting a revolutionary ideology, the country became identified with an international revolutionary community of countries, which gave it an identity as well as 'international visibility'.[46] In addition to revolutionary discourse, the country borrowed from Cuba the model of a single party in order to close the political space to grassroots initiatives. These constitutional and ideological rearrangements reflected the confusion of a postcolonial society unable to stabilise its internal tensions and face its external dangers on its own. Regionally, these rearrangements represented for neighbouring countries an act of 'disobedience' because Equatorial Guinea refused to identify itself politically with the rest of the Gulf of Guinea region. In fact, Equatorial Guinea broke with the prevailing ideological orthodoxy in the region which was based on networks of alliances with those countries' former colonial masters.

Military cooperation between Cuba and Equatorial Guinea took the form of military advisers. In 1977, there were between 150 and 200 Cuban advisers in Equatorial Guinea, a number that was reduced in 1980 to 100.[47] This Cuban presence would serve to deter attempts at annexation by neighbouring countries and the 'recolonization of Equatorial Guinea by Spain'.[48] Furthermore, in1977 Equatorial Guinea broke its ties with the Western bloc and signed a defence treaty with Cuba and the Soviet Union in exchange for the installation of a submarine base and a radar and transmitting station. Port facilities were granted to Cuba and the Soviet Union in Annobón and Fernando Po. Equatorial Guinea then developed a network of alliances with countries of the Eastern bloc. The relations were part of a logic of opposition to the extension of the US sphere of influence in Africa. Control of territories in the Gulf of Guinea would allow Cuba and the Soviet Union to monitor shipping in that part of the South Atlantic.

This alliance with communist and socialist countries in the 1970s opened a long history of relations between Equatorial Guinea and Cuba. These intensified with the accession to power of Obiang Nguema Mbasogo on 3 August 1979 after a coup against Macías Nguema. When Obiang Nguema took over power in 1979, he inherited a very poor country. To address the country's economic, political and social problems, he decided to turn to Morocco (traditionally, the presidential guard was composed of Moroccan soldiers) and Central African states. He also sought the integration of his country into the regional grouping of Central Africa. While Cuba remained an ally, Equatorial Guinea's foreign policy now looked to regional integration, and the country became a member of the Customs and Economic Union of Central African states in 1983. Cooperation between Cuba and Equatorial Guinea was reanimated in the 1990s when oil was discovered off the African coast.

CUBAN TRAINERS IN THE HEALTH AND EDUCATION SECTORS

From the 1990s, Cuba became one of Equatorial Guinea's preferred partners in bilateral cooperation. The education sector is a major focus of cooperation between the two countries. Cuban teachers have contributed to the training of large numbers of students at universities, technical schools and primary schools in the country.[49] At the same time, students from Equatorial Guinea have been sent on scholarships to study in Cuba. In 2013, about 110 Equatorial Guinean students were studying in various academic institutions in Cuba, in the fields of computer science, law, technology, health, biology, geology and sport.[50]

Cuba plays an important role in the extension of literacy in Equatorial Guinea. In August 2013 the two states signed an agreement on female literacy, which involved the training of twenty literacy supervisors over a two-month period. The programme aimed to counter the illiteracy of more than 2000 women who were not in school because of early marriage, financial difficulties or for other reasons. The training was funded by the first lady of Equatorial Guinea, Constancia Mangue de Obiang. According to government statistics, the illiteracy rate among women is 80 per cent as against 35 per cent for men.[51]

Cuba and Equatorial Guinea also signed a cooperation agreement in respect of the creation of the National University of Equatorial Guinea in 1995. A further agreement signed on 22 January 2013 in Malabo was aimed at increasing the number of Cuban teachers at the National University.[52]

Cuban teachers represent a high proportion of the foreign staff at the university. Of the 731 permanent teachers for the academic year 2015–16, 44 were foreigners, making up 6 per cent of the workforce. Table 3.1 shows the level of qualification of the permanent staff at the university. Most permanent teachers do not hold PhDs, which is indicative of the low levels of education and of the challenges facing the country. The bulk of the workforce – 450 staff members – are holders of bachelor degrees (*licenciados*).

Table 3.1: Level of qualification of permanent teachers at the National University of Equatorial Guinea for the academic year 2015–16.

No.	Academic diplomas of lecturers			Quantity	Percentage
1.	Medical doctor	Nationals	25	44	6
		Foreigners	19		
2.	Master's degree	Nationals	86	95	11
		Foreigners	9		
3.	Bachelor degree	Nationals	442	450	62
		Foreigners	8		
4.	Engineer	Nationals	88	96	14
		Foreigners	8		
5.	1st University degree	Nationals	46	46	7
		Foreigners	-		
Total				**731**	**100**

Source: National University of Equatorial Guinea, http://unge.education/main/?page_id=437 Accessed May 2016.

The Medical Sciences faculty at the university is headed by a Cuban national, Doña Zoila de la C. Fernández Montequin. This faculty was established in August 2000 at the instigation of Presidents Nguema and Fidel Castro.[53] Medical education began in 2000–1 with Cuban teachers and 30 students. In 2012, the teaching faculty comprised a total of 86 teachers including 46 Guineans and 40 Cubans, 63 men and 23 women; among them were 4 with PhDs, 79 with bachelor degrees, 1 with a first degree and 1 engineer. Training takes six years to complete: there is a three-year core curriculum in medicine and three years of specialisation in medicine or two specialisations in nursing.[54] The faculty works closely with the Havana

University Medical School and trains students in general medicine and nursing. It consists of five departments, namely the departments of basic clinical sciences, surgical sciences, public health, complementary medicine and related courses.

AN EQUATORIAL GUINEAN HEALTH SECTOR WITH A STRONG CUBAN PRESENCE

Apart from the training of doctors and nurses, Cuba is also heavily involved in the general health sector in Equatorial Guinea. After the end of Soviet aid to Cuba and the beginning of the 'special period', a programme was set up in Cuba to send physicians, nurses, dentists and other professionals to more than 52 countries in the developing world.[55] This policy is viewed domestically in Cuba as a continuation of the internationalism that began in the early 1960s.[56] In 1999 the Latin American School of Medicine was created in Havana and is currently providing free medical education to over 6000 students from around the developing world.[57] In 2008, there were more than 3000 Cuban doctors providing services in Africa, at no cost to the beneficiaries.[58] In more than thirty developing countries, including Equatorial Guinea, the total number of Cuban doctors giving their services free is close to 30 000.[59] This would be the equivalent of the United States sending 900 000 doctors to work for free in the developing world.[60]

Cuba has signed agreements with Equatorial Guinea on cooperation in the field of health since the 1970s. In 2013, this cooperation was reviewed and an agreement was signed to strengthen the health services of Equatorial Guinea and increase the number of Cuban doctors working in the country in different specialties.[61]

Cuba also played an important role in the health sector at the time of the Africa Cup of Nations in 2015. Morocco was due to host this event but, because of an outbreak of the Ebola epidemic during the previous year, it decided to withdraw. Equatorial Guinea then undertook to host the games, assuming this role just a few months before they began. To deal with the epidemic, the government of Equatorial Guinea called on the expertise of its Cuban ally. A team of 15 Cuban specialists arrived in Malabo on 6 December 2014 with advanced equipment to prevent the spread of the virus, focusing especially on securing airports and football stadiums.[62] Cuban specialists largely 'helped prevent the entry of the pandemic through rigorous checks in the stadiums, in the air, land and sea borders, and awareness campaigns for the population'.[63] At the departure ceremony for the Cuban medical specialists, the Equatorial Guinean government warmly thanked Cuba for this act of solidarity.

As part of his 'Horizon 2020' programme, Obiang Nguema built two major hospitals in the main cities of Malabo and Bata. Given that there are few trained

Equatorial Guinean doctors, Cuban and Spanish medical doctors currently form the bulk of medical personnel in these referral hospitals.

The Equatorial Guinean authorities are aware that Cuba has greatly changed the health landscape in the country. According to the Equatorial Guinean ambassador to Cuba, Lourdes Mba Ayecaba, speaking in November 2013, 'Before the arrival of the Cuban doctors, there was about one doctor for 4000 people, and curable diseases decimated the population. Today, the social situation is different and we can talk about successes in which Cuban professionals have their share.'

POLITICAL COOPERATION

Cooperation between Cuba and Equatorial Guinea is underscored by high-ranking visits between the two countries. Obiang Nguema, for instance, paid a visit to Cuba in September 2014 during which he met with his Cuban counterpart, Raúl Castro. During the visit, the president described the Cubans as internationalists: 'they do not have borders, and they are everywhere'.[64] In Equatorial Guinea the anniversaries of the attack by Fidel Castro on the Moncada barracks (on 26 July 1953) and the Cuban Revolution are celebrated publicly. Each time, the occasion lends itself to mention of the US blockade on Cuba, to which Equatorial Guinea is openly opposed. In various speeches, members of the government have supported their ally against the US embargo. When Cuba and the United States discussed a possible lifting of sanctions against Cuba, the president of Equatorial Guinea expressed the hope that diplomatic negotiations between the two countries would lead to the end of the embargo. Obiang Nguema has also stressed how seriously the blockade impacts on the lives of Cubans.[65]

THE CUBAN PRESENCE IN OTHER SECTORS IN EQUATORIAL GUINEA

The Cuban presence in Equatorial Guinea is to be found not only in the spheres of health and education. Cuba also cooperates in the fields of telecommunications, fisheries and agriculture. In the telecommunications sector, Cuban workers help maintain the broadcasting network for the Equatorial Guinean ministry of telecommunications. In the domain of electricity generation and transmission, the Equatorial Guinean electricity company, the Sociedad de electricidad de Guinea Ecuatorial (SEGESA), works in collaboration with its Cuban counterpart, the

Sociedad mercantil servicios de ingeniería eléctrica (SIECSA). Equatorial Guinea is also developing the field of aviation with Cuban expertise.

According to the Equatorial Guinean ambassador to Cuba, the cooperation between their two countries is 'disinterested', as neither country asks for anything in return. In 2016, there were '421 Cuban *cooperantes* [aid workers] working in Equatorial Guinea, and the presence of doctors, counsellors, teachers and technicians is an act of solidarity, friendship and fraternity that strengthens bilateral relations'.[66]

The Cuban presence in Equatorial Guinea, which dates from 1969, was made official on 27 December 1972 through the exchange of diplomatic representatives between the two countries. The bilateral cooperation between the two states focuses on the educational, health, political and technical sectors. The rapidly growing Cuban presence in Equatorial Guinea can be explained by several factors. Firstly, it was prompted by the quarrel between Equatorial Guinea and Spain, the former colonial power, which did not fulfil its promises after independence. Disappointed by Spain, Equatorial Guinea sought an alternative and aligned itself with the communist bloc countries including Cuba. Secondly, the Cuban presence in Equatorial Guinea can be seen as a result of the Cold War. Thirdly, the Cuban presence in Equatorial Guinea was made possible by the fact that Cuba found itself isolated by the major powers, and turned to African countries in order to build an effective foreign policy at a time when African states were focused on the eradication of colonisation. There, Cuba found a welcome response among anti-colonial movements and fought alongside national liberation movements like the FLN in Algeria. Since 1972, Equatorial Guinea has signed cooperation agreements with Cuba, which is still a major ally and provides aid in the areas of health and education in particular. In turn, Equatorial Guinea has supported Cuba in its struggle for the lifting of the embargo imposed by the United States. The relationship between Cuba and Equatorial Guinea may be seen as an instance of the foreign policy of small states that need allies in order to deal with external threats. The Cuban presence in Equatorial Guinea is also an instance of South–South cooperation, a major issue for researchers in international relations.

NOTES

1. Nicole Sarmiento Oddveig, 'A Postcolonial Analysis of Cuban Foreign Policy towards South African Liberation Movements, 1959–1994,' MA thesis, Stellenbosch University, 2010, 3.
2. Piero Gleijeses, 'Moscow's Proxy? Cuba and Africa 1975–1988,' *Journal of Cold War Studies* 8, no. 2 (2006): 3–51.

3 Richard Cooper, Joan Kennelly, and Pedro Orduñez-Garcia, 'Review: Health in Cuba,' *International Journal of Epidemiology* 35 (2006): 817–24; Julie Feinsilver, *Healing the Masses: Cuban Health Politics at Home and Abroad* (Berkeley: University of California Press, 1993).

4 Oddveig, 'A Postcolonial Analysis,' 5.

5 Oddveig, 'A Postcolonial Analysis,' 10.

6 Michael Erisman and John Kirk, *Cuban Foreign Policy Confronts a New International Order* (London: Lynne Rienner Publishers, 1991).

7 Gleijeses, 'Moscow's Proxy?', 3.

8 Piero Gleijeses, *Conflicting Missions: Havana, Washington, and Africa: 1959–1976* (Chapel Hill, NC: University of North Carolina Press, 2002), 328; Piero Gleijeses, 'From Cassinga to New York: The Struggle for the Independence of Namibia,' in *Cold War in Southern Africa: White Power, Black Liberation*, ed. Sue Onslow (London: Routledge, 2009), 201–24; Isaac Saney, 'African Stalingrad: The Cuban Revolution, Internationalism, and the End of Apartheid,' *Latin American Perspectives* 33, no. 5 (2006): 81–117; Isaac Saney, 'Homeland of Humanity: Internationalism within the Cuban Revolution,' *Latin American Perspectives* 36, no. 1 (2009): 111–23.

9 Piero Gleijeses, 'Cuba's First Venture in Africa: Algeria, 1961–1965,' *Journal of Latin American Studies* 28, no. 1 (1996): 159–95; Gleijeses, *Conflicting Missions*; Gleijeses, 'Moscow's Proxy?'; Piero Gleijeses, 'The First Ambassadors: Cuba's Contribution to Guinea-Bissau's War of Independence,' *Journal of Latin American Studies* 29 (1997): 45–88.

10 Edgard Dosman, 'Countdown to Cuito Cuanavale: Cuba's Angola Campaign,' in *Beyond the Border War: New Perspectives on Southern Africa's Late-Cold War Conflicts*, ed. G. Baines and P. Vale (Pretoria: Unisa Press, 2008), 207–28.

11 Hedelberto López Blanch, 'Cuba: The Little Giant against Apartheid,' in *The Road to Democracy in South Africa:* vol. 3, *International Solidarity, Part 2*, ed. SADET (Pretoria: Unisa Press, 2008), 1155–210.

12 William LeoGrande, *Cuba's Policy in Africa, 1959–1980*, Policy Papers in International Affairs, No. 13 (Berkeley: University of California, Institute of International Studies, 1980).

13 Isaac Saney, *Cuba: A Revolution in Motion* (Halifax: Fernwood Publishing, 2004).

14 See Gretchen Bauer and Scott Taylor, *Politics in Southern Africa: State and Society in Transition* (Boulder: Lynne Rienner, 2005); Greg Mills, ed., *From Pariah to Participant: South Africa's Evolving Foreign Relations, 1990–1994* (Johannesburg: SAIIA, 1994); Patrick McGowan and Philip Nel, eds, *Power, Wealth and Global Equity: An International Relations Textbook for Africa* (Cape Town: UCT Press, 2002).

15 Carlos Alzugaray, 'Anti-Hegemony in Theory and Practice: The Exceptional Case of Cuba,' paper presented at the 2004 International Studies Association Convention held at Montreal, Quebec, Canada, 17–21 March 2004, 3.

16 Oddveig, 'A Postcolonial Analysis,' 37.

17 Alzugaray, 'Anti-Hegemony in Theory and Practice,' 3.

18 LeoGrande, *Cuba's Policy in Africa*, 9.

19 Gleijeses, 'Cuba's First Venture in Africa,' 188.

20 LeoGrande, *Cuba's Policy in Africa*, 1. See as well the chapters by Alcaraz, and Kiriakou and André in this volume.

21 Michael T. Kaufman, 'Russia and Cuba Trying to End African Role of U.S. and China,' *New York Times*, 13 March 1977: 3; David B. Ottaway, 'Castro Seen as Mediator in Africa Talks,' *Washington Post*, 18 March 1977: 5.

[22] Oddveig, 'A Postcolonial Analysis,' 3.

[23] Randolph Persaud, *Counter-Hegemony and Foreign Policy: The Dialectics of Marginalized and Global Forces in Jamaica* (Albany: State University of New York Press, 2001); Gleijeses, 'Moscow's Proxy?', 3.

[24] Richard Saull, 'Locating the Global South in the Theorisation of the Cold War: Capitalist Development, Social Revolution and Geopolitical Conflict,' *Third World Quarterly* 26, no. 2 (2005): 253–80.

[25] Oddveig, 'A Postcolonial Analysis,' 40.

[26] E. Eduardo Galeano, *Open Veins of Latin America: Five Centuries of the Pillage of a Continent* (New York: Monthly Review Press, 1997 [1973]); Cyril Lionel Robert James, *The Black Jacobins: Toussaint L'Ouverture and the San Domingo Revolution* (London: Penguin Books, 1980 [1963]; Mark Laffey and Jutta Weldes, 'Decolonizing the Cuban Missile Crisis,' *International Studies Quarterly* 52, no. 3 (2008): 555–77.

[27] Max Liniger-Goumaz, *Brève histoire de la Guinée Équatoriale* (Geneva: Éditions des Peuples Noirs, 1986).

[28] Liniger-Goumaz, *Brève histoire de la Guinée Équatoriale*, 84.

[29] Rudolph Joseph Rummel, *National Attributes and Behavior* (Beverly Hills: Sage, 1978).

[30] Cited by Max Liniger-Goumaz, *La Guinée Équatoriale: Un pays méconnu* (Paris: L'Harmattan, 1979).

[31] José Antonio Garcia Trevijano Fos, from Granada, was born in Valencia. When Equatorial Guinea was seeking an economic adviser to the constitutional conference of 1968 in Madrid, he was presented by Gonzales Armijo. However, he was suspected of funding the electoral campaign of Macías Nguema, and after independence he became the great adviser and sponsor of Nguema.

[32] Carrero Blanco was the secretary general to the Presidency of Spain and number two in Franco's government.

[33] Bonifacio Ondo Edú-Aguong was the president of the autonomous government of Spanish Guinea from 1964 to 1968. During the first democratic presidential elections, he emerged second in the second round after Macías Nguema.

[34] During the Constitutional Conference of 1967–8 Carrero Blanco defended Ondo Edú and Garcia defended Macías Nguema. But in the elections, Macías defeated Ondo Edú. This is what explains the disagreements between Spain and Equatorial Guinea because Carrero Blanco, being a minister and attached to Franco, did not want to cooperate with the candidate of his opponent. Cooperating with him was seen as treason. See Liniger-Goumaz, *Brève histoire de la Guinée Équatoriale*, 1986.

[35] Paul Gerard Nsah-Voundy, 'Le petit État dans les relations internationales: La Guinée Équatoriale et ses voisins,' PhD diss., International Relations Institute of Cameroon (IRIC), Yaoundé, 1990, 136.

[36] To protest against the refusal of Spain to reduce the number of places where it hoisted its flags, Equatorial Guinea tore them down in March 1969.

[37] Liniger-Goumaz, *La Guinée Équatoriale*, 14.

[38] Jean Koufan and Casimir Tchudjing, 'Sur la voie de l'intégration sous-régionale en Afrique centrale: Les facteurs d'adhésion de la Guinée Équatoriale à l'UDEAC,' in *Dynamiques d'intégration régionale en Afrique centrale: Actes du colloque de Yaoundé 26–28 Avril 2000*, vol. 1, ed. Daniel Abwa, Joseph Marie Essomba, Martin Njeuma and Charles de la Roncière (Yaoundé: PUY, 2001), 227.

[39] Simon Baynham, 'Equatorial Guinea: The Terror and the Coup,' *World Today* 36 (February 1980): 65–71.

40 Nsah-Voundy, 'Le petit État,' 55.
41 Nsah-Voundy, 'Le petit État,' 137.
42 Mba Ayecaba, Lourdes, 'Je considère le peuple cubain comme le mien.' Interview de l'Ambassadeur équato-guinéen à Cuba par Nuria Barbosa, Granma Internacional, accessed 3 May 2016, http://www.france-guineeequatoriale.org/lourdes-mba-ayecaba-je-considere-le-peuple-cubain-comme-le-mien/.
43 Nsah-Voundy, 'Le petit État.'
44 Nsah-Voundy, 'Le petit État,' 143.
45 Laïdi Zaki, 'Les problèmes de consolidation de l'influence soviétique en Afrique,' *Politique Africaine* II, no. 7 (September 1982): 82.
46 Jean Leca and Yves Shemeil, 'Clientélisme et patrimonialisme dans le monde arabe,' *Revue Internationale de Science Politique* 4 (1983): 455–94.
47 LeoGrande, *Cuba's Policy in Africa*, 69
48 Macías Nguema, *Address to the Nation*, 12 March 1977, Malabo.
49 Tania Hernández, 'Le président de la Guinée Équatoriale remercie Cuba de sa coopération,' accessed 12 April 2016, http://www.radiohc.cu/fr/noticias/nacionales/75898-le-president-de-la-guinee-equatoriale-remercie-cuba-de-sa-cooperation.
50 Mba Ayecaba, 'Je considère le peuple cubain comme le mien.'
51 http://www.journaldemalabo.com/article.php?aid=1265, accessed 15 May 2016.
52 Jorge Dominguez, 'Signing of the Cooperation Agreement between Cuba and Equatorial Guinea,' accessed 18 March 2016, https://www.foreignaffairs.com/authors/jorgue-dominguez.
53 http://unge.education/main/?pageid=447, accessed 3 May 2016.
54 Embassy of France in Equatorial Guinea, 2012.
55 Oddveig, 'A Postcolonial Analysis,' 6.
56 Cooper, Kennelly, and Orduñez-Garcia, 'Review,' 821; Feinsilver, *Healing the Masses.*
57 Cooper, Kennelly, and Orduñez-Garcia, 'Review,' 821.
58 Baffour Ankomah, 'Fidel Castro, the Verdict … How the West Reacted to His Resignation,' *New African*, no. 472 (2008): 20–5.
59 Carlos Alberto Montaner and Ignacio Ramonet, 'Was Fidel Good for Cuba? A Debate between Carlos Alberto Montaner and Ignacio Ramonet,' *Foreign Policy* 158 (2007): 62.
60 Montaner and Ramonet, 'Was Fidel Good for Cuba?', 62.
61 Reynaldo Henquen, 'La Guinée Équatoriale remercie Cuba de sa collaboration médicale,' accessed 12 March 2016, http://www.radiohc.cu/fr/noticias/nacionales/77836-la-guinee-equatoriale-remercie-cuba-de-sa-collaboration-medicale.
62 Michele Claverie, 'Des experts cubains arrivent en Guinée Équatoriale pour faire face au virus Ebola,' accessed 25 February 2016, http://www.radiohc.cu/fr/noticias/nacionales/41216-des-experts-cubains-arrivent-en-guinee-equatoriale-pour-faire-face-au-virus-ebola.
63 Henquen, 'La Guinée Équatoriale remercie Cuba de sa collaboration médicale.'
64 Reynaldo Henquen, 'Le président Raúl Castro reçoit ses homologues de Guinée Équatoriale et de Namibie,' accessed 25 April 2016, http://www.radiohc.cu/fr/noticias/nacionales/35079-le-president-raul-castro-recoit-ses-homologues-de-guinee-equatoriale-et-de-namibie.
65 Reynaldo Henquen, 'Le président de la Guinée Équatoriale exprime sa confiance dans la levée du blocus étasunien,' accessed 2 April 2016, http://www.radiohc.cu/fr/noticias/nacionales/71265-le-president-de-la-guinee-equatoriale-exprime-sa-confiance-dans-le-levee-du-blocus-etasunien.

[66] Mba Ayecaba, 'Je considère le peuple cubain comme le mien.' Interview of the Ambassador of Equatorial Guinea in Cuba by Granma Internacional, accessed 3 May 2016, http://www.france-guineeequatoriale.org/lourdes-mba-ayecaba-je-considere-le-peuple-cubain-comme-le-mien/.

REFERENCES

Alzugaray, Carlos. 'Anti-Hegemony in Theory and Practice: The Exceptional Case of Cuba.' Paper presented at the 2004 International Studies Association Convention held at Montreal, Quebec, Canada, 17–21 March 2004.

Ankomah, Baffour. 'Fidel Castro, the Verdict . . . How the West Reacted to His Resignation.' *New African*, no. 472 (2008): 20–5.

Bauer, Gretchen and Scott Taylor. *Politics in Southern Africa: State and Society in Transition*. Boulder: Lynne Rienner, 2005.

Baynham, Simon. 'Equatorial Guinea: The Terror and the Coup.' *World Today* 36 (February 1980): 65–71.

Blanch, Hedelberto López. 'Cuba: The Little Giant against Apartheid.' In *The Road to Democracy in South Africa: vol. 3, International Solidarity, Part 2*, edited by SADET, 1155–210. Pretoria: Unisa Press, 2008.

Cooper, Richard, Joan Kennelly and Pedro Orduñez-Garcia. 'Review: Health in Cuba.' *International Journal of Epidemiology* 35 (2006): 817–24.

Deutschmann, David, ed. *Angola and Namibia: Changing the History of Africa*. Melbourne: Ocean Press, 1989.

Dosman, Edgard. 'Countdown to Cuito Cuanavale: Cuba's Angola Campaign.' In *Beyond the Border War: New Perspectives on Southern Africa's Late-Cold War Conflicts*, edited by G. Baines and P. Vale, 207–28. Pretoria: Unisa Press, 2008.

Erisman, Michael and John Kirk. *Cuban Foreign Policy Confronts a New International Order*. London: Lynne Rienner Publishers,1991.

Feinsilver, Julie. *Healing the Masses: Cuban Health Politics at Home and Abroad* (Berkeley: University of California Press, 1993).

Galeano, Eduardo. *Open Veins of Latin America: Five Centuries of the Pillage of a Continent*. New York: Monthly Review Press, 1997 [1973].

Galvez, Milliam. *Che in Africa: Che Guevara's Congo Diary*. Melbourne and New York: Ocean Press, 1999.

Gleijeses, Piero. *Conflicting Missions: Havana, Washington, and Africa: 1959–1976*. Chapel Hill, NC: University of North Carolina Press, 2002.

Gleijeses, Piero. 'Cuba's First Venture in Africa: Algeria, 1961–1965.' *Journal of Latin American Studies* 28, no. 1 (1996): 159–95.

Gleijeses, Piero. 'The First Ambassadors: Cuba's Contribution to Guinea-Bissau's War of Independence.' *Journal of Latin American Studies* 29 (1997): 45–88.

Gleijeses, Piero. 'From Cassinga to New York: The Struggle for the Independence of Namibia.' In *Cold War in Southern Africa: White Power, Black Liberation*, edited by Sue Onslow, 201–24. London: Routledge, 2009.

Gleijeses, Piero.'Moscow's Proxy? Cuba and Africa 1975–1988.' *Journal of Cold War Studies* 8, no. 2 (2006): 3–51.

James, Cyril Lionel Robert. *The Black Jacobins: Toussaint L'Ouverture and the San Domingo Revolution*. London: Penguin Books, 1980 [1963].

Julie, Feinsilver. *Healing the Masses: Cuban Health Politics at Home and Abroad*. Berkeley: University of California Press, 1993.

Kaufman, Michael T. 'Russia and Cuba Trying to End African Role of U.S. and China.' *New York Times*, 13 March 1977: 3.

Koufan, Jean and Casimir Tchudjing. 'Sur la voie de l'intégration sous-régionale en Afrique centrale: Les facteurs d'adhésion de la Guinée Équatoriale à l'UDEAC.' In *Dynamiques d'intégration régionale en Afrique centrale: Actes du colloque de Yaoundé 26-28 avril 2000*, vol. 1, edited by Daniel Abwa, Joseph Marie Essomba, Martin Njeuma and Charles de la Roncière, 215–30. Yaoundé: PUY, 2001.

Laffey, Mark and Jutta Weldes. 'Decolonizing the Cuban Missile Crisis.' *International Studies Quarterly* 52, no. 3 (2008): 555–77.

Leca, Jean and Yves Shemeil. 'Clientélisme et patrimonialisme dans le monde arabe.' *Revue Internationale de Science Politique* 4 (1983): 455–94.

LeoGrande, William. *Cuba's Policy in Africa, 1959–1980*. Policy Papers in International Affairs, No. 13. Berkeley: University of California, Institute of International Studies, 1980.

Liniger-Goumaz, Max. *Brève histoire de la Guinée Équatoriale*. Geneva: Éditions des Peuples Noirs, 1986.

Liniger-Goumaz, Max. *La Guinée Équatoriale: Un pays méconnu*. Paris: L'Harmattan, 1979.

McGowan, Patrick and Philip Nel, eds. *Power, Wealth and Global Equity: An International Relations Textbook for Africa*. Cape Town: UCT Press, 2002.

Mills, Greg, ed. *From Pariah to Participant: South Africa's Evolving Foreign Relations, 1990–1994*. Johannesburg: SAIIA,1994.

Montaner, Carlos Alberto and Ignacio Ramonet. 'Was Fidel Good for Cuba? A Debate between Carlos Alberto Montaner and Ignacio Ramonet.' *Foreign Policy* 158 (2007): 56–64.

Nsah-Voundy, Paul Gerard. 'Le petit État dans les relations internationales: La Guinée Équatoriale et ses voisins.' PhD diss., International Relations Institute of Cameroon (IRIC), Yaoundé, 1990.

Oddveig, Nicole Sarmiento. 'A Postcolonial Analysis of Cuban Foreign Policy towards South African Liberation Movements, 1959–1994.' MA thesis, Stellenbosch University, 2010.

Ottaway, David B. 'Castro Seen as Mediator in Africa Talks.' *Washington Post*, 18 March 1977: 5.

Persaud, Randolph. *Counter-Hegemony and Foreign Policy: The Dialectics of Marginalized and Global Forces in Jamaica*. Albany: State University of New York Press, 2001.

Rummel, Rudolph Joseph. *National Attributes and Behavior*. Beverly Hills: Sage, 1978.

Saney, Isaac. 'African Stalingrad: The Cuban Revolution, Internationalism, and the End of Apartheid.' *Latin American Perspectives* 33, no. 5 (2006): 81–117.

Saney, Isaac. *Cuba: A Revolution in Motion*. Halifax: Fernwood Publishing, 2004.

Saney, Isaac. 'Homeland of Humanity: Internationalism within the Cuban Revolution.' *Latin American Perspectives* 36, no. 1 (2009): 111–23.

Saull, Richard. 'Locating the Global South in the Theorisation of the Cold War: Capitalist Development, Social Revolution and Geopolitical Conflict.' *Third World Quarterly* 26, no. 2 (2005): 253–80.

Zaki, Laïdi. 'Les problèmes de consolidation de l'influence soviétique en Afrique.' *Politique Africaine II*, no. 7 (September 1982): 82–90.

ELECTRONIC SOURCES, PRESS AND MEDIA

Aranega, Francisco Rodríguez. 'Cuba et la Guinée Équatoriale envisagent de signer un accord de coopération dans le domaine de l'aéronautique.' Accessed 25 April 2016. http://www.radiohc.cu/fr/noticias/nacionales/89032-cuba-et-la-guinee-equatoriale-envisagent-de-signer-un-accord-de-cooperation-dans-le-domaine-de-l'aeronautique.

Claverie, Michèle. 'Des experts cubains arrivent en Guinée Équatoriale pour faire face au virus Ebola.' Accessed 25 February 2016. http://www.radiohc.cu/fr/noticias/nacionales/41216-des-experts-cubains-arrivent-en-guinee-equatoriale-pour-faire-face-au-virus-ebola.

Dominguez, Jorge. 'Signing of the Cooperation Agreement between Cuba and Equatorial Guinea.' Accessed 18 March 2016. https://www.foreignaffairs.com/authors/jorgue-dominguez.

Henquen, Reynaldo. 'La Guinée Équatoriale condamne le blocus étasunien contre Cuba.' Accessed 25 April 2016. http://www.radiohc.cu/fr/noticias/nacionales/69953-la-guinee-equatoriale-condamne-le-blocus-etasunien-contre-cuba.

Henquen, Reynaldo. 'La Guinée Équatoriale remercie Cuba de sa collaboration médicale.' Accessed 12 March 2016. http://www.radiohc.cu/fr/noticias/nacionales/77836-la-guinee-equatoriale-remercie-cuba-de-sa-collaboration-medicale.

Henquen, Reynaldo. 'Le président de la Guinée Équatoriale exprime sa confiance dans la levée du blocus étasunien.' Accessed 2 April 2016. http://www.radiohc.cu/fr/noticias/nacionales/71265-le-president-de-la-guinee-equatoriale-exprime-sa-confiance-dans-le-levee-du-blocus-etasunien.

Henquen, Reynaldo. 'Le président de la Guinée Équatoriale met en exergue l'aide des professeurs cubains à l'éducation dans son pays.' Accessed 29 February 2016. http://www.radiohc.cu/fr/noticias/nacionales/5568-le-president-de-la-guinee-equatoriale-met-en-exergue-l'aide-des-professeurs-cubains-a-l'education-dans-son-pays.

Henquen, Reynaldo. 'Le président Raúl Castro reçoit ses homologues de Guinée Équatoriale et de Namibie.' Accessed 25 April 2016. http://www.radiohc.cu/fr/noticias/nacionales/35079-le-president-raul-castro-recoit-ses-homologues-de-guinee-equatoriale-et-de-namibie.

Hernández, Tania. 'Le président de la Guinée Équatoriale remercie Cuba de sa coopération.' Accessed 12 April 2016. http://www.radiohc.cu/fr/noticias/nacionales/75898-le-president-de-la-guinee-equatoriale-remercie-cuba-de-sa-cooperation.

Hounkpe. 'Cuba et son allié africain, un partenariat émergent pour le développement.' Accessed 25 April 2016. http://terangaweb.com/pour-une-cooperation-emergente-entre-cuba-et-lafrique/.

http://unge.education/main/?pageid=447. Accessed 3 May 2016.

http://www.journaldemalabo.com/article.php?aid=1265. Accessed 15 May 2016.

Marrero, Lisandra. 'La Guinée Équatoriale réitère sa position en faveur de la levée du blocus de Cuba.' Accessed 25 April 2016. http://www.radiohc.cu/fr/noticias/nacionales/56862-la-guinee-equatoriale-reitere-sa-position-en-faveur-de-la-levee-du-blocus-de-cuba.

Mba Ayecaba, Lourdes. 'Je considère le peuple cubain comme le mien.' Interview de l'Ambassadeur équato-guinéen à Cuba par Nuria Barbosa, Granma Internacional. Accessed 3 May 2016. http://www.france-guineeequatoriale.org/lourdes-mba-ayecaba-je-considere-le-peuple-cubain-comme-le-mien/.

CHAPTER

4

Cuban Internationalism in Africa: Civil cooperation with Angola and its aftermath

Christine Hatzky

Cuba and Africa have a long, rich and complex history with a trajectory of probably more than five hundred years since the time when, together with the Spanish conquistadors, the first Africans set foot on the island. Cuba has particularly close links to Africa because of the transatlantic slave trade, which started in the early sixteenth century. Of the estimated 10 to 12 million Africans who survived the Middle Passage across the Atlantic to the Americas, about one million came to Cuba. This history became even more complicated in the nineteenth century, in the era of 'Second Slavery',[1] when the Cuban colonial plantation economy became the world's first producer of sugar for the world based on mass slave labour. The majority of Africans in Cuba – slaves, former slaves and their descendants – fought actively in Cuba's long independence struggle (1868–98) against Spanish colonial rule.[2] Cuba's post-emancipation history (after 1886) illustrates that the connection with Africa was not merely a unidirectional movement from Africa to the Americas resulting from the forced migration of Africans.[3] It was the start of a process of exchange and reciprocity. Beginning in the late 1950s, Cuba's civil and military South–South cooperation with different African countries coincided politically with the dynamics of massive decolonisation in Africa. Nevertheless, this cooperation would not have been possible without the long-term connections between Africa and the Americas since the age of European expansion into the Atlantic.

The involvement of Africans and their descendants in Cuba's independence struggle constitutes the historical framework for the official explanation of support for Angola's anti-colonial movement, the Popular Movement for the Liberation of Angola (MPLA). Castro's justification for Operation Carlota,[4] the military engagement that started the cooperation with Angola in autumn 1975, referred to the 'historical duty' of Cubans to support the Angolan independence struggle. Castro created an interactive transatlantic space and went as far as defining Cuba as an 'Afro-Latin American nation' – and was indeed the first to invent, *avant la lettre*, what the British cultural studies academic Paul Gilroy later called the 'Black Atlantic'[5] – a turning point in the study of African diasporas. While the Cuban leader did not intend to bring about a paradigm shift in Atlantic history, nevertheless it was an expression of the conviction that Cuba was part of something bigger than its own nation. In late 1975 Castro called on the Cuban people to show internationalist solidarity and to commit themselves to military and civil engagement in Africa. He based his argument also on the blood ties between Cubans and Africans, formed through their shared colonial past. His conclusion was that every Cuban was compelled not only by anti-colonial and anti-imperialist but also by anti-racist principles to defend Angola's independence against the attacks of the South African apartheid regime.

This recourse to history with the 'invention of a tradition'[6] was significant because, especially after the Cuban Revolution, the cultural and national identity of all Cubans emerged from the war of independence firmly rooted in the collective memory of the Cuban people. Several hundred thousand Cubans followed Castro's call and served as military and civil 'internationalists' in Africa until the early 1990s and afterwards in a great variety of inter-state cooperation and development aid programmes. But this did not automatically mean that Castro's notion of transnational and transcultural identity motivated them to go to Africa. The answers that my interviewees[7] gave to me represented a break with the official discourse and could not have been more unambiguous: regardless of whether or not my interviewees had African ancestry, the majority of them stated that they had no special connection to Africa or Angola. Almost no one wished to be identified with Africa and Angola.

The special ties between Cuba and Africa did not mean that within Cuba racism had vanished, although it was legally banned and mitigated through manifold social, economic and educational programmes. Nowadays it is clear that racism has survived all progressive social experiments in Cuba. It was even reinforced during the Cuban economic crisis after 1990 when Soviet support stopped, and today Cubans of African descent still have to deal with inequality, racial prejudice and racism.[8] I became aware of this during a visit to Havana with a group of my students in early 2017, exploring the history of Cuba and the traces of Africa in Cuba. Inequality had become even more visible in the last decade, but we heard equally clear criticism of ethnic discrimination within Cuban society and a diminishing knowledge of Africa, its history and its culture. We were astonished. In retrospect the intensity, quantity and quality of the Cuban engagement in Angola in the civil sphere acquired even greater significance. And, above all, the majority of those who served as internationalists in Africa are still alive, and a broader public discussion about Cuba's massive solidarity engagement in Africa could be a meaningful contribution to decoding the complexity of racism, identity and inclusion within Cuban society. There is no doubt that the engagement in Angola had great reverse social and cultural effects on Cuban society – though sociological, anthropological and cultural research on this is largely still lacking.[9] In the following reflections on the civil engagement of Cuba in Africa and the transfer and circulation of knowledge in the global South, based on the findings of my empirical study of Cuba's civil cooperation in education with postcolonial Angola between 1975 and 1991,[10] I can only give a small insight into the magnitude of this South–South cooperation.

When I started researching the topic one and a half decades ago, there was no awareness whatsoever of the extent and impact of Cuban civil cooperation in Africa, and even less about that in Angola. There was not only an absence of data and of relevant academic studies and publications, but also a prevailing view, shaped by the perspective of the Cold War, that the Cuban engagement in Angola was a purely military operation, a proxy war in which the Cuban government had acted on behalf of the Soviet Union. In Cuba any attempt to historicise its engagement in Angola is hindered to this day by an ideologically charged discourse and an equally polarised version that still portrays it as part of the official success story of the Cuban Revolution. During my research in Cuba, Portugal, Angola and the US, I realised that Cuba's cooperation with Africa as a whole, and specifically in Angola, was probably the world's most comprehensive example of civil (and military) cooperation between two formerly colonised countries. In the beginning, the official motive for Cuba's engagement in Africa was internationalist solidarity in its 'old' signification: revolutionary export with a firm political goal, the establishment of an anti-colonial and anti-imperialist South–South axis that extended towards the young, independent African nation-states and even towards Asia, with Havana as the central hub. It was a specific form of political and military aid for anti-colonial and independence movements and governments. After the failure of Che Guevara's Congo expedition in 1965, this policy shifted to include more and more pragmatic visions of solidarity and, finally, in view of the concrete and extensive needs of independent Angola in order to build an independent state, Cuba's civil engagement in Angola became a kind of socialist development aid, starting as a progressive empowerment programme with 'help for self-help'.

A look at the extent of the cooperation shows how impressive Cuban support for Angola was, in quantitative terms alone: according to official figures, around 400 000 Cuban soldiers and approximately 50 000 civilians (all kinds of experts, for example technicians, civil engineers, doctors, teachers, professors and aid workers) worked in Angola between 1975 and 1991.[11] Moreover, from the 1960s onwards, Cuba had also provided civil development aid and military support to many other countries in Africa, Latin America and Asia, both to help anti-colonial movements and to assist fledgling postcolonial governments. Among others, Algeria, Ethiopia, Benin, Ghana, Guinea-Bissau, Yemen, Cape Verde, Congo-Brazzaville, Mozambique, São Tomé and Príncipe, Zambia and Zimbabwe received Cuban civil support from 1963 up to 1991.[12] Such undertakings provide firm evidence that, following worldwide decolonisation after the Second World War, if not before, knowledge transfer and development aid were not unidirectional from North to South but included a definite component of knowledge circulation and mutual aid within South–South relations.[13] Here too, the South–South cooperation projects issuing from Cuba towards Africa opened up a completely new perspective.

As I have discussed in a recently published article on the role of the so-called Third World in the Cold War,[14] despite the numerous publications on military cooperation between Cuba and Angola that appeared during the Cold War era, there has been little research on the huge civilian support programmes – though now, at least, more research is being done on this subject and a number of works have appeared in recent years, some of them taking into account the development of Cuban internationalism after 1990.[15] The studies of Cuba's military cooperation that were published before 1990 claimed to be scientifically based, but seldom revealed any new findings. Furthermore, they persistently repeated the prevailing parameters of Cold War discourse, conjuring up a communist threat to the US and the rest of the Western world from the involvement of the Soviet Union in Angola's postcolonial war. Interest therefore focused almost exclusively on the extent of ostensible (or supposed) Soviet backing for military cooperation between Cuba and Angola. Although several critical studies have since taken issue with this version of history, the presence of Cuban troops is still regarded with very few exceptions as an example of Cuban military 'intervention' in Angola. Time and again, the role of Soviet proxy has been ascribed to the Cuban government.[16] US academics and publicists in particular have interpreted Cuba's support for the MPLA almost exclusively in terms of the global interests of the Soviet regime, and in so doing have frequently underestimated the role of Cuba as an independent protagonist.[17] Even those historians who have rightly emphasised the importance of Cuba's political activity in the international arena[18] have tended to concentrate on Cuba's foreign military operations and disregard the fact that, particularly after Angola, its civil engagement abroad became increasingly significant.[19]

To the present day, ideological premises obscure the role played by civil cooperation in Angola, during which Cuban experts and aid workers contributed to the construction of the postcolonial nation-state in education, health, administration, industry, and civil engineering. Furthermore, the engagement now has to be judged by its long-term results and in the light of subsequent developments in Angolan history. These include the postcolonial war that, even after the withdrawal of Cuban military forces and civilians in 1991, raged until 2002 with unbelievably destructive power, and the descent of the MPLA government into a kind of corrupt family enterprise that is plundering the country today at the cost of the majority of the population. Nevertheless, the Cuban government itself continues to disseminate a narrative firmly anchored in the dichotomies of the Cold War, dividing the protagonists into the 'good' (the Cubans demonstrating heroic solidarity with the people of Angola) and the 'bad' (the imperialists, neo-colonialists and racists). Amazingly, this narrative also almost ignores the civilian aspects of cooperation and reduces the Cuban engagement in Angola to the political and military successes that secured Angola's territorial integrity, accelerated the collapse of the South African apartheid regime, and helped bring about Namibia's independence.

SPECIAL FEATURES OF CUBAN–ANGOLAN CIVIL COOPERATION

Cuba's cooperation with the friendly, left-wing, anti-colonial MPLA from 1975 on is unique because of its scope, impact and character. It came into being under the banner of 'internationalist solidarity', which was propagated by the Cuban government especially with regard to the countries of the Tricontinental, the three continents of Asia, Africa and Latin America. It is not within the scope of this chapter to make any conclusive assessment of the military cooperation and its political implications; I will rather focus on the special features and challenges of civil cooperation. At the end of the colonial era, the challenges Angola faced were similar to those of revolutionary Cuba: high levels of illiteracy and the lack of a trained workforce. Cuba's successes in modernising its education system – which has been regarded as the 'revolutionary government's most impressive achievement'[20] – and the principle of educating 'new men' pointed the way for Angola's postcolonial education policy. The Cuban–Angolan cooperation in education was founded on a common consensus. The 'success story' of Cuba's education policy, which created sustainable literacy levels and involved the people in the national and revolutionary project, was to be transferred to Angola. Unlike previous political and military cooperation, Cuba's involvement in Angola therefore led quickly to an extensive professionalisation, which in turn triggered numerous structural, organisational and institutional changes within Cuba itself.

The study of Cuba's cooperation with Angola demonstrates surprising features. Contrary to previous assumptions deriving from a Cold War perspective, the dynamics of this cooperative relationship were determined by the Angolan side: the Cuban government always acted in response to Angolan requests. At least with respect to civil cooperation in the education sector, a mechanism of 'demand and supply'[21] established itself, which runs like a thread through the history of this cooperation. It is probable that this pattern can be equally applied to other sectors of cooperation. The very start of the Cuban involvement can be clearly traced back to Angolan initiative: at the request of the MPLA even before Angola's independence in November 1975, Cuba provided military assistance to overcome its rivals, the National Union for the Total Independence of Angola (UNITA) and the National Front for the Liberation of Angola (FNLA),[22] and help fight against the intervention of the South African apartheid regime. Shortly after the MPLA came to power in postcolonial Angola with Cuba's assistance, it requested that, in addition to military aid, Cuba dispatch the first civilian experts so that they could push ahead together with the construction of the socialist People's Republic of Angola at all levels. Cuban expertise was intended to fill the gap that had been left behind by the hurried exodus after independence of the Portuguese settlers who had occupied almost all key positions in politics, administration and the economy within the Portuguese colonial system.

From then on, the Angolan government repeatedly asked for help from specialists and aid workers, and the Cuban government met its requests. This 'demand and supply' mechanism functioned far into the 1980s. The Cuban government constantly endeavoured to respond to Angolan demands and provide the desired manpower and know-how. A major feature of this cooperation pattern was the Economic, Scientific and Technical Cooperation Framework Agreement signed in Havana in July 1976 by both heads of state, Agostinho Neto and Fidel Castro. This marked the beginning of the cooperation's bilateral legalisation and institutionalisation.[23] The agreement was based on reciprocity and comprised the framework sub-agreements governing Cuba's undertaking to provide aid in health, education, industry and agriculture, and to help improve infrastructure. It also included a number of agreements on economic cooperation that benefited Cuba's economy, for example quotas for Cuban sugar imports into Angola and a fisheries agreement.[24] The two signatories further agreed that Cuba would receive financial compensation for the civil aid that it would provide in the future and had already provided. The Framework Agreement served as the basis for bilateral negotiations to determine the details, implementation and monitoring of cooperation. This process took place at various levels in bilateral committees and was characterised by open dialogue and solution-oriented debate.[25] Since the Angolan government was paying for Cuba's involvement, the amount of influence it had on the quality and quantity of cooperation was not negligible.

The engagement in Angola became the springboard for Cuba's export of workforce and knowledge that we are familiar with today: with great personal commitment, doctors, educationists and teachers (education experts in the broadest sense) make an important contribution to health and literacy programmes in many countries of Latin America and Africa. Such projects have earned Cuba the unique reputation of a 'nation of solidarity' primarily in Africa, but also in Latin America. Cuban doctors, teachers, technicians and aid workers are also becoming increasingly present in international NGOs, where they are appreciated for their extensive foreign experience, their dedication, and their sound education and training tailored towards the needs of developing countries. One of the most striking examples of this unique engagement and dedication in recent years is the unprecedented work of hundreds of Cuban doctors after the earthquake in Haiti in 2010, and in the case of the Ebola epidemic in West Africa in 2014, where the Cubans were among the first who dared engage in the crisis area and were even praised for this by the US government.[26]

Since the experience of massive civil cooperation in Angola, Cuban civil engagement abroad has become an important part of the Cuban economy. An almost unknown fact is that already at the time of cooperation, the Angolan government was paying the salaries of Cuban *cooperantes* – experts and aid workers – directly to the Cuban government, depending on their qualifications. That the Cuban government accepted payment from the Angolan government in return for skilled labour is by no means reprehensible. My investigation shed light, on the one hand, on the high costs and effort involved in the civilian engagement in Angola and, on the other hand, the constant economic and financial constraints faced by the Cuban government, which was by no means able to meet the costs of such an extensive engagement. On the contrary, it would have been surprising had the Cubans not demanded recompense for their assistance. It is true that the cooperation in education (and in all other civil sectors) primarily involved experts, skilled workers and know-how rather than goods or materials, which nominally cost the Cuban state nothing. Nevertheless, there were indirect costs involved, as over a period of more than fifteen years the Cuban national economy was drained of thousands of young, well-educated, skilled workers. However, double standards seem to have been at work in the practice of remunerating according to qualifications. In the state-controlled Cuban economy, workers were paid a uniform salary regardless of their qualifications and could only supplement their pay with performance-related bonuses. The socialist principles of the planned economy obviously did not apply to cooperation abroad – even though this was not a question of private gain but of profit for the sole good of the state.

The salient point is not that the aid was paid for, as this is completely justified, but that the Cuban 'internationalists', as the aid workers were known in the jargon of the time, have been led to believe to this day that they were providing altruistic help out of solidarity, and have no idea that the value of their work in Angola was many times higher than their salaries in Cuba, and that the state kept the difference. Apart from a small allowance, the 'internationalists' only received compensation in kind, in the form of transport, food and accommodation. But they could keep their salaries at home to maintain the family and they had the guarantee that their jobs in Cuba would remain open to them on their return – they were, after all, acting out of solidarity. Today, experts and aid workers receive at least a small salary, while the Cuban government benefits, depending on the recipient country, from raw materials (like crude oil from Venezuela) or hard currency. By means of human capital, the paid deployment of specialists, the Cuban government tried to compensate for its enormous financial and trade deficit that resulted from the ending of Soviet subsidies. Here the civil South–South cooperation in Angola was the decisive test case for all subsequent major engagements, which could not have been carried out without this huge human experience and without structural and infrastructural preparations. Long-term cooperation with Venezuela deriving from the 'oil-for-doctors' agreement, including projects like the Mission into the Neighbourhood (Misión Barrio Adentro), in which health care for the Venezuelan population of poor quarters (*barrios*) and remote regions was established with the help of Cuban doctors and health workers from the late 1990s, would not have been conceivable without the Angolan mission. In the same way, Operation Milagro (free eye operations) and the Robinson Mission (literacy and post-literacy training) involved making available on a temporary basis Cuban specialists, for whom financing was agreed between the governments and for whom the payment of salaries was essentially based on deliveries of crude oil.[27] These programmes in particular have benefited also people from Africa, Asia and even Europe.[28] The Cuban specialists themselves receive to this day only about a tenth of the payment that is made bilaterally, but through this they were able to keep their families going during the Cuban economic crisis (from 1991), and gain additional earnings that remain important for their survival today. The deployment of specialist Cuban workers, now on an ideology-free, pragmatic basis, has seen an astonishing revival between Cuba and Angola.

But back to the 1970s. It is clear that the ultimate driving force of Cuban cooperation with Angola was at that time the political cause of internationalist solidarity and mutual support in the global South to provide protection against imperialist demands, but in a way also against the predominant power of the socialist 'big brother'. Politics and pragmatism received equal importance, and Cuba's cooperation with Angola therefore combined both 'revolutionary export', as espoused by the Cuban revolutionaries of the 1960s, and specific, practical and day-to-day development aid during the upheaval of this historic transition from the colonial era to independence. The challenge of this transformation was huge and involved not only overcoming the legacy of colonialism in the midst of an armed decolonisation struggle, but also the revolutionising of society and the establishment of a new national culture.

Cooperation also incorporated elements of 'socialist development aid', with both Cuba and the MPLA pursuing a classic modernisation and national reconstruction programme. There were, however, considerable differences between this and Western, North–South development aid, especially considering the 'institutionalised know-it-all arrogance' inherent in this hierarchy-based North–South transfer of knowledge.[29] Just as in North–South relationships, there was indeed a gap in knowledge between the Cubans and the Angolans, and there were asymmetries and dissonances resulting from the day-to-day operations of the cooperation programme. Nevertheless, there is a clear distinction to be made. The peculiarities of Cuban–Angolan cooperation described above indicate that, unlike North–South development projects, both governments worked together at eye level, always endeavouring to maintain a mutual balance of interests. The Angolan government was well aware of its own deficits and comparative lack of knowledge, but it seems to have been astute in making use of the various options and offers that arose from the systems existing in the Cold War era. Its decision to purchase Cuban know-how to rebuild Angola was a conscious one, because it realised that the Cuban government was a suitable partner, able to support a socialist development model that would help stabilise its power and that could be adjusted practically to suit the specific requirements of a developing country. When the MPLA chose to work with the Cuban government, it was also assuming that Cuba would refrain from becoming too heavily involved in Angola's domestic affairs, despite its massive presence. Both were members of the Non-Aligned Movement and strove to follow an independent socialist path, which added to the mutual personal and political trust that already existed between the two governments – at least in the initial phase. During an interview that I held in 2006 with the Angolan minister of education, António Burity da Silva, he characterised the cooperation with Cuba wisely as an example of 'internationalism with reciprocal benefits'.[30]

THE *COOPERANTES*:[31] CUBAN SPECIALISTS AND AID WORKERS IN ANGOLA

The mass deployment of civilian 'internationalists' in Angola from around 1978 to 1985 had not been planned from the outset, but was rather a consequence of the dynamic of 'demand and supply'. The Cuban government had certainly not envisaged a long-term engagement, either in the military or civilian sector, but intended to withdraw their personnel as quickly as possible in the first half of 1976. Cuban society had then by no means overcome its own brain drain in the wake of the triumph of the revolution, and in the 1970s Cuba, like Angola, was suffering from a lack of specialists, experts and skilled workers in all sectors. But President Neto pre-empted Cuba's withdrawal by asking the Cuban government to extend both military and civil cooperation, thus frustrating Cuban plans. Cuba had originally envisaged a programme of 'help for self-help', which is why the project initially concentrated on sending advisers and providing Angolans with specialised training. Part of the intention behind this was to minimise the number of civilians sent to Angola, because already by spring 1976 it was becoming clear that there was no end in sight to the postcolonial war. The first special agreements between Cuba and Angola still reflected the original premise of empowerment. In the main, specialists were to go to Angola to work at national level advising Angolan ministers and providing specialised training for Angolans. In the education sector, these were people qualified in teaching or education science who already had considerable experience in education and teaching or had been involved in developing Cuba's own education policy.

The majority of education specialists who were first sent to Angola had participated as pupils and students in Cuba's 1961 national literacy campaign and then continued to specialise in educational sciences, a growing field in revolutionary Cuba. In fact, the literacy campaign was one of the seminal experiences that qualified Cubans as education experts for the Angolan project. Approximately 250 000 young Cuban men and women had participated in the literacy campaign alone. Those who were sent to Angola were able to build on their experience and their own education and training. In most cases, there was a further criterion that counted towards their selection: revolutionary commitment and uncompromising support for the aims of the revolution, which in the 1970s generally entailed membership of the Communist Party of Cuba.[32]

In Angola, they worked on behalf of the Angolan government, and so again their proximity to decision-makers was crucial to their expert status and the authority they commanded to solve problems. It is, however, precisely at this point that asymmetries and dissonances occurred. The Angolan partners depended on foreign expertise to find solutions for the Angolan situation, and they therefore requested help from Cuban advisers.[33] Particularly in the education sector, this involved very fundamental tasks. Independent Angola's constitution stipulated that every Angolan citizen had the basic right to education and culture, which involved the right to eight years of free education.[34] A new, emancipated education system was to help overcome the legacy of colonialism, racism, discrimination and paternalism in the consciousness of the Angolan population. This necessitated a completely new education system, for which the foundations and structures still had to be put in place – an enormous task. The very basics required to realise this ambitious plan were lacking: experience, educationists, qualified teachers, teacher training programmes, teaching materials, curricula, school buildings. To make matters worse, in 1975 approximately 85 per cent of the Angolan population was illiterate.

In the first years of cooperation Cuban advisers were active at all cardinal points in the early days of the new Angolan education system. In the 1980s, their importance continually declined, partly because Angolan education planners and educationists were able to establish themselves, and partly because – again at the behest of the Angolan government – the focus of cooperation turned to the mass deployment of Cuban teachers to make up for the dearth of local teaching staff. Nevertheless, Cuban advisers continued to serve as education experts until the end of the period of cooperation, although as early as 1978 Angolan education planners had insisted that their number be reduced and limited to the purely technical and administrative level.

The evaluation of all interviews I conducted concluded that the Cubans who were sent to Angola were not always as skilled as they should have been for the task. Angolan complaints about the Cuban advisers' lack of skill were probably not completely unfounded. Many of those sent to Angola as advisers may well have possessed the relevant qualifications in theory but in practice lacked the experience needed to function in an expert capacity. My study backs this: most of my respondents, whether teachers, doctors, professors or technicians, went to Angola while they were still young. They signed up so that they could gain more professional experience under the difficult conditions in Angola and thus better their qualifications for their career in Cuba. Many of my interviewees volunteered as inexperienced professionals, and during their stint abroad were able to become experts in their field. Whoever had worked in Angola in a position of responsibility for two years had proved themselves able to cope with a completely foreign environment and unforeseen challenges, and they had learned to find solutions by collaborating with Angolan partners and colleagues.

FROM KNOWLEDGE TRANSFER TO CIRCULATION: CUBAN TEACHERS AT ANGOLAN SCHOOLS

The majority of Cubans who went to Angola on behalf of the cooperation arrangements in education carried on working in their usual professions, as primary and secondary school teachers, university professors, doctors and nurses, engineers and construction workers. Unlike the advisers, who were deployed at key national and regional positions in the emerging social system, they worked at local level in schools, universities, hospitals and factories, and on farms and construction sites. These were the people who came into closest contact with the daily lives and working environments of the Angolan population. They shared the often-dire shortages, particularly in the provinces, and they, too, experienced war. It was their work on the ground that proved crucial in putting into practice the policies drawn up at national level by Cuban and Angolan specialists in education.

Between 1978 and 1983 (and finally till 1991), cooperation in education focused on employing Cuban teachers at Angolan schools. They worked there for one to two years from the sixth grade of primary school, and at secondary and polytechnic schools. Owing to the differences between Spanish and Portuguese, the Angolan Ministry of Education (MED) determined that Cuban teachers should not teach below the sixth grade. In general, the Cuban teachers were only able to speak *portuñol*, a cross between Spanish and Portuguese. Angolan education experts rightly considered the language barrier detrimental to the teaching of literacy to primary school children, many of whom did not even speak Portuguese but an African language as their mother tongue. With few exceptions the Cuban teachers were permitted to teach only natural sciences (mathematics, biology, chemistry, physics), history, geography and the obligatory 'Marxism-Leninism', because in these subjects their language deficit was considered less serious. Portuguese (and

Brazilian) teachers were called in to teach language-related classes at elementary level and Portuguese in the higher grades.[35]

The Cuban teachers subsequently played a major role in the Angolan school system. According to an internal MED report from 1982, 80 per cent of middle and higher education was conducted by foreign teachers, the majority of whom were Cubans.[36] Approximately a quarter of the teachers were student teachers who had been mobilised for the student brigades of the Che Guevara International Educational Detachment, established in 1977. In mid-1982, the number of Cuban teachers reached its absolute height: of a total of 2309 foreign teachers, 1779 came from Cuba.[37] The statistics from the MED's Department for International Cooperation (GICI/GII) show that just under 10 per cent of foreign teachers were Portuguese, while the rest came mainly from socialist countries like Bulgaria, the German Democratic Republic, the Soviet Union and Vietnam. Because of the much greater language barrier that these teachers faced, they worked almost exclusively in higher education or as advisers. A small number of teachers were recruited from other African countries or other countries in the West.[38]

Angola's urban areas profited most from their presence, as the majority of the teachers worked in Luanda, followed by the cities of Huambo and Benguela. Unlike their Portuguese or Eastern bloc and African colleagues, Cuban teachers also taught in 16 of the 18 Angolan provinces. The advantage they had over Angolan and other foreign teachers was their extreme flexibility, because they had no say whatsoever in where they would be deployed. Nevertheless, the distribution of teachers remained unequal, which was particularly noticeable in the remotest parts of the country. In 1980, only 6 Cuban primary teachers were working in the south-east province of Cuando Cubango, 22 were teaching in the north-east province of Lunda Norte, and 33 in the north-west province of Zaire.[39] Because of frequent military attacks from South African forces, the south-western province of Cunene was considered a war zone, and no foreign teachers at all were sent there. Between 1983/4 and 1991, the teachers were gradually withdrawn from Angola, at first mainly from the provinces at war. From 1985, they taught almost exclusively in the towns and cities, mainly at secondary level, at polytechnic schools and at the university. This withdrawal of teachers seriously undermined the running of schools.[40]

The Cuban teachers were not only there to impart knowledge. They also played key educational and political roles in carrying out the nationwide education reforms of the MPLA government. Their duties therefore included using education to integrate the population into the new political, social and national cause of the independent nation-state. At this time, Angola was still a highly unstable entity which UNITA, opponents of the MPLA government, wished to take over, having military control over considerable areas of the country. Despite the reservations of Angolan education planners, the curricula, teaching methods and educational aims developed by the MED essentially adhered to Cuban principles and methods of education. Cuban teachers were therefore ideal for carrying out this 'mission' in education policy. In order to achieve this, the Cuban teachers enthusiastically introduced modern, interactive teaching and learning methods that had been developed and tested in Cuba. Indeed, this new approach did away with the authoritarian 'chalk-and-talk' teaching style of colonial times that had prevailed in Angolan schools.[41]

My Angolan interviewees who had been taught by Cubans in the 1970s and 1980s generally had very positive memories of their classes. Above all, the pupils had enjoyed the new, interactive teaching methods. Against a social background that was marked by war, poverty and insecurity, the committed and motivating lessons of the Cuban teachers provided a glimmer of hope for the future. For the school children, the ideology behind the teachers' dedication was of no importance. What they cared about was education, knowledge and social improvement. All my Angolan interviewees did indeed manage to better their social situation thanks to the new education system, and not least thanks to the instruction given by Cubans. They became either teachers themselves or university lecturers, businessmen, professionals and artists or entered the priesthood, the elite of contemporary Angola. One of my interviewees was the Angolan writer Ondjaki, who describes in his novel *Bom día camaradas* the complex school situation of the 1980s and the great personal commitment of Cuban teachers to improving it. Ondjaki's novel, written from the point of view of an Angolan school pupil with Cuban teachers, reflects much of what my Cuban interviewees reported about their experience of school in Angola. Ondjaki has thus honoured the memory of his Cuban teachers in a sensitive, positive way that also raises a smile. In the interview with me he expressed the opinion that the Cubans had educated at least a whole generation of Angolans.[42]

***

The conclusions to be drawn from this extraordinary South–South cooperation are many and, because of its complexity, ambiguous. Neither Cuban military nor civil cooperation was able to solve the conflict between Angola's internal rivals. On the other hand, Cuba's military engagement was able to secure the territorial integrity of Angola, and the Cuban civil cooperation laid the foundations for political structures in postcolonial Angola. And together with military support, it proved instrumental in the long-term consolidation of the MPLA's position of power in Angola.

The establishment of a national education system was furthermore decisive in establishing the MPLA's political influence throughout the country. But despite this massive Cuban support until the beginning of the 1990s, Angola today still suffers from an acute shortage of skills, a consequence, partly, of Portuguese colonialism and of the war footing the country had to maintain until 2002. The MPLA government has also failed on other measures of development, such as poverty reduction and improving health care, since the postcolonial war ended. One of the most frequent complaints by investors today – other than the state of the bureaucracy and corruption – is that there is only a small pool of trained Angolan workers that they can draw from. Companies like the Brazilian enterprise Odebrecht have reluctantly stepped in to fill the gap left by poor state education and have trained tens of thousands of Angolans since the late 1980s. In the early post-conflict period of 2002–5, international NGOs remained in Angola and the government relied on them heavily to support the poor.

In summer 2009, the Cuban president Raúl Castro, during a state visit to meet his counterpart, José Eduardo dos Santos, signed an agreement to continue civil and economic cooperation. During the visit, the Cuban daily newspaper *Granma* reported that since 2007 the number of Cuban aid workers in Angola had been rising steadily. Nowadays it is estimated that eight to ten thousand Cuban experts, teachers, doctors, and technicians work temporarily in Angola. In the field of education, the new Cuban literary campaign, entitled 'Yes I can', is praised by UNESCO as outstanding in basic education,[43] and in 2014 a World Bank study found Cuba's education system to be 'high performing', especially in rural areas developed since the early 1960s under the Cuban literacy campaign.[44] This renewed civil cooperation with Angola, which would not have been possible without the former stage from 1976 to 1991, indicates that in the long term the Cuban–Angolan cooperation is a success story after all and despite everything – at least from this perspective. But who is profiting from this renewed Cuban–Angolan cooperation? Although the Angolan state has the resources to take full responsibility for building an educational and health system to benefit its people, this has not happened. There is no better illustration of this than the poor response of the Angolan government to the public health crisis caused by the 2016 yellow fever epidemic. The corruption and mismanagement of the Angolan government today cannot be blamed on the Cuban government.

Despite all the bitter criticism about the behaviour of the MPLA government and its broken promises about improving the situation of the majority of the population after independence and the end of the civil war in 2002, a few conclusions that go beyond this can be drawn. The Cuban–Angolan cooperation presented here not only comprised a cooperative relationship, and a knowledge transfer, but included, moreover, a form of knowledge circulation in the global South, between Cuba and Angola and also between Africa and Latin America in general. This can be seen in projects such as the international school complex on the Cuban Isla de la Juventud, founded in 1977, where children and adolescents from Latin America, Africa and Asia to this day are still able to receive free school education, vocational training and university degrees. The experience that Cuba gained in Angola flowed into other Cuban cooperation projects at that time and later. The quantitative and qualitative dimensions of Cuba's engagement in Angola, and its resulting formalisation and institutionalisation, marked the starting point for Cuba's export of a specialised workforce in return for payment, which it has been successfully pursuing since 1990. Knowledge and experience also continued to circulate in the various institutions established in Cuba and Angola as a result of cooperation. The aid workers and specialists who had been involved in Angola often went on to serve in other countries, for example, Mozambique, Ethiopia and Nicaragua and, from the late 1990s until today, in Venezuela.

NOTES

1 Dale Tomich, *Through the Prism of Slavery: Labor, Capital, and World Economy* (Lanham: Rowman & Littlefield, 2004).

2 The best analysis of this Afro-Cuban engagement in the Cuban independence struggle is still Ada Ferrer's *Insurgent Cuba: Race, Nation, and Revolution, 1868–1898* (Chapel Hill, NC: University of North Carolina Press, 1999).

3 The first historical studies about African slaves that returned from Cuba, the Caribbean or Brazil to West Africa in the nineteenth century have been written by the Cuban historian Rodolfo Sarracino; see Rodolfo Sarracino, *Los que volvieron a África* (Havana: Editorial de Ciencias Sociales, 1988).

4 One of the largest slave uprisings in colonial Cuba was led in 1843 by a slave named Carlota. In 1975, the rebellious slave gave her name to Operation Carlota and she became the 'patron saint' of Cuban military engagement in Angola.

5 Paul Gilroy, *The Black Atlantic: Modernity and Double Consciousness* (London: Verso, 1993).

6 Eric Hobsbawm and Terence Ranger, *The Invention of Tradition* (Cambridge: Cambridge University Press, 1983).

7 Sources and information for this research consisted not only of extensive archival material from Cuban, Portuguese, American and particularly Angolan archives, but also from interviews with 139 Cuban and Angolan eyewitnesses who lived in Angola and Portugal, in Cuba and in exile. With the exception of interviews with persons in public life, the eyewitnesses have been kept anonymous in these notes.

8 Katrin Hansing, 'Race and Inequality in Cuba,' *Current History* 117, no. 796 (February 2018): 69–72; Katrin Hansing, 'Race and Inequality in the New Cuba: Reasons, Dynamics, and Manifestations,' *Social Research: An International Quarterly* 84, no. 2 (2017): 331–49.

9 One exception to the perspective of cultural studies is by Christabelle Peters, *Cuban Identity and the Angolan Experience* (New York: Palgrave Macmillan, 2012), which

among other things tries to establish links between the engagement in Angola and (Afro-)Cuban identity on the basis of (literary) texts, in which Cubans wrote about their experiences in Angola. See also the chapter by Rodríguez Ruiz in this volume.

10 Christine Hatzky, *Cubans in Angola: South–South Cooperation and Transfer of Knowledge 1976–1991* (Madison: University of Wisconsin Press, 2015). The unclassified documents used in this chapter are listed as evidence with letterhead, date, reference, and content and signature (if available). Most of them are digitalised and in my private archive.

11 Edward George, *The Cuban Intervention in Angola 1965–1991: From Che Guevara to Cuito Cuanavale* (London: Cass, 2005). The author refers to a public speech given by Raúl Castro to mark the final return of soldiers and civilians from Angola on 27 May 1991, in which he mentioned that 377 033 soldiers and approximately 50 000 civilians had been involved in Angola since 1975. See also Susan Eva Eckstein, *Back from the Future: Cuba under Castro* (Princeton: Princeton University Press, 1995), 172. My own research proved that it is difficult to give exact numbers, as many Cubans worked in different functions in Angola as civilians (with their civil occupations) and in the armed forces, and some of the internal statistics provide years of duty and not persons. The average stay in Angola for civilians was two years.

12 Until today the only reliable official Cuban source providing a survey of quantitative details of the deployment of civilian experts and aid workers is an unpublished manuscript by the historian Angel García Perez-Castañeda, *El internacionalismo de Cuba en la colaboración económica y científico-técnica: Esbozo histórico de un cuarto de siglo de la Revolución socialista cubana 1963–1988* (Havana: Instituto de Historia de Cuba, n.d.). Only the archive of the Instituto de Historia de Cuba (Institute of Cuban History) seems to hold more documents on 'Cuban Internationalism' but they are still unclassified.

13 David Featherstone, *Solidarity: Hidden Histories and Geographies of Internationalism* (London: Zed Books, 2012). Featherstone outlines the various geographical directions of solidarity and knowledge circulation from South to South and South to North, which according to him began not after the Second World War but already in the nineteenth century with the abolitionist and international workers' movements.

14 Christine Hatzky, 'Cubans in Angola: Internationalist Solidarity, Transfers and Interactions in the Global South 1975–1991,' in *Neutrality and Neutralism in the Global Cold War: Between or Within the Blocs?*, ed. S. Bott, J. Hanhimäki and M. Wyss (London and New York: Routledge, 2016), 196–212.

15 See for example Anne Hickling-Hudson, Jorge Corona González and Rosemary Preston, eds, *The Capacity to Share: A Study of Cuba's International Cooperation in Educational Development* (New York: Palgrave Macmillan, 2012); Catherine Krull, ed., *Cuba in a Global Context: International Relations, Internationalism, and Transnationalism* (Gainesville: University Press of Florida, 2014); Kepa Artaraz, 'Cuba's Internationalism Revisited: Exporting Literacy, ALBA, and a New Paradigm for South–South Collaboration,' in *Rethinking the Cuban Revolution Nationally and Regionally: Politics, Culture and Identity*, ed. P. Kumaraswami (Chichester: Wiley-Blackwell, 2012), 22–37; Max Azicri, 'The Cuba–Venezuela Alliance and Its Continental Impact,' in *Cuba in a Global Context: International Relations, Internationalism, and Transnationalism*, ed. C. Krull (Gainesville: University Press of Florida, 2014), 127–44; Jonas Jürgens, 'Kuba: Exportschlager Ärzte,' in *Einblicke in das kubanische Gesundheits- und Sozialsystem*, ed. J. Becker (Münster: Westfälisches Dampfboot, 2015), 234–63; Hauke Dorsch,

'Trans-Atlantic Educational Crossroads: Experiences of Mozambican Students in Cuba,' in *Transatlantic Caribbean: Dialogues of People, Practices, Ideas*, ed. I. Kummels, C. Rauhut, S. Rinke and B. Timm (Bielefeld: Transcript, 2014), 77–97.

16 This applies particularly to all studies that were published during the Cold War era. Compare Arthur Jay Klinghoffer, *The Angolan War: A Study in Soviet Policy in the Third World* (Boulder: Westview Press, 1980); Cole Blasier and Carmelo Mesa-Lago, eds, *Cuba in the World* (Pittsburgh: University of Pittsburgh Press, 1979); William LeoGrande, 'Cuban–Soviet Relations and Cuban Policy in Africa,' in *Cuba in Africa*, ed. C. Mesa-Lago and J. Belkin (Pittsburgh: Center for Latin American Studies, 1982), 13–50; William LeoGrande, *Cuba's Policy in Africa 1959–1980: Policy Papers in International Affairs* (Berkeley: Institute of International Studies, University of California, 1980).

17 Compare Mesa-Lago's and Belkin's anthology *Cuba in Africa*, which contains solid political analyses of the aims of Cuban foreign policy and a wide range of opinions, above all of Cuban-American academics; see also Blasier and Mesa-Lago, *Cuba in the World*; LeoGrande, 'Cuban–Soviet Relations,' and LeoGrande, *Cuba's Policy in Africa*; Jorge I. Domínguez, *Cuba: Internal and International Affairs* (Beverly Hills: Sage Publications, 1982); Michael H. Erisman, *Cuba's International Relations: The Anatomy of a Nationalistic Foreign Policy* (Boulder: Westview Press, 1985).

18 The publications by Piero Gleijeses are an exception to the Cold War interpretations. See Piero Gleijeses, *Conflicting Missions: Havana, Washington, and Africa, 1959–1976* (Chapel Hill, NC: University of North Carolina Press, 2002). Gleijeses here refers only to the political and military level of cooperation. Only in his recent publication does he also devote a short chapter to Cuba's civil support for the MPLA; see Piero Gleijeses, *Visions of Freedom, Havana, Washington, Pretoria, and the Struggle for Southern Africa, 1976–1991* (Chapel Hill, NC: University of North Carolina Press, 2013).

19 The sociologist Susan Eva Eckstein and the political scientist Sergio Díaz-Briquets pointed out back in the 1980s the significance of Cuba's civil cooperation projects across the globe; see Eckstein, *Back from the Future*; Susan Eva Eckstein, 'Cuban Internationalism,' in *Cuba: Twenty-Five Years of Revolution, 1959–1984*, ed. S. Halebsky and J.M. Kirk (New York: Prager, 1985), 175–203; Sergio Díaz-Briquets, ed., *Cuban Internationalism in Sub-Saharan Africa* (Pittsburgh: Duquesne University Press, 1989).

20 Jorge I. Domínguez, 'Cuba since 1959,' in *Cuba: A Short History*, ed. L. Bethell (Cambridge: Cambridge University Press, 1993), 95–148.

21 Compare Hatzky, *Cubans in Angola*, 151–69.

22 See the chapter by Kiriakou and André in this volume.

23 The text of the Framework Agreement was not available at the time of my research. Therefore, details of the agreement have been brought together from internal documents and especially from the subsequent cooperation agreements drawn up on its basis between the Cuban and Angolan ministries. Parts of the Framework Agreement were also published in the Angolan and Cuban press; see *Jornal de Angola*, 31 July 1976, 2; *Bohemia*, no. 32 (6 August 1976): 55–56.

24 *Jornal de Angola*, 31 July 1976, 2.

25 Compare Hatzky, *Cubans in Angola*, 170–8.

26 Matthias Rüb, 'Kubas Kampf gegen Ebola: Die Chefärzte der internationalen Solidarität,' *Frankfurter Allgemeine*, 10 October 2014, http://www.faz.net/aktuell/politik/ausland/amerika/kuba-und-der-kampf-gegen-ebola-die-chefaerzte-der-internationalen-solidaritaet-13224214.html.

27 Compare Azicri, 'The Cuba–Venezuela Alliance and Its Continental Impact,' 128; Jürgens, 'Kuba: Exportschlager Ärzte,' 237.

28 Azicri, 'The Cuba–Venezuela Alliance and Its Continental Impact,' 129; Jürgens, 'Kuba: Exportschlager Ärzte,' 238.

29 Philipp H. Lepenies, 'Lernen vom Besserwisser: Wissenstransfer in der "Entwicklungshilfe" aus historischer Perspektive,' in *Entwicklungswelten: Globalgeschichte der Entwicklungszusammenarbeit*, ed. H. Büschel and D. Speich (Frankfurt am Main: Campus-Verlag, 2009), 33–59.

30 Interview Angola 2006, No. 23, Luanda, 22 March 2006 (António Burity da Silva).

31 Angolan files refer to all civil aid workers as *cooperantes*.

32 Hatzky, *Cubans in Angola*, 193–206. Much of the information about the internal organisation of cooperation in education was given to me during my interviews with former *cooperantes* specialists and aid workers involved in Angola. I have only given the names of the interviewees if they are public persons; in all other cases I have kept my sources anonymous for their own protection. Compare Interview Angola 2006, No. 8, Luanda, 1 February 2006; Interview Cuba 2006, No. 11, Havana, 16 June 2006; Interview Cuba 2006, No. 8, Havana, 10 June 2006; Interview Cuba 2006, No. 4, Havana, 25 May and 31 May 2006.

33 Interview Angola 2006, No. 6, Luanda, 27 January and 17 March 2006 (Artur Pestana, pen name 'Pepetela'), writer and former deputy minister of education, 1977–81. He was one of the architects of the new Angolan education system. Along with the minister of education Ambrôsio Lukoki (1977–81), he pushed through the new education policy across the country.

34 Ministério da Informação, Angola, 11 de Novembro de 1975, 'Documentos da Independência, Luanda, 1975'.

35 Interview Angola 2006, No. 7, Luanda, 27 January and 17 March 2006 (Artur Pestana, 'Pepetela').

36 RPA, MED, Direcção Nacional do Ensino Médio e Pré-universitário, 'Relatório sobre a situação do Ensino Médio na R.P.A. - Período 1978–1982', undated, approx. 1983, 12 pages, 3 (MED Archive); RPA, Secretaria do Estado da Cooperação, 'Comissão de avaliação da cooperação ao Cda. Ministro da Educação, Luanda, Circular No. 1/CACI/SEC/Maio de 1982, Assunto: Avaliação da cooperação', 2 pages (MED archive).

37 RPA, Secretaria do Estado da Cooperação, 'Comissão de avaliação da cooperação ao Cda. Ministro da Educação, Luanda, Circular No. 1/CACI/SEC/Maio de 1982, Assunto: Avaliação da cooperação', 2 pages (MED archive), 2.

38 RPA, Secretaria do Estado da Cooperação, 'Comissão de avaliação da cooperação ao Cda. Ministro da Educação, Luanda, Circular No. 1/CACI/SEC/Maio de 1982, Assunto: Avaliação da cooperação', 2 pages (MED archive).

39 See RPA statistic, MED, GICI/GII, 'Existência de Trabalhadores Estrangeiros, 09 de Novembro de 1981', 1 (MED archive).

40 RPA, MED, GICI/GII, 'Memorandum: Problemática da retirada da cooperação Cubana da RPA, Luanda aos 15 de Agosto de 1990', 5 pages, 1 (MED archive).

41 For example, '2nd Jornada Pedagogica del Contingente Educacional Cubano en la RPA (Programa), Mayo 1983', 6 pages; '2nd Jornada Pedagogica del Contingente Educacional Cubano en la RPA (Libro de Resumen), Mayo 1983', 21 pages (both MED archive); Interview Cuba 2004, No. 10, Santiago de Cuba, 4 November 2004.

42 Interview Angola 2006, No. 28, Luanda, 29 November 2006 (Ondjaki).

[43] In 2006, the outstanding test results of the Laboratorio Latinoamericano de Evaluación de Calidad de la Educación (Latin American Laboratory for the Assessment of the Quality of Education) since the late 1990s have been confirmed in maths and literacy; see UNESCO, *Student Achievement in Latin American and the Caribbean Results of the Second Regional Comparative and Explanatory Study* (Santiago, Chile: Regional Bureau for Education in Latin America and the Caribbean/UNESCO Santiago, 2008).

[44] Barbara Bruns and Javier Luque, *Great Teachers: How to Raise Student Learning in Latin America and the Caribbean* (Washington, DC: World Bank Group, 2014), 226.

REFERENCES

Artaraz, Kepa. 'Cuba's Internationalism Revisited: Exporting Literacy, ALBA, and a New Paradigm for South–South Collaboration.' In *Rethinking the Cuban Revolution Nationally and Regionally: Politics, Culture and Identity*, edited by P. Kumaraswami, 22–37. Chichester: Wiley-Blackwell, 2012.

Azicri, Max. 'The Cuba–Venezuela Alliance and Its Continental Impact.' In *Cuba in a Global Context: International Relations, Internationalism, and Transnationalism*, edited by C. Krull, 127–44. Gainesville: University Press of Florida, 2014.

Blasier, Cole and Carmelo Mesa-Lago, eds. *Cuba in the World*. Pittsburgh: University of Pittsburgh Press, 1979.

Bruns, Barbara and Javier Luque. *Great Teachers: How to Raise Student Learning in Latin America and the Caribbean*. Washington, DC: The World Bank Group, 2014.

Díaz-Briquets, Sergio, ed. *Cuban Internationalism in Sub-Saharan Africa*. Pittsburgh: Duquesne University Press, 1989.

Domínguez, Jorge I. *Cuba: Internal and International Affairs*. Beverly Hills: Sage Publications, 1982.

Domínguez, Jorge I. 'Cuba since 1959.' In *Cuba: A Short History*, edited by L. Bethell, 95–148. Cambridge: Cambridge University Press, 1993.

Dorsch, Hauke. 'Trans-Atlantic Educational Crossroads: Experiences of Mozambican Students in Cuba.' In *Transatlantic Caribbean: Dialogues of People, Practices, Ideas*, edited by I. Kummels, C. Rauhut, S. Rinke and B. Timm, 77–97. Bielefeld: Transcript, 2014.

Eckstein, Susan Eva. *Back from the Future: Cuba under Castro*. Princeton: Princeton University Press, 1995.

Eckstein, Susan Eva. 'Cuban Internationalism.' In *Cuba: Twenty-Five Years of Revolution, 1959–1984*, edited by S. Halebsky and J.M. Kirk, 175–203. New York: Prager, 1985.

Erisman, Michael H. *Cuba's International Relations: The Anatomy of a Nationalistic Foreign Policy*. Boulder: Westview Press, 1985.

Featherstone, David. *Solidarity: Hidden Histories and Geographies of Internationalism*. London: Zed Books, 2012.

Ferrer, Ada. *Insurgent Cuba: Race, Nation, and Revolution, 1868–1898*. Chapel Hill, NC: University of North Carolina Press, 1999.

García Perez-Castañeda, Angel. *El internacionalismo de Cuba en la colaboración económica y científico-técnica: Esbozo histórico de un cuarto de siglo de la Revolución socialista cubana 1963–1988*. Havana: Instituto de Historia de Cuba, n.d.

George, Edward. *The Cuban Intervention in Angola 1965–1991: From Che Guevara to Cuito Cuanavale*. London: Cass, 2005.

Gilroy, Paul. *The Black Atlantic: Modernity and Double Consciousness*. London: Verso, 1993.

Gleijeses, Piero. *Conflicting Missions: Havana, Washington, and Africa, 1959–1976*. Chapel Hill, NC: University of North Carolina Press, 2002.

Gleijeses, Piero. *Visions of Freedom, Havana, Washington, Pretoria, and the Struggle for Southern Africa, 1976–1991*. Chapel Hill, NC: University of North Carolina Press, 2013.

Hansing, Katrin. 'Race and Inequality in Cuba.' *Current History* 117, no. 796 (February 2018): 69–72.

Hansing, Katrin. 'Race and Inequality in the New Cuba: Reasons, Dynamics, and Manifestations.' *Social Research: An International Quarterly* 84, no. 2 (2017): 331–49.

Hatzky, Christine. 'Cubans in Angola: Internationalist Solidarity, Transfers and Interactions in the Global South 1975–1991.' In *Neutrality and Neutralism in the Global Cold War: Between or Within the Blocs?*, edited by S. Bott, J. Hanhimäki and M. Wyss, 196–212. London and New York: Routledge, 2016.

Hatzky, Christine. *Cubans in Angola: South–South Cooperation and Transfer of Knowledge 1976–1991*. Madison: University of Wisconsin Press, 2015.

Hickling-Hudson, Anne, Jorge Corona González and Rosemary Preston, eds. *The Capacity to Share: A Study of Cuba's International Cooperation in Educational Development*. New York: Palgrave Macmillan, 2012.

Hobsbawm, Eric and Terence Ranger. *The Invention of Tradition*. Cambridge: Cambridge University Press, 1983.

Jürgens, Jonas. 'Kuba: Exportschlager Ärzte.' In *Einblicke in das kubanische Gesundheits- und Sozialsystem*, edited by J. Becker, 234–63. Münster: Westfälisches Dampfboot, 2015.

Klinghoffer, Arthur Jay. *The Angolan War: A Study in Soviet Policy in the Third World*. Boulder: Westview Press, 1980.

Krull, Catherine, ed. *Cuba in a Global Context: International Relations, Internationalism, and Transnationalism*. Gainesville: University Press of Florida, 2014.

LeoGrande, William. 'Cuban–Soviet Relations and Cuban Policy in Africa.' In *Cuba in Africa*, edited by C. Mesa-Lago and J. Belkin, 13–50. Pittsburgh: Center for Latin American Studies, 1982.

LeoGrande, William. *Cuba's Policy in Africa 1959–1980: Policy Papers in International Affairs*. Berkeley: Institute of International Studies, University of California, 1980.

Lepenies, Philipp H. 'Lernen vom Besserwisser: Wissenstransfer in der "Entwicklungshilfe" aus historischer Perspektive.' In *Entwicklungswelten: Globalgeschichte der Entwicklungszusammenarbeit*, edited by H. Büschel and D. Speich, 33–59. Frankfurt am Main: Campus-Verlag, 2009.

Mesa-Lago, Carmelo and June Belkin, eds. *Cuba in Africa*. Pittsburgh: Center for Latin American Studies, 1982.

Peters, Christabelle. *Cuban Identity and the Angolan Experience*. New York: Palgrave Macmillan, 2012.

Rüb, Matthias. 'Kubas Kampf gegen Ebola: Die Chefärzte der internationalen Solidarität.' *Frankfurter Allgemeine*, 10 October 2014. http://www.faz.net/aktuell/politik/ausland/amerika/kuba-und-der-kampf-gegen-ebola-die-chefaerzte-der-internationalen-solidaritaet-13224214.html.

Sarracino, Rodolfo. *Los que volvieron a África*. Havana: Editorial de Ciencias Sociales, 1988.

Tomich, Dale. *Through the Prism of Slavery: Labor, Capital, and World Economy*. Lanham: Rowman and Littlefield, 2004.

UNESCO. *Student Achievement in Latin American and the Caribbean Results of the Second Regional Comparative and Explanatory Study*. Santiago, Chile: Regional Bureau for Education in Latin America and the Caribbean/UNESCO Santiago, 2008.

PART II

TRAJECTORIES

CHAPTER

5

The Experience of Multidisciplinary Research into Angola's National Question: Anthropology in a war context

Pablo Rodríguez Ruiz

It is astonishing that a small country such as Cuba, located in the middle of the Caribbean Sea, thousands of kilometres from Africa, with an underdeveloped economy and economically and financially hemmed in by the policy of the most powerful country in the world, has achieved such a remarkable influence on the African continent. This has been the result of several factors. First and foremost, it is based on a certain cultural proximity, derived from shared roots, from which spring common identities and interests.[1] Undoubtedly this facilitated dialogue, the exchange of influence and mutual understanding between Cuba and Africa. Furthermore, the representations that result from cultural proximity were heightened by a shared experience of victimhood through the domination of historically configured structures. Cuba and the African continent share the socio-economic location of an underdeveloped South that has been exploited and oppressed. Their collective memory retains the pain of the forced removal of entire populations, snatched from their contexts to be flung, without hope or resources, into a strange and oppressive environment in which they had to re-create their identities. One was a place of departure, the other a place of arrival – but both participated in a single overarching process. Both continue to suffer from the effects and barriers of colonialism, neocolonialism, unfair exchange, dispossession of their natural and human resources, and the consequences of the concentration of wealth, technologies and knowledge in the hands of a few individuals and a few countries. There is, thus, a common stance that makes mutual acquaintance easier.

Furthermore, the Cuban Revolution of the late 1950s coincided with the worldwide struggle for decolonisation and revolution. The popular and nationalist character of the policies of the revolutionary government led to an open confrontation with capitalism and the American companies that owned a substantial part of Cuba's land, industry, services and banks. This confrontation took the form on the part of the US of a state policy towards Cuba, still in place today, that damaged the mainstays of popular support, and led to the country's isolation and international opprobrium.[2] In the shark–sardine situation of confrontation imposed by these circumstances, the Cuban revolutionary process developed and showed great ingenuity in circumventing these structures of domination, which, although global, have concrete local expressions. In the global context of the time, such realities did not go unnoticed by the new nation-states and anti-colonial movements of the Third World, creating premises of identification that sprang from not only shared ideals and goals, but also similar difficulties.

In these uneven conditions of confrontation, the victories achieved by Cuba, and its stance of rebelliousness and discursive disobedience, acquired a particular character. This could be seen in the dismantling of internal opposition, the defeat of the invasion at Playa Girón (Bay of Pigs), Fidel Castro's visit to the United Nations – during which a tent was erected in Central Park and the revolutionary leader ended up staying at a hotel in Harlem (the Hotel Theresa), after accommodation for the Cuban delegation was blocked – the neutralisation of attempts at subversion, the unyielding defence of national sovereignty and Third World interests, and the subsequent engagement in African wars. This long list of events helped to frame a legend of rebelliousness and an aura of victory for the Cuban revolution. For the peoples of the Third World, historical and structural victims and losers, the chance to be seen as winners encouraged the feeling that it was possible, and thus their views inclined towards Cuba. In 1970, President Sékou Touré of the Republic of Guinea declared 26 July – the anniversary of the Cuban Revolution – a paid public holiday in his country, an act of deep symbolism that illustrates the kind of image of Cuba that flourished among the anti-colonial movements of the time.[3]

In international relations, all Latin American countries, with the exception of Mexico, bowed to pressure from the US government to cut diplomatic ties to Cuba, while some European countries adopted a low profile. This isolation was supposed to subdue the island, and was successful to some extent, but it compelled the revolutionary leadership to reorient its international relations in order to find spaces of legitimacy and support. The wave of new states created by decolonisation and the rise of anti-colonialist movements proved fertile ground, and Africa, because of its cultural proximity, came to enjoy a privileged position.[4]

In practice, Cuba had been trying to build a system of international relations based on respect, commitment and mutual assistance, focused on social aspects and away from economic interests and cost-benefit analysis. It established an ethic that was distinct from that which had formerly prevailed in relations with the nations of the South. President Fidel Castro made this clear when, speaking of Cuban participation in the Angolan war, he quoted Guinean revolutionary leader Amílcar Cabral: 'Cuban combatants are ready to sacrifice their lives for the liberation of our countries, and in exchange for this help to our freedom and to the progress of our population the only one thing they will take back from us are the combatants who fell fighting for freedom.'[5]

In fact, Cuban collaboration with Africa has taken place in many fields: military, education, public health,[6] culture, official and human resource development, technical, and so on. In many cases, these links developed before the advent of African postcolonial states, and served as structures for a multi-purpose system of sharing and cooperation.

There is, however, a completely unknown chapter in this story of collaboration. It relates to scientific and academic collaboration, especially in the social sciences, and concerns a multidisciplinary study of Angola's national question. The work was undertaken by a team of Cuban and Angolan scientists in Angola, at the request of the politburos of Angola's Popular Movement for the Liberation of Angola (MPLA) and Cuba's Communist Party (PCC). This chapter describes the author's experience of this effort.

There is no doubt that, for many Cuban social scientists, the Angolan experience was a 'rite of passage' far beyond their country's participation in the military conflict. At the time, Cuban anthropology fell under the Cuban Academy of Sciences, through bulwark institutions such as the Department for Archaeology and Ethnology, heir to the Institute of Ethnology and Folklore (IEF), created in 1961 as part of the wave of institutionalisation triggered by the Cuban Revolution.[7]

Since the nineteenth century Cuban anthropology had been mainly focused on the study of its own Cuban society. However, during the 1980s, many students of anthropology in Cuba went to study natural and social sciences in the Soviet Union, thanks to international scholarships made available as a result of the collaboration between the socialist republics. Their academic training was thus marked by the Soviet ethnographic school, and by such classic works such those of Y. Bromley[8] on ethnos theory and of S.A. Tokarev[9] and E.G. Aleksandrenkov.[10] These authors exerted a significant influence on the adoption of theoretical paradigms in the Cuban academy, as was evident in Cuban–Soviet scientific collaboration projects such as *The Ethnographical Atlas of Cuba*.[11] In this context, the collective investigation of Angola's national question described here represents 'an entirely unprecedented chapter' of scientific collaboration,[12] and a serious contribution to the discipline in Cuba.[13] In my own case, I had graduated in philosophy and, as I explain elsewhere,[14] I arrived at anthropology 'by chance' through my experience in Angola, which acted for me as a real *in situ* academic training.

DESCRIPTION OF THE PROJECT

According to our colleague, sociologist María Isabel Domínguez, the collaboration was a kind of 'multi' investigation in several respects. It was multidisciplinary because of the commitment to the social and human sciences. It was multinational because of the number of specialists involved from both countries. And, in its aims and interests, it was multidimensional. It also had the peculiarity of being developed during the Angolan civil war, which made the research more complex and added a specific character to it.

The Cuban participation in this research turned out to be path-breaking, posing real challenges to the social sciences in general, and to its developers in particular. In the Cuban social landscape, there is not the same ethnic and linguistic diversity that is common to many African or Latin American countries. Thus, there is no scientific tradition focused on the relation between ethnic issues and the national question. In Cuban national thinking, the starting point is the premise of a consolidated nationality, which is the result of deep and intense processes of transculturation.[15] The few studies of ethnic and inter-ethnic relations have looked at the question from a historical viewpoint, focusing on Cuban culture and nationality, on the existence of small groups of immigrants that have persisted in the social environment, or on the remaining vestiges of native cultures.

It is possible that the increasing request for Cuban specialists in the mid-1980s was influenced more by the relations established with the MPLA since its beginnings as a guerrilla movement[16] than by any recognition of a scientific tradition relating to the national question. When one reflects on the feasibility of such research, one must recall that Cuban troops had already been involved in Angola's armed conflict for more than ten years, long enough for the Cubans to acquire experience of and a perspective on that country. For the nascent Angolan nation-state, there was an urgent need to define policies aimed at managing ethnic diversity in order to build national unity.[17] In Cuba at that time, the experience of the Organisation of Solidarity with the Peoples of Asia, Africa and Latin America (OSPAAAL) had led to growing awareness of the real differences between Latin America and Africa on the issue of ethnicity. And so on both sides there were reasons and motives for participating in the project.

The request for assistance in the project was sent to Cuban social scientists by way of an agreement between the ruling parties of both countries. It was presented, therefore, as a series of ideas and general concerns of a political type rather than in the form of a research question. The organisation and design of the research were supposed to provide an answer to the request of the two parties and governments.

It was Juan Luis Martin, at that time chief of the Department of Sociology in the Social Sciences Institute of the Academy of Sciences of Cuba, who received the request directly. He was responsible for deciding on the basic approach to solving the two questions that were immediately posed: the choice of the research team, and how to turn these ideas into a research project. The two questions were closely related. Being in charge of selecting the people to take part in the research, he naturally became its scientific head and chief organiser.

Cuba had no experience of carrying out a research project of this magnitude, one that extended beyond the perspective of a single discipline. It was evident that in addition to sociology, the resources and knowledge of other disciplines would be required. In view of this, it became necessary to select people to head the different teams that would make up the project, namely, sociologists, psychologists, linguists, economists, historians, political scientists and anthropologists. These would form the core of the research effort, with specialists in sample design and programmers acting as support personnel.

The coordinators of the scientific disciplines that would work in the field were Dr. Juan Luis Martin (sociology); Dr. Fernando González Rey (psychology); Dr. Sergio Valdés Bernal[18] (linguistics); and Dr Rafael Leovigildo López Valdés (anthropology).[19] They were in charge of the selection of team members, among whom was the author of this chapter. The historian Joel James Figarola[20] participated as well in this research plan, but later on he postponed his trip to Angola in order to conduct research on the impact of the armed conflict there.[21]

Once this first stage was resolved, the rest of the preliminary work focused in a collective way on the research design. The government's request contained a general idea, but this had to be transformed into a scientific approach to the problem, with variables and explanatory categories, and then into a concrete research plan. Moreover, the researchers had little knowledge of conditions on the ground or of the context in which they would work. Thus, two exploratory trips were made to Angola to obtain a more detailed idea of local conditions. The material and the

Figure 5.1: From left to right: Pablo Rodríguez Ruiz, a Cuban bodyguard and two Angolan soldiers. © Pablo Rodríguez Ruiz, south-east Angola, 1985.

information collected during these trips helped to devise the initial premise and to develop an action plan.

The formulation of a general scientific question relevant for all the disciplines involved was an indispensable starting point. This was to be agreed with the Angolan side, as it would become a common platform of action. There were two basic questions that the inquiry would attempt to answer:

a) If an Angolan nation really exists, what level or expression of integration exists in the country?
b) In these conditions, is it possible to build a socialist project in the country?

On the whole, the scientific evidence suggested that the slogan current at the time in Angola, 'From Cabinda to Cunene a single people, a single nation', as proclaimed by Agostinho Neto, was more of an aspiration than a reality. Strong bonds of belonging and ethnic consciousness persisted at the level of communities and ethnolinguistic groups, which overlapped and interfered with national sentiment. These grew stronger in settlements far from the cities and from the hubs of colonial capitalism in industry and agriculture. Such a reality found expression in, and was reinforced by, the persistence of links relying on lineages in the life and activities of many groups. These included a preference for using native languages in everyday life, and even an ignorance of Portuguese as a language of communication; the existence of systems of classificatory kinship; forms of preferential marriage and polygamous family organisation; the existence of matrilineal filiation; the presence and functionality, alongside governmental structures, of traditional power hierarchies, together with a strong group endogamy, which in some cases came to be restrictive. Faced with this socio-cultural scheme, the insistence on a socialist project seemed to invite contradiction.

In parallel with the formulation of the research question, consensus was reached on a host of ideas around the organisation of the research work, which guided the process as a whole. First and foremost, in 1985 a coordinating group was formed, consisting of Cuban and Angolan specialists, whose task would be to coordinate actions and, in the final phase, to collate the material contributed by the different disciplines. This model of organisation is, no doubt, useful in the work of large research groups. The experience later proved to be useful in the organisation of another multidisciplinary investigation requested by the Cuban state, into criminal violence, the black market, and administrative corruption.[22]

It was decided that each participating discipline would retain its independence, objectives and approach, but everyone's research would be oriented towards answering the basic questions posed for the project as a whole. Consequently, the research plan of each discipline would be in line with its specific objective, looking at its field of study and the kind of variables and information appropriate to each. The idea was to reach a consensus with the rest of the team so that, from the outset, each discipline would contribute information on the main problems outlined. In this sense, a limited time frame for executing the research was imperative, which for certain disciplines such as anthropology implied the need to bring methods into line with the time available for research.

The techniques and methodologies to be used by those disciplines requiring field information would be developed through the participation of Angolan partners. In this way, not only would the general design and basic methodological premises arise from a joint effort, but so also would the whole process. At the same time, the knowledge that the Angolans had about their own reality was essential to the project. Without their participation, it would not have been possible to move the project forward as scheduled.

In the case of anthropology, the participation of the Angolan anthropologists Enrique Abranches[23] and Julio Artur de Morais[24] over long days of discussion during the process of preparing questionnaires was not only an essential contribution to the project, but also a real education for the younger researchers who took part. This was an important moment in which the theory of ethnos,[25] the starting point for most of the Cuban participants, began to reveal its shortcomings for understanding the African reality. Some of the premises had to be adjusted. Issues that were important in terms of the theory, such as kinship, the role of traditional hierarchies and the interaction between 'modern' and 'traditional' economies, among others, were found to lack significant weight, in contrast to the socio-cultural reality we encountered on the ground.

The other problematic issue was how to combine participation in fieldwork, by at least four different disciplines, in a country fighting a war on two fronts (an external war with the apartheid government of South Africa and an internal civil war). Much of Angola's communication infrastructure was affected by the war situation and by the operations of the rival opposition groups. These were mostly conducted, it can be said, as part of a 'war of roads and lanes', in which the use of landmines and ambushes provided the most common tactics. To avoid the periodic raids made by the South African military, no location could be selected that was beyond the advanced lines of defence of Cuban troops.[26] In this context, support for mobility and coordination with the military were indispensable. To overcome such difficulties, multidisciplinary groups were created that would operate from bases established in specific regions. In this way, disciplines engaged in fieldwork could share a common space.

The work of these groups in such spaces demanded a certain division of labour, especially between sociologists and anthropologists. The former would focus their attention on urban areas, while the latter would centre their work on rural areas and traditional communities. The linguists and psychologists who were part of these groups moved in both spaces. In this way, each discipline could clearly define its zone of research. History, economics and political science, for their part, organised their work around documentary and archival sources, with these specialists working in the capital city, Luanda.

The research had to be comprehensive, and had to include the country's main social agents and actors. It included, therefore, different strata of the urban and rural population, the set of existing ethnolinguistic communities, the socio-class structure, and the institutions. There was also specific research designed for the army. To carry this out in the last-mentioned sphere, the researchers had to accompany combat units of FAPLA, Angola's armed forces, which were often stationed in remote locations.[27]

It was my task to work with FAPLA's 92 Brigade, operating in the province of Huambo. Given the operational situation, the region was accessible only by helicopter, which was used to support combat missions, evacuate wounded soldiers and provide logistical support. To protect themselves from anti-aircraft missiles fired by guerrilla groups, helicopters were only permitted to fly in pairs at certain times of the day.

Two experiences characterised my stay in this region. One has to do with psychological flexibility and the speed at which human beings adapt to extreme situations, creating mechanisms to naturalise them or, at least, establish distance from those unusual predicaments. Under such conditions, the physical and psychological effects of lived tension are experienced only at the end of the situation. Something similar happens with the apprehension of events: with distance, these acquire significance.

The other experience is related to space. When the pilot signalled our arrival at the base where I would be working, pointing at a spot on the ground, what I saw was a deserted place, the only feature being a circular construction made of wood and straw, some two metres in diameter. This turned out to be the kitchen of the brigade's general staff. The whole existence of the soldiers was spent underground, in shelters and trenches. During the research period, the dimensions of time and space acquired a certain normality. The days were spent visiting soldiers at various defensive positions, talking with them, filling in questionnaires. At night, because of the accumulated fatigue, I was grateful to be able to lie on my bed – a wooden door removed from a house. The problem began when the work ended and we had to wait for our return journey, because the helicopters were busy with more important missions. The space became smaller and smaller, the days seemed endless, and the nights became a torture on my hard bed. These were two ways of experiencing time and space in the same situation.

In the end, the involvement of disciplines and specialists took place as the research demanded. Thus it happened, for example, that the programmers and specialists in sample design, having worked on the design from Havana, did not join the team in Angola until the final phase.

ANTHROPOLOGY AND THE SITE OF OUR RESEARCH

The basic questions posed, the ethnic diversity of the country, and the influence of these factors on the social process made anthropology central to the research conducted in Angola. The ethnic question provided nuances to the socio-class structure, institutions, and other elements of organisation and social action. The discipline made its mark also in the design of the fieldwork and the definition of the concrete scenarios in which this would take place.

The organisation of the fieldwork was characterised by two levels of complexity. One came from the heterogeneous ethnic-linguistic condition of a country with a great expanse of territory, and the other had to do with the war situation.

In terms of space, Angola is an immense country, with an area of 1 247 700 square kilometres – around eleven times larger than Cuba – and a population (estimated at the time) of 11 million, encompassing great ethnolinguistic diversity. There is a significant group of ethnic communities of Bantu origin, which were called, using the categories of the time, the Bakongo, Ambundu or Kimbundu, Mbundu or Ovimbundu, Lunda-Chokwe, Ganguela, Nyaneka-Khumbi, Ovambo and Herero.[28] Each of these ethno-linguistic communities, whose members shared cultural features and some common history, was fragmented into a significant number of subdivisions in which consciousness of self-belonging was often stronger than membership in the larger community. For instance, before defining themselves as Nyaneka, the people considered themselves mainly as Muila or Gambo. To all this were added a white population of Portuguese origin, people of mixed race, and the Khoisan groups,[29] as well as groups native to other African nations who had been displaced by regional conflicts.

What was fundamental to everything was that the different ethnic communities had historically occupied certain territories. Their distribution roughly corresponded to the political-administrative divisions of the country, which were inherited from the colonial administrative divisions. From a practical point of view, this solved the problem of how to cover such a vast space, even though we were trapped in this way in a pre-established model. On the other hand, from a methodological and conceptual perspective, two similar concepts, from different schools, were put into practice: the Soviet historical-cultural concept of M.G. Levin and N.N. Cheboksarov,[30] and the concept of cultural area drawn from the school of Franz Boas.[31] Both concepts referred to the spatial distribution of cultural traits, and both linked ethnic identity to territoriality. The work already done by Portuguese anthropologists offered an account of these realities, and thereby facilitated – and simultaneously predetermined – the research.

These premises determined the specific regions where the research would be carried out. One group would be located in the Cabinda region, where the presence of the Bakongo is strong. Another group would operate in the centre of the country, in Huambo and Bié provinces, the traditional territory of the Ovimbundu, one of the larger communities of Angola, to which UNITA[32] leader Jonas Savimbi belonged and where he could count on a certain support base. The east, the home of the Lunda-Chokwe and Ganguela, would be entrusted to another group, which would base itself in Lunda Sul province. The last group would operate in the south-east, home to the settled agro-pastoralist and transhumant communities of the Nyaneka-Khumbi, Ovambo and Herero. This group would move between the provinces of Huíla, Namibe and Cunene. This model of work organisation was a departure from the premise that the anthropologist should work with smaller observed units, as these can be covered more easily. Instead, each researcher was confronted with a large area – in most cases, larger than his home country.

How to determine specific points to study in each region was decided according to a plan drawn from the research design. They were selected on certain criteria, such as the concentration and pre-eminence of different groups within the ethno-linguistic communities, and their distance from urban centres and communication networks. Also included were regions affected by harsh inter-ethnic conflicts. Though these locations had been selected previously, each group, depending on conditions of access and the imperatives of the war situation, could adjust the selection in the field, provided that the replacement corresponded to the defined criteria. One example occurred in Cahama, in Cunene province, where the operational situation led the military to oppose the research, and so another district was chosen. The fact that the research was carried out at the request of both governments made it easier to find solutions to such situations.

The war context, as well as the displacement of large numbers of people to peri-urban areas or regions with less military activity, generated pockets of intense inter-ethnic contact in which conflict sometimes arose. These circumstances reduced the space for transhumance, particularly for the half-nomadic pastoralists of the south, who also faced the growing problem of desertification, and sometimes generated rivalry and troubled relationships with other groups.

Throughout the period of preparation and execution of the research, the constant war situation had a direct effect on the research objective, its organisation, and the researchers themselves. The war affected the entire territory, but in Luanda events were constantly reproduced as anecdotes and accounts that intensified their effects. News flowing in about the war sometimes gave rise to rumours suggesting that every inch of territory contained a mine, a grenade or a UNITA guerrilla party, or *cuaches*, ready to massacre you and put you in a 'Savimbi vest'.[33] Overcoming rumours and the fear that they provoked was one of the first personal challenges we had to face. Those who overcame them took an important step forward. The reality in the field, even if there were risks, turned out to be quite different.

On the other hand, anything to do with logistics and the movement of researchers required support from the military and the local authorities. Even within the national territory, movement was generally by military aircraft. I remember that my journey from Luanda to southern Angola took place aboard a military cargo aircraft. At the airport, we negotiated directly with the pilot, who allowed us to take some boxes of fish to Namibe. The journey from Namibe to Lubango was by road. Work plans had to be coordinated with the military before researchers could move to the places where they would begin research.

Coordination with the military not only gave us important information about conditions in our areas of activity, but also had an effect on the movements of the groups. Transfers to relatively distant areas more affected by armed conflict were approved only if done as part of the military convoys organised to provide logistical support to combat units. This generated tensions, delays and inconvenience. To get to Matala, for instance, the group had to wait many days until a military convoy could depart from Lubango. After several days spent working in the field, the return journey was subject to the same process. The waiting and the uncertainty resumed, since for obvious security reasons the date and time of a convoy departure could be announced only a few hours in advance. At the scheduled time, there was a problem when the group delayed its departure for three to five hours. If the military were informed, they would not allow us to leave until the next convoy (between ten and fifteen days ahead); if we did not inform them, we would be taking the risk of travelling on our own, without military protection. We opted for the latter solution.

On another occasion, in Namibe province, the research called for a trip to the deep south of the country. In discussions with the regional military command, it was judged that we would require an escort with anti-aircraft capability in order to reach the area safely. They were eager to support us, and the date for the trip to the area was agreed. The day of departure coincided with an inspection by the high command, so the regional command was not authorised to release the necessary

Figure 5.2: Ethnographic research among the Nyaneka-Khumbi: meeting the residents of the village to present the project. © Pablo Rodríguez Ruiz, south-east Angola, 1985.

weapons. After some discussion, we were allowed to travel to the area. For protection, we were assigned one soldier and two Second World War-vintage German pistols. That is to say, there was planning and coordination, but ultimately the imponderables of life defined the situation. Everything became more flexible, and the fear that was felt in Luanda was replaced in the field by a certain indifference, confidence even, and a normalising of the tension.

ENTRY INTO THE FIELD AND CONTACT WITH THE POPULATION

Going out into the field and coming into direct contact with the population also presented a number of challenges that had to be factored into the research design. These challenges ranged from previous knowledge of the ethnic particularities of each space to communications and details that should not be overlooked.

The published sources gave researchers a sense of the landscape of the country. Similarly, monographs, previous research reports and archive materials, gathered by region, made it possible to become familiar with the reality that each group would face on the ground. But it did leave empty spaces that had to be filled through contact with reality and the people living that reality. It was precisely in this area that the main challenges were encountered.

Communication was a limiting factor and one of the greatest challenges that the project faced. Because of the planned time frame, it was impossible to train the specialists in local languages. In the case of Portuguese, given its linguistic proximity to Spanish and the close contact of the population with the Cuban *cooperantes*, the issue turned out to be less of a problem. In a short time, people adopted a kind of *portuñol* (mixture of Portuguese and Spanish), which facilitated communication. The need to master a broad range of written material in Portuguese and to ensure mutual comprehension between Cuban and Angolan specialists during long work sessions was a strong incentive to improve this process. By the time the researchers went into the field, they could all communicate in this language. A greater difficulty emerged, especially for anthropologists working in rural areas, with the use of national languages. From the beginning, though, there was a recognition of this problem.

The development of a standardised questionnaire for all groups responded to the need not only to formulate the research by means of scientific questions, but also to mitigate the adverse effects of communication difficulties. The inclusion of Angolan assistants who were familiar with the national languages of the various regions, and who were trained in the use of the questionnaire, was one remedy that was applied.

At the same time, in order to satisfy specific communities, the researchers attempted, as far as possible, to follow a gradual process that included knowledge both contributed by scientific sources and derived from interviews and previous contacts with experts. As such, the input of local officials, traders, priests, and other notables was considered, because their long contact with the inhabitants could provide an outsider's view, which was valuable in itself and which could be triangulated with information obtained in the field.

In the field, it was almost impossible to move around unarmed or, on some rare occasions, without military escort. This added obstacles to the work, even though the soldiers stayed out of the villages while we were working with the people. The presence of the military was potentially intimidating, but was unavoidable in the circumstances. Weapons were carried by researchers for self-defence and by escorts, when in the rare cases this occurred – a condition imposed by military commanders for access to particular areas. The escorts were responsible to the high command for every dead, wounded or captured Cuban in their defensive area. The solution to both issues was always the same: to conceal weapons for as long as possible. Rifles were kept hidden in the vehicle, which would be parked at a discreet distance, but were accessible in case a dangerous situation arose, and pistols were concealed in clothes or backpacks. Whenever we were compelled to have bodyguards with us, we always dealt with their commander to ensure that they set up camp at a discreet distance from the hamlet where the research would take place, to ensure that their presence would not be visible to the villagers.

Whether in African hamlets or Havana 'shanty towns',[34] contact with people beaten down by an existence that condemns them to anonymity and obscurity is always marked by easy conversation and by their gratitude for being heard and treated thoughtfully. It was the pressing need to speak that is felt by those who lack or have been long deprived of speaking and being heard. There is an African proverb that says, 'When two elephants have a fight, the big loser is the grass.' Those who suffer, and who find themselves trapped in a state of profound shock or social turmoil, are generally not taken into consideration in the meta-story of a history that, however, would not exist without them, and such people are always grateful when they are listened to. In the village of Cainde, deep in the south of Angola, in the middle of the Namib Desert, a *soba*[35] invited us to lunch in his humble grass hut. The menu consisted of baked sweet potatoes, fish with sauce, and, on occasion, *coporoto*,[36] kept in a transparent bottle that, though dirty, gave information about how it was made. This hospitality, in conditions of great poverty and amid all the shortages caused by the war and the aridity of the territory, meant a lot to us.

Despite all the difficulties, imponderables and tensions, every one of the chosen areas was studied. The fieldwork was completed, and contributed valuable information. This allowed the team to move to the next phase, the processing of the information and the writing of the final report. The writing of the reports followed a disciplinary perspective. Based on the information gathered in the field, a report was prepared on each ethnic region or community studied. These would all contribute to a general anthropological report, which would be integrated with the findings of the other disciplines. The report was supposed to contain recommendations in line with the basic lines of inquiry described above. These recommendations were organised by following hierarchical criteria, and included both strictly local content and content of regional and national significance.

The process did not make use of all the material gathered. A significant part was left aside, whether as the personal belonging of the individual researcher or just as an archive of the collective work. In this way, individual and collective interests were combined. In my particular case, following the research effort I was able to use the material gathered to write a monograph, 'The Angolan Nyaneka-Khumbi, Economy and Society'. The Angolan Book Institute planned to publish it, but once that institution collapsed, the material, already translated into Portuguese, was lost. Nevertheless, a chapter of it was prepared as a monograph and was awarded the Pinos Nuevos prize. It was published in 1996 under the title *The Angolan Nyaneka-Khumbi: Ethno-Social Process*. These have been the only works to emerge from the research. In my book, I aimed to reconstruct the formative process of the groups studied through an ethno-historical approach. I outlined their ethnogenesis from the study of their ethno-dividing process (*procesos etnodivisorios*) and I re-examined the epistemological meaning of concepts.[37] Other issues worth recalling include intra-ethnic and inter-ethnic relations, treated as units revealing multiple and varied dimensions of the object, functioning like cultural hubs. It was important to proceed to this level of analysis in order to address the national question. Thanks to this approach, I reached the conclusion that the hubs that configured elements of sameness at the inter-ethnic level are the ones that allowed participation in a shared identity. However, these hubs were dissolved because of the growing distinction between 'we' and 'them' due to jealousy, prejudice and inter-ethnic hatred accentuated by internal wars. All this created a discontinuity between social and economic relations and ancestral links; at the level of the ethnic group, this revealed the difficulty of conceiving of a 'national unity'.

SOME FINAL REFLECTIONS, BY WAY OF CONCLUSION

The multidisciplinary research into Angola's national question was an important moment for the social sciences in Cuba and Angola. However, the material that was gathered remains forgotten as it sinks into oblivion. Much of the field material and all the work elaborated from it is locked away in the archives of the institutions that commissioned the project, under the control of a bureaucracy that is always busy with 'more important issues'. Another part of the research remains in the experiences or personal notes of the participants, some of whom have moved abroad or have died. There is the risk, therefore, of all this richness being diluted into anecdotal accounts or the lecture notes of the participants. There is some interest, not only mine, in keeping the matter alive and in trying to join forces, among those who are still alive, to reconstruct these experiences and to draw useful conclusions about the organisation, the methodological concepts and, ultimately, the adventure (always challenging) of investigating and creating new knowledge.

Like all human processes, the research work had its achievements and its limitations, many of them imposed by circumstances. Notwithstanding, it left a body of experiences that have marked us and our subsequent work. From a personal viewpoint, everyone who took part in this initiative, particularly those who took part in the fieldwork, agrees that the experience of rising to the occasion in a short period of time enriched us on a human level. After the Angolan experience, we were all different and better people. At a scientific level, the research helped to reaffirm the view that what exists in society are problems, and that these

Figure 5.3: Pablo Rodríguez Ruiz in front of the hut built for him by villagers. © Pablo Rodríguez Ruiz, south-east Angola, 1985.

need multiple viewpoints rather than a range of different disciplines. Traditional thinking alone cannot provide answers to the complex issues that derive from human interaction. Similar methods were used in our collective research into criminal violence during the crisis of the 1990s, as well as into racism, the black market, social prevention, and administrative corruption – all undertaken following requests from the state.

In addition, with respect to the multidisciplinary interactions, the Angolan effort taught that teamwork demands some conceptual flexibility and a willingness to renounce some of the individual ego that makes dialogue difficult. Some methodological flexibility is required so that, rather than starting from certain pre-existing conceptual or doctrinal premises, one allows the line of inquiry to be determined by the problem itself. Subsequently, my work has followed a logic by which I start the research with certain essential premises or concepts, but I place them in dialogue with the results and end up by reformulating the concepts. At the same time, in the particular case of anthropology, this was an important moment to rediscover other traditions of thinking and to establish the limits of ethnos theory, thus making possible the enrichment of the discipline.

NOTES

1. See the Introduction to this volume, as well as the chapters by Grabli and Argyriadis.
2. These measures included the withdrawal of the US sugar quota, to deprive the country of financial resources; the prohibition or reduction of exports to Cuba of basic products, including food, to create shortages and discontent, a process that became an entire commercial and financial embargo; logistical, media and financial support to counterrevolutionary groups, especially to those that opted for irregular armed conflict in different parts of the country; the recruiting and training of Cuban exile brigades to attack the island militarily; the promotion of internal subversion in every way possible, to which effort was added the creation of the biggest operational base in the history of US intelligence, from which was hatched a plan of action code-named Operation Mongoose. These actions were, among other things, designed to thwart the rising revolution, which had to dodge such obstacles in order to move forward.
3. Fidel Castro Ruz, 'Discurso pronunciado en la concentración efectuada en la Plaza de la Revolución "José Martí", para conmemorar el XVIII Aniversario del ataque al Cuartel Moncada, el 26 de julio de 1971,' in *Discursos e intervenciones del Comandante en Jefe Fidel Castro Ruz, Presidente del Consejo de Estado de la República de Cuba* (Havana: Departamento de versiones taquigráficas del gobierno revolucionario, 2 December 2005), http://www.cuba.cu/gobierno/discursos/.
4. See the chapters by Alcaraz, and Kiriakou and André in this volume.
5. Castro Ruz, 'Discurso pronunciado en la concentración efectuada en la Plaza de la Revolución "José Martí".

6 There were some 6000 doctors in Cuba before 1959. Many left the country after the revolution, and only some 3000 remained. Despite this, some of those who stayed in Cuba eventually served in Algeria in 1963.

7 Niurka Núñez González, 'La antropología sociocultural en Cuba: Apuntes para una historia necesaria,' *Perfiles de la Cultura Cubana*, no. 18 (2015), http://www.perfiles.cult.cu/inicio_c.php?numero=18; Pablo Rodríguez Ruiz, 'La antropología sociocultural en Cuba: Historia y actualidad,' in *Antropologías en América Latina: Prácticas, alcances y retos*, ed. Jairo Tocancipá-Falla (Popayán: University of Cauca, 2017), 205–40.

8 Yulian Bromley, *Etnografía teórica* (Moscow: Ed. Nauca, 1986).

9 Sergei Aleksandrovich Tokarev, *Historia de las religiones* (Havana: Editorial de Ciencias Sociales, 1975); Sergei Aleksandrovich Tokarev, *Historia de la etnografía* (Havana: Editorial de Ciencias Sociales, 1989).

10 Eduard Grigorevich Aleksandrenkov, *Poniéndose cubano: Problemas de formación de la identidad étnica (siglos XVI–XIX)* (Moscow: Institute of Ethnology and Anthropology of the Academy of Sciences of Russia, 2005).

11 Colectivo de autores, *Atlas etnográfico de Cuba: Cultura popular tradicional* (Havana: CIDCC Juan Marinello/Centro de Antropología/CEISIC, CD-ROM, 2000).

12 Pablo Rodríguez Ruiz, 'Hacer antropología en un contexto de conflicto armado: La experiencia de la investigación multidisciplinaria acerca de la cuestión nacional en Angola,' in *XIII Conferencia Internacional Antropología* (Havana: Editorial Filosofía@.cu, Instituto Cubano de Antropología, CD-ROM, 2016).

13 Adrián Fundora García and Dmitri Prieto Samsónov, 'No hay hombre sin cultura como no hay cultura sin hombre: Itinerario intelectual de Pablo Rodríguez Ruiz y sus contribuciones a la antropología sociocultural desarrollada en Cuba' (Havana: Departamento de Etnología, Instituto Cubano de Antropología, 2017), 84.

14 García and Samsónov, 'No hay hombre sin cultura,' 79.

15 Fernando Ortiz, *Contrapunteo cubano del tabaco y el azúcar* (Havana: Editorial de Ciencias Sociales, 1963 [1940]), 99.

16 In 1965 Ernesto 'Che' Guevara, while in the Congo, made the first contacts with the MPLA and its leader, Agostinho Neto. As Fidel Castro declared in 2005, 'In that context began, in the year 1965, our collaboration with the pro-independence fight in Angola and Guinea-Bissau, which consisted mainly in the training of officials, the dispatching of instructors and material aid' (Fidel Castro Ruz, 'Discurso en el acto conmemorativo por el aniversario 30 de la Misión Militar cubana en Angola y el aniversario 49 del desembarco del Granma Día de las FAR'). The contacts and collaborations endured through the independence period. Jorge Risquet, a former revolutionary fighter, was the representative of the Cuban Communist Party and the Cuban government in Angola between 1975 and 1979. He was entrusted with the coordination of the work related to the Angolan research. Thereafter, he was in charge of relations with the African continent at the Ministry of Foreign Affairs; he headed the Cuban delegation participating in the negotiations in 1988.

17 The fact of opposing ethnicity to the nation or to modernity contributed to reifying a dichotomy that is far from the reality. Nonetheless, we should not deny the fact that cultural diversity or ethnic identification, when instrumentalised by inadequate policies, can give way to conflicts having a negative impact on social coexistence. It is with this conceptual framework that the nascent Angolan nation-state questioned ethnicity and national unity.

18 A distinguished Cuban linguist and main expert on linguistic anthropology in Cuba.

19 A Cuban anthropologist who specialised in the ethnic composition of slaves brought to Cuba and in the religious practices of African origin; he was the first to consider these at a theoretical level as a complementary system, also including spiritism and popular Catholicism.

20 A Cuban historian who made an original contribution to identity construction and religion in Cuba, and whose work is transdisciplinary (anthropological, sociological, philosophical and historiographical).

21 García and Samsónov, 'No hay hombre sin cultura.'

22 I coordinated the research requested by the office of the General of the armies, Raúl Castro Ruz, who was then the second secretary to the Central Committee of the CCP. The results of the research were presented in two reports: *La violencia criminal durante la crisis y los ajustes económicos de los noventa* (2002) and *El mercado negro en Cuba* (2002). My research on administrative corruption was conducted years later. All these results were presented as documents for the use of state institutions and are not public.

23 Born in Portugal in 1932 (he died in South Africa in 2004), Enrique Abranches was an Angolan writer, anti-colonialist and anthropologist of high renown. He was the founder, with the writer Artur Carlos Maurício Pestana dos Santos ('Pepetela'), of the Centre for Angolan Studies, in Algeria in 1963. He also was director of the National Museum of Slavery, established in Luanda in 1977. His most famous work is *A konkhava de Feti* (1981).

24 For a doctorate in eco-anthropology, he defended a dissertation at the University Paris VII in 1974 on the Herero pastoralists (*Contribution à l'étude des écosystèmes pastoraux: Las Vakuval du Chingo*). De Morais was deputy minister of agriculture in 1981.

25 This is the theoretical core of the Soviet ethnographic school developed in the former USSR, which, contrary to Western anthropology, considered 'ethnos people' as its main object of study. Yulian Bromley was a major proponent of that school. Simultaneously, we considered other theoretical positions like those of Fredrik Barth and Hector Diaz Polanco.

26 As of 1984, Cuban troops in the south-west occupied a defensive line running from Cahama to Otchinjau, that is to say, next to the 17th parallel.

27 Our fieldwork on military units was distinct from an instrumentalisation of anthropology for the sake of war by invading armies (as we can find in US military manuals like *Guerrilla Warfare and Special Forces Operations: Field Manual 21–31* (Washington DC, Defense Department of the United States, 1961) or *Counterinsurgency: Field Manual 3–24* (Washington DC, Army Department, Defense Department of the United States, 2003). In our case, military units constituted a research subject, in addition to the others.

28 The traditional settlement zones of the Herero and Ovambo share their territories in Namibia and Angola. The Herero population considered here is different from the group who suffered genocide in Namibia at the hands of the Germans in the early twentieth century.

29 The Khoisan, also known as the Bushmen and in Angola as Musankala or Musenkele, are hunter-gatherer groups of the Kalahari Desert, who live scattered across territories in southern Angola.

30 See Maksim Grigorevich Levin and Nikolai Nikolaievich Cheboksarov, 'Tipos económicos culturales y región histórica etnográfica,' in *Lecturas de etnología* (Havana: Academia de Ciencias de Cuba, 1972).

[31] The concept of cultural area had its origin in the practical exigencies of American ethnographical investigation, which elaborated it as a heuristic instrument to classify and represent cartographically the tribal groups of North America and South America.

[32] UNITA (National Union for the Total Independence of Angola), created in 1966 by Jonas Savimbi, in Moxico province, became the main movement of armed opposition against the MPLA government. It used guerrilla tactics and enjoyed the direct support of the United States (especially during the Reagan administration), several European countries and South Africa. At a regional level, Mobutu Sese Seko's Republic of Zaire (today the Democratic Republic of Congo) supported UNITA directly. The group's position brought it face to face with the Cuban civil and military contingent.

[33] Among the legends circulating in Angola, that of the 'Savimbi vest' was the most terrifying. This consisted, according to the tales, of cuts made to the abdominal region, through which the arms were introduced, and finished by cutting off the genitalia, which were put into the corpse's mouth.

[34] In Cuba, these are called *llega y pon* (literally, 'come and put it') while in other Latin American contexts they are called as well *villas miserias*, *favelas*, etc. These are urban spaces where houses are built with various materials and without any urban development planning. On this, see Pablo Rodríguez Ruiz, *Los marginales de las Alturas del Mirador: Un estudio de caso* (Havana: Fundación Fernando Ortiz, 2011).

[35] The term for traditional chiefs in Angola.

[36] A homemade beverage obtained by fermenting sorghum, corn or another cereal, which, in the version described here, is distilled to obtain a kind of eau de vie. Drinking this beverage can be harmful because the locals sometimes use acid from electric batteries, which contains high levels of arsenic, to speed up the fermentation process. In southern Angola, according to the prosecutor in Huíla province, at least one Cuban aid worker died after consuming this drink.

[37] Pablo Rodríguez Ruiz, *Los Nhaneca-Humbi de Angola, procesos etnosociales* (Havana: Editorial de Ciencias Sociales, 1996).

REFERENCES

Aleksandrenkov, Eduard Grigorevich. *Poniéndose cubano: Problemas de formación de la identidad étnica (siglos XVI–XIX)*. Moscow: Institute of Ethnology and Anthropology of the Academy of Sciences of Russia, 2005.

Bromley, Yulian. *Etnografía teórica*. Moscow: Ed. Nauca, 1986.

Castro Ruz, Fidel. 'Discurso en el acto conmemorativo por el aniversario 30 de la Misión Militar cubana en Angola y el aniversario 49 del desembarco del Granma, Día de las FAR.' In *Discursos e intervenciones del comandante en Jefe Fidel Castro Ruz, Presidente del Consejo de Estado de la República de Cuba*. Havana: Departamento de versiones taquigráficas del gobierno revolucionario, 2 December 2005. http://www.cuba.cu/gobierno/discursos/.

Castro Ruz, Fidel. 'Discurso pronunciado en la concentración efectuada en la Plaza de la Revolución "José Martí", para conmemorar el XVIII Aniversario del ataque al Cuartel Moncada, el 26 de Julio de 1971.' In *Discursos e intervenciones del comandante en jefe Fidel Castro Ruz, presidente del Consejo de estado de la República de Cuba*. Havana: Departamento de versiones taquigráficas del gobierno revolucionario, 2 December 2005. http://www.cuba.cu/gobierno/discursos/.

Colectivo de autores. *Atlas etnográfico de Cuba: Cultura popular tradicional*. Havana: CIDCC Juan Marinello/Centro de Antropología/CEISIC, CD-ROM, 2000.

Fundora García, Adrián and Dmitri Prieto Samsónov. 'No hay hombre sin cultura como no hay cultura sin hombre: Itinerario intelectual de Pablo Rodríguez Ruiz y sus contribuciones a la antropología sociocultural desarrollada en Cuba.' Havana: Departamento de Etnología, Instituto Cubano de Antropología, 2017.

Levin, Maksim Grigorevich and Nikolai Nikolaievich Cheboksarov. 'Tipos económicos culturales y región histórica etnográfica.' In *Lecturas de etnología*. Havana: Academia de Ciencias de Cuba, 1972.

Núñez González, Niurka. 'La antropología sociocultural en Cuba: Apuntes para una historia necesaria.' *Perfiles de la Cultura Cubana*, no. 18 (July–December 2015). http://www.perfiles.cult.cu/inicio_c.php?numero=18.

Ortiz, Fernando. *Contrapunteo cubano del tabaco y el azúcar*. Havana: Editorial de Ciencias Sociales, 1963 [1940].

Rodríguez Ruiz, Pablo. 'Hacer antropología en un contexto de conflicto armado: La experiencia de la investigación multidisciplinaria acerca de la cuestión nacional en Angola.' In *XIII Conferencia Internacional Antropología*. Havana: Editorial Filosofía@.cu, Instituto Cubano de Antropología, CD-ROM, 2016.

Rodríguez Ruiz, Pablo. 'La antropología sociocultural en Cuba: Historia y actualidad.' In *Antropologías en América Latina: Prácticas, alcances y retos*, edited by J. Tocancipá-Falla, 205–40. Popayán: University of Cauca, 2017.

Rodríguez Ruiz, Pablo. *Los marginales de las Alturas del Mirador: Un estudio de caso*. Havana: Fundación Fernando Ortiz, 2011.

Rodríguez Ruiz, Pablo. *Los Nhaneca-Humbi de Angola, procesos etnosociales*. Havana: Editorial de Ciencias Sociales, 1996.

Tokarev, Sergei Aleksandrovich. *Historia de la etnografía*. Havana: Editorial de Ciencias Sociales, 1989.

Tokarev, Sergei Aleksandrovich. *Historia de las religiones*. Havana: Editorial de Ciencias Sociales, 1975.

CHAPTER

6

Cuban-Congolese Families: From the Fizi-Baraka underground to Havana

Michel Luntumbue

Well before the Cuban intervention in Angola in November 1975 and Havana's decisive contribution to the liberation of southern Africa, the present Democratic Republic of Congo (DRC) was a test bed for Cuba's geopolitical projection into the heart of Africa. Indeed, in April 1965, four years after the assassination of prime minister Patrice Lumumba in January 1961, Che Guevara crossed Lake Tanganyika in secret to lend support to the resistance fighters of the National Council of Liberation (CNL), led by Gaston Soumialot, Christophe Gbenye and Laurent-Désiré Kabila. For Havana, the focus of the revolution turned to Africa, then considered the underbelly of the 'Western imperial system'.

Cuba's leaning towards Africa relied equally on considerations of identity, linked to the African footprint and presence on the Caribbean island: Afro-Cubans (slaves and free people of colour) made up an important part of the *mambises*, the guerrilla fighters of the late-nineteenth-century Cuban wars of independence.[1] Likewise, the origins of one of the main Cuban syncretic movements, the *palo-monte* cult,[2] lay in the Congo Basin and north-western Angola. But, more importantly, 'Cuba's African odyssey'[3] aimed at enlarging, thanks to the alliance with 'African progressive movements', the scope of a world revolution in line with the Guevarist vision.[4]

From April 1964, the seizure of three-quarters of Congolese territory[5] by the supporters of Patrice Lumumba gave strength to the notion that a revolution in

Congo would herald a much vaster movement of emancipation. Nevertheless, the disorganisation of the Congolese rebels and the differences of views between their leaders, as well as an inadequate assessment of the balance of power on both the regional and international scale, got the better of the guerrillas of eastern Congo. The Congolese revolutionaries, supported by a Cuban expeditionary force of barely a hundred advisers, faced a vast coalition consisting of the Congolese regular army, joined by European, South African and Rhodesian mercenaries, as well as anti-Castro elements who had escaped the failed Bay of Pigs expedition.[6] The Western powers, who detected a communist menace behind the ongoing crisis in the Congo, consequently lent decisive support to the government in Léopoldville (now Kinshasa).

Despite the failure of the Cuban incursion into eastern Congo, its sequel is still poorly understood. Dozens of young Congolese fighters from the underground (*maquis*) in Fizi-Baraka,[7] as well as a number of the families of Lumumbist leaders, left for Cuba following the withdrawal of the Cuban expeditionary force, in November 1965. Today there is a Cuban-Congolese community, the children of the former guerrillas of eastern Congo, present in Cuba, and the children born of 'Cuban Pan-Africanism' have often chosen to return to Congo-Kinshasa, as doctors or managers, notably since Laurent-Désiré Kabila's seizure of power in 1997. This little-known trajectory – though similar to that of the thirty to fifty thousand *Afrocubanos*[8] trained in Cuban schools since 1961 – has left a certain Cuban influence and presence, beyond that of language, family ties and exchanges, with members of these groups settled on the Caribbean island.

By following the progress of the former *guerrilleros* of eastern Congo and their families, this chapter sets out to reconstitute the elements of a Cuban-Congolese memory, which remains largely oral, apart from eyewitness accounts of feats of arms recorded in Guevara's Congo diary.[9] This chapter is also the account of the author's encounter with the dramatis personae of this story. Indeed, when I was a child my family spent time in Cuba, for quite other reasons, and developed ties with families from this community. These personal contacts facilitated the conduct of interviews, done in Havana in 2003, and in Kinshasa between 2007 and 2010, that complete my memories from childhood, and that have been followed by regular exchanges.

Making sense of this journey requires a brief summary of the local political context and the geopolitical stakes, both regional and international, that accompanied the Congo crisis, from the day after independence was achieved on 30 June 1960. This context sheds light on the motivations and limits of Cuban policy towards the Congo. The failure to transplant the revolution to eastern Congo, followed by Cuba's relative disengagement from the country, and the return to their place of origin of a few Cuban-Congolese, particularly in the late 1990s, became part of the individual journeys that a number of them experienced, quite distinct from the voluntarist and internationalist politics of the 1960s.

CUBA'S INTEREST IN THE CONGO: GENESIS OF AN AFRICAN DOCTRINE

The beginnings of Cuban policy towards the Congo are becoming better known, in particular thanks to the declassification of certain secret documents of the 1960s, such as the much-acclaimed *Pasajes de la guerra revolucionaria* (Episodes of the Revolutionary War) by Guevara. This posthumously published campaign diary is a critical account of 'the first Cuban international mission and the unfulfilled dream of helping African countries to free themselves from colonialism'.[10] In the early 1960s, indeed, the African continent, then in the throes of decolonisation, became the setting for a double confrontation: that of the Cold War, pitting American power and the Western bloc against the supposed ambitions of the communist bloc on the African continent,[11] as well as a trial of strength that pitted Washington against Havana given the risks posed to the US by an extension of the Cuban revolutionary model to other Latin American countries.[12] In a way, the Cuban incursion on the African continent seemed also like compensation for the difficulties encountered in attempting to implant this model in other settings in Latin America.[13] As tensions with the United States rose – leading to the imposition by the Americans of a total commercial embargo at the end of 1960 – the search for new allies outside the western hemisphere became imperative for the survival of the young Cuban revolution, particularly after the attempted invasion of the island, in April 1961, by Cuban exiles supported by the CIA.[14]

The Algerian precedent

Between 1959 and 1964, contacts established with various Third World revolutionary leaders during official visits or discreet missions led by Guevara paved the way for the implementation of Cuba's internationalist doctrine outside the western hemisphere.[15] More particularly, the friendly ties established between Guevara and the Egyptian and Algerian presidents – Gamal Abdel Nasser and Ahmed Ben Bella, respectively – would serve as a shortcut to sub-Saharan Africa by facilitating dialogue between Cuba and various African liberation movements. Ben Bella's Algeria and Nasser's Egypt were among the main supporters of the Lumumbist rebellion of 1963–5 in Congo-Kinshasa.

From 1961, the Department of Special Operations, established within Cuba's Ministry of the Interior to support other Latin American liberation movements,[16] put in place the first African operations: African guerrillas were trained in Cuba,[17] while military aid – rifles, machine guns and mortars – was sent to the Algerian FLN (National Liberation Front) during its struggle for independence; moreover, a Cuban military mission was opened in Algiers after Algerian independence in July 1962 (see the chapter by Alcaraz in this book). And in May 1963, Cuba sent its 'first internationalist medical brigade', consisting of 50 doctors and nurses, to Algeria.[18] Finally, in October of the same year, a contingent of 686 Cuban soldiers, with 20 tanks and artillery pieces, was dispatched to Algeria, alongside Egyptian troops, at the request of President Ben Bella, following the outbreak of a border dispute with Morocco. This was Cuba's first foreign military intervention. However, a ceasefire was signed between the two countries even before the Cuban troops went into action. Apart from a display of solidarity with the Algerian government, this operation showed above all Cuba's capacity to assemble and transport, in an extremely short period of time, an important military force for the African continent. A decade later, the Algerian experience would serve as a model for the much larger military intervention in Angola.

A second Cuba in the heart of Africa?

Cuba's interest in Congo-Kinshasa derived mostly from the latter's geopolitical role in the context of the Cold War, and particularly from the symbolic character of the Congo crisis, after the assassination of Lumumba in January 1961, and then the Belgian–American intervention of November 1964 in Stanleyville (today Kisangani) against the Lumumbist partisans.[19] In his speech of 11 December 1964 before the 19th session of the United Nations General Assembly in New York, Guevara highlighted the Congo crisis to denounce the denial of the rights of the Congolese people and the greed of foreign powers:

> I wish to refer specifically to the painful affair of the Congo, unique in the history of the modern world, which shows how, with complete impunity, and with the most insolent cynicism, the rights of peoples can be ridiculed. The direct reason for all this is the enormous wealth of the Congo, which the imperialist countries want to keep under their control ... How can we forget the betrayal of the hope that Patrice Lumumba placed in the United Nations?

> How can we forget the machinations and manoeuvres that followed in the wake of the occupation of that country by United Nations troops, under the auspices of which the assassins of this great patriot acted in all impunity? All free men of the world should be ready to avenge the crime of the Congo.[20]

The immense mineral resources of the Congo indeed constituted a central stake in the tensions between East and West, both in economic and strategic terms. Various minerals essential for, in particular, the defence and aerospace industries – uranium, coltan, cobalt – were available almost solely in the Congolese province of Katanga.[21] Moreover, the first American atomic bombs (dropped on Hiroshima and Nagasaki) were built using uranium from the Shinkolobwe mine in Katanga. Western dependence on Congolese mineral resources explains the fierce effort to preserve access to these in the face of the growing (or supposed) influence of the Soviet Union and China on African progressive movements and governments.[22] In addition, after the loss of Cuba to the communist bloc, the American administration was determined to block all Soviet–Chinese competition on African soil, so as to forestall 'a second Cuba' in the heart of Africa. In consequence, the nationalist position of Patrice Lumumba, in spite of his repeated denials of communist allegiance, aroused hostility and renewed efforts by the United States and its Western European allies to remove from the Congolese political stage the only leader capable of uniting the country after independence.[23]

In early 1964, the rebellion by Lumumba's supporters against the central government in Léopoldville gained in strength, and by April the rebels controlled up to three-quarters of the country, forcing Washington to intervene in favour of the Léopoldville government.[24] Indeed, at the beginning of October 1963, at a meeting in Brazzaville, Lumumba's nationalist heirs formed the CNL, which brought together around the MNC–L (National Congolese Movement – Patrice Lumumba), founded by Lumumba, all the political forces that remained loyal to him. Its programme of liberation, breaking with the pro-Western alignment of the Léopoldville government, called for a second independence for the Congo. On 3 October 1963, Pierre Mulele (former minister of public education in the Lumumba government) and his travel companion, Théodore Bengila, who had gone underground some weeks earlier, triggered the first great peasant uprising in the Congo, in the western province of Kwilu.[25] In April 1964, Kivu and Nord-Katanga provinces in turn broke away, under the direction of Gaston Soumialot and Laurent Kabila, who created an eastern front. In August, Lumumbist forces from the eastern front, known as Simbas, seized Stanleyville. In September 1964, the government in Léopoldville called in mercenaries and organised a counteroffensive by the government army. Stanleyville was finally retaken in November, with the help of Belgian para-commandos and mercenaries of various nationalities, including anti-Castro Cuban pilots, who came to counter what was seen as an attempt by communists to seize the Congo.

In a context marked by a powerful nationalist current and by the struggles for the emancipation of territory still under European control, Congo-Kinshasa appeared to Guevara the ideal terrain as the focus for an African uprising, in line with his theory of the *guerrilla madre*, a base that would spread the revolutionary dynamic to other regions of the continent.[26] In addition, because of its strategic location in the heart of the continent and its extensive forests, Congolese territory offered almost perfect cover for a guerrilla force. Moreover, the Lumumbist forces controlled a vast liberated zone in the east of the country, particularly in the mountainous areas along the western bank of Lake Tanganyika, guaranteeing the guerrillas relatively invulnerable areas to base themselves, as well as secure areas for resupply.[27]

For an African revolution

After his intervention at the UN in December 1964, Guevara undertook a two-month tour of his closest allies and the revolutionary movements of the African continent. His journey took him from Algiers to Bamako in Mali, by way of Congo-Brazzaville and then Dar es Salaam, in Tanzania.[28] According to the testimony of Jorge Serguera Riberi, the Cuban ambassador in Algeria, the main goal of the Algerian leg 'was to create an alliance between Cuba and Algeria to support liberation movements and already independent nations against colonialism and imperialism in Africa, in the economic, political and military spheres'.[29] Guevara's idea, then still a closely guarded secret, was to support the formation of an African force made up of fighters from various liberation movements, which would train in the base area of eastern Congo.[30] In January 1965, during conversations with the authorities in Congo-Brazzaville, President Alphonse Massamba-Débat, then on bad terms with the Léopoldville government, and fearing an imminent invasion, asked Cuba for military assistance in training a Congolese militia intended for use in defending Brazzaville (see Kiriakou and André in this volume). From the perspective of Guevara's revolutionary project in Congo-Kinshasa, Brazzaville therefore became a rear base for the eventual dispatch of troops, arms and supplies.[31] The Brazzaville stage of Guevara's journey also saw the finalising of a military alliance with the Popular Movement for the Liberation of Angola (MPLA), which would last more than a quarter of a century. Cuba and the MPLA had maintained discreet contacts since the end of the 1950s.

At the beginning of February 1965, Guevara met with the leadership of the Congolese CNL in Dar es Salaam, along with 50 other representatives of African liberation movements, from at least ten countries. The meeting with two of the main representatives of the CNL, Gaston Soumialot and Laurent Kabila, left Guevara with contrasting first impressions. Gaston Soumialot seemed quite reserved, whereas Laurent Kabila was enthusiastic and, in further conversations, he enabled Guevara to identify what set him apart from the other leaders of the rebellion.

> Kabila's presentation was clear, concrete, solid; he allowed a glimpse of his opposition to Gbenye and Kanza and his poor relations with Soumialot. Kabila's position was that one could not speak of the Congolese government in as much as Mulele, the initiator of the struggle, had not been consulted, and that in consequence the president was nothing more than the leader of the government of northeastern Congo. This affirmation permitted him to shield the influence of Gbenye from his own southeastern zone, which he controlled as vice president of the party.[32]

Taking care not to inform his Congolese interlocutors of his real identity or his intentions, particularly regarding the planned offensive in the Congo, Guevara tried to convince Kabila of the international importance of the Congolese question:

> We spoke at length with Kabila about what our government considered as a strategic mistake of our African friends: in the face of the manifest aggression of the imperialist powers, their watchword was 'The problem of the Congo is an African problem', and they acted accordingly. But we ourselves thought that the problem of the Congo was a problem that concerned the whole world, and Kabila agreed. I offered him, in the name of the government, 30 instructors and whatever arms we could find, and he gladly accepted. He asked that the shipment be effected quickly, which Soumialot equally demanded during another conversation; the latter recommended that the instructors should be black,[33] so that they could 'pass' for Congolese.

After this meeting with the CNL, Guevara met with the leaders of other African liberation movements based in Dar es Salaam, but failed to convince them of the merits of incorporating their fighters into a single common front in eastern Congo. Believing that the qualities of a guerrilla were forged more on the battlefield than in an academy, Guevara strongly criticised the relevance of the demand, expressed unanimously by the representatives of the various movements, that combatants be trained in Cuba, in spite of the consequent investment of time and money that this represented:[34] 'I tried to show them that it was not about struggle within frontiers, but rather of a war against a common enemy, omnipresent, whether this was in Mozambique, in Malawi, in Rhodesia or in South Africa, in the Congo or in Angola. But no one understood it in that way.'[35] The leaders of the liberation movements preferred to concentrate on the struggles within their respective countries.[36] The struggle for liberation in the Congo would be pursued by the Congolese alone, with the support of a Cuban expeditionary force: 'From that moment, we decided to proceed to the selection of a group of black Cubans and to send them, as volunteers obviously, to reinforce the struggle in the Congo.'[37] In reality, from early February 1965, nearly 500 black Cuban militiamen were already assembled in training camps, some of whom would be chosen to join the internationalist contingent departing for Africa.[38] Altogether, 113 combatants were selected to go to the Congo, including 11 officers, 19 sergeants, 11 corporals and 72 soldiers.[39]

THE MISSED RENDEZVOUS: GRANDEUR AND MISERY OF THE CONGOLESE REVOLUTION

In April 1965, sometime after the arrival of the Cuban military contingent in the CNL's liberated zone in Fizi-Baraka, the political leadership of the CNL found itself in a delicate diplomatic situation when it was informed of the presence of Guevara himself. After he had entered the Congo in secret, it was decided that the needs of the mission required him to conceal his real identity by disguising his physical appearance. While rumours[40] circulated in Cuba for many weeks as to the reasons for his physical disappearance, there was great fear among the CNL leadership that the discovery of Guevara's presence would lead to a strong response on the part of the United States and its allies against the Lumumbist supporters, at a moment when the balance of power had been upset following the loss of Stanleyville in November 1964. Laurent Kabila, who was in charge of the south-eastern zone for the CNL, held off informing the Tanzanian government, without whose consent Cuban aid to the Congolese underground would not have been possible. Nevertheless, following the Belgian–American operation against Stanleyville, in support of the government army, external aid to the Lumumbist rebellion intensified at the end of December 1964. Algeria and Egypt promised to provide equipment, while Sudan, Uganda and Tanzania were natural transit zones for the regions still controlled by the People's Army of Liberation (APL), the armed wing of the CNL.[41] April 1965 seems to represent a turning point in the balance of forces on the ground, with the resumption of the initiative by the government army, which pursued a strategy of progressive reconquest of the zones bordering Sudan and Uganda. The arrival of the Cuban contingent in the Fizi-Baraka liberated area also coincided with the departure for Cairo of all the members of the revolutionary government for a series of discussions on the unity of the struggle and the new structure of the revolutionary organisation. Indeed, the Cairo meeting was an attempt to smooth over the tensions within the rebel leadership, revived more than ever by the loss of Stanleyville.[42] Nevertheless, in the war zone the political void translated into a situation of relative standstill on the front line and long periods of waiting and inaction, made more onerous by Guevara's clandestine status. The recurrent absence of rebel leaders on the ground, and Laurent Kabila's reluctance to let the Cuban leader take part in combat operations, became a source of misunderstanding and strategic indecision during the first two months.

The first use of Cuban combatants in CNL military operations took place from June. The tactics used by the Simbas in the fighting against the army of General Mobutu and the mercenaries of Prime Minister Tshombe attracted attention and raised suspicions about the presence of foreign fighters in the ranks of the CNL:

> The foreign management from which they benefit remains very hypothetical: there is no decisive proof. On the other hand, the convergence of military operations that they effect, the skill with which they elude any patrols on the lake and the practice of barter trade with Tanzania leads to the belief in the existence of an organisation that exceeds the anarchy that one typically attributes to them.[43]

The Cuban presence was confirmed when the body of a Cuban fighter killed in fighting with mercenaries of the Congolese national army was recovered by the latter and his identity established thanks to the label on his underwear, which said *Hecho en Cuba* (made in Cuba).

From then on, the government counteroffensive increased in intensity. In the face of the retreat of rebel troops, harried by aircraft flown by anti-Castro pilots and the attacks of a reorganised government army, the political leadership of the CNL decided to withdraw the Cuban combatants. The regional political context changed after General Mobutu took power on 24 November 1965. Mobutu undertook a policy of normalising diplomatic relations with neighbouring countries, signing cooperation agreements that weakened the regional support enjoyed by the CNL up to that point. The government in Léopoldville combined military action with a campaign to demoralise the rebel troops, offering an amnesty to those who left the ranks of the CNL. Moreover, the coup d'état that took place in Algeria in June 1965 deprived the rebellion of one of its strongest supporters. Soon afterwards, the

Organisation of African Unity (OAU) summit held in Accra, Ghana, in October 1965, which was supposed to debate the Congo crisis, condemned the foreign military presence in the Congo on both sides. The summit's final declaration demanded the withdrawal of foreign troops from the Congo.

The Cuban expeditionary force stayed for seven months in total, and participated in more than fifty military actions.[44] At the height of the withdrawal of revolutionary forces on the ground, Guevara put forward the idea of joining up with the western front under Pierre Mulele, but this could not be carried out because of the gradual encirclement of the rebel strongholds. In consequence, unless they sacrificed themselves in vain, in situations where the Cubans sometimes found themselves the only ones fighting, Guevara and the military instructors had no other option but to leave the Congo and return to Cuba. Guevara's Congo diary points to the principal factors that weighed in the failure to transplant the revolution to this region of the Congo, namely the socio-cultural and geopolitical context that prevailed there at that time.[45] In strictly military terms, despite its initial successes, the eastern liberated zone suffered from damaging rivalries within its leadership and from its dispersal over an extended territory, which hampered interaction between its various components; above all, the movement was deprived of a real unified command that would have permitted the formulation of a coherent overall strategy.

In his account, Guevara underlined the lack of political and military preparation among most of the core militants, as well as the strength of esoteric beliefs in the power of amulets, the *dawa* supposed to ensure their invulnerability to bullets.[46] With the CNL leadership absorbed in the tasks of representing their organisation and of external diplomacy, it became apparent that there were few or insufficient intermediate-level cadres to ensure discipline among the troops on the ground and to help instil the Lumumbist political doctrine, as laid out in the *Catéchisme du MNC*.[47] Finally the language barrier and intercommunal prejudices, both among the Congolese and between Congolese and Cuban, also represented obstacles to achieving group cohesion, in a context characterised by a harsh climate and insufficient food. The fate of the Congolese revolution played out not only in serious local weaknesses, but also in the evolution of the balance of power between the two great-power blocs and their capacity to influence African actors at the regional level.

Cuba's internationalist mission in the Congo remains one of Havana's most audacious initiatives in the southern hemisphere before Operation Carlota, carried out a decade later in Angola.[48] As Piero Gleijeses emphasises: 'more Cubans fought in the Congo than in the whole of Latin America during the first two decades of the Castro regime. The major importance that Cuba attributed to the Congo is attested by the choice to entrust the command of the operation to one of Cuba's principal leaders, and one of Castro's closest comrades.'[49]

TRAJECTORY AND DESTINY OF THE CUBAN-CONGOLESE

At the time of the withdrawal of the Cuban expeditionary corps, between November and December 1965, 17 young Congolese fighters travelled to Havana without, it seems, the knowledge of the CNL leadership. Even though no formal military assistance agreement existed between Cuba and the CNL, particularly around the training of Congolese combatants in Cuba, it seems that Che Guevara took the initiative to bring to Cuba this group of young Simbas, distinguished by their fighting spirit or personal qualities; 'the goal was to train them militarily and politically, as politico-military cadres capable of continuing the revolutionary war in the Congo.'[50] Eleven came from the liberated zone in the east, and six from Pierre Mulele's western front.

An unforeseen exile

Among the Simbas who accompanied Guevara to Havana were, notably, Freddy Ilanga Yaite, 17, who has passed into posterity as Guevara's Swahili teacher in eastern Congo,[51] and Godefroid Tchamulesso, the CNL's main contact with the Cuban expeditionary force, who would become a Cuban press representative in the Caribbean. Others included Joseph Yangala (known as Kassoulé), Adolphe Idwabuse Mukombozi, Frédéric Ilho Longomo, Alexis Selemani (known as Mukishi), Elias Mwalandume (known as Nino) and Salumu 'Boumediene'. Much less is known about François Tambwe, Jérôme[52] and Fidel, three Rwandan fighters from the eastern zone. All of them were supposed to return to the Congo after politico-military training in Cuba. However, the changing military situation in eastern Congo and the progressive loss of territory held by the CNL transformed what should have been a temporary stay into exile. Indeed, when General Mobutu toppled President Joseph Kasa-Vubu on 24 November 1965, the new head of state rapidly normalised relations between the Congo and its neighbours, to the detriment of the CNL. Reversing their political position, all the former sponsors of the CNL proceeded to sign security agreements with the Kinshasa government. As a result, there were no more entry points to pursue revolutionary war in the Congo. The former Simbas therefore concentrated on studies or professional training in their new host country.

In the years that followed the revolution, Cuba indeed was a destination for thousands of young people, from various countries, who came to complete their training in the country.[53] For the Cuban leadership, educational cooperation was a way to support these sister countries in their efforts to ensure their independence and development.[54] During the 1970s, more than 52 000 young people from Africa and Latin America benefited from bursaries enabling them to study at Cuba's *escuelas internacionalistas* (internationalist schools).[55] To mention a few notable Congolese examples,[56] Freddy Ilanga became a paediatrician and neurosurgeon; Frédéric Ilho Longomo became an electro-medical engineer; Joseph Yangala earned a degree in sports science; Adolphe Idwabuse Mukombozi became a dental equipment technician; Elias Mwalandume became a doctor; and so on. For these former Simbas, mainly from rural backgrounds, participation in the 'revolutionary war' of 1964 and departure for Cuba represented an unexpected opportunity to obtain training and jobs that they would never have had in the Congo. Many of these combatants had no previous training and were practically illiterate.

Maintaining the revolutionary myth

In Cuba, the former Simbas and their families enjoyed access to professional opportunities and the tranquillity of their new life. For some of them, however, the dream of revolutionary engagement on African soil remained alive. On 14 August 1980, Léopold Soumialot, son of Gaston Soumialot, and Dr Freddy Ilanga created in Havana the Front for the Liberation of Congo – Patrice Lumumba (FLC-L), a political–military party aiming to unite the exiled Lumumbist forces with the goal of relaunching the unfinished war of liberation begun by the CNL. The founders of the FLC-L visited Libya many times in the mid-1980s and formed contacts with their compatriots in Tripoli, such as François Lumumba, son of Patrice Lumumba, who represented the MNC-L outside the country, and General Nathanaël Mbumba, leader of the *Tigres Katangais*,[57] with whom the leaders of the FLC-L and the MNC-L soon formed a national unity coalition. The FLC-L recruited hundreds of volunteers from the pool of Congolese exiles in Tanzania, Burundi, Uganda, Kenya and Congo-Brazzaville. They were sent to Libya for military training, with the unconditional support of Libyan strongman Muammar Gaddafi. After vain attempts at infiltration into Zaire (Congo) during the 1980s, starting from the borders of Burundi and Uganda, some of them would rejoin the coalition of the Alliance of Democratic Forces for the Liberation of Congo (AFDL), under the aegis of André Kisase Ngandu (a former Simba who had received military training in East Germany before earning a medical degree in West Germany), which toppled

Mobutu in April 1997, with the active support of Rwanda and Uganda. Léopold Soumialot was the only Cuban-Congolese national to rejoin the AFDL from Cuba and return to Congo as a fighter, and he took part in the liberation of Kinshasa. Freddy Ilanga was forced to remain in Cuba because of health problems. Godefroid Tchamulesso,[58] a former CNL cadre in the eastern liberated zone, did not reach Kinshasa until after the AFDL's military victory, as was the case with many other Lumumbist figures, such as Abdoulaye Yerodia, who would go on to occupy high office in the government of Laurent Kabila. The assassination of Kabila in January 2001, and the change in policy of his son and successor, Joseph, led to a break between the latter and a portion of the Lumumbist young guard, who did not see themselves working in the compromise institutions that resulted from the Sun City agreement between the warring parties in 2002.[59]

With the ending of the Cold War the Cuban authorities would look kindly on, though without interfering in, the military initiatives supported first by Libya and then by neighbouring states in the subregion, with the supposed sponsorship of the major powers in the new configuration of forces since the end of the bipolar world system. After its engagements in Ethiopia and Angola, and after signing tripartite agreements – with Angola and South Africa – to guarantee peace in southern Africa, Cuba was no longer in a position to embark on new African military adventures. As Léopold Soumialot emphasised: 'They knew of our movements in Cuba and our movements overseas; they facilitated our access to Cuban passports, as a cover for our overseas trips, but they did not get involved in our affairs. They encouraged us without compromising themselves … They behaved only as interested spectators, without taking part.'[60]

Family ties

Around the time of the arrival in Cuba of the former Congolese guerrillas, the families and close relatives of the CNL leadership were also invited to settle in Cuba, both for the sake of their children's education and to boost the morale of the combatants, freeing them from worries about the safety of their families. The first to arrive in Cuba, from Egypt, was the Soumialot family in December 1965. They were followed by five other families of CNL cadres, the Nkumu, Mukwidi, Balongi, Nima and Katasa families, who came from Congo-Brazzaville in July 1966. Then came the Mongali and Kitungwa families, from Albania and Egypt, respectively. In Havana they found Edouard Sumbu Mulenda, the CNL representative to the Cuban government, as well as Albert Lopepe and his wife, Lucie Olenga. Captain Lopepe was in Cuba to undergo treatment for blindness caused by a grenade explosion during the fighting for Stanleyville in November 1964.

Figure 6.1: From left to right: Joseph Yangala Shabani (aka Kassoulé) and his son Kazudi, Maman Marguerite Tumba Nkumu (Maman Margot) holding the hand of Ilho Longomo (son of Frédéric Ilho Longomo), Isabelle Nkumu, Henriette Nkumu, Rose Mwamini Kyondo Soumialot (Maman Rose) carrying in her arms Milili 'Kabibi' Nkumu (daughter of Séraphine Nkumu). In the forefront the other children are Safi Soumialot (daughter of Marcel Soumialot) and Nadine Nkumu (daughter of Isabelle Nkumu). © Amisi Soumialot, Havana, c.1980.

This Congolese presence, along familial lines, largely reproduced the organisational hierarchy of the CNL. Thus, we find the family of Gaston Soumialot, president of the Supreme Council of the Revolution (CSR), the highest political organ of the liberation movement, set up during the Cairo meeting of April 1965. The family of Camille Nkumu, one of the leaders of the eastern guerrillas, who was killed in combat, was also linked to the political leadership of the CNL. Nkumu was part of the CNL delegation on various political missions in Cuba, particularly during the conference Organisation of Solidarity with the Peoples of Asia, Africa and Latin America (OSPAAAL, also known as the Tricontinental), which was held in Havana from 3 to 15 January 1966. Thomas Mukwidi and Barthélemy Balongi were both leaders of the resistance fighters on the western front, which was headed by Pierre Mulele. Michel Mongali was in charge of finance and logistics within the CNL,

Figure 6.2: From left to right: Léopold Soumialot (son of Gaston Soumialot), Marcel Soumialot carrying Kazudi Yangala (son of Joseph Yangala), Rita Kitenge, spouse of Dr Kitenge, carrying his daughter Ricel Kitenge, Dr Marcel Kitenge and Safi Soumialot (daughter of Marcel Soumialot), Rose Mwamini Kyondo Soumialot (wife of Gaston Soumialot). In front of Maman Rose, Aracely (daughter of Marcel and Rita Kitenge). In the forefront, Carolina, the mother-in-law of Marcel Soumialot. Behind Carolina, Marcel Soumialot carrying his son Tenzi; on the right, Iliana, the former wife of Patricio Soumialot carrying their son Yosman. © Amisi Soumialot, Havana, 1985, two years after his return from his first military training in Libya.

before being entrusted with diplomacy and relations with friendly states that supported the movement. Finally, during the Tricontinental, Mongali became the CNL representative with this organisation. Placide Kitungwa, the cadre directing the eastern front of the resistance, was first the secretary of Gaston Soumialot, then secretary-general of the CNL, before representing the CNL at OSPAAAL, replacing Michel Mongali. Kitungwa would himself be replaced in the post of CNL representative to OSPAAAL by Antoine Kazimbura, a CNL cadre from the western underground.

The turnover of CNL representatives with OSPAAAL was linked particularly to the return of certain families to Africa during the first ten years of their stay in Cuba. The Mukwidi, Balongi, Nima, Katasa and Mongali families chose to return to Congo-Brazzaville in 1969, out of homesickness for Africa, having lived in Cuba for four years. The Kitungwa family returned to Cairo in 1974 because Kitungwa's Egyptian-born wife wished to go back there. Members of the Soumialot and Nkumu families returned to Congo-Kinshasa, of their own free will, after the fall of Mobutu, with the assistance of the United Nations High Commissioner for Refugees, which assumed the costs of their relocation. The Cuban government did not intervene. Nevertheless, we can follow back-and-forth movements that indicate the mobility of individuals in two directions, particularly between Brazzaville and Havana. Some Cuban-Congolese held Congo-Brazzaville passports, by the simple fact of having lived there before settling in Cuba.[61] It is for this reason that members of the Nkumu family changed residence frequently, between Cuba and Congo-Brazzaville, as did Séraphine Nkumu, who left Cuba to go into business in Congo-Brazzaville, but would return to Cuba after living in Brazzaville for ten years.[62] 'Families' therefore must be understood as households made up most often of minor children and later of children born in Cuba from unions between Congolese and Cubans. The first marriages between Cubans and Congolese exiles involved the core of young resistance fighters who arrived after the withdrawal of the Cuban expeditionary corps, as well as individuals who arrived as minors during the first wave of family reunions, which principally involved the families of CNL cadres. The term Cuban-Congolese thus includes 'Cubanised' Congolese as much as children born out of unions with Cuban partners.

Heritage and parentage

> The principal legacy that we have retained from Cuba rests probably in the professional training received in various fields, and which allows us today to live honestly in any country in the world.[63]

The Cuban-Congolese are today settled on both sides of the Atlantic, from the Caribbean to the African continent, and in Europe and North America. Not everyone professes absolute commitment to the 'humanist internationalist' ideals extolled by the Cuban government. Nevertheless, the trajectory of the new generations is still marked by their experience of life in Cuba, and offers a range of diverse experiences. Careers in medicine and engineering are the professional threads most represented, in accord with the Cuban ideal of universal access to health and social welfare. Thus, Amisi Soumialot Lezcano,[64] eldest son of Léopold Soumialot, is a doctor, and found himself involved in an 'internationalist mission' in Costa Rica during 2016. Marie-Thérèse Soumialot, granddaughter of Gaston Soumialot, was, in this period, director-general of hygiene and epidemiology in the municipality of Marianao, in Havana, while her eldest son was an officer of the Cuban immigration service. The two children of Dr Freddy Ilanga, Ilya and Yaile, both live and work in Cuba, Ilya as a doctor – a neurosurgeon like his father – and Yaile (Freddy Junior) as an engineer. The daughter of Séraphine Nkumu, Milili Nkumu (granddaughter of Camille Nkumu), born of a Cuban father, is an obstetrician in a hospital in Havana. The daughter of Salumu Boumediene, Yamila, lives in Cuba and works at the Ghanaian embassy as an assistant to the ambassador. Ilho and Longomo, the children of Frédéric Ilho Longomo, live in Spain and the United States, respectively. Ilho is a non-commissioned officer in the US Army.[65] In 2014, he spent time in Guinea-Conakry as part of an American military mission to that country, while his brother Longomo was settled in Spain with his mother. Choma, Edouard and Zaina, the children of Edouard Sumbu Mulenda, live in Bosnia, Costa Rica and Cuba, respectively. Choma is a professor of Afro-Cuban dance in Bosnia; Edouard has a degree in hotel management, is married to a Spanish woman, and owns a hotel in Costa Rica; Zaina is a lawyer in Cuba.

Yosmiel Soumialot, son of Ambroise Soumialot and grandson of Gaston Soumialot, lives in Cuba, where he is a civil engineer. Kazudi, son of Joseph Yangala Shabani (known as Kassoulé), holds a degree in sports science, like his father, and lives in Germany with his Russian wife. As for the sons of Adolphe Idwabuse Mukombozi, Adolphito and Imuka, they live in the United States and Switzerland, respectively. Adolphito is a choreographer and dancer in Las Vegas, while Imuku lives and works in Geneva.

In the Democratic Republic of Congo (DRC), the daughters of Dr Marcel Kitenge (a cousin of Gaston Soumialot), Rose and Ricel, live and work in Kinshasa; Rose is a doctor in a hospital founded by her father, while Ricel is an international businesswoman and is married to a Congolese politician currently in office in Kinshasa. Yosman Soumialot, the son of Patricio Soumialot and grandson of Gaston Soumialot, is a highway engineer and works in the infrastructure programme called the 'policy of modernity' initiated by Joseph Kabila.

Henriette Nkumu, who returned to Kinshasa with part of the family, is a doctor and works with an international humanitarian NGO. Among the individuals who have returned to the Congo, only three Cuban-Congolese of the second generation – in the mechanical and juridical fields – have encountered difficulties in adapting to the less diverse and more unstable professional and institutional landscape of the DRC.

A Cuban-Congolese identity?

> When we were still in Cuba, we spoke Swahili or Lingala among ourselves, but once in the Congo, Spanish naturally became the language of communication between us. In this way, even the children of our families, born in the Congo and who have never travelled to Cuba, express themselves in Spanish.[66]

> To be Latino is a matter of pride, but to be Cuban is a privilege.[67]

For the Congolese who have returned from Cuba, the transmission of their adopted language is one of the most distinctive traits of the Cuban-Congolese community. Language conveys a whole imaginary: 'Everyone, even those in Kinshasa, is there only physically; mentally they are in Cuba … they act, think and do as Cubans do … Cuba is their model of comparison in evaluating good and bad.'[68] Culinary practices and habits also reinforce this process of superposition and interpenetration between the two worlds. 'We eat mainly Congolese food, because in Cuba our mothers prepared only the cuisine of the country, so much so that even our Cuban wives have adopted Congolese food from Cuba.'[69] But it is also often the case that families who have settled in the Congo acquire the ingredients needed to prepare typical Cuban recipes.[70]

Music represents another, no less important, space of hybridisation, given the place of musical arts in the daily expression of both Cubans and Congolese. Music echoes the twin-like relationship between Cuba and the Congo: 'We love Congolese music, because, in Cuba, we have never cut ties with Congolese culture, whose music reached us via the students from Congo-Brazzaville.'[71] During the 1950s, it was recordings of Cuban music, which crossed the Atlantic on merchant ships, that contributed to the emergence of African urban musical forms, such as 'Congolese rumba' (see Grabli in this volume). The shared musical roots of Cuban *son* and rumba were recalled by the approach of musicians such as Ricardo Lemvo, or by the encounter between the Congolese and Cuban guitarists Papa Noel and Papi Oviedo.[72] But today the Cuban-Congolese families in Kinshasa are probably the only keen listeners to music from Cuba and Latin America, in a cultural environment dominated by new and hegemonic forms of contemporary Congolese music.

More fundamentally, the peculiarity of the Cuban-Congolese identity has also been shaped by the way these families and their children were socialised within the Cuban revolutionary project and model:

> We grew up over there … I arrived in Cuba, at age 11, and I left Cuba when I was over 40 … my younger brother, Patricio, arrived there when he was just two and a half. All of our childhood friends were Cuban … culturally, we are more Cuban than Congolese, but politically we are today more inclined towards Congolese politics than that of Cuba. We have a Cuban culture without having lost our Congolese identity.[73]

In Cuba, the Cuban-Congolese families were housed in Havana's most comfortable residential neighbourhoods, particularly Miramar, Siboney and Vedado; family members who have stayed on still occupy the same houses that were granted to them by the Cuban government when all the families were living in Cuba. Taking into account the groups of combatants from the eastern and western fronts, as well as the families of the leaders, this community numbered more than 500 individuals during the 1960s and 1970s. But their number fluctuated with new births and as certain families and combatants left the island to return to Africa. The task of undertaking a census to establish the exact number of individuals of Cuban-Congolese ancestry living in Cuba and outside the island today still needs to be carried out.

In a chapter of his Congo campaign diary, Guevara highlights the arrogant behaviour of certain Cuban combatants towards the Congolese in the underground zone of the east.[74] But in Cuba, the families settled in Havana seem never to have heard of or experienced prejudice or flagrant discrimination towards Africans or Cuban-Congolese: 'The Cubans never saw or treated us as foreigners, and always regarded us as Cubans.'[75] Although we need to question the idea of an absence of prejudice in any society, the experience of the Cuban-Congolese seems to represent a model of successful integration: 'All the nationals of our generation in Cuba, all skin colours mixed, grew up together in the same boarding schools, in the same schools, with the same rights of access to education, and to all aspects of social, economic and political life.'[76]

In principle, anyone living in Cuba can attain positions of responsibility in student, trade union and professional institutions, except for institutions of a political character, for which Cuban nationality is required. This is acquired after ten years of residence, but on condition that one gives up one's nationality of origin. Godefroid Tchamulesso is the only member of the generation of the eastern underground to become a naturalised Cuban, thanks to his work. As a journalist, he represented the Cuban international news agency, La Prensa Latina, in the Caribbean, Latin America and the United States. Even though he would later assume the position of presidential adviser, then minister of defence, under Laurent-Desiré Kabila, before becoming Congolese ambassador to Angola under the government of Joseph Kabila, he held on to his Cuban nationality.

Foreigners who marry Cubans or who have children with Cuban citizens can also apply for nationality. Most Congolese who arrived in Cuba as children or adults have nevertheless opted for the status of permanent residents, which confers the same social rights with respect to schooling, health and employment as those enjoyed by Cuban citizens. At the same time, some Cuban-Congolese of the generation born in Cuba, such as Marie-Thérèse Soumialot and the children of Dr Freddy Ilanga and Amisi Soumialot Lezcano, became members of the Young Communist League (UJC) or are members of the Cuban Communist Party (PCC).

Furthermore, schooling in Cuba has constituted a powerful factor in mixing young Cubans and young Afro-Cubans from various backgrounds. The group of children of the CNL leadership, who arrived in Cuba during the 1960s, were trained in the Cuban educational model, which involves military training in parallel with the school curriculum, from primary school to secondary school and university.[77] The Cuban Ministry of the Interior was responsible for the families of the CNL leaders, while the Simbas were the responsibility of the Ministry of Defence – at least during the first years of their Cuban stay, as long as the project of a revitalised revolutionary struggle in the Congo continued. The children of the CNL leaders mixed with the children of the leaders of other liberation movements – African, Latin American and Asian – in institutions where they met the children of Cuban leaders and children of the 'martyrs of the Cuban revolution', killed during Fidel Castro's 'war of the liberation of Cuba'. 'Every Friday, a car from the ICAP [Instituto Cubano de Amistad con los Pueblos, or Cuban Institute of Friendship with Peoples] came to fetch us from the boarding school to take us to a residence situated at that time in Miramar, from where cultural activities were suggested, such as visits to Playa Girón, Playa Larga or Varadero.'[78]

Even today, continuing the children's schooling in Cuba, even for families settled in Africa, remains a way of avoiding a break with the Cuban frame of reference, a way of defending the memory of the struggles of the 1960s. 'All of our children know the history of the Congo well, but in its Lumumbist and anti-imperialist version.' Thus, school careers begun in Kinshasa have been, in many cases, completed in Cuba. 'My daughter Cherylin began her medical studies in Kinshasa, and she is now in the process of finishing in Cuba; when she was still in Kinshasa, in secondary school, she was in the habit of debating with her history teacher, who was surprised to find an adolescent had mastered certain aspects of national history that he himself was not familiar with.'[79]

A singular collective memory

> What I retain from the story of my grandfather is that he was a determined man, a man of integrity, who knew what a country is.[80]

The final distinctive characteristic of the Cuban-Congolese is probably their sharing of a singular collective memory, distinct from the account of the official history forged during the reign of Mobutu. It is a collective memory marked by figures from the struggles of the 1960s, and above all by references and attachments to Cuba, which remains an ever-present source of inspiration: 'The socialist ideals received in childhood mark you throughout life.'[81]

For some of the older Cuban-Congolese, the attachment to Cuban soil manifests itself particularly in the explicit expression of a wish to be buried in Cuba, if they should die while away from the island. At the height of a long illness, Henry Nkumu, eldest of the Nkumu siblings, who settled in Spain, his wife's country of origin, expressed the wish to be buried in Cuba, where his only son lives. Joseph Yangala (known as Kassoulé) and Freddy Ilanga, both of whom died in the early 2000s, are also buried in Cuba. Shortly before his death in November 2005, at the age of 57, Freddy Ilanga confided to his son a notebook outlining a plan to return and engage in the service of the people of the eastern Congo, a continuation of the unfinished dream of the struggles of the 1960s.[82]

However, in the absence of institutional links and of a new account shared by all Congolese integrating the peculiar trajectory of the Cuban-Congolese, the preservation of this collective memory takes place through the formation of associative links. This is particularly the choice made by the *Africubanos* of Congo-Brazzaville. Brazzaville and its 'twin', Kinshasa, share a common cultural and musical heritage, and their relationship can at times be described as one of rivalry or emulation.[83] The establishment of Los Amigos de Cuba in Brazzaville, in July 2013, has brought together former diplomats, students and managers from Congo-Brazzaville who were trained in Cuba.[84] The association defines itself as socio-economic in character, and aims to place the expertise of its members in the service of the modernisation of the Republic of Congo. The goal is also to reinforce ties of friendship and solidarity with Cuba. Isabelle Nkumu, a long-time resident of Brazzaville, and widow of a Congo-Brazzaville national, is a member of this association.

There is no equivalent association in Kinshasa, but the Cuban embassy seems to have developed close personal relations with members of the city's Cuban-Congolese community. Most are invited to activities organised by the embassy, particularly receptions marking official Cuban holidays, such as the national day. The ambassador, as well as diplomats stationed in Kinshasa, regularly makes personal visits to Cuban-Congolese families.[85] But, at the official level, it is difficult to identify a coherent approach to relations between the two countries, or a strategy that makes use of the skills and contribution of the Cuban-Congolese community for the benefit of exchanges between the two countries.

Under the short presidency of Laurent-Désiré Kabila, the Cuban ambassador in Kinshasa made available, in the name of the Cuban government, several hundred grants for Congolese to pursue studies in Cuba in the areas of human and veterinary medicine, agronomy and mining engineering: 'It was not about a response to a request by the government of Laurent Kabila, but rather an initiative of the Cuban ambassador aiming to help the agricultural, breeding and fishing programme of President Laurent-Désiré Kabila.'[86]

The Congolese president, who was assassinated in January 2001, did not have the time to develop a coherent policy of multi-sectoral cooperation with Cuba. This is why Cuba and the DRC have still not formalised an official reception policy for students. Nevertheless, in June 2010 the two countries signed an agreement in the area of sport, which envisaged particularly joint programmes for the training and improvement of coaches and exchanges of specialists in different sporting disciplines.[87] The future trajectory of Congolese sport in the disciplines framed by this bilateral agreement will point the way to further joint programmes planned between the two countries.[88]

EPILOGUE: FIZI-BARAKA–HAVANA–KINSHASA, AND BACK

> The return to Africa was the occasion everyone was waiting for to bring their contribution to the reconstruction of the Congo. But the reality was very far from that which most of us imagined from Cuba. It was not at all favourable to us. The fate of the Lumumbist revolutionaries, at the time Laurent-Désiré Kabila came to power (1997), depended on participation in the AFDL's war against the Mobutu regime. There was no place in the political system of Laurent-Désiré Kabila for those who did not take part in the AFDL war. Moreover, the level of underdevelopment we encountered in the technical and professional sectors in the Congo sowed the seeds of disappointment for many of us. But with the education we received in Cuba, one can adapt to all situations![89]

The failure of the attempt to transplant the revolution to eastern Congo was accompanied by Cuba's relative disengagement from the country, which was to the benefit of other parts of Africa (Guinea-Bissau and Angola in particular). Especially after being involved in Ethiopia and Angola, and having signed the Tripartite Accords (New York Accords) with Angola and South Africa to bring about peace in southern Africa, Cuba was no longer in a position to embark on new military adventures in Africa. Moreover, in the new configuration of international relations following the end of the Cold War, its model of intervention in other Third World countries had to be rethought. Interventions in support of liberation movements were themselves justified by the necessity to apply pressure to ongoing struggles, as well as by the wish to contribute to the training of cadres from friendly countries in the three priority sectors: education, medicine and the military.[90] The last-mentioned is apparently no longer applicable in the context of a post-Cold War world and the start of normalisation of relations with the United States. However, Cuba still possesses considerable soft power in the form of cooperation in the medical and health fields, and in education through the hosting of students from partner countries.

In a way, Cuba has allowed thousands of young people from all over Africa to come closer to the Pan-African dream of the fathers of African independence and the founders of the OAU, forerunner of the African Union; it is in Cuba that young people of southern Africa, from the former 'front-line states' (Angola, Mozambique, Zimbabwe), have been able to fraternise with young people from West Africa (Mali, Guinea-Bissau, Guinea-Conakry), Central Africa (Congo-Brazzaville, São Tomé and Príncipe, Equatorial Guinea), and East Africa (including Ethiopia and Tanzania).

The 'pointillist' memory of the Cuban-Congolese bears witness to a counter-model that Cuba still represents for many of the *Africubanos*. Indeed, the Cuban trajectory remains a reference for societies seeking dignity for the many: 'Kinshasa is not Fidel Castro's Cuba, where everyone was assured of a minimum to live decently and with dignity. Here is capitalism! You have to be on the move every day in order to live at the day's rate.'[91]

During a working visit to Cape Verde in 2006, then to the Central African Republic in 2011, I met Cuban-trained engineers from Guinea-Bissau, Angola and São Tomé, and we recalled the liberation struggles of yesteryear, at the same time predicting the inevitable advent of new generations of struggles for collective emancipation, nourished by our Cuban legacies. Everyone shared a strongly Pan-Africanist sensibility, and the dream of reshaping our societies on a basis other than competition and fractured identity.

Postscript

Since the conference where the paper on which this chapter is based was first presented, in Cape Town in 2016, three Cuban-Congolese families were plunged into mourning. Placide Kitungwa, member of CNL and cadre of the eastern front underground, later CNL representative to OSPAAAL, passed away on 22 May 2016 in Kinshasa. Yosman Soumialot, son of Patricio Soumialot and grandson of Gaston Soumialot, civil engineer and technician, passed away in Kinshasa on 24 December 2018. Godefroid Tchamulesso, former cadre of CNL who was the representative of the Cuban press agency, Prensa Latina, for North America and the Caribbean for over 15 years, passed away in Spain on 28 December 2018 at the age of 77. Tchamulesso asked for his remains to be transferred to Cuba, which he considered his second homeland.

NOTES

1. Ada Ferrer, *Insurgent Cuba: Race, Nation and Revolution, 1868–1898* (Chapel Hill, NC: University of North Carolina Press, 1999).
2. Erwan Dianteill, 'Kongo à Cuba: Transformations d'une religion africaine,' *Archives de Sciences Sociales des Religions* 117 (2002): 59–80.
3. To paraphrase the title of the edifying documentary by director Jihan El-Tahri, 'Cuba: Une odyssée africaine,' Artevideo, March 2012.
4. Edward George, *The Cuban Intervention in Angola, 1965–1991* (New York: Frank Cass, 2005); Piero Gleijeses, *Conflicting Missions: Havana, Washington and Africa, 1959–1976* (Chapel Hill, NC: University of North Carolina Press, 2002).
5. It was in fact an occupation of the main urban centres and their immediate surroundings, in the wake of the collapse of Congolese national army, which was demoralised, poorly equipped and weakened by a succession of mutinies and two territorial secessions, immediately following the country's independence on 30 June 1960.
6. Frank R. Villafaña, *Cold War in the Congo: The Confrontation of Cuban Military Forces, 1960–1967* (New Brunswick: Transaction Publishers, 2012); Patrick S. Baker, 'Mercenaries and the Congo Crisis,' *Saber and Scroll* 2, no. 1 (January 2013): 89–103. The involvement of mercenary legions, among them anti-Castro Cubans, rested principally on ideological justifications, a number of them having experienced the Congolese conflict as an 'anti-communist crusade.'
7. The term *maquis* in French is translated throughout the chapter as 'underground', 'liberated zone' or 'liberated area.'
8. 'De África a España, vía Cuba,' *El Pais*, 3 December 2008. In an article devoted to the relations between Cuba and African Americans, 'Back to the Future: African-Americans and Cuba in the Time(s) of Race', *Contributions in Black Studies* 12 (1994): 9–32, Lisa Brook, professor of African history and Diaspora studies at Columbia College in Chicago, cites other sources estimating at more than 80 000 the number of doctors, engineers and African students trained in Cuba from the 1960s to the 1980s.
9. The beginnings of a written history were made with the publication in 2015, in Cuba, of a biography devoted to Freddy Ilanga.
10. William Gálvez, *Le rêve africain du Che* (Brussels: EPO, 1998).
11. Villafaña, *Cold War in the Congo*, 97.
12. George, *The Cuban Intervention in Angola.*
13. Particularly in Argentina and Peru. See George, *The Cuban Intervention in Angola*, 18–19.
14. George, *The Cuban Intervention in Angola*, 19.
15. Gálvez, 'Le rêve africain du Che,' 41–8; George, *The Cuban Intervention in Angola*, 24.
16. George, *The Cuban Intervention in Angola*, 18–19.
17. Particularly those of the Zanzibar Nationalist Party, led by John Okello, who overthrew the sultan in 1964. See Gleijeses, *Conflicting Missions*, 75–80; George, *The Cuban Intervention in Angola*, 18.
18. Gleijeses, *Conflicting Missions*, 36–8; George, *The Cuban Intervention in Angola*, 21.
19. J. Gérard-Libois and J. van Lierde, *Congo 1964* (Brussels: C.R.I.S.P. and Léopoldville: I.N.E.P., 1965), 397–411.
20. Che Guevara at the United Nations, 11 December 1964, 19th General Assembly of the United Nations in New York.

[21] The Congo held 80 per cent of the world's reserves of coltan, 65 per cent of cobalt, 15 per cent of copper, 40 per cent of germanium and 78 per cent of diamonds. See Villafaña, *Cold War in the Congo*, 18.
[22] Villafaña, *Cold War in the Congo*, 18–19.
[23] Villafaña, *Cold War in the Congo*, 22.
[24] Gleijeses, *Conflicting Missions*, 66.
[25] Gérard-Libois and Van Lierde, *Congo 1964*, 9–53.
[26] George, *The Cuban Intervention in Angola*, 21–4.
[27] George, *The Cuban Intervention in Angola*, 21–4.
[28] Che Guevara visited a total of seven countries, including Dahomey, Guinea-Conakry, Ghana, Egypt and Zanzibar, which was not yet part of Tanzania. See Gálvez, 'Le rêve africain du Che,' 50.
[29] Gálvez, 'Le rêve africain du Che,' 41.
[30] Gálvez, 'Le rêve africain du Che,' 52–3.
[31] George, *The Cuban Intervention in Angola*, 21–2.
[32] Ernesto Guevara, *Journal du Congo* (Paris: Mille et Une Nuits, 2009), 50.
[33] Guevara, *Journal du Congo*, 51.
[34] Guevara, *Journal du Congo*, 51–2.
[35] Guevara, *Journal du Congo*, 53.
[36] For Amisi Soumialot, son of Congolese leader Gaston Soumialot, this exclusively nationalist approach to the struggle on the part of Guevara's interlocutors represented a crippling pitfall of this revolutionary enterprise in eastern Congo. Interview, London, February 2016.
[37] Guevara, *Journal du Congo*, 53.
[38] Gálvez, 'Le rêve africain du Che,' 67.
[39] Gálvez, 'Le rêve africain du Che,' 68.
[40] Gálvez, 'Le rêve africain du Che,' 144.
[41] Gérard-Libois and Van Lierde, *Congo 1964*, 48.
[42] The Cairo meeting decided on the restructuring of the liberation movement with the creation of the Supreme Council of the Revolution (CSR), the political organ of the CNL, that is, its political wing, while the CNL became the general assembly of the movement. Gaston Soumialot assumed the presidency of the CSR. Laurent Kabila became vice-president of the CSR and was put in charge of the eastern front. Pierre Mulele was promoted to vice-president and placed in charge of the western front. Christophe Gbenye was ousted from the movement's executive.
[43] Gérard-Libois and Van Lierde, *Congo 1964*, 58.
[44] Initially, the intervention was conceived of as lasting for at least five years, a period Guevara thought essential in order to form strong revolutionary forces and to tip the regional balance of power.
[45] Gálvez, 'Le rêve africain du Che,' 125–8.
[46] The esoteric practices led to veritable slaughter among the Simbas, who were sent to attack the Congolese army and mercenary forces with rudimentary weapons.
[47] Gérard-Libois and Van Lierde, *Congo 1964*, 66–7.
[48] Gabriel García Márquez, 'Cuba en Angola: Operación Carlota,' *Proceso*, 8 January 1977: 6–15.
[49] Gleijeses, *Conflicting Missions*, 105.
[50] Amisi Soumialot and Patricio Soumialot, interviews in London and Kinshasa, April 2016. Certain elements of the account relative to the journey of the former Simbas rest

equally on fragments of eyewitness testimony heard, as children, from the very mouths of the protagonists of the *maquis* of the east. In these eyewitness accounts the presence of Guevara on Congolese soil is curiously overshadowed.

51 'Freddy Ilanga: Che's Swahili Translator,' a film by Katrin Hansing, Icarus Films, 2009.

52 In 2008, a Belgian radio host, Hilde Baele, met fortuitously in Rwanda a certain Jérôme Sebasoni, who turned out to be one of those young Rwandan fighters on the eastern front. Sebasoni was one of Guevara's guides in the underground. After graduating in Cuba, where he worked as a physiotherapist, he returned to Rwanda in 1975 and died at the age of 70 without being able to return to Cuba. A film was dedicated to him in 2016: Jeroen Janssen and Hilde Baele, 'The Unlikely but True Story of the Rwandese Who Took Part in the African Expedition of Che Guevara,' https://drawingthetimes.com/story/the-unlikely-but-true-story-of-the-rwandese-who-took-part-in-the-african-expedition-of-che-guevara/, accessed 5 February 2020.

53 'África en una Isla cubana: 40 aniversario de la escuelas internacionalistas,' *Mesa Redonda*, 16 October 2017.

54 'La odisea educativa de África en Cuba,' *El Mundo*, 13 December 2015.

55 'África en una Isla cubana.' During the 1990s, close to 35 000 African students, from different African countries (such as Angola, Burkina Faso, Ethiopia, Democratic Republic of Congo, South Sudan), were given grants to study at Cuban universities. In 2015, more than half of the grant holders, out of some 2500 African grant holders registered in the faculties of the Island, were in the medical stream. See 'La odisea educativa de África en Cuba.'

56 On account of a restrictive political education under colonial rule, the Congo had few university graduates on the eve of independence, apart from theologians. See Moïse Léonard Jamfa Chiadjeu, *Comment comprendre la 'crise' de l'État postcolonial en Afrique? Un essai d'explication structurelle à partir des cas de l'Angola, du Congo-Brazzaville, du Congo-Kinshasa, du Libéria et du Rwanda* (Bern: Publications Universitaires Européennes, 2005).

57 These former supporters of Moïse Tshombe, exiled in Angola, then the fighters of the two wars in Katanga against the Mobutu regime, in 1977 and 1978, would be more or less demobilised following a security agreement between the Angolan and Zairian (Congolese) authorities, and their leader Nathanaël Mbumba would be expelled from Angola.

58 In reality, in his foreign press mission Tchamulesso provided two missions at the same time; as 'overseas representative of Prensa Latina' and 'agent of the Cuban intelligence service, G2', according to the testimony of a member of the Cuban-Congolese community who has requested anonymity.

59 Signed on 12 December 2002 in South Africa, between the Congolese government, the main armed movements, the political opposition and civil society, the agreement allowed for a political transition and the end of the war, and set up a government led by a president and four vice-presidents. This led to the organisation of the presidential and legislative elections of 2006.

60 Interviews with Léopold Soumialot, London, February 2016.

61 Interviews, Havana, December 2003.

62 Interview, Milili Nkumu, Havana, December 2003.

63 Interview, Patricio Soumialot, Kinshasa, February 2016.

64 His maternal grandfather is Jorge Lezcano, the Cuban ambassador to Brazil, member of the Central Committee of the Cuban Communist Party, and member of the 26 July

Movement which carried Fidel Castro to power. He has also been vice-president of the Council of Ministers and of State, member of the party politburo, ambassador to the United Kingdom, and vice-president of the Cuban parliament.

65 Married to the daughter of an anti-Castro dissident imprisoned in Havana, Ilho has benefited (with his wife) from the American law relating to 'family reunification', at the time of the negotiated release of his father-in-law and other Cuban political prisoners. A naturalised American, Ilho chose a career in the military, not having found other work. He would have, according to certain accounts, participated in the 2003 US invasion of Iraq.

66 Interview, Amisi Soumialot, London, February 2016.

67 Safi Soumialot, granddaughter of Gaston Soumialot, born in Cuba to a Cuban mother, of Cuban nationality, lives and works in Kinshasa.

68 Interviews, Patricio Soumialot, Kinshasa, February 2016.

69 Interviews, Patricio Soumialot, Kinshasa, February 2016.

70 *Arroz Congri* – a typical recipe of rice and black beans – and soup with Cuban flavours are often served with Congolese-style manioc leaves and plantain.

71 Interviews, Patricio Nkumu, Kinshasa, March 2016.

72 Maud Hand, 'Papa Noel and Papi Oviedo, *Bana Congo*: Two Master Guitarists from Cuba and Congo: A Fluid and Welcome Treat,' review, BBC Music, 2002, www.bbc.co.uk/music/reviews.

73 Interview, Amisi Soumialot, London, December 2015.

74 Gálvez, 'Le rêve africain du Che,' 364.

75 Interview, Patricio Soumialot, Kinshasa, December 2015.

76 Interview, Marcel Soumialot, Kinshasa, March 2017.

77 Many African students would, moreover, spend time in the first Escuelas Secundarias Básicas en el Campo (ESBEC), or basic secondary schools in the country, set up from 1969, and based on an idea put forward by José Martí according to which a child must 'handle a notebook in the morning and a hoe in the afternoon'.

78 Interview, Amisi Soumialot, London, April 2016. The ICAP, founded in 1960, played a major role in cultural programmes and the welcoming of volunteers and solidarity groups from friendly countries. Playa Girón was the site of the attempted invasion by anti-Castro mercenaries in April 1961. Playa Larga is located in the Bay of Pigs (Bahía de Cochinos) on the south coast of Cuba, on the Caribbean Sea; it is part of the national ecological park on the Zapata Peninsula. Varadero is one of Cuba's major seaside resorts, situated on the north coast on the Atlantic Ocean.

79 Interview, Léopold Soumialot, London, February 2016.

80 Safi Soumialot, granddaughter of Gaston Soumialot, born in Cuba, of Cuban nationality, lives and works in Kinshasa.

81 Nadine Nkumu, granddaughter of Camille Nkumu. Born in Brazzaville, raised in Cuba, then settled in Congo-Brazzaville upon the return of her parents in the early 1990s. She lives and works in Brazzaville.

82 Interview, Yaile Ilanga, Havana, March 2017.

83 Located 4.76 kilometres apart, Kinshasa and Brazzaville are the closest capital cities in the world.

84 Los Amigos de Cuba created their association, ADIAC, on 6 July 2013.

85 During the funeral of Gaston Soumialot, in the spring of 2007, the presence of the Cuban ambassador to Kinshasa was particularly noticed.

[86] Interview, Amisi Soumialot, London, February 2016.

[87] 'DRC–Cuba: Cooperation Agreement for the Promotion of Sports,' Radio Okapi, 24 June 2016; 'End of the Official Visit of the Vice President of the State Council of Cuba in the DRC,' Congolese News Agency (ACP), 12 October 2016..

[88] The bilateral relations between the two countries have been marked by the official visit of Joseph Kabila to Havana in September 2011, then by the visit of the vice-president of the Council of State, Salvador Valdes Mesa, to Kinshasa in October 2016.

[89] Interview, Amisi Soumialot, London, February 2016.

[90] El-Tahri, 'Cuba: Une odyssée africaine.'

[91] Interview, Marcel Soumialot, Kinshasha, April 2017. 'To live at the day's rate' is an informal Congolese expression to describe the difficulty of daily survival in a 'dollarised' economy subject to the fluctuations of the Congolese franc.

REFERENCES

'África en una Isla cubana: 40 aniversario de la escuelas internacionalistas.' *Mesa Redonda*, 16 October 2017.

Baker, Patrick S. 'Mercenaries and the Congo Crisis.' *Saber and Scroll* 2, no. 1 (January 2013): 89–103.

Brook, Lisa. 'Back to the Future: African-Americans and Cuba in the Time(s) of Race.' *Contributions in Black Studies* 12 (1994): 9–32.

'De África a España, vía Cuba.' *El Pais*, 3 December 2008.

Dianteill, Erwan. 'Kongo à Cuba: Transformations d'une religion africaine.' *Archives de Sciences Sociales des Religions* 117 (2002): 59–80.

'DRC–Cuba: Cooperation Agreement for the Promotion of Sports.' Radio Okapi, 24 June 2016.

El-Tahri, Jihan. 'Cuba: Une odyssée africaine.' Artevideo, March 2012.

'End of the Official Visit of the Vice President of the State Council of Cuba in the DRC.' Congolese News Agency (ACP), 12 October 2016.

Ferrer, Ada. *Insurgent Cuba: Race, Nation and Revolution, 1868–1898*. Chapel Hill, NC: University of North Carolina Press, 1999.

Gálvez, William. *Le rêve africain du Che*. Brussels: EPO, 1998.

García Márquez, Gabriel. 'Cuba en Angola: Operación Carlota.' *Proceso*, 8 January 1977: 6–15.

George, Edward. *The Cuban Intervention in Angola, 1965–1991*. New York: Frank Cass, 2005.

Gérard-Libois, J. and J. van Lierde. *Congo 1964*. Brussels: C.R.I.S.P. and Léopoldville: I.N.E.P., 1965.

Gleijeses, Piero. *Conflicting Missions: Havana, Washington and Africa, 1959–1976*. Chapel Hill, NC: University of North Carolina Press, 2002.

Guevara, Ernesto. *Journal du Congo*. Paris: Mille et Une Nuits, 2009.

Hand, Maud. 'Papa Noel and Papi Oviedo, *Bana Congo*: Two Master Guitarists from Cuba and Congo: A Fluid and Welcome Treat.' BBC Music, 2002. www.bbc.co.uk/music/reviews.

Hansing, Katrin. *Freddy Ilanga: Che's Swahili Translator*. Icarus Films, 2009.

Jamfa Chiadjeu, Moïse Léonard. *Comment comprendre la 'crise' de l'État postcolonial en Afrique? Un essai d'explication structurelle à partir des cas de l'Angola, du Congo-*

Brazzaville, du Congo-Kinshasa, du Libéria et du Rwanda. Bern: Publications Universitaires Européennes, 2005.

Janssen, Jeroen and Hilde Baele. 'The Unlikely but True Story of the Rwandese Who Took Part in the African Expedition of Che Guevara.' Accessed 5 February 2020. https://drawingthetimes.com/story/the-unlikely-but-true-story-of-the-rwandese-who-took-part-in-the-african-expedition-of-che-guevara/.

'La odisea educativa de África en Cuba.' *El Mundo*, 13 December 2015.

Villafaña, Frank R. *Cold War in the Congo: The Confrontation of Cuban Military Forces, 1960–1967*. New Brunswick: Transaction Publishers, 2012.

PART III

VOICES

CHAPTER

7

Atlantic Voices: Imagination and sound dialogue between Congolese and Cuban singers in the 1950s

Charlotte Grabli

In 1990, Tropicana y Cubartista, a Cuban ensemble of seventy singers, musicians and dancers came to Kinshasa to pay tribute to Joseph Kabasele, the Congolese singer and bandleader of African Jazz. Several female and male singers performed Kabasele's hits, including Tabu Ley Rochereau's compositions 'Africa elati pili' and 'Kaji bolingo', singing the original version in Lingala and adapted lyrics in Spanish. The show also included a special tribute by Cuban singer Miriam Bayard entitled 'Matanga ya Kabasele'[1] – *matanga* denoting the Congolese celebration for the end of mourning. Why, then, did a Cuban dance troupe take part in an African tribute to one of the most famous singers of Congolese rumba?[2] Why did it seem significant to celebrate Kabasele and his African Jazz's musical work with Cuban artists singing in Lingala, Kinshasa's vernacular and musical language?[3] Part of the answer is that the reciprocal appropriation of languages by popular singers has been a recurrent feature of Cuban and Congolese popular music.

From an African perspective, compositions sung in Spanish reflected the diffusion of Cuban music as a global phenomenon reaching international audiences from the early twentieth century. However, the Tropicana ballet's performance in Lingala also demonstrates the acknowledgement of Congolese rumba as an 'Afro-Cuban'[4] creation arising from a transatlantic sound dialogue. In many ways, indeed,

Congolese music can be seen as the most beautiful outcome of musical cross-fertilisation between Cuba and Africa.[5] As Congolese rumba grew in popularity throughout much of the continent, it became one of the three major sources of musical influence in Africa, along with European and American music.[6] In Havana and Léopoldville (the colonial name of Kinshasa), the use of African languages and Spanish respectively in popular music represents an interesting case for the study of the historical formation of this 'sound dialogue.' By putting Congolese and Cuban musicians' experiences in perspective, one can better understand how sounds, music and languages shaped Afro-Atlantic musical imaginaries on the eve of independence in the Belgian Congo (30 June 1960). Here, Cuban music had a significant influence 'not only on the musical style of the country, but also onstage presentation, clothing, and even the artists' names'.[7]

Following the Brazilian samba fad,[8] the influence of Cuban records, which first reached Africa in the early 1930s, was a result of the increasing output of ethnic records by US labels, which sought to expand their markets overseas.[9] In particular, the success of one song – 'El manisero' (The peanut vendor) by Don Azpiazú and his Havana Casino Orchestra – prompted the music label RCA Victor to distribute throughout Africa its Latin American GV series, with over 200 titles of mostly Cuban *son* music.[10] By the 1940s, this musical genre 'had become the rage throughout much of Africa, even more so than in Europe and the USA, where the "*mambo* craze" was in full swing'.[11] Also known as 'South American music', Cuban records represented the most influential musical source of the time, along with *biguine* records from Brazzaville, the capital of neighbouring French Congo, where French Caribbean music was imported.

In this context, the dissemination of Spanish among Congolese musicians is worthy of study. In the colonial press and that of the *évolués* – the nascent African bourgeoisie – of the late 1950s, a wealth of articles dealt with this phenomenon and the Congolese quest for a musical identity. However, while Cuban artists' use of African languages such as Kikongo is well known,[12] African singers' use of Spanish has never been studied in a systematic way. The few studies dealing with the 'Latin' motifs that surfaced in African culture present them as 'an alternative modernity to the Europeanized models'.[13] More specifically, in late colonial Léopoldville, these motifs were seen 'as an alternative to a particular form of cosmopolitanism – Belgian colonialism – that was strict and stiff, if not cruel and in many ways anti-cosmopolitan'.[14] On the increasing use of Spanish in Senegal, Ibrahima Thioub significantly comments, 'Power in Senegal talked in French. The people talked back in Spanish.'[15] However, as Brian Larkin suggests, the study of global cultural flows 'within and between non-Western countries' cannot be reduced to a response to Western domination.[16]

By observing how Africans city-dwellers listened to Afro-Cuban music, 'we can trace the genealogies of a modern [African] sensibility'[17] beyond national cultural history. This approach can serve to illuminate how transcultural sounds shaped the 'live dialogue'[18] between Congolese and Afro-Cuban musicians and listeners.[19] In particular, Marcel Mauss's conception of the body allows us to explore the voice as the narrow space through which an essential part of the Atlantic imaginary is revealed.[20] My focus here is thus on 'the micro politics of emplaced, embodied, and voiced identity'.[21] In my understanding, the voice is the materiality and musicality of human vocal sound and not a metaphorical connotation of agency, as in the expression 'having a voice.'

How then did the global change of musical conditions determine the way early Cuban records were listened to within the 'colonial situation'?[22] Cuban records first reached Léopoldville in the early 1930s, while the invention of phonographic recording, public address systems and the expansion of radio created the conditions of what Murray Schafer calls 'schizophonia'. Referring to 'the split between an original sound and its electroacoustical transmission or reproduction', the concept of schizophonia reveals a key dimension of the changing sociality of vocal practice.[23] The 'illusion of seamless, unbroken spatial and temporal contiguity'[24] generated by acoustic reproduction has been critical for musical creation on both sides of the Atlantic. Schizophonia opened up new possibilities to fuel, express and merge two major aspects of the Atlantic imaginary: a pre-existing fascination with acoustic dislocations and re-spatialisation, and the desire to defy the material and symbolic separation engendered by slavery and sustained by colonisation.

STAGE NAMES OF AN IMAGINED AFRO-CUBAN COMMUNITY

Well before the actual encounter of African and Cuban musicians, artists from various parts of the continent expressed a sense of belonging to an imagined Afro-Cuban community. Just as insightful as songs, objects of popular and material cultures, artists' names suggest a shared perception of Cuba as a hub of Atlantic creativity.[25] In southern Africa, the Latin 'ballroom' dance craze as well as the diffusion of Mills Brothers records and Carmen Miranda films contributed to a perception of Cuba linked to US representations of tropical romance. Reflecting this, Miriam Makeba started to sing in the 1950s with a band called the Cuban Brothers.

Figure 7.1: Advertisement for *Week-End in Havana* with Carmen Miranda and Cesar Romero, film by Walter Lang, 1941. Source: Bibliothèque Nationale de France (BNF, Paris), the French National Library.

According to her autobiography, this name was a 'fantasy': 'no one is Cuban/none of us have even met a Cuban. From the movies, though, we know they look like Cesar Romero and Carmen Miranda.'[26]

Although these actors had starred in the film *Week-End in Havana* (1941), Miranda 'was born in Portugal, first became popular in Brazil, and then entered US popular culture in the context of the Good Neighbour Policy, and the US culture industry's interest in selling exoticism.'[27] As Arjun Appadurai points out, as more people saw their reality 'through the prisms of possible lives offered by the mass media', fantasy became 'a social practice; it entered, in a host of ways, into the fabrication of social lives.'[28]

Another kind of reference to Cuba could be found in West and Central Africa where audiences were attuned to Cuban sound. In these regions, musicians changed their name to sound more Spanish – in Sierra Leone, Gerald Pine adopted the name Geraldo Pino in the 1960s,[29] while in Belgian Congo the whole musical scene had been transformed in the 1950s: 'an Edward became Edo, a François became Franco, a Nicolas became Nico, and a Baloji became Baroza.'[30] The bands' names could also refer to a specific musical style, as in M'Bengwe et ses Cha-cha-cha Boys from

Dakar, one of the rare West African bands touring the Congo in 1957.[31] Although the reasons that led this Latin Senegalese band to visit the capital of Belgian Congo remain unclear, we know that the ensemble's horn section took this opportunity to record with the great guitarist and bandleader Franco Luambo Makiadi.[32] Thus, the Afro-Cuban imagined community was not merely the result of transatlantic circulations – it was also framed by the Pan-African acknowledgement and celebration of this new, emerging Africa that created its own map through sound organisation.

As the Latin imaginary and fantasy followed multiple trajectories on the continent in the late 1950s, Cuban musicians also renamed themselves to connect with this Afro-Atlantic community. In this respect, Arsenio Rodríguez's song 'Yo nací del Africa' (I was born of Africa), recorded in New York in 1960 for his LP *Cumbanchando con Arsenio: Fiesta en Harlem* (SMC-1074), is the most significant example.

Arsenio Rodríguez, a songwriter who was born in 1911 in Matanzas, one of the Cuban provinces with the largest slave populations, is known for having developed a critique of the Cuban discourse on African inferiority from the 1930s onwards.[33] Besides mastering the rhythms and instruments of his African heritage, such as the

Figure 7.2: *Cumbanchando con Arsenio* (SMC 1074), LP cover, 1960. Source: Bibliothèque Nationale de France (BNF, Paris), the French National Library.

Congo-derived drumming tradition known as *yuka*, he developed a new synthesis of the *son* 'by incorporating the inflections and syncopations characteristic of the ritual music of the Cuban *palo-monte* religion of Kongo origin'.[34] He created the *son montuno*, the basic template of both Congolese rumba and modern-day salsa. Enjoying great popularity as a bandleader and composer, he settled in New York in the mid-1950s and participated in symbolic events such as the 1969 Festival of American Folklife in Washington, DC, where his musical discourse resonated with Black Power activism and the civil rights movement.[35] Performing in a programme titled 'Black Music through Languages of the New World', he insisted on the Africanness of his compositions sung in Kikongo, the Bantu language his grandfather taught him, which is known for having contributed to the development of Cuban Spanish.[36]

This transnational and diasporic perspective on issues of Afro-Cuban identity clearly appears in the lyrics of 'Yo nací del Africa'. In 1960, the international popularity of Cuban *son* and the mass acceptance of certain forms of black music and dance by Cuban society did not imply greater social equality among Afro-Cubans themselves.[37] This made particularly significant Arsenio's rejection of his Spanish surname while praising his Congolese roots in his lyrics:

> Maybe I'm from Congo … Maybe I'm *Congo real* … I'm not a Rodríguez / I'm not a Travieso … Maybe I'm a Lumumba, maybe I'm a Kasavubu / I was born of Africa / Yes! Africa! I am from the Congo / You are my homeland / My beautiful homeland.[38]

In the early 1930s, Arsenio had first changed his stage name from Travieso ('naughty') to his mother's maiden name, Rodríguez. In the song of 1960 just quoted, he mentions two leaders of the Congo's independence movement, Lumumba and Kasavubu, as his possible real names, thus redeploying Congo as a modern entity. The recent political events in Congo appear alongside the Afro-Cuban resistance that Arsenio identified in the line 'Maybe I'm *Congo real*'. This was one of the mutual aid societies formed by slaves (*cabildos*) and based on a common language that allowed Cubans of Congo origin to preserve certain linguistic, cultural and religious traditions.[39] His song asserted that Afro-Cuban and Congolese people were facing a similar domination, a transnational view also expressed in 'Aquí como allá' (It's the same here as it is over there), a 1950 song that emphasised the shared black experience of segregation in Cuba and the US.[40] As 'Yo nací del Africa' served for the performance of an Afro-Atlantic identity, the act of renaming himself allowed Arsenio to reduce both temporal and geographical distance between Spanish and Belgian colonialism.

As the stage names quoted by the Cuban performer Benny Moré in his song 'Rumberos de ayer' illustrate, using Africanised names, whether 'inherited' or invented, was very common among Afro-Cubans.[41] In Cuba, such a sonic act was fostered by the fact that these musicians were direct descendants of African slaves – slavery was finally abolished in 1886 though the trade really ended in the 1870s. In the Belgian Congo, meanwhile, African musicians changed their names to express their belonging to an imagined Afro-Latin community. This African and Cuban act of renaming oneself helped to map a new cartography of the African and Afro-Cuban experience and to create symbolic possibilities of a transatlantic dialogue beyond the colonial situation.

SPANISH AND TRANSOCEANIC IMAGINATION IN CONGOLESE MUSIC

Like the act of renaming oneself, the increasing use of Spanish in popular music revealed the social reality of fantasy and imagination in Léopoldville.[42] In the 1950s Belgian Congo, the popularity of Latin tunes and Congolese compositions in Spanish broadcast and sold on records reached its height. This phenomenon can be explored by the notion of cover, a practice rarely analysed, probably because the study of African music has been influenced by the idea of authenticity. Yet, in respect of Congolese songs composed during the post-war 'golden age' of the covers, this notion is helpful in revealing embodied practices through which African covers not only echo a pre-existing tune, but also 'inhale one vision, exhale another'.[43]

Listening to Cuban singers in Léopoldville

Besides the African-influenced rhythm of Cuban *son*, which is often used to explain Congolese audiences' fondness for this music, the vocal field seems to have been dedicated to the exploration of the Atlantic imaginary. In the context of schizophonia, it is interesting to start with the seemingly anecdotal interpretation of the abbreviation GV inscribed on the first Cuban records played in Léopoldville. Listeners referred to this series as that of the *Grands Vocalistes* (great singers).[44]

The expression *Grands Vocalistes* indicates listeners' attention to singing and a perception of the body implied by or intuited from the Cuban voice – it supports Steven Connor's contention that 'there are no disembodied voices'.[45] As the physical sound of the voices in the GV series communicated 'the true, vital, and perceptible uniqueness of the one who emit[ted] it',[46] singing, more than the music itself, created an intimate connection with Cuban musicians. Moreover, the US phonographic industry's production of the series was bypassed to imply an immediate relation between Congolese listeners and Cuban singers.

The meaning of covers

At the same time, successive waves of Cuban and Latin music such as cha-cha-cha, calypso and mambo caused disarray among Congolese musicians in the mid-1950s.[47] Indeed, Kabasele and his African Jazz, who are now regarded as the creators of a Congolese equivalent of the Ghanaian high-life atmosphere, with its connotations of good living and sophistication,[48] at first struggled to cater for their audience's new musical taste.

As the double bass player Roitelet remembered: 'Not only that Cuban music had an influence upon us, it also fought against us. One brought out new records in Léopoldville and then people stopped dancing to our songs. Then we began to study and we managed to convince them … not by imitating them, but by adding new ways of playing.'[49] When Roitelet mentioned that his band had to 'study' Cuban records, he was referring to mimicry as a learning process. In another context, Walter Benjamin highlighted the significance of this conception: 'Only the copied text thus commands the soul of him who is occupied with it, whereas the mere

Figure 7.3: Joseph Kabasele (in the centre) and his African Jazz playing imported instruments. Source: Photographer unknown, in Lonoh Malangi and Michel Bokelenge (eds), *Hommage á Grand Kallé*, Kinshasa, Lokole (coll. Témoignages), 1985: 60.

reader never discovers the new aspects of his inner self that are opened by the text.'[50] Evidently, the idea of discovering one's inner self was central to the 1950s Congolese debates on musical identity.

As musicians sang along with records, they learned Spanish phonetically: in the 1950s, 'no one flinched upon hearing a series of OK Jazz songs sung in Spanish with titles such as *Es mi cumpleanos* and *Corre yo te llamo*'.[51] When the growing use of Spanish became an issue discussed in newspapers such as *Actualités Africaines* (African News), in 1958 a Congolese journalist published a 'Letter to a Musician Friend' about the pervasive presence of Latin music in the township's soundscape.[52] In his letter, ironically addressed to his dear 'Amigo Senorita de Canto Bayla', the journalist mentioned a show in the prestigious bar Air France in the *cité indigène* (native quarters). He recalled that, after having listened to 'a cocktail of montuno riffs entitled Bayla, Demi-Amor' (*sic*), he wondered if 'Congolese music was not in distress'. The journalist attested to local knowledge of Cuban music. In Congolese music, the influence of *son montuno* resulted in 'the emergence of a two-part song structure, [a] progression from a slow lyrical introduction to an improvised solo section which in Kinshasa is called *seben* or *chauffé*'. According to Bob White, this is one of the three formal aspects of Congolese music that reflect its proximity to Cuban music to this day.[53]

In the journalist's opinion, however, this proximity was the result of a confusion: 'you become unable to distinguish rhythms of our own country, rhythms proper to our temperament, from those of Tito Puente and Perez Prado'. This loss of identity could find its equivalent in the realm of language: 'what will happen to us if all of your fans suddenly decide to only express themselves in this incoherent Spanish that loudspeakers pour over the *cité*?' He observed that even the most educated songwriters mixed Lingala, Spanish and French in the same sentence. Musicians, he said, did not care anymore about the meaning of their songs – they were only fascinated by the magic of Spanish words.

Indeed, while other cultural contexts such as the 1930s Parisian dance venues (*les guinguettes*) produced similar adaptations of Cuban songs,[54] the Congolese taste for Spanish seemed to exceed its exotic appeal. In 1958, another article enthusiastically pointed out the primacy of Spanish sonority and emotion in listeners' perception: 'This magical, mysterious, language! Spanish, rich in musical melodies, a language with sonorous syllables, has captivated all our singers. All the latest musical hits, the latest successful records have Spanish as a theme and cha-cha-cha as a rhythm. Evidence of this is songs like "*Rossignol Cantador*" of the master José Rossignol, "*Primera*" of the clarinettist Essou, "*La Fiesta*" of the sorcerer Franco, and many others.'[55] This perception of the melodic quality of Spanish may have been enhanced by similarities between Lingala and Cuban Spanish, especially the presence of vowels at the end of words.

At the same time, criticism about the loss of meaning of the lyrics may be understood in relation to the social role that songs usually played in the everyday life of the *cité*.[56] While Congolese songs had become popular because of their engagement with the disjunctures of social change, Léopoldville's 'social' soundscape was altered by the growing number of songs which had nonsense lyrics, consisting of words that sounded like Spanish but meant nothing. However, by examining this soundscape through the prism of the voice, one can observe, following Greil Marcus, that in much popular music 'words are sounds we can feel before they are statements to understand'.[57] Indeed, Congolese songwriters elaborated a poetic approach in which 'the realm of sounds turns out to be the musical side of language, soliciting bodily pleasure'.[58]

Kabasele's version of Miguel Matamoros's '*El que siembra su maíz*' (He who sows his corn) is a good example. The original song was recorded in the US by RCA Victor and became Trío Matamoros' first hit in 1928 – 64 000 copies were sold in ninety days.[59] Kabasele's version added Lingala lyrics and retained only the Spanish title, itself part of the chorus. As Kabasele turns 'Huye', the interjection that opens the original song, into 'Ouh yes!', and then cheerfully performs the chorus, this version makes perceptible the pleasure of covering a song. Singing the chorus in Spanish, a language foreign to the Congo, could fuel this pleasure of 'singing otherness'. In an almost explicit illustration of this playful practice, the North American star Stevie Wonder sang in 1972: 'I speak very very fluent Spanish, *todo está bien chébere*, you understand what I mean? ¡*Chévere*!'[60] The song revolved around the Abakuá[61] term *chévere* (or *chébere*) commonly used by Afro-Cuban singers and popularised in the US through Cuban *son* and its derivatives.

As for the Lingala lyrics, Kabasele's cover was an adaptation rather than a translation. These mixed-language songs were produced at an early stage of the process of cultural appropriation, before a growing weariness set in.[62] Though the Cuban lyrics and Kabasele's adaptation are linked by themes of love and money, it is hard to say if Kabasele's aim was to reproduce the general mood of the original lyrics, given that these were the most recurrent themes of popular music.[63] There may be no commonality at all. The most significant aspect of this cover lies in the synthesis of Lingala lyrics and a Spanish chorus sung by a famous Congolese voice to a popular Cuban tune.

Musical address and listeners' emplacement

As these Cuban compositions grew in popularity, Spanish integrated the musicians' 'oneiric universe' and contributed to the circulation of a Lingala blended with

Spanish expressions beyond the musical scene.[64] As in post-war Ghanaian concert parties, the way Congolese rumba addressed its audience implicitly assigned to the public a certain relationship to musical experience through language. The listeners were identified not just as Lingala speakers but as 'citizens of a polyglot nation able to operate mixed codes'.[65] Although the notion of 'a polyglot nation' is inaccurate, the idea of an implicit assignation through mixed sound codes is helpful in understanding how the iconic properties of Spanish (and of African languages in Cuba) became central in listeners' experience of the Afro-Atlantic imagined community.

In his first recorded and most familiar song, 'Bruca maniguá' (1936), Arsenio Rodríguez artfully combined languages to express the historical legacy of maroonage. The lyrics freely alternate between Kikongo and Spanish to such an extent that the piece was only intelligible to those familiar with Afro-Cuban slang.[66] This combination relates to the *maniguá*, the bush, which speaks 'of a space of refuge and reconstruction for fugitives from slavery within Afro-diasporan structure of memory'.[67] Embracing the slave's perspective, the lyrics condemn the '*mundele*' – the 'white man' (or woman) in Kikongo and Lingala:

> *Yo son carabalí* [I am Carabalí] / *Negro de nación* [Black man of a nation] / *Sin libertad* [Without freedom] / *No pueo viví* [I cannot live] /*Mundele cabá* [White man finished off] / *Con mi corasón* [My heart] / *Tanto maltratá* [So mistreated] / *Cuerpo ta'fuirí eh* [They kill my body] / *Mundele cum bafiote* [The white man with his hostility] / *Siempre ta'nguara'cha* [He's always deceiving] / *Etá po mucho que lo ndinga* [He's saying many things I don't understand].[68]

According to Miller, although Arsenio was not of Calabari origin – the Abakuá society established in Cuba by Africans from old Calabar, in south-eastern Nigeria – he refers to 'the Calabari, legendary for their rebelliousness, to voice the desire of all black Cubans for self-determination'.[69] Like most of the songs recorded during the 1930s, 'Bruca maniguá' was not new music, but old music captured and disseminated by a new technology.[70] Arsenio used the new possibility the phonographic industry offered to amplify the significance of *afro-sones*, which served a dual purpose: 'to reach an international dancing public, and to communicate in codes with those Cubans whose sentiments are attuned to African-derived religions'.[71] According to the Abakuá construction of Cuba as a sacred land, the song does not, however, refer to Africa as the homeland – in this 'double performance' the reference to Abakuá represented a return 'toward the I, toward the Caribbean Self, intending...

to assume its marginality vis-à-vis the West and to speak of its Calibanesque Otherness'.[72]

That the *soneros* were able to simultaneously address local and international, Afro-Cuban and non-African audiences, was largely the result of the permeability between Cuban secular and ritual music and the 'easy oscillation between Abakuá chants and the rumba'.[73] Besides the broad circulation of African languages spoken by descendants of slaves, Lingala, the language of Congolese modern music, also crossed the Atlantic – in 1957, a Puerto Rican band did covers of Kabasele's most famous hits, 'Parafifi' and 'Ambiance'.[74] Although the uses of African languages in Caribbean music, and Spanish in Congolese rumba, came about through different social and cultural trajectories, this example shows that, in the late 1950s, both American and African musicians sang the 'Afro-Cuban otherness'. Listeners and dancers experienced alternative Afro-Atlantic identities in live sonic spaces that communicated across a transoceanic bridge.

The historical elaboration of this sound dialogue thus demonstrates how Cuban and Congolese singers constituted their worlds through the imagination of other place-times. They created what Michel Foucault calls the 'utopian body': 'they place the body into another space. They usher it into a place that does not take place in the world directly. They make of this body a fragment of imaginary space, which will communicate with the universe of divinities, or with the universe of the other.'[75] In the 1950s, however, even though utopian performances were already based on a mutual acknowledgement, the local form of Congolese rumba, emerging from among other expressive cultures of the black Atlantic, had to find its place within contemporary narratives of music and racial representations.

RUMBA GOES BLACK

As the journalist's 'Letter to a Musician Friend' illustrates, the colonial question of authenticity was crucial to Congolese debates about musical creation in the 1950s. Criticism of urban musicians referred not only to the disappearance of local traditions, but also to the essentialist view that all Africans were attuned to jazz. The idea that Latin music, and so Congolese modern music, did not match with the representation of blackness can be found as early as 1947 in colonial newspaper headlines such as 'About the Recording of Native Music: Where We Found Out that the Black Man Hates "Jazz"'.[76]

More significantly, the same criticism came from black musicians visiting the two Congos, such as the Martinican trumpeter and bandleader Hubert Pontat, who had been hired by the Belgian and French governments to train musicians in Léopoldville and Brazzaville. Commenting on the attraction of Franco and OK Jazz to Cuban music, Pontat pointed out the band's lack of musical technique and concluded that the Congolese did not enjoy jazz music because they were unable to understand it. He added, 'Fundamentally, they love it without knowing it. Because for the Black man, regardless of whether he is from the Caribbean, the United States or Africa, it is through jazz that he would best express his feelings.'[77]

Although jazz started to influence Cuban music as early as the 1920s,[78] the opposition of these two genres seems to fall partly into the Cold War cultural framework. Indeed, in the Cuban context, where the country faced a barrage of North American merchandise, *son* represented an important symbol of national identity and a 'weapon against [American] jazz'.[79] Conversely, in the late 1950s, the US considered jazz performances helpful in their offensive against communist influence in Africa – jazz musicians such as Louis Armstrong thus 'served as international "race artists" who performed at venues in Kenya, Ghana, Nigeria, the Congo, Morocco, and Tunisia from 1956 to 1960'.[80] As sound remained the 'master signifier of black creativity' and had not yet been 'supplanted by eyes and visuality',[81] Congolese used the same notion of blackness to cope with the difficulty of apprehending that various syncretic cultural formations might coexist in Africa.

In Léopoldville, where each successive wave of Latin and Caribbean music brought a new look and a new dance step,[82] this discourse could relate either to musical or dance practices. Indeed, in some ways, the compelling appeal of Latin dances appeared similar to the 'exotic dansomania' in Paris during the interwar years.[83] Unlike the French phenomenon, however, the learning process involved in each dance imported to the Congo implied a degree of subjectivisation and self-knowledge far from the notion of exoticism. For instance, as many comments on the introduction of the cha-cha-cha dance demonstrate, discussion of the local fondness for Cuban dance music reveals less an aestheticisation of distance than a process of identification. A journalist, for instance, evoked the African beauty of the cha-cha-cha dance (a variation of the *son*) while speculating on its cultural origins: 'This dance would have been invented by slaves. Because they were chained together, they were only able to move laterally or backward and forward. This explains why this dance is so appealing, especially to black people.'[84] While dancing and listening, Congolese audiences thus speculated about the origin of Afro-Cuban music to build an Afro-Atlantic memory and address their lack of historical knowledge. At the end of his article, the journalist added that cha-cha-cha dance strongly resembled the *sakata* round dance of the Budza, a people from the north of Congo. He emphasised the Africanness of Latin music, as did many others at the time, who pointed, for instance, to the confusing sameness of the Dominican *merengue* rhythms and those of Batetela songs from Bena Dibele, in the centre of the Belgian Congo.[85]

According to Richard Shain, such descriptions spoke of the aesthetic jolt involved in hearing familiar music in new contexts.[86] Despite the fact that cha-cha-cha dance and *merengue* rhythms were the product of toing and froing between both sides of the Atlantic, they were introduced as having originated from Congo, as artistic forms endemic to the region. In her study of *champeta*, an African-influenced musical genre, Elisabeth Cunin made a similar point about discourses referring to this music as a 'cultural renaissance' occurring in Cartagena, on the Colombian Caribbean coast. As 'the emphasis on filiation follows the path of racialisation', this discourse conflated cultural and biological strands to show that *champeta* fell into a racialised continuity.[87] As Congolese observers played with notions of original copy and original (Africa), they made a turnabout and presented the dance-learning process as a natural, almost necessary appropriation.

Usually associated with diasporic cultural formations,[88] this discourse claiming 'sameness' with the homeland was equally significant in Congolese representations of Cuban dance music. As with diasporic cultural formations dependent on heritage, the longevity of Congolese rumba lies in the recognition of social continuities across space and time.

The study of Cuban and Congolese musical scenes demonstrates how racialised and cultural identities are 'indexed and expressed in the intertwining of musical and verbal practices'.[89] Besides historical continuities between the African continent and the African diaspora, Congolese and Cuban singers emphasised a transatlantic Afro-Cuban community, exploring the new possibilities offered by the phonographic industry from the 1930s onwards. In Havana, in the US, and later in Congo, Cuban culture-bearers of Central African descent held onto musical and linguistic aspects of their cultural identity, not only in the context of (post) colonial society, but also to communicate with the emerging Afro-Cuban community in Congo. In Léopoldville, after the discovery of the Cuban *Grands Vocalistes*, the GV series, Congolese rumba voices made of the singers' body a fragment of imaginary space connected to the Afro-Latin world. From their audiences' perspective, Congolese musicians both conveyed and filtered Cuban sound, inaugurating a multi-voiced and pleasurable harmony, mixing Lingala and Spanish. This inventiveness resulted in the Congolese rumba's Pan-African appeal in Puerto Rico, in Cuba and throughout the larger part of the continent.

Although this popularity enhanced and re-established the social position of musicians such as Kabasele and African Jazz, Congolese rumba remained at odds with the representation of jazz as the master signifier of black creativity. In contrast, the Congolese discourses emerging in the late 1950s presented local music as an outcome of black Atlantic history, ensuring the legitimacy and longevity of the local scene through narratives emphasising slavery. Such narratives, along with embodied practices and travelling records, framed later encounters between Cuban and Congolese musicians, such as the 1990 tribute to Kabasele mentioned above, or Tabu Ley Rochereau's musical work, which received an award at the World Festival of Music in Varadero, Cuba, in 2008. Further research on Congolese musicians' tours in Cuba could be helpful in expanding the question of the social link between processes based on memory, aesthetic experience and embodiment.

NOTES

1 Mengi Massamba, personal communication. TV footage reporting on this event is available online: https://www.youtube.com/watch?v=oPGOFLxpuXM. See also Antoine Manda Tchebwa, *Terre de la chanson: La musique zaïroise, hier et aujourd'hui* (Louvain-la-Neuve: Duculot, 1996), 105.

2 'Rumba' was the generic label used by the US record industry for any Latin American music, including *son montuno*. Afro-Cuban rumba, which has had little impact in Africa, is a distinctly Cuban genre performed by singers and percussionists. According to Bob White, in Congo the term 'rumba' is associated with 'a particular style of dancing and a particular rhythm that was common in the early years of Congolese dance music (1940s–1960s), but it is also used as a generic term to refer to Congolese popular dance music in general, "*la rumba congolaise*"'. See Bob W. White, 'Congolese Rumba and Other Cosmopolitanisms,' *Cahiers d'Études Africaines* 168 (2002): 665.

3 The band chose the word 'Jazz' in agreement with the label owner to refer to 'the time of the gentlemen of American Jazz' even though their music had little to do with jazz; see Gary Stewart, *Rumba on the River: A History of the Popular Music of the Two Congos* (London: Verso, 2001), 45. This applies to another famous band of Congolese rumba that we mention below, Franco and OK Jazz.

4 The term 'Afro-Cuban' (*afrocubano*) was first coined by Fernando Ortiz in *Los negros brujos* (1906) to refer to the few thousands of Africans living in Cuba when writing his book. By extension, it came to refer to all Cubans of African descent. See Kali Argyriadis, 'Les batá deux fois sacrés: La construction de la tradition musicale et chorégraphique afro-cubaine,' *Civilisations* no. 53 (2006): 47.

5 Achille Mbembe, 'Variations on the Beautiful in the Congolese World of Sounds,' *Politique Africaine* 100, no. 4 (2005): 69–91.

6 Peter Manuel, *Popular Musics of the Non-Western World: An Introductory Survey* (Oxford: Oxford University Press, 1988), 86.

7 Kazadi wa Mukuna, 'Latin American Musical Influences in Zaire,' in *Garland Encyclopedia of World Music*, ed. Ruth M. Stone (New York: Garland, 1998), 387. On this influence on Congolese rumba, see also White, 'Congolese Rumba and Other Cosmopolitanisms'; and Isabela de Aranzadi, 'La rumba congoleña en el diálogo afroatlántico: Influencias caribeñas desde 1800,' *Methaodos: Revista de Ciencias Sociales* 4, no. 1 (2016): 100–18.

8 With the invention of the gramophone, a succession of black dance crazes, such as the 1920s Brazilian samba, struck Africa. Since then, and especially after 1945, there has been a continuous stream of black dance music styles to Africa. See John Collins, 'Jazz Feedback to Africa,' *American Music* 5, no. 2 (1987): 177.

9 Allan Sutton, *Recording the 'Thirties: The Evolution of the American Recording Industry, 1930–39* (Denver: Mainspring Press, 2011), 3.

10 Ivor Miller, 'A Secret Society Goes Public: The Relationship between Abakuá and Cuban Popular Culture,' *African Studies Review* 43, no. 1 (2000): 174; Richard M. Shain, 'Roots in Reverse: Cubanismo in Twentieth-Century Senegalese Music,' *International Journal of African Historical Studies* 35, no. 1 (2002): 87. RCA stands for Radio Corporation of America. As several interpretations of the abbreviation GV existed, I discuss the popular Congolese nickname '*Grand Vocaliste*' (great singer) below.

11 Manuel, *Popular Musics of the Non-Western World*, 87.

12 Most of the studies about African languages in Cuban music deal with the field of Afro-Cuban religious practices. See Maureen Warner-Lewis, *Central Africa in the Caribbean: Transcending Time, Transforming Cultures* (Kingston: University of the West Indies Press, 2003). See also the study of the renowned linguist Sergio Valdés-Bernal, *Lenguas africanas y el espanol de America* (Havana: Editorial de Ciencias Sociales, 2016). As a member of the scientific Cuban team sent to Angola in the 1980s (see Pablo Rodriguez's account in this volume), Valdés-Bernal was the first Cuban linguist to study Bantu languages in the African context; see also the pioneer work of Fernando Ortiz, *Los bailes y el teatro de los negros en el folklore de Cuba* (Madrid: Música Mundana Maqueda, 1998 [1951]); and *La africanía de la música folklórica de Cuba* (Madrid: Música Mundana Maqueda, 1998 [1950]); Lydia González-Huguet and Jean René Baudry, 'Voces "bantú" en el vocabulario "palero",' *Etnologia y Folklore* 3 (1967): 31–64; Lydia Cabrera, *Anagó: Vocabulario lucumí, el yoruba que se habla en Cuba* (Havana: Ediciones C.R., 1957).

13 Shain, 'Roots in Reverse,' 84. See also his recent book, *Roots in Reverse: Senegalese Afro-Cuban Music and Tropical Cosmopolitanism* (Middletown: Wesleyan University Press, 2018).

14 White, 'Congolese Rumba and Other Cosmopolitanisms,' 678.

15 Quoted by Shain, 'Roots in Reverse,' 91.

16 Brian Larkin, 'Indian Films and Nigerian Lovers: Media and the Creation of Parallel Modernities,' *Africa* 67 (1997): 407–8.

17 Shain, *Roots in Reverse*, xxi.

18 J. Lorand Matory, 'Afro-Atlantic Culture: On the Live Dialogue between Africa and the Americas,' in *Africana: The Encyclopedia of the African and African American Experience*, ed. Henry Louis Gates and Kwame Appiah, vol. 1 (New York: Basic Civitas Books), 36–44. For another take on this live dialogue between Malian and Cuban musicians during the Cold War period, see the chapter by Djebbari in this volume.

19 For a reflection on the aesthetics of sounds as a global phenomenon in the case of World music, see Veit Erlmann, 'The Aesthetics of the Global Imagination: Reflections on World Music in the 1990s,' *Public Culture*, no. 8 (1996): 468–9.

20 David Le Breton, 'Mauss et la naissance de la sociologie du corps,' *Revue du MAUSS* 36, no. 2 (2010): 371.

21 Steven Feld, Thomas Porcello, Aaron A. Fox and David Samuels, 'Vocal Anthropology: From the Music of Language to the Language of Song,' in *A Companion to Linguistic Anthropology*, ed. Alessandro Duranti (Malden, MA: Blackwell, 2006), 340.

[22] Georges Balandier, 'La situation coloniale: Approche théorique,' *Cahiers Internationaux de Sociologie* 110, no. 1 (2001): 9–29.

[23] In this chapter, I put aside Schafer's anxious view of the impact of technology. R. Murray Schafer, *The Tuning of the World* (New York: Knopf, 1977), 90.

[24] Steven Feld, 'From Schizophonia to Schismogenesis: The Discourses and Practices of World Music and World Beat,' in *Traffic in Culture: Refiguring Art and Anthropology*, ed. George E. Marcus and Fred R. Myers (Berkeley: University of California Press, 1995), 97–8.

[25] For a discussion of the importance of naming in the Congolese colonial experience, see Osumaka Likaka, *Naming Colonialism: History and Collective Memory in the Congo, 1870–1960 (Africa and the Diaspora)* (Madison: University of Wisconsin Press, 2009).

[26] Quoted by Carol A. Muller, *Focus: Music of South Africa* (New York: Routledge, 2008), 93.

[27] Thomas Turino, 'Are We Global Yet? Globalist Discourse, Cultural Formations and the Study of Zimbabwean Popular Music.' *British Journal of Ethnomusicology* 12, no. 2 (2003): 67.

[28] Arjun Appadurai, 'Global Ethnoscapes: Notes and Queries for a Transnational Anthropology,' in *Modernity at Large* (Minneapolis: University of Minnesota Press, 1996), 54.

[29] Naomi Ware, 'Popular Music and African Identity in Freetown, Sierra Leone,' in *Eight Urban Musical Cultures: Tradition and Change*, ed. Bruno Nettl (Urbana: University of Illinois Press, 1978), 303.

[30] Kazadi wa Mukuna, 'Latin American Musical Influences in Zaire,' 387.

[31] *Actualités Africaines*, 20 September 1957.

[32] Graeme Ewens, *Congo Colossus: The Life and Legacy of Franco and OK Jazz* (North Walsham: Buku Press, 1994), 80.

[33] David F. García, *Arsenio Rodríguez and the Transnational Flows of Latin Popular Music* (Philadelphia: Temple University Press, 2006), 20; Robin Moore, *Nationalizing Blackness: Afrocubanismo and Artistic Revolution in Havana,1920–1940* (Pittsburgh: University of Pittsburgh Press, 1997), 110; and Raúl A. Fernández, *From Afro-Cuban Rhythms to Latin Jazz* (Berkeley: University of California Press, 2006), 38–9.

[34] Fernandez, *From Afro-Cuban Rhythms to Latin Jazz*, 39.

[35] See García, *Arsenio Rodríguez and the Transnational Flows of Latin Popular Music*, 17.

[36] See Marlen A. Domínguez Hernández, *La lengua en Cuba: Estudios* (Santiago de Compostela: University of Santiago de Compostela, 2007), 44.

[37] Moore, *Nationalizing Blackness*, 2–7.

[38] 'Tal vez sea del Congo … Tal vez sea congo real … Yo no soy Rodríguez, yo no soy Travieso … Tal vez soy Lumumba, Tal vez soy Kazavubu/Yo nací del Africa/¡Sí! ¡Africa! … yo soy del Congo/tu eres mi tierra/mi tierra linda.' Partly translated in García, *Arsenio Rodríguez and the Transnational Flows of Latin Popular Music*, 12.

[39] Initially, the Spanish government had encouraged African slaves in urban areas to form these *cabildos*, or 'nations', according to their ethnic group. See Rafael Leo López Valdés, *Componentes africanos en el etnos cubano* (Havana: Editorial de Ciencias Sociales, 1985), 190.

[40] García, *Arsenio Rodríguez and the Transnational Flows of Latin Popular Music*, 23.

[41] Singer and songwriter Benny Moré (1919–63), the most revered star in Cuban musical history, also gave prominence to his Kongo family lineage and contributed to the acknowledgement and diffusion of Afro-Cuban musical forms. Robin Moore, *Music and Revolution: Cultural Change in Socialist Cuba* (Berkeley: University of California Press, 2006), 49–50; and Miller, 'A Secret Society Goes Public,' 170.

42 Appadurai, 'Global Ethnoscapes,' 53–4.

43 Nick Tosches, *Where Dead Voices Gather* (Boston; New York and London: Little, Brown and Company, 2009), 56.

44 For possible meanings of this title, see White, 'Congolese Rumba and Other Cosmopolitanisms,' 669.

45 Steven Connor, 'Panophonia,' Public Conference, Centre Pompidou: Paris, 22 February 2012, 1–2, accessed 22 May 2017, http://www.stevenconnor.com/panophonia/panophonia.pdf.

46 Adriana Cavarero, 'Multiple Voices,' in *The Sound Studies Reader*, ed. Jonathan Sterne (New York: Routledge, 2012), 523.

47 *Quinze*, 11 July 1957. All translations from English and Spanish are by the author.

48 Ewens, *Congo Colossus*, 75.

49 Interview with 'Roitelet' Augustin Moniania, Kinshasa, 19 July 2014. 'Brazzos' Armand Moango and 'Petit Pierre' Yantula, respectively the guitarist and the drummer, made a similar point in the interviews I conducted with them. See also Gary Stewart, *Rumba on the River*, 15.

50 Walter Benjamin, *One-Way Street*, trans. Edmund Jephcott (Cambridge, MA: Harvard University Press, 2016), 28.

51 White, 'Congolese Rumba and Other Cosmopolitanisms,' 673.

52 *Actualités Africaines*, 2 May 1958.

53 White, 'Congolese Rumba and Other Cosmopolitanisms,' 665.

54 Kali Argyriadis and Sara Le Menestrel, *Vivre la guinguette* (Paris: PUF, 2003), 136.

55 *Actualités Africaines*, 19 June 1958.

56 Sylvain Bemba, *Cinquante ans de musique du Congo-Zaïre (1920–1970): De Paul Kamba à Tabu-Ley* (Paris: Présence Africaine, 1984), 105.

57 Quoted by Gerry McGoldrick, 'From Annie Laurie to Lady Madonna: A Century of Cover Songs in Japan,' *Volume!* 7, no. 1 (2010): 158.

58 Cavarero, 'Multiple Voices,' 527.

59 Tabu Ley Rochereau, another prominent singer, also covered this Cuban song: Jean Mpisi, *Tabu Ley 'Rochereau': Innovateur de la musique africaine* (Paris: L'Harmattan, 2003), 43; Ned Sublette, *Cuba and Its Music: From the First Drums to the Mambo* (Chicago: Chicago Review Press, 2007), 367.

60 Stevie Wonder, 'Don't You Worry About a Thing,' Innervisions, Talma, 1973.

61 Abakuá is a Cuban mutual aid society for men founded in the nineteenth century to resist slavery. These secret societies are identified as black even though participation has long been racially inclusive and, as Ivor Miller demonstrates, their performances influenced nearly every genre of Cuban popular music. The word 'Abakuá' itself 'is apparently a Cuban creolised rendering of the Efik or Ejagham term Abakpa,' reported to be an Ekoi subgroup from the southern part of present-day Nigeria. See Ennis B. Edmonds and Michelle A. Gonzalez, *Caribbean Religious History: An Introduction* (New York and London: New York University Press, 2010), 107; and Miller, 'A Secret Society Goes Public.'

62 McGoldrick, 'From Annie Laurie to Lady Madonna,' 136–64. After mastering the Cuban style in the early 1960s, Senegalese musicians also proceeded to sing in Wolof, one of Senegal's major languages. As Shain observes, however, the fact that musical groups such as the Star band were singing in Cuban lyrics in their original form 'struck the Dakar public as a great advance in the nation's cultural development.' See *Roots in Reverse*, 61.

63 See Joseph Trapido, 'Love and Money in Kinois Popular Music,' *Journal of African Cultural Studies* 22, no. 2 (2010): 121–44. See also Charles Didier Gondola, 'Popular

Music, Urban Society, and Changing Gender Relations in Kinshasa, Zaire (1950–1990),' in *Gendered Encounters: Challenging Cultural Boundaries and Social Hierarchies in Africa*, ed. Maria Grosz-Ngate and Omari Kokole (New York: Routledge, 2014), 65–84.

64 Bemba, *Cinquante ans de musique du Congo-Zaïre (1920–1970)*, 108.

65 Karin Barber,'Preliminary Notes on Audiences in Africa.' *Africa* 67, no. 3 (1997): 354.

66 Moore, *Nationalizing Blackness*, 110.

67 Jerome C. Branche, *The Poetics and Politics of Diaspora: Transatlantic Musings* (New York: Routledge, 2014), 70. The word *maniguá* first appeared in Esteban Pichardo's *Diccionario provincial de voces cubanas* in 1836. Nowadays, Cuban musicians use 'Bruca maniguá!' or 'Bruca!' in tribute to Arsenio, as an interjection during their performance (Kali Argyriadis, personal communication).

68 Translated by García, *Arsenio Rodríguez and the Transnational Flows of Latin Popular Music*, 20.

69 Miller, 'A Secret Society Goes Public,' 170.

70 On this point, see Michael Denning, *Noise Uprising: The Audiopolitics of a World Musical Revolution* (London: Verso, 2015).

71 Miller, 'A Secret Society Goes Public,' 172.

72 Antonio Benitez-Rojo, *The Repeating Island: The Caribbean and the Postmodern Perspective* (Durham, NC, and London: Duke University Press, 1997), 210.

73 Miller, 'A Secret Society Goes Public,' 174.

74 *Actualités Africaines*, 7 February 1957.

75 Michel Foucault, 'Utopian Body,' in *Sensorium: Embodied Experience, Technology, and Contemporary Art*, ed. Caroline A. Jones (Cambridge, MA: MIT Press, 2006), 232–1.

76 *Le Courrier d'Afrique*, 14 October 1947.

77 *Quinze*, 26 July 1957.

78 Kali Argyriadis, 'Les batá deux fois sacré,' 49.

79 Moore, *Nationalizing Blackness*, 105.

80 Karen B. Bell, 'Developing a "Sense of Community": U.S. Cultural Diplomacy and the Place of Africa during the Early Cold War Period, 1953–64,' in *The United States and West Africa Interactions and Relations*, ed. Alusine Jalloh and Toyin Falola (Rochester, NY: Boydell and Brewer, 2008), 139. See also Penny M. von Eschen, *Satchmo Blows Up the World: Jazz Ambassadors Play the Cold War* (Cambridge, MA: Harvard University Press, 2009).

81 Paul Gilroy, '". . .To Be Real": The Dissident Forms of Black Expressive Culture,' in *Let's Get It On: The Politics of Black Performance*, ed. Catherine Ugwu (London: ICA, 1995), 29.

82 White, 'Congolese Rumba and Other Cosmopolitanisms,' 673.

83 Anne Décoret-Ahiha, *Les danses exotiques en France: 1880–1940* (Pantin: Centre National de la Danse, 2004), 63–75.

84 *Actualités Africaines*, 5 June 1958.

85 *Quinze*, 11 July 1957.

86 Shain, 'Roots in Reverse,' 91.

87 Élisabeth Cunin, 'De Kinshasa à Cartagena, en passant par Paris: Itinéraires d'une "musique noire", la champeta,' *Civilisations* 53 (2005): 105.

88 Cunin, 'De Kinshasa à Cartagena, en passant par Paris,' 105.

89 Feld, Porcello, Fox and Samuels, 'Vocal Anthropology: From the Music of Language to the Language of Song,' 340.

REFERENCES

Appadurai, Arjun. 'Global Ethnoscapes: Notes and Queries for a Transnational Anthropology.' In *Modernity at Large: Cultural Dimensions of Globalization*, 48–65. Minneapolis: University of Minnesota Press, 1996.

Aranzadi, Isabela de. 'La rumba congoleña en el diálogo afro-atlántico: Influencias caribeñas desde 1800.' *Methaodos: Revista de Ciencias Sociales* 4, no. 1 (2016): 100–18.

Argyriadis, Kali. 'Les batá deux fois sacrés: La construction de la tradition musicale et chorégraphique afro-cubaine.' *Civilisations*, no. 53 (2006): 45–74.

Argyriadis, Kali and Sara Le Menestrel. *Vivre la guinguette*. Paris: PUF, 2003.

Balandier, Georges. 'La situation coloniale: Approche théorique.' *Cahiers Internationaux de Sociologie* 110, no. 1 (2001): 9–29.

Barber, Karin. 'Preliminary Notes on Audiences in Africa.' *Africa* 67, no. 3 (1997): 347–62.

Bell, Karen B. 'Developing a "Sense of Community": U.S. Cultural Diplomacy and the Place of Africa during the Early Cold War Period, 1953–64.' In *The United States and West Africa: Interactions and Relations*, edited by Alusine Jalloh and Toyin Falola, 125–46. Rochester, NY: Boydell and Brewer, 2008.

Bemba, Sylvain. *Cinquante ans de musique du Congo-Zaïre (1920–1970): De Paul Kamba à Tabu-Ley*. Paris: Présence Africaine, 1984.

Benitez-Rojo, Antonio. *The Repeating Island: The Caribbean and the Postmodern Perspective*. Durham, NC, and London: Duke University Press, 1997.

Benjamin, Walter. *One-Way Street*. Translated by Edmund Jephcott. Cambridge, MA: Harvard University Press, 2016.

Branche, Jerome C. *The Poetics and Politics of Diaspora: Transatlantic Musings*. New York: Routledge, 2014.

Cabrera, Lydia. *Anagó: Vocabulario lucumí, el yoruba que se habla en Cuba*. Havana: Ediciones C.R., 1957.

Cavarero, Adriana. 'Multiple Voices.' In *The Sound Studies Reader*, edited by Jonathan Sterne, 520–32. New York: Routledge, 2012.

Collins, John. 'Jazz Feedback to Africa.' *American Music* 5, no. 2 (1987): 176–93.

Connor, Steven. 'Panophonia.' Public Conference, Centre Pompidou: Paris, 22 February 2012. Accessed 22 May 2017. http://www.stevenconnor.com/panophonia/panophonia.pdf.

Cunin, Élisabeth. 'De Kinshasa à Cartagena, en passant par Paris: Itinéraires d'une "musique noire", la champeta.' *Civilisations* 53 (2005): 97–117.

Décoret-Ahiha, Anne. *Les danses exotiques en France: 1880–1940*. Pantin: Centre National de la Danse, 2004.

Denning, Michael. *Noise Uprising: The Audiopolitics of a World Musical Revolution*. London: Verso, 2015.

Domínguez Hernández, Marlen A. *La lengua en Cuba: Estudios*. Santiago de Compostela: University of Santiago de Compostela, 2007.

Edmonds, Ennis B. and Michelle A. Gonzalez. *Caribbean Religious History: An Introduction*. New York and London: New York University Press, 2010.

Erlmann, Veit. 'The Aesthetics of the Global Imagination: Reflections on World Music in the 1990s.' *Public Culture*, no. 8 (1996): 467–87.

Eschen, Penny M. von. *Satchmo Blows Up the World: Jazz Ambassadors Play the Cold War*. Cambridge, MA: Harvard University Press, 2009.

Ewens, Graeme. *Congo Colossus: The Life and Legacy of Franco and OK Jazz*. North Walsham: Buku Press, 1994.

Feld, Steven. 'From Schizophonia to Schismogenesis: The Discourses and Practices of World Music and World Beat.' In *Traffic in Culture: Refiguring Art and Anthropology*, edited by George E. Marcus and Fred R. Myers, 96–126. Berkeley: University of California Press, 1995.

Feld, Steven, Thomas Porcello, Aaron A. Fox and David Samuels. 'Vocal Anthropology: From the Music of Language to the Language of Song.' In *A Companion to Linguistic Anthropology*, edited by Alessandro Duranti, 321–46. Malden, MA: Blackwell, 2006.

Fernández, Raúl A. *From Afro-Cuban Rhythms to Latin Jazz*. Berkeley: University of California Press, 2006.

Foucault, Michel. 'Utopian Body.' In *Sensorium: Embodied Experience, Technology, and Contemporary Art*, edited by Caroline A. Jones, 229–34. Cambridge, MA: MIT Press, 2006.

García, David F. *Arsenio Rodríguez and the Transnational Flows of Latin Popular Music*. Philadelphia: Temple University Press, 2006.

Gilroy, Paul. '"...To Be Real": The Dissident Forms of Black Expressive Culture.' In *Let's Get It On: The Politics of Black Performance*, edited by Catherine Ugwu, 12–33. London: ICA, 1995.

Gondola, Charles Didier. 'Popular Music, Urban Society, and Changing Gender Relations in Kinshasa, Zaire (1950–1990).' In *Gendered Encounters: Challenging Cultural Boundaries and Social Hierarchies in Africa*, edited by Maria Grosz-Ngate and Omari Kokole, 65–84. New York: Routledge, 2014.

González-Huguet, Lydia and Jean René Baudry. 'Voces "bantú" en el vocabulario "palero".' *Etnologia y Folklore* 3 (1967): 31–64.

Larkin, Brian. 'Indian Films and Nigerian Lovers: Media and the Creation of Parallel Modernities.' *Africa* 67 (1997): 406–40.

Le Breton, David. 'Mauss et la naissance de la sociologie du corps.' *Revue du MAUSS* 36, no. 2 (2010): 371–84.

Likaka, Osumaka. *Naming Colonialism: History and Collective Memory in the Congo, 1870–1960 (Africa and the Diaspora)*. Madison: University of Wisconsin Press, 2009.

López Valdés, Rafael Leo. *Componentes africanos en el etnos cubano*. Havana: Editorial de Ciencias Sociales, 1985.

Manuel, Peter. *Popular Musics of the Non-Western World: An Introductory Survey*. Oxford: Oxford University Press, 1988.

Matory, J. Lorand. 'Afro-Atlantic Culture: On the Live Dialogue between Africa and the Americas.' In *Africana: The Encyclopedia of the African and African American Experience*, edited by Henry Louis Gates and Kwame Appiah, vol. 1, 36–44. New York: Basic Civitas Books.

Mbembe, Achille. 'Variations on the Beautiful in the Congolese World of Sounds.' *Politique Africaine* 100, no. 4 (2005): 69–91.

McGoldrick, Gerry. 'From Annie Laurie to Lady Madonna: A Century of Cover Songs in Japan.' *Volume!* 7, no. 1 (2010): 136–64.

Miller, Ivor. 'A Secret Society Goes Public: The Relationship between Abakuá and Cuban Popular Culture.' *African Studies Review* 43, no. 1 (2000): 161–88.

Moore, Robin. *Music and Revolution: Cultural Change in Socialist Cuba*. Berkeley: University of California Press, 2006.
Moore, Robin. *Nationalizing Blackness: Afrocubanismo and Artistic Revolution in Havana, 1920–1940*. Pittsburgh: University of Pittsburgh Press, 1997.
Mpisi, Jean. *Tabu Ley 'Rochereau': Innovateur de la musique africaine*. Paris: L'Harmattan, 2003.
Mukuna, Kazadi wa. 'Latin American Musical Influences in Zaire.' In *Garland Encyclopedia of World Music*, ed. Ruth M. Stone. New York: Garland, 1998.
Muller, Carol A. *Focus: Music of South Africa*. New York: Routledge, 2008.
Ortiz, Fernando. *La africanía de la música folklórica de Cuba*. Madrid: Música Mundana Maqueda, 1998 [1950].
Ortiz, Fernando. *Los bailes y el teatro de los negros en el folklore de Cuba*. Madrid: Música Mundana Maqueda, 1998 [1951].
Schafer, R. Murray. *The Tuning of the World*. New York: Knopf, 1977.
Shain, Richard. 'Roots in Reverse: Cubanismo in Twentieth-Century Senegalese Music.' *International Journal of African Historical Studies* 35, no. 1 (2002): 83–101.
Shain, Richard. *Roots in Reverse: Senegalese Afro-Cuban Music and Tropical Cosmopolitanism*. Middletown: Wesleyan University Press, 2018.
Stewart, Gary. *Rumba on the River: A History of the Popular Music of the Two Congos*. London: Verso, 2001.
Sublette, Ned. *Cuba and Its Music: From the First Drums to the Mambo*. Chicago: Chicago Review Press, 2007.
Sutton, Allan. *Recording the 'Thirties: The Evolution of the American Recording Industry, 1930–39*. Denver: Mainspring Press, 2011.
Tchebwa, Antoine Manda. *Terre de la chanson: La musique zaïroise, hier et aujourd'hui*. Louvain-la-Neuve: Duculot, 1996.
Tosches, Nick. *Where Dead Voices Gather*. Boston, New York and London: Little, Brown and Company, 2009.
Trapido, Joseph. 'Love and Money in Kinois Popular Music.' *Journal of African Cultural Studies* 22, no. 2 (2010): 121–44.
Turino, Thomas. 'Are We Global Yet? Globalist Discourse, Cultural Formations and the Study of Zimbabwean Popular Music.' *British Journal of Ethnomusicology* 12, no. 2 (2003): 51–79.
Valdés-Bernal, Sergio. *Lenguas africanas y el espanol de America*. Havana: Editorial de Ciencias Sociales, 2016.
Ware, Naomi. 'Popular Music and African Identity in Freetown, Sierra Leone.' In *Eight Urban Musical Cultures: Tradition and Change*, edited by Bruno Nettl, 296–320. Urbana: University of Illinois Press, 1978.
Warner-Lewis, Maureen. *Central Africa in the Caribbean: Transcending Time, Transforming Cultures*. Kingston: University of the West Indies Press, 2003.
White, Bob W. 'Congolese Rumba and Other Cosmopolitanisms.' *Cahiers d'Études Africaines* 168 (2002): 663–86.

CHAPTER

8

Cultural Diplomacy in the Cold War: Musical dialogues between Cuba and West Africa, 1960–1970

Elina Djebbari

One Saturday evening in January 2015 in Cotonou, Benin, the Malian musician Boncana Maïga arrived on the stage at the grand finale of the second Benin International Salsa Festival.[1] After words of praise from the festival organisers to introduce their guest of honour to the audience, Maïga ceremoniously displayed the transverse flute he was about to play. He accompanied the gesture with an account explaining that this very flute was presented to him as a gift by the Cuban government during his music studies in Havana in the mid-1960s. By making the flute the symbol of his high-level musical training that led him to developing a successful international career, the Malian musician showed how much he had benefited from the cultural exchanges established between Mali and Cuba in the context of a post-colonial diplomatic rapprochement. Moreover, the eloquent gesture of showing off the flute and the accompanying words indicated not only how much this experience had shaped him as an accomplished musician but that it was also still very vivid in his memory more than fifty years later.

The intertwinement of the musician's personal journey and the political interests fostered during the Cold War era between Cuba and Mali features at the core of this chapter. It explores the political, musical and interpersonal relationships revealed by the criss-crossing of Malian and Cuban musicians across the postcolonial Atlantic.

It therefore sheds light on the cultural exchanges initiated between Cuba and newly independent African countries throughout the 1960s and 1970s.

During the Cold War, numerous African countries adopted a socialist policy at their independence in the 1960s. This was the case of the Republic of Mali, which became independent from France on 22 September 1960. Such anti-imperialist positioning led to the development of privileged relationships with other socialist countries worldwide. In addition to offering an ideological and political model opposed to Western imperialism, these new economic and political partnerships also took the form of cultural exchanges. USSR, China, North Korea and Cuba became Mali's main partners in the realm of culture. The cultural exchanges consisted mainly of sending Malian students and civil servants abroad for training; building cultural infrastructure; organising cultural events; and reciprocally facilitating tours of national artistic ensembles.[2] For instance, Malian choreographers were sent to Moscow, youth managers to China and North Korea, while musicians were trained in Cuba.

In the context of the new political alliances fostered during the Cold War (such as the Non-Aligned Movement), Cuba developed a foreign cultural policy towards African countries. Within this framework, Cuba signed several cultural conventions with different African countries: with Egypt and Guinea in 1960; with Ghana, Mali and Algeria in 1964; and with the Democratic Republic of Congo, Sierra Leone and Tanzania in 1974.[3] The Mali–Cuba cultural convention signed on 14 January 1964 stipulated that one of its purposes was to 'develop the cultural relations in the realm of science, culture and art between the two countries in the interest of strengthening the friendship and mutual comprehension between Cuban and Malian people'.[4]

MUSIC, DECOLONISATION AND CULTURAL DIPLOMACY IN THE COLD WAR

Cultural diplomacy is conceived of as a means of 'soft power', that is a way to establish and sustain the influence of a given political, social and cultural model abroad.[5] In the era of the Cold War, cultural outreach was seen as an index of state power and prosperity. As Lisa Davenport puts it, 'culture itself became a measure of a nation's wealth and power'. [6] Many cultural initiatives became the forum where such issues were conveyed under the guise of a debate of ideas. The Congress for Cultural Freedom, largely supported covertly by the CIA from 1950 onwards, is an example of the way artists and intellectuals were brought to take a stand against Soviet communism in the name of culture and freedom of thought.[7] The Congress had more than 30 branches all over the world and was particularly active in Western Europe and the Americas.[8] In another example, the Congress of Black Writers and Artists held in Paris in 1956 was seen as an intellectual follow-up to the Bandung Conference of 1955, that is, a means for Non-Aligned Movement stakeholders to be active as well at the cultural level in order to support their political positioning. Although the issues at stake regarding the cultural Cold War have been addressed by scholars in the case of Europe, North and Latin America, their implications for Africa remain to be fully investigated.[9]

The African continent was indeed a field where Cold War tensions arose, especially in the situation of decolonisation struggles.[10] Several bilateral cultural conventions were signed at the time between African countries and socialist countries elsewhere: the USSR with Egypt in 1957 for example; and Cuba with a number of West African countries.[11] Based on political alliances established through the Non-Aligned Movement and the Tricontinental conference held in Cuba in 1966, these cultural partnerships with African countries sustained anti-imperialist ideologies and intellectual movements in the context of the Cold War. The major Pan-African festivals of the 1960s and 1970s (Dakar 1966, Algiers 1969, Kinshasa 1974, Lagos 1977) formed diplomatic spaces where a symbolic staging of Cold War political rivalries and alliances could be performed.[12]

In the field of cultural diplomacy, music and musicians have been involved in many diplomatic strategies aimed at developing foreign policies and international relations over different periods of time and between various stakeholders.[13] A wealth of scholarly works have investigated, for instance, the US State Department's cultural diplomacy during the Cold War, showing the key role of music, and especially jazz, in these international exchanges.[14] However, the musical exchanges developed between Cuba and Africa as well as, more broadly, Cuba's involvement in Africa at the level of cultural diplomatic exchanges have not yet been explored at length. With regard to music, such programmes involved sending Cuban artists abroad as well as welcoming foreign artists and productions in Cuba. Interestingly, the development of cultural relations with foreign countries featured as an important point addressed at the first National Congress of Culture held in Havana in 1962:

> Todo espectáculo de artistas extranjeros será programación de especial atención para los organismos de masa y deberán lograrse llenos totales en esos presentaciones, tanto por el valor político de esa conducta como por el alto valor cultural y artístico que representa para nuestra masa, el contacto con los mejores artistas del extranjero, antiguo privilegio de la burguesía.[15]
>
> [Every show by foreign artists will be a programme of special attention for mass organisations and they will have to be fully present on those occasions,

> both for the political value of that behaviour and for the high cultural and artistic value that represents for our mass the contact with the best artists from abroad, a former privilege of the bourgeoisie.]

This statement acknowledged both the 'political' and 'cultural and artistic' values that were attached to the welcoming of foreign artists in Cuba. It also presented their shows as a way to reclaim a 'former privilege of the bourgeoisie'. Communist and anti-imperialist ideologies thus blended together to provide the masses with access to culture and art.

In cultural exchanges with Africa, Cuban political leaders drew on the history of the slave trade to enhance and legitimate the new political relationships with African countries. In various speeches and writings, Fidel Castro referred to the contribution of Africans to Cuban culture and to the sharing of 'common blood'.[16] As Hauke Dorsch comments on the education programmes established between Cuba and Mozambique, 'ideas of an Afro-Atlantic connection' informed them.[17] The reference to a shared history was an important trope in postcolonial cultural diplomacy between Cuba and Africa.

Independently of these formal initiatives, Cuban music had already come to play a key role in cultural decolonisation in Africa. In 1960s Mali, rock, jazz, twist and Cuban music were the main sounds to which people danced in urban nightclubs.[18] Music dance styles from the New World were so popular that 'Latin American music came to be the soundtrack of the independence era'.[19] Cuban music was already well established all over the continent during the era of colonisation. Its spread was particularly facilitated in the 1930s and 1940s with the arrival of the GV series of 78rpm records that mainly brought Cuban *son* and *son montuno* to African ears (see Grabli in this volume).[20] Cuban music considerably influenced the creation of many genres of modern African popular music, of which Congolese rumba is certainly the most renowned example.[21] What the diplomatic exchanges fostered with Cuba did was to increase the popularity of Cuban music within the framework of processes of cultural decolonisation.

At a time of African independence and Cold War rivalry, Cuban music was deemed to be both modern and capable of offering a musical alternative to the Western music dance styles. It also accompanied a cosmopolitan lifestyle and social behaviour that appealed to the African urban youth.[22] As Richard Shain remarks about the success of Cuban music in Senegal, 'Cuban music provided a progressive alternative to both traditional African music and the hegemonic culture of the colonizers', by 'enacting an alternative modernity to the Europeanized models so prevalent in post-war Senegal'.[23]

Moreover, this music was not considered foreign but rather as a genre repatriated after centuries of slavery and colonisation, a development Shain identifies as 'roots in reverse'.[24] Numerous African musicians and dancers shared this assumption.[25] Ato Quayson noticed how Ghanaian *salseros* in Accra 'feel salsa is a return back home of something that was taken away from its source in the course of slavery'.[26] Because of this, Cuban music could be included in the nationalist ideologies of the independence era. As Bob White points out, 'the success of Afro-Cuban music was due in part to this structural ambiguity, which made it possible to function as a torch of authenticity for some and as a marker of cosmopolitan modernity for others'.[27] Indeed, this 'musical cosmopolitanism' did not prevent the construction of postcolonial Africa's national identities.[28] Cuban sounds and instruments were actually incorporated into the repertoires played by national 'modern orchestras' that flourished all over the continent.[29] For newly independent African countries where strong cultural policies were established to support the nation-building process, the emphasis on 'traditional' and local music dance practices could at the same time accommodate Cuban music as the marker of an aspirational cosmopolitan modernity.

FROM MALI TO CUBA: LAS MARAVILLAS DE MALI IN HAVANA

As part of the cultural convention signed between Cuba and Mali in 1964, ten Malian students received scholarships to study music in Havana. The Malian state also wanted to constitute a corps of music professionals to serve the nascent artistic institutions of the new nation.[30] The young Malians spent about ten years in Havana, from the mid-1960s to the beginning of the 1970s, studying music at the Conservatorio Alejandro García Caturla after having learned Spanish. During the course of their studies, they created a band called Las Maravillas de Mali in 1965 and recorded a disc at EGREM (Musical Recording and Publishing Company) studio in 1967.[31]

Their music met with success in Cuba and in Africa, and their most famous song is 'Chez Fatimata'. Las Maravillas de Mali's eponymous album shows how they adopted the format of the *charanga* to play different kinds of Cuban music, from *guajira* to *bolero* via *danzón* and *chachachá*.[32] The famous Cuban Orquesta Aragón was a major influence on their musical style. In an interview held in Cotonou, where I met the former Maravillas leader, Boncana Maïga, in February 2015, the only surviving member of the band acknowledged how much the Cuban orchestra had influenced their style:

> J'étais à Cuba, on arrive, on allume la télé un dimanche. Le premier orchestre qu'on voit c'est l'orchestre Aragón. On découvrait comme ça à la télévision Aragón. J'ai vu la flûte [he mimics the flute playing]. C'est là, c'est là que j'ai choisi, c'est ça qui m'a séduit, Richard Eguës, le flûtiste de l'orchestre Aragón. J'ai vu, j'ai dit 'c'est la Aragón, je veux faire la flûte,' c'est comme ça. Et on a eu l'idée de faire la charanga [he mimics the violin playing]. Vous écoutez Maravillas de Mali, vous allez jurer que vous écoutez l'orchestre Aragón. Parce que je les ai trop copiés, je les ai trop imités, à ma façon, avec les violons et tout, c'est presque comme Aragón.[33]
>
> [I was in Cuba, we arrive, we turn on the TV on a Sunday. The first orchestra we see is the Aragón orchestra. We were like that discovering Aragón on TV. I saw the flute [he mimics the flute playing]. That was it, I chose at that moment, it was what seduced me, Richard Eguës, the flautist of Aragón orchestra. I saw, I said 'this is Aragón, I want to play the flute', it was like that. And we got the idea to do the *charanga* [he mimics the violin playing]. You listen to Maravillas de Mali, you will swear that you are listening to Aragón orchestra. Because I copied them so much, I mimicked them so much, in my own way, with the violins and all, it is almost like Aragón.]

Orquesta Aragón, whose music was already very popular in Africa, inspired the creation of the Malian *charanga* in Havana. Aragón's musicians advised their Malian counterparts about ways of playing Cuban music during their studies.[34] In addition to the musical interactions, the two orchestras also fostered personal relationships between the musicians that were to continue on both sides of the Atlantic over several decades.[35]

Notwithstanding Orquesta Aragón's influence on Maravillas de Mali's album, the Malian musicians managed to Africanise or even 'Malianise' their music through the themes addressed in the songs as well as the languages they used: they sang not only in Spanish but also in French and Bambara (*bamanan kan*), the Malian national language. For instance, 'Chez Fatimata', sung in French, evokes the nightlife of the urban African youth; 'Soubalé' recounts part of the epic of Sundiata Keïta, the founder of the Empire of Mali in the thirteenth century; 'Lumumba' celebrates Patrice Lumumba's fight for the independence of Congo from Belgian rule; 'Africa mia', in Spanish, is a Pan-Africanist ode that reflects the intellectual currents of the independence era.[36] Moreover, the lyrics of the last-mentioned song are particularly telling, in a subtle way, of the encounter with the Cubans that the Malian musicians experienced:

África
África mía
Que bella te sueño
Tierra de ensueño
Y melancolía
África mía

Tu embrujo sentimental
Tu nombre es mi ideal
Yo soy africano
No tengo rival
Y tengo mi hermano que me trata igual /
Y tengo mi hermano si me trata igual

¡Oye mi hermano, trátame igual!
Sí, sí, sí, me trata igual (x 3)

[Africa
My Africa
How beautiful I dream you
Land of dreams
And melancholy
My Africa

Your sentimental spell
Your name is my ideal
I am African
I have no rival
And I have my brother who treats me the same /
And I have my brother if he treats me the same

Hey, my brother, treat me the same!
Yes yes yes, he treats me the same (x 3)]

Interestingly, the lyrics signal how, from Cuba, the musicians claim their Africanity and their love for Africa, yet by singing in Spanish ('Yo soy africano').[37] At the same time, they explain how they met their alter ego on the island. The idea of a trans-atlantic brotherhood ('And I have my brother who treats me the same') shared between the Malians and the Cubans echoes the political discourses of the time, of both Pan-Africanism and Cuban internationalism towards Africa. It also implicitly relates to the history of the transatlantic slave trade; the lyrics refer to Africa as both a 'land of dreams and melancholia', a source of longing and suffering at once. When the singer declares 'I am African / I have no rival', this statement seems to assert his sense of authenticity vis-à-vis his Cuban 'brothers'. Yet at the same time, there is a search for validation when he asks to be treated as an equal ('¡Oye mi hermano, trátame igual!') to which the chorus responds assertively that he is indeed treated as such ('Sí, sí, sí, me trata igual'). These lyrics are particularly striking in the way they convey the emotions felt by the Malians, their yearning for Africa and their sense of solidarity with the islanders. The latter could well become their 'brothers' if only they spoke to each other on equal terms: 'And I have my brother if he treats me the same.'

Later generations of Malian students would also benefit from these cultural exchange programmes. One of the members of Las Maravillas, the percussionist Bah Tapo, even came back to Cuba in the 1980s to obtain his PhD in musicology. In the introduction to his dissertation, written in Spanish, about a Malian performance genre, the author acknowledged the role played by both Cuba and Mali in his academic achievements.[38] His graduation made him, he wrote, 'the first musicologist of [his] country and the first African to be trained in this speciality by Cuba', which constituted for him 'a great historical responsibility'.[39] In this way Bah Tapo expressed a sense of duty and a national pride shared with the Malian musicians sent to Cuba in the aftermath of Mali's independence.

On their return to Mali at the beginning of the 1970s the students experienced great disillusionment. Modibo Keïta's government had been overthrown by a military coup led by General Moussa Traoré in 1968. The cultural policies of the deposed government were suspended and the state-sponsored artistic ensembles and festivals were temporarily abandoned.[40] In this unfavourable political situation, they either joined the national orchestra or left the country.[41] This was the case of Boncana Maïga, Maravillas' leader, who settled in Ivory Coast. In Abidjan, he continued to play an important role in the development of an African *salsa*, not least as one of the founder members of Africando at the beginning of the 1990s.[42] All the same, the disillusionment that faced Las Maravillas on their return did not darken the bright vitality of Cuban music, which continued to inspire the great Malian orchestras of the 1970s such as the Rail Band du Buffet de la Gare de Bamako, Les Ambassadeurs du Motel, Super Biton de Ségou and Kanaga de Mopti.[43]

FROM CUBA TO AFRICA: ORQUESTA ARAGÓN'S TOURS

Although Orquesta Aragón was certainly the most famous Cuban orchestra in 1960s Africa, it was only in the 1970s that the band started touring on the continent.[44] Tanzania and Zanzibar were the first to welcome Orquesta Aragón to Africa in December 1971. The band then toured in Congo-Brazzaville, Guinea, Mali and Algeria in January 1972 before spending another three months the following year in Guinea, Sierra Leone and Mali. In 1977 a new tour took the orchestra to Guinea-Bissau, Guinea, Mali, Benin, Congo-Brazzaville and Angola; and to Ivory Coast and Guinea in 1979.[45] In the 1970s, Mali was one of the countries most visited by Orquesta Aragón.[46]

Many newspapers in Africa and Cuba recounted the success of the orchestra's concerts in West Africa.[47] Besides its popularity, the newspapers also mentioned the political framework within which these tours were organised, thereby acknowledging the diplomatic links established on the basis of socialist camaraderie. For instance, on the visit to Benin by Orquesta Aragón in 1977, a local journalist noted how much 'the head of state did thereafter underline the profound meaning of the visit by the Cuban orchestra in the People's Republic of Benin. A visit that is indeed inscribed in the context of the reinforcement of the friendship and solidarity links between the Cuban and Beninese revolutions.'[48] In another news item, the journalist Mensah Ekué commented on the success of the Cuban orchestra whose songs 'remind one so much our local rhythms' (*rappellent tant les rythmes de chez nous*).[49]

On the occasion of Orquesta Aragón's concert in Cotonou in November 1977, Benin's president Mathieu Kérékou gave a speech. Having adopted a Marxist-Leninist political orientation, the new government sought to strengthen diplomatic relationships with Cuba.[50] While expressing his admiration for Fidel Castro's revolution, Kérékou referred to the statement by one of the Cuban musicians that they were returning home to Africa: 'Our comrades come from afar, their young representative well said that they were born in Africa and coming back home.'[51]

These quotations show how much the sense of musical familiarity as well as the acknowledgement of socialist political orientation renewed the shared transatlantic history between Cuba and Benin. These instances of a transatlantic cultural diplomacy programme enacted 'a South–South dialogue that buil[t] on historical connections yet also establishe[d] new resonances in musical evocations of Atlantic affinities.'[52]

In terms of musical creativity, Orquesta Aragón's members benefited from this encounter with African music on the continent itself. The cellist Alejandro Tomás

Valdés is said to have created the *chaonda* rhythm after their visit to Guinea.[53] The president of Guinea, Sékou Touré, apparently suggested to Aragón's director, Rafaël Lay, that they share this creation.[54] In an album recorded at EGREM studios in 1976, Aragón released two songs to promote this new rhythm.[55] When Aragón toured Guinea again in 1977, the musicians presented this new rhythm to the audience. Valdés recalls:

> Yo pensaba que, como este ritmo era mas bien africanista – por las acepciones folklóricas de su línea – iba a ser de menos interés para el pueblo africano. Sin embargo, luego de la presentación, recibí una de mis grandes emociones: los Consejos de Ministros y Cultura, y la Jeunesse, o sea, la Juventud de ese país, me hicieron objeto de un reconocimiento por haber evolucionado su música y llevarla a ámbitos modernos e internacionales de música popular.[56]
>
> [I thought that, since this rhythm was rather Africanist – because of the folkloric acceptations of its lineage – it would be of less interest to the African people. However, after the presentation, I received one of my greatest emotions: the representatives of the Ministries of Culture, and of the Jeunesse, that is, the Youth of that country, gave official recognition to me for having made their music evolve and taken it to the level of modern and international popular music.]

The example of the creation of the *chaonda* rhythm inspired by Aragón's stay in Guinea shows how the political context not only strengthened the reciprocal diplomatic exchanges but also nourished the orchestra's musical creativity. A new layer of influences from the African continent transformed in this way the already creolised Cuban music played by Orquesta Aragón. After the *chaonda* rhythm entered Aragón's repertoire in the late 1970s, it inspired many other songs whose lyrics always mentioned the African source of inspiration from which they drew. For instance, the song 'A bailar mi chaonda' recorded by Aragón for their 2001 album *En Route* declares:

> ¡Chaonda!
> Oye lo bien
> Llegó el chaonda
> De pura esencia africana y música cubana
> Es el legado de un ritmo fuerte
> Que ha recorrido cuatro continentes
> Y fue creado
> Por Alejandro Tomás Valdés

> [Chaonda!
> Hey good
> The chaonda arrived
> Of pure African essence and Cuban music
> It is the legacy of a strong rhythm
> That has travelled four continents
> And it was created
> By Alejandro Tomás Valdés]

The *chaonda* rhythm is here presented as the creative product of an encounter between African and Cuban music – 'de pura esencia africana y música cubana' – yet mediated by Alejandro Tomás Valdés. This encounter between African and Cuban music replicates some musical encounters of the past. Yet the creation of the *chaonda* rhythm is also directly connected to contemporary Africa, with Aragón's musicians having newly rediscovered this Guinean rhythm. Interestingly, the song also mentions the success of this rhythm, which 'has travelled four continents', as a result of Aragón's tours over the world.

These different strata of 'African essence and Cuban music' represent several layers and movements of Africanisation, Cubanisation and re-Africanisation. The combination of these musical elements and their creative results can be seen as a process of mutual enrichment and cross-fertilisation as they criss-cross the Atlantic.[57]

On another note, I was told an anecdote by Aragón's Dagoberto González about a concert in Mali in 1973 where they again met Maravillas de Mali's members, who had just returned from Cuba.[58] When Aragón's percussionist Guido Sarría fell ill, his place was taken by Bah Tapo, Maravillas' percussionist.[59] This unexpected replacement attests to the links sustained between the Cuban and Malian musicians, this time not in Cuba but in Mali.

ROOTS, BELONGING AND DIASPORIC INTIMACY

These accounts of the members of Orquesta Aragón and Las Maravillas de Mali as well as their songs about their experiences – in Africa for the former, in Cuba for the latter – emphasise a shared sentiment of feeling 'at home' both here and there. For instance, Rafael Bacallao, Orquesta Aragón's singer and dancer, expressed his surprise at discovering the dancing skills of young women in Africa:

> A toda el África le gusta mucho la Orquesta Aragón, le gusta mucho el ritmo cubano. Yo gozo de bastante popularidad allí y no puedo decir donde me

siento mejor, porque soy agasajado en todos los lugares. Tu sabes que nuestro folklore viene de las raíces africanas. Encuentras en África una muchacha, la sacas a bailar y los pasos son exactamente iguales a los de una joven de aquí. Te sientes al rato como si estuvieras bailando con una cubana. Tienen un poder ritmatico fantástico. Ellos tocan un son parecido al nuestro.[60]

[All Africa enjoys very much Orquesta Aragón, enjoys the Cuban rhythm. I was quite popular there (in Africa) and I cannot say where I feel better, because I am honoured in all places. You know that our folklore comes from the African roots. You find a girl in Africa, invite her to dance and the steps are exactly the same as a young girl from here. You feel like you're dancing with a Cuban for a little while. They have fantastic rhythmic power. They play a sound similar to ours.]

This musical, rhythmical and kinetic familiarity expresses a sense of 'diasporic intimacy that has been a marked feature of transnational Black Atlantic creativity'.[61] These exchanges involved individuals who engaged fully with the music and at the same time developed deep emotional feelings towards the land that welcomed them. Malian percussionist Bah Tapo wrote a short poem to end the acknowledgements section of his PhD thesis, which he dedicated to his 'adoptive Cuban parents':[62]

A Cuba le digo
Que mi tierra me llama:
Tengo que partir.
Me siento cubano,
Lo llevo en mi sueño
Y es todo un tormento
Para mí,
Fuera de ella vivir.

[To Cuba I say
That my land is calling me:
I have to leave.
I feel Cuban,
I carry it in my dreams
And this is a real torment
For me
To live away from it.]

The poem emphasises how the musician feels torn between his sense of duty to return to Mali and his emotional link to Cuba. It shows how much the political agenda developed in the cultural field during the Cold War was not only symbolic but was actually embodied, to the extent of marking the musicians at an intimate level.[63]

Moreover, this feeling of being 'at home' relied not only on the musical familiarity felt on both sides but also on the acknowledgement of a shared history characterised by the experience of slavery and colonialism. Boncana Maïga thus explains:

> On avait la chance d'avoir tous les musiciens cubains avec nous tout le temps, tout le temps parce que nous étions les premiers Noirs à Cuba et les Cubains voulaient s'approcher des Noirs pour en fait connaître leur histoire quoi. Ils sont à Cuba, on leur dit vous êtes venus descendants des esclaves et tout, mais voilà, les authentiques sont là, ils sont nés en Afrique.[64]
>
> [We were lucky to have the Cuban musicians with us all the time, all the time ... Because we were the first Blacks in Cuba and Cubans wanted to approach Blacks in order to, actually, learn their own history. They are in Cuba, they are told that they came from slave descent and so on, but there you go, the authentic ones are here, they were born in Africa.]

In this excerpt, Maïga positions himself as an 'authentic' black African whose presence would have offered to the Cuban musicians he encountered the chance to reconnect to their history. In this way, historical traumas were re-embodied through the journey of the Malian musicians to Cuba, somehow mirroring the original forced displacement of the Middle Passage. At the same time, we can recall that the Malian students travelled to Havana in the 1960s for training in music. The journey testifies to the popularity of Cuban music in Africa at that time and also offers an alternative account of the African influences on Cuban music.[65]

In President Kérékou's speech of 1977, where he greeted Orquesta Aragón's members as 'hijos de Africa' (children of Africa) returning to their home and birthplace ('ellos habían nacido de África'), we can see another layer of spatio-temporal conflation. The entanglement of space and time features at the heart of the dialectic of return in the realm of diaspora experience. As James Clifford puts it:

> In diaspora experience, the co-presence of 'here' and 'there' is articulated with an antiteleological (sometimes messianic) temporality. Linear history is broken, the present constantly shadowed by a past that is also a desired, but obstructed, future: a renewed, painful yearning. For Black Atlantic diaspora

> consciousness, the recurring break where time stops and restarts is the Middle Passage.[66]

Different historical phases of circulation across the Black Atlantic are thus reimagined and even compressed in an elusive temporality.[67] The feelings of the people who experienced these actual criss-crossings complicate further and challenge notions of 'sources', 'roots', 'belonging' and identity formation. This complex process of *allers-retours* (round trips) or 'roots in reverse' clearly shows the paradoxical mobility of the notion of roots, which are displaced from one side of the Atlantic to the other, according to various interlocutors.[68] As Ariana Hernandez-Reguant notes, World music producers 'took contemporary African music as a starting point, tracing a genealogy back to Cuba as its source'.[69] The musical journeys of Las Maravillas de Mali in Cuba and the Orquesta Aragón's tours in West Africa demonstrate the elusive malleability of both 'roots' and 'routes', challenging Clifford's assumption that 'roots always precede routes'.[70] Indeed, it seems that routes in fact precede roots.

Whether it be through the musical and political exchanges that occurred between Cuba and Africa during the Cold War or, later, through World music networks, the multidirectional circulations, the interplay of influences and 'creative appropriation', the 'boomerang' effect and the 'cross-fertilisation' between Cuban and African music clearly reverse and challenge long-settled musical genealogies and discourses.[71] At the same time, the related discourses reactivate and legitimise the historical links between Africa and the Caribbean. Yet the reversal of the expected senses of circulation in the cultural flows across the Black Atlantic complicate some Afro-centred ideologies for which Africa is not only conceived of as a place of origin, but also as a place to which to return.[72] Marcus Garvey's Back to Africa movement and other intellectual currents and social movements made the idea of the return to Africa both a philosophical issue and a political project. In these movements, the idea of return also implies that there is a 'before' (before slave trade, before colonisation), where 'Africa' exists as a lost paradise. Nostalgic feelings and fantasised idealisation of the continent are one of the 'diasporic responses' that shape the dialectic of the return, for 'the potentiality of a return is intertwined with a longing for the homeland'.[73] Yet, as we have seen, the Malian and Cuban musicians' journeys across the Atlantic show in fact how shifting the apprehension is of where the homeland exists.

CONCLUSION

During the Cold War and while African countries were becoming independent, the postcolonial alliances fostered between socialist countries involved the bypassing of former imperial hegemonies by the creation of new South–South trajectories. These routes helped to strengthen the incessant musical circulation back and forth across the Atlantic. Both African and Cuban musical creativity benefited from these exchanges throughout the postcolonial Atlantic. The political exchanges also assisted the development of the artistic careers of cosmopolitan musicians. In addition to proposing an alternative modernity, the appropriation of Cuban music in Africa reactivated historical transatlantic linkages between Africa and the Caribbean and inscribed them in the intellectual and political framework of the independence era.

The creation of the band Las Maravillas de Mali by young Malians sent to Cuba for musical training in the 1960s, and the tours in Africa by the famous Cuban Orquesta Aragón from the 1970s, personified these transatlantic diplomatic exchanges. Personal accounts by both orchestras' members shed light on how the political measures relied on individuals who were deeply and emotionally engaged with their music and its values. This process challenged notions of roots and belonging in a political context otherwise saturated with competing nationalist ideologies.

Interestingly enough, the musical exchanges initiated during the Cold War seem to have heralded artistic collaborations that subsequently developed within different frameworks. Whether they were shaped by the socialist diplomatic interplay during the Cold War, or by World music networks later on, many contemporary musical productions continue to draw on the Cuba–Mali connections. For instance, the release of the album *Afrocubism* by the World Circuit label in 2010 featured famous Cuban and Malian musicians. This project was the long-awaited realisation of an encounter that should have taken place 15 years earlier at the initiative of music producer Nick Gold. The initial project was intended to create an album with Cuban and Malian musicians, but the latter did not get their visas on time. The album featured as a result only the Cuban musicians. This accident eventually produced the album *Buena Vista Social Club* (1997), one of the most successful World music productions.[74]

If musical encounters between Cuban and African musicians are now part of the 'global imagination', they have a long, multifaceted and multilayered history that also involves a continuous 'Afro-Atlantic dialogue'.[75] By considering different scales and levels of perception, the chapter has offered a diffracted approach to understanding the convergence of different kinds of musical circulation, political relations and individual trajectories. What it reveals is the complex history of a form of transatlantic musical globalisation as well as the role of particular political dynamics in the postcolonial world in shaping new music and identities.

NOTES

1. The research presented here was undertaken as part of postdoctoral research within the project Modern Moves funded by the European Research Council and led by Prof. Ananya Jahanara Kabir at King's College London. Some parts of the research data included here appeared in French in Elina Djebbari, 'Guerre froide, jeux politiques et circulations musicales entre Cuba et l'Afrique de l'Ouest: Las Maravillas de Mali à Cuba et la Orquesta Aragón en Afrique,' *Afrique Contemporaine* 2, no. 254 (2015): 21–36. All translations from French and Spanish to English are by the author.
2. Younoussa Touré, 'La Biennale artistique et culturelle du Mali (1962–1988): Socioanthropologie d'une action de politique culturelle africaine,' PhD diss., EHESS, 1996, 76–77.
3. Ministry of Foreign Relations (MINREX), *Convenios culturales suscritos por Cuba 1959–1975* (Havana: Ministerio de Relaciones Exteriores, Dirección Jurídica, 1975).
4. Original quote in Spanish: 'desarrollar las relaciones culturales en el dominio de la ciencia, de la cultura y del arte entre sus países con el interés del reforzamiento de las relaciones amistosas y de la comprensión mutua entre los pueblos cubano y maliense,' MINREX, *Convenios culturales*, n.p.
5. Joseph Nye, *Power in the Global Information Age* (London: Routledge, 2004).
6. Lisa Davenport, *Jazz Diplomacy: Promoting America in the Cold War Era* (Jackson: University Press of Mississippi, 2009), 148.
7. Frances Stonor Saunders, *Who Paid the Piper? The CIA and the Cultural Cold War* (London: Granta Books, 1999); Volker R. Berghahn, *America and the Intellectual Cold Wars in Europe: Shepard Stone between Philanthropy, Academy, and Diplomacy* (Princeton: Princeton University Press, 2001).
8. Karina C. Jannello, 'El Congreso por la Libertad de la Cultura: El caso chileno y la disputa por las "ideas fuerza" de la Guerra Fría.' *Revista Izquierdas*, no. 14 (December 2012): 25–8.
9. Some works nevertheless address the relationships developed between the USSR and certain African countries. See among others, Kate Baldwin, *Beyond the Color Line and the Iron Curtain: Reading Encounters between Black and Red, 1922–1963* (Durham, NC: Duke University Press, 2002); Allison Blakely, *Russia and the Negro: Blacks in Russian History and Thought* (Washington, DC: Howard University Press, 1986); Constantin Katsakioris, 'L'Union soviétique et les intellectuels africains: Internationalisme, panafricanisme et négritude pendant les années de la décolonisation, 1954–1964,' *Cahiers du Monde Russe* 47, no. 1–2 (2006): 15–32; and Constantin Katsakioris, 'Transferts Est-Sud: Echanges éducatifs et formation de cadres africains en Union soviétique pendant les années soixante,' *Revue d'Histoire d'Outre-Mers* 95, no. 354–5 (2007): 80–103.
10. Piero Gleisjeses, *Conflicting Missions: Havana, Washington, and Africa, 1959–1976* (Chapel Hill, NC: University of North Carolina Press, 2002).
11. Katsakioris, 'Transferts Est-Sud,' 87; Djebbari, 'Guerre froide,' 24.
12. Andrew Apter, 'Beyond Négritude: Black Cultural Citizenship and the Arab Question in FESTAC 77,' *Journal of African Cultural Studies* 28, no. 3 (2015): 1–14; Éloi Ficquet and Lorraine Gallimardet, 'On ne peut nier longtemps l'art nègre,' *Gradhiva* 2, no. 10 (2009): 134–55. Regarding Kinshasa 1974 and Lagos 1977, see the chapters by Gonçalves and Argyriadis in this volume.
13. Antoine Marès and Anaïs Fléchet, 'Introduction,' *Relations Internationales* 3, no. 155 (2013): 3–9; Mario Dunkel and Sina A. Nitzsche, eds, *Popular Music and Public*

Diplomacy: Transnational and Transdisciplinary Perspectives (Bielefeld: Transcript Verlag, 2018); Anne Dulphy, Marie-Anne Matard-Bonucci and Pascal Ory, eds, *Les relations culturelles internationales au XXe siècle: De la diplomatie culturelle à l'acculturation* (Brussels: Peter Lang, 2011).

14 Davenport, *Jazz Diplomacy*; Danielle Fosler-Lussier, *Music in America's Cold War Diplomacy* (Oakland: University of California Press, 2015); Penny M. von Eschen, *Satchmo Blows the World: Jazz Ambassadors Play the Cold War* (Cambridge, MA: Harvard University Press, 2004).

15 *1° Congreso nacional de cultura: Guía para la discusión del proyecto del plan de cultura para 1963 con los organismos de masa*, 1962, p. 20. National Archives, Havana, Fondo Especial, caja 1, no. 169.

16 Fidel Castro, 'We Are United by Blood,' in *Changing the History of Africa: Angola and Namibia*, ed. David Deutschmann (Melbourne: Ocean Press, 1989), 61–4; Nelson Mandela and Fidel Castro, *How Far We Slaves Have Come! South Africa and Cuba in Today's World* (New York: Pathfinder, 1991).

17 Hauke Dorsch, 'Black or Red Atlantic? Mozambican Students in Cuba and Their Reintegration at Home,' *Zeitschrift für Ethnologie* 136, no. 2 (2011): 295.

18 Ophélie Rillon, 'Corps rebelles: La mode des jeunes urbains dans les années 1960–1970 au Mali,' *Genèses* 4, no. 81 (2010): 64–83.

19 Hauke Dorsch, 'Indépendance Cha Cha: African Pop Music since the Independence Era,' *Africa Spectrum* 45, no. 3 (2010): 131.

20 Dorsch, 'Indépendance Cha Cha,' 132; Richard M. Shain, 'Roots in Reverse: *Cubanismo* in Twentieth Century Senegalese Music,' *International Journal of African Historical Studies* 35, no. 1 (2002): 86–7; Bob W. White, 'Congolese Rumba and Other Cosmopolitanisms,' *Cahiers d'Études Africaines* 4, no. 168 (2002): 669–70. 'GV series' was the name given to the gramophone records produced in Europe and the United States between 1933 and 1958 and specifically exported to Africa.

21 Bob W. White, *Rumba Rules: The Politics of Dance Music in Mobutu's Zaïre* (Durham, NC: Duke University Press, 2008). The song 'Independence chacha' by Grand Kalle and African Jazz is often considered the hymn of the independence era; see also Dorsch, 'Indépendance Cha Cha'. For more information on Congolese rumba, see Grabli in this volume.

22 Rillon, 'Corps rebelles.'

23 Shain, 'Roots in Reverse,' 91, 84.

24 Shain, 'Roots in Reverse.'

25 See for instance accounts on Senegal: Timothy Roark Mangin, 'Mbalax: Cosmopolitanism in Senegalese Urban Popular Music,' PhD diss., Columbia University, 2013, and Shain, 'Roots in Reverse'; on Benin: Ananya Jahanara Kabir, 'Afro-Latin-Africa: Movement and Memory in Benin,' in *The Routledge Companion to World Literature and World History: Circulation, Movement, Encounters*, ed. May Hawas (New York: Routledge, 2018), 234–45; on DRC: White, 'Congolese Rumba,' 673; and on Ghana: Ato Quayson, *Oxford Street, Accra: City Life and the Itineraries of Transnationalism* (Durham, NC: Duke University Press, 2014), 159–82.

26 Quayson, *Oxford Street*, 166.

27 White, 'Congolese Rumba,' 668.

28 Martin Stokes, 'On Musical Cosmopolitanism,' The Macalester International Roundtable, Paper 3 (2007): 1–19; Marissa J. Moorman, *Intonations: A Social History of Music and Nation in Luanda, Angola, from 1945 to Recent Times* (Athens: Ohio University Press,

2008), 18; Thomas Turino, *Nationalists, Cosmopolitans, and Popular Music in Zimbabwe* (Chicago: Chicago University Press, 2000).

29 Florent Mazzoleni, *Musiques modernes et traditionnelles du Mali* (Bègles: Le Castor Astral, 2011).

30 Ryan Skinner, 'Artistiya: Popular Music and Personhood in Postcolonial Bamako, Mali,' PhD diss., Columbia University, 2009, 23. The creation of a national conservatoire was already a project in the early 1960s (Touré, 'Biennale,' 90), but the Conservatoire des Arts et Métiers Multimédia Balla Fasséké Kouyaté eventually opened in Bamako in 2014.

31 EGREM: Empresa de grabaciones y ediciones musicales (Musical recording and publishing company). Based in Havana, EGREM studios are the Cuban national recording institution. The information given here appears on the cover (verso) of Las Maravillas de Mali's record (Las Maravillas de Mali, *Les Merveilles du Mali*, EGREM, Areito, Cuba, LDA-3344, 1967).

32 The term *charanga* refers to an orchestra consisting mainly of piano, violin, flute, double bass and percussion.

33 Interview with Boncana Maïga, Cotonou, 21 February 2015.

34 José Loyola Fernández, *La charanga y sus maravillas: Orquesta Aragón* (Barranquilla: Fondo Editorial del Caribe, 2013), 362.

35 Djebbari, 'Guerre froide,' 28.

36 For Ryan Skinner, the song 'Soubalé' adapted to a Cuban *danzón* shows the patriotism of the Malian musicians who, while being in Cuba, proved their attachment to their fatherland as well as to the regime of President Modibo Keïta, considered an heir of this historical figure (Skinner, 'Artistiya,' 100–2).

37 I thank Kali Argyriadis for her help in translating the lyrics. This song echoes quite strikingly Arsenio Rodríguez's song 'Yo nací del Africa', analysed by Charlotte Grabli in this volume.

38 Bah Tapo, 'El kotebá: Complejo cultural de la etnia bamanán o bambará en la Republica de Mali,' PhD diss., Instituto Superior de Arte, 1989.

39 Original quote in Spanish: 'para así hacer de mi el primer musicólogo de mí país y el primer africano formado en dicha especialidad por Cuba. Esto constituye para mí una gran responsabilidad histórica' (Tapo, 'El kotebá,' n.p.).

40 Elina Djebbari, 'Le Ballet National du Mali: Créer un patrimoine, construire une nation: Enjeux politiques, sociologiques et esthétiques d'un genre musico-chorégraphique, de l'indépendance du pays à aujourd'hui,' PhD diss., EHESS, 2013, 142.

41 Skinner, 'Artistiya,' 105.

42 The group Africando was created in 1992 by Guinean producer Ibrahima Sylla and Malian musician Boncana Maïga. The group defined itself as a Pan-African orchestra aimed at developing an 'African salsa' (interview with Boncana Maïga, Cotonou, 21 February 2015).

43 Mazzoleni, *Musiques modernes et traditionnelles du Mali.*

44 It is often considered that Orquesta Aragón was the first Cuban orchestra to visit Africa, yet Orquesta Jorrín preceded it in 1965. See François-Xavier Gomez, *Orquesta Aragón: The Story 1939–1999* (Paris: Lusafrica, 1999), 15; and Ariana Hernandez-Reguant, 'World Music Producers and the Cuban Frontier,' in *Music and Globalization: Critical Encounters*, ed. Bob White (Bloomington and Indianapolis: Indiana University Press, 2012), 115.

45 Gaspard Marrero, *La Orquesta Aragón* (Havana: Editorial José Marti, 2008), 243–6.

46 Other tours organised in the 1980s and later kept bringing Orquesta Aragón to West Africa; see Marrero, *Orquesta Aragón*, 243–6.

47 Ilse Bulit, 'Debuto la Orquesta Aragón en el Palacio del pueblo de Conakry ante tres mil espectadores,' *Granma*, 1 October 1977; Ilse Bulit, 'Ritmos cubanos en Africa,' *Bohemia* 69, no. 41 (14 October 1977): 27; Ilse Bulit, 'Aragón: Un visa para Africa,' *Bohemia* 69, no. 52 (30 December 1977): 4–7; Hector Hernandez Pardo, 'Impresionados los integrantes de la "Aragón" por la simpatia que goza nuestra musica en los pueblos de Africa,' *Granma*, 15 March 1972; Marrero, *Orquesta Aragón*, 130–2, 142.

48 Excerpt from a Beninese news item entitled 'Fin du séjour en République populaire du Bénin de l'orchestre Aragón de Cuba,' featured in Ilse Bulit, 'Aragón: Un visa para Africa,' 5 ('Le chef de l'État devait par la suite dégager le sens profond de la visite de l'orchestre cubain en République populaire du Bénin: Une visite qui entre effectivement dans le cadre du renforcement des liens d'amitié et de solidarité entre les révolutions cubaine et béninoise').

49 Mensah Ekué, 'L'international Aragon Orchestra au Bénin: Des maîtres incontestables de la musique afro-cubaine,' *Ehuzu*, 25 October 1977, 3.

50 Kérékou took over from the previous regime after a military coup on 26 October 1972. Dahomey became the People's Republic of Benin in 1975.

51 Original quote: 'Estos compañeros vienen de muy lejos, el joven representante de ellos bien decía, que ellos habían nacido de África y que volvían a ella.' Archives of the Ministry of Foreign Affairs, Havana, Cuba, box Benin, 1970–1983, ordinario 1.

52 Frederick Moehn, 'New Dialogues, Old Routes: Emergent Collaborations between Brazilian and Angolan Music Makers,' *Popular Music* 30, no. 2 (2011): 175.

53 The term *chaonda* derives from *cha* (referring to *chachachá*) and *onda* (wave), denoting that this rhythm announced a 'new wave' (*onda nueva*) (Marrero, *Orquesta Aragón*, 135).

54 Bulit, 'Debuto la Orquesta Aragón en el Palacio del pueblo de Conakry ante tres mil espectadores.'

55 *Orquesta Aragón*, Areito, LD 3600, 1976, 33rpm LP.

56 Quoted in Marrero, *Orquesta Aragón*, 141.

57 Denis-Constant Martin, 'The Musical Heritage of Slavery: From Creolization to "World Music",' in *Music and Globalization: Critical Encounters*, ed. Bob White (Bloomington: Indiana University Press, 2012), 26.

58 Interview, Havana, 2 December 2014.

59 Marrero, *Orquesta Aragón*, 134.

60 Marrero, *Orquesta Aragón*, 142.

61 Paul Gilroy, *The Black Atlantic: Modernity and Double Consciousness* (London: Verso, 1993), 16.

62 Tapo, 'El kotebá,' n.p. Original quote in Spanish: 'Dedico este trabajo de diploma a mis queridos padres adoptivos cubanos.'

63 This process has been acknowledged by scholars such as Danielle Fosler-Lussier, who accurately describes how the jazz musicians involved in diplomatic circuits managed to create personal connections with local musicians, who in turn influenced their own musical style (Fosler-Lussier, *Music in America's Cold War Diplomacy*, 147, 149).

64 Interview with the author, Cotonou, 21 February 2015.

65 Hernandez-Reguant, 'World Music,' 117.

66 James Clifford, *Routes: Travel and Translation in the Late Twentieth Century* (Cambridge, MA: Harvard University Press, 1997), 264.

67 Gilroy, *Black Atlantic*.

68 Shain, 'Roots in Reverse.'

69 Hernandez-Reguant, 'World Music,' 117.

[70] Clifford, *Routes*, 3. For instance, Senegambian singer Laba Sosseh 'located his fount of authenticity *outside* Africa, in Cuba itself and in the *barrios* of Latin New York, whereas other African performers such as Franco (Luambo Makiadi) of OK Jazz in Kinshasa, either through encouragement or state-sponsored coercion, found cultural authenticity in re-embracing their indigenous musical roots' (Richard M. Shain, 'Trovador of the Black Atlantic: Laba Sosseh and the Africanization of Afro-Cuban Music,' in *Music and Globalization: Critical Encounters*, ed. Bob White (Bloomington and Indianapolis: Indiana University Press, 2012), 138).

[71] Peter Manuel, 'Puerto Rican Music and Cultural Identity: Creative Appropriation of Cuban Sources from Danza to Salsa,' *Ethnomusicology* 38, no. 2 (1994): 249–80; Shain, 'Trovador,' 146–7; Martin, 'The Musical Heritage of Slavery,' 26.

[72] Giulia Bonacci, 'La fabrique du retour en Afrique: Politiques et pratiques de l'appartenance en Jamaïque (1920–1968),' *Revue Européenne des Migrations Internationales* 29, no. 3 (2013): 33.

[73] Emmanuel Akyeampong, 'Africans in the Diaspora: The Diaspora and Africa,' *African Affairs* 99, no. 395 (2000): 185.

[74] To learn more about this story from Nick Gold himself, see Lucy Durán, 'Our Stories, from Us, the "They": Nick Gold Talks to Lucy Durán about the Making of Buena Vista Social Club,' *Journal of World Popular Music* 1, no. 1 (2014): 135–55.

[75] Veit Erlmann, 'The Aesthetics of the Global Imagination: Reflections on World Music in the 1990s,' *Public Culture* 8, no. 3 (1996): 467–87, and J. Lorand Matory, 'Afro-Atlantic Culture: On the Live Dialogue between Africa and the Americas,' in *Africana: The Encyclopedia of the African and African American Experience*, ed. Kwame A. Appiah and Henry L. Gates Jr. (New York: Basic Civitas Books, 1999), 93–103.

REFERENCES

Akyeampong, Emmanuel. 'Africans in the Diaspora: The Diaspora and Africa.' *African Affairs* 99, no. 395 (2000): 183–215.

Apter, Andrew. 'Beyond Négritude: Black Cultural Citizenship and the Arab question in FESTAC 77.' *Journal of African Cultural Studies* 28, no. 3 (2015): 1–14.

Baldwin, Kate. *Beyond the Color Line and the Iron Curtain: Reading Encounters between Black and Red, 1922–1963*. Durham, NC: Duke University Press, 2002.

Berghahn, Volker R. *America and the Intellectual Cold Wars in Europe: Shepard Stone between Philanthropy, Academy, and Diplomacy*. Princeton: Princeton University Press, 2001.

Blakely, Allison. *Russia and the Negro: Blacks in Russian History and Thought*. Washington, DC: Howard University Press, 1986.

Bonacci, Giulia. 'La fabrique du retour en Afrique: Politiques et pratiques de l'appartenance en Jamaïque (1920–1968).' *Revue Européenne des Migrations Internationales* 29, no. 3 (2013): 33–54.

Castro, Fidel. 'We are United by Blood.' In *Changing the History of Africa: Angola and Namibia*, edited by David Deutschmann, 61–4. Melbourne: Ocean Press, 1989.

Clifford, James. *Routes: Travel and Translation in the Late Twentieth Century*. Cambridge, MA: Harvard University Press, 1997.

Davenport, Lisa E. *Jazz Diplomacy: Promoting America in the Cold War Era*. Jackson: University Press of Mississippi, 2009.

Djebbari, Elina. 'Guerre froide, jeux politiques et circulations musicales entre Cuba et l'Afrique de l'Ouest: Las Maravillas de Mali à Cuba et la Orquesta Aragón en Afrique.' *Afrique Contemporaine* 2, no. 254 (2015): 21–36.

Djebbari, Elina. 'Le Ballet National du Mali: Créer un patrimoine, construire une nation: Enjeux politiques, sociologiques et esthétiques d'un genre musico-chorégraphique, de l'indépendance du pays à aujourd'hui.' PhD diss., EHESS, 2013.

Dorsch, Hauke. 'Black or Red Atlantic? Mozambican Students in Cuba and Their Reintegration at Home.' *Zeitschrift für Ethnologie* 136, no. 2 (2011): 289–309.

Dorsch, Hauke. 'Indépendance Cha Cha: African Pop Music since the Independence Era.' *Africa Spectrum* 45, no. 3 (2010): 131–46.

Dulphy, Anne, Robert Frank, Marie-Anne Matard-Bonucci and Pascal Ory. *Les relations culturelles internationales au XXe siècle: De la diplomatie culturelle à l'acculturation*. Brussels: Peter Lang, 2011.

Dunkel, Mario and Sina A. Nitzsche, eds. *Popular Music and Public Diplomacy: Transnational and Transdisciplinary Perspectives*. Bielefeld: Transcript Verlag, 2018.

Durán, Lucy. 'Our Stories, from Us, the "They": Nick Gold Talks to Lucy Durán about the Making of Buena Vista Social Club.' *Journal of World Popular Music* 1, no. 1 (2014): 135–55.

Erlmann, Veit. 'The Aesthetics of the Global Imagination: Reflections on World Music in the 1990s.' *Public Culture* 8, no. 3 (1996): 467–87.

Ficquet, Éloi and Lorraine Gallimardet. 'On ne peut nier longtemps l'art nègre.' *Gradhiva* 2, no. 10 (2009): 134–55.

Fosler-Lussier, Danielle. *Music in America's Cold War Diplomacy*. Oakland: University of California Press, 2015.

Gilroy, Paul. *The Black Atlantic: Modernity and Double Consciousness*. London: Verso, 1993.

Gleisjeses, Piero. *Conflicting Missions: Havana, Washington, and Africa, 1959–1976*. Chapel Hill, NC: University of North Carolina Press, 2002.

Gomez, François-Xavier. *Orquesta Aragón: The Story 1939–1999*. Paris: Lusafrica, 1999.

Hernandez-Reguant, Ariana. 'World Music Producers and the Cuban Frontier.' In *Music and Globalization: Critical Encounters*, edited by Bob White, 111–33. Bloomington and Indianapolis: Indiana University Press, 2012.

Jannello, Karina C. 'El Congreso por la Libertad de la Cultura: El caso chileno y la disputa por las "ideas fuerza" de la Guerra Fría.' *Revista Izquierdas*, no. 14 (December 2012): 14–52.

Kabir, Ananya Jahanara. 'Afro-Latin-Africa: Movement and Memory in Benin.' In *The Routledge Companion to World Literature and World History: Circulation, Movement, Encounters*, edited by May Hawas, 234–45. New York: Routledge, 2018.

Katsakioris, Constantin. 'L'Union soviétique et les intellectuels africains: Internationalisme, panafricanisme et négritude pendant les années de la décolonisation, 1954–1964.' *Cahiers du Monde Russe* 47, no. 1–2 (2006): 15–32.

Katsakioris, Constantin. 'Transferts Est-Sud: Echanges éducatifs et formation de cadres africains en Union soviétique pendant les années soixante.' *Revue d'Histoire d'Outre-Mers* 95, no. 354–55 (2007): 80–103.

Loyola Fernández, José. *La charanga y sus maravillas: Orquesta Aragón*. Barranquilla: Fondo Editorial del Caribe, 2013.

Mandela, Nelson and Fidel Castro, *How Far We Slaves Have Come! South Africa and Cuba in Today's World*. New York: Pathfinder, 1991.

Mangin, Timothy Roark. 'Mbalax: Cosmopolitanism in Senegalese Urban Popular Music.' PhD diss., Columbia University, 2013.

Manuel, Peter. 'Puerto Rican Music and Cultural Identity: Creative Appropriation of Cuban Sources from Danza to Salsa.' *Ethnomusicology* 38, no. 2 (1994): 249–80.

Marès, Antoine and Anaïs Fléchet. 'Introduction.' *Relations Internationales* 3, no. 155 (2013): 3–9.

Marrero, Gaspard. *La Orquesta Aragón*. Havana: Editorial José Marti, 2008.

Martin, Denis-Constant. 'The Musical Heritage of Slavery: From Creolization to "World Music".' In *Music and Globalization: Critical Encounters*, edited by Bob White, 17–39. Bloomington: Indiana University Press, 2012.

Matory, J. Lorand. 'Afro-Atlantic Culture: On the Live Dialogue between Africa and the Americas.' In *Africana: The Encyclopedia of the African and African American Experience*, edited by Kwame A. Appiah and Henry L. Gates Jr., 93–103. New York: Basic Civitas Books, 1999.

Mazzoleni, Florent. *Musiques modernes et traditionnelles du Mali*. Bègles: Le Castor Astral, 2011.

Moehn, Frederick.'New Dialogues, Old Routes: Emergent Collaborations between Brazilian and Angolan Music Makers.' *Popular Music* 30, no. 2 (2011): 175–90.

Moorman, Marissa J. *Intonations: A Social History of Music and Nation in Luanda, Angola, from 1945 to Recent Times*. Athens: Ohio University Press, *2008*.

Nye, Joseph. *Power in the Global Information Age*. London: Routledge, 2004.

Quayson, Ato. *Oxford Street, Accra: City Life and the Itineraries of Transnationalism*. Durham, NC: Duke University Press, 2014.

Rillon, Ophélie. 'Corps rebelles: La mode des jeunes urbains dans les années 1960–1970 au Mali.' *Genèses* 4, no. 81 (2010): 64–83.

Shain, Richard M.'Roots in Reverse: *Cubanismo* in Twentieth Century Senegalese Music.' *International Journal of African Historical Studies* 35, no. 1 (2002): 83–101.

Shain, Richard M.'Trovador of the Black Atlantic: Laba Sosseh and the Africanization of Afro-Cuban Music.' In *Music and Globalization: Critical Encounters*, edited by Bob White, 135–56. Bloomington and Indianapolis: Indiana University Press, 2012.

Skinner, Ryan. 'Artistiya: Popular Music and Personhood in Postcolonial Bamako, Mali.' PhD diss., Columbia University, 2009.

Stokes, Martin. 'On Musical Cosmopolitanism.' The Macalester International Roundtable, Paper 3 (2007): 1–19. http://digitalcommons.macalester.edu/cgi/viewcontent.cgi?article=1002&context=intlrdtable.

Stonor Saunders, Frances. *Who Paid the Piper? The CIA and the Cultural Cold War*. London: Granta Books, 1999.

Tapo, Bah. 'El kotebá: Complejo cultural de la etnia bamanán o bambará en la República de Mali.' PhD diss., Instituto Superior de Arte, 1989.

Touré, Younoussa. 'La Biennale artistique et culturelle du Mali (1962–1988): Socioanthropologie d'une action de politique culturelle africaine.' PhD diss., EHESS, 1996.

Turino, Thomas. *Nationalists, Cosmopolitans, and Popular Music in Zimbabwe*. Chicago: Chicago University Press, 2000.

Von Eschen, Penny M. *Satchmo Blows the World: Jazz Ambassadors Play the Cold War*. Cambridge, MA: Harvard University Press, 2004.

White, Bob W. 'Congolese Rumba and Other Cosmopolitanisms.' *Cahiers d'Études Africaines* 4, no. 168 (2002): 663–86.

White, Bob W. *Rumba Rules: The Politics of Dance Music in Mobutu's Zaïre*. Durham, NC: Duke University Press, 2008.

PART IV

RECONSTRUCTING HISTORY, RECONNECTING ROOTS

CHAPTER

9

The Construction of a Spiritual Filiation from Havana to Ile-Ife

Kali Argyriadis

'I have always cared about Nigeria because it was our Motherland.'
— Rodolfo Sarracino, interview, 25 February 2016

Cuba was the second-last country in America to abolish slavery for good in 1886. The actual slave trade had continued until at least 1873, the year of the last-known arrival of a clandestine slave ship on the island[1]. It was long accepted that this date also marked the end of all direct links between Cuba and the African continent. However, the oral history of several ritual lineages of *santeros/santeras*, *babalaos* and *omó añá*[2] – Cuban practitioners of religions of Yoruba origin – collected and published at the end of the 1930s by the Cuban anthropologist Fernando Ortiz, or compiled in the manuals and handbooks written during the same period by the practitioners themselves, attested to some instances of initiated ancestors who had arrived at the end of the nineteenth century, or had gone to and then come back from Yorubaland. It was not until the end of the 1980s that these stories were clarified or corroborated in Cuba thanks to research by historians and anthropologists.[3]

When Fernando Ortiz published his first book on the 'witchcraft' practised by Africans and their descendants in Cuba,[4] he drew extensively on the work of the Brazilian anthropologist Raimundo Nina Rodrigues.[5] Like Nina Rodrigues, Ortiz was influenced by the racist ideas of the time, which considered Yoruba culture to be one of the 'most civilised in Africa', and by the dictionaries produced by missionaries in Nigeria who were part of the Lagos cultural renaissance movement involved in the construction of identity and the standardisation of the 'Yoruba' language in the nineteenth century.[6] This led Ortiz to search for traces of this culture on the island, but it was not until 1916 that he formally identified the culture, using the generic ethnonym of the time: Lucumí. From the 1920s onwards, against a background of protest against United States interference and a vogue for primitivism and Art Nègre, the thinking of this key Cuban writer took a radically different turn. He joined the artistic and social AfroCubanismo movement and paved the way for a revision of the history of the 'coloured' population, highlighting its specific forms of political organisation and the wealth of its religious and artistic expression.[7] He went on to found several research associations in this field, calling for the creation of an institute whose sole focus would be safeguarding Afro-Cuban 'folklore', which he felt was being corrupted by the entertainment and tourist industries.

Did direct contacts exist, at the time, between Cuban religious practitioners and their counterparts from the Bight of Benin? According to James Lorand Matory, at least one of the authors of the manuals drew on the books and pamphlets on the Yoruba religion written in the wake of the Lagos cultural renaissance movement between 1899 and 1931; access would have been possible via the postal and commercial services that linked Cuba and West Africa in the 1950s.[8] In this connection, Lydia Cabrera cites elderly informants who claim that in the 1940s a number of traders from the Canary Islands regularly imported cowrie shells, kola nuts, plants, feathers, animal teeth, skins and horns, and other essential ritual objects 'from Guinea'.[9] In 1956, when the ethnographers Pierre Verger and Alfred Métraux spent time in Cuba at the invitation of Cabrera, Verger brought ritual ingredients from Dahomey to Cabrera's informants, as he regularly did for his co-religionists in Salvador.[10]

According to our current state of knowledge, it appears that it was not until the 1960s, in the context of African independence movements and the advent of the Cuban Revolution, that 'reconnections' began to be made. I would like to explore these 'reconnections' in this chapter in order to understand how such links gradually led to highly controversial changes in ritual and to the late but significant incorporation of Cuban ritual lineages into the transnational social field of the Orisha religion. I will focus particularly on the triple process of 'heritagisation', translocal and trans-class diffusion of the practice, and the reconstruction of ritual kinship with Nigerian 'Yoruba' through the work of various actors from Cuban academic, diplomatic, artistic and religious communities.

FROM FOLKLORE TO YORUBA CULTURE: FIRST 'RECONNECTIONS'

'I put a name to things, and by naming them I capture their essence.'
— Rogelio Martínez Furé[11]

In 1959, under the influence of Pierre Verger, the Centre for Afro-Oriental Studies (CEAO) was founded in Brazil, and a Yoruba language professorship established at the University of Salvador in Bahia state. At the request of the Candomblé *pais* and *mães de santo* – Afro-Brazilian religious practitioners – who studied there, the courses became more religious in nature. In the favourable climate of cultural exchanges with newly independent Nigeria and with the support of UNESCO, the CEAO also sent some of its young researchers and initiates to Africa.[12] As Stefania Capone has shown, these initiatives generated a movement of 'return to the roots' in Brazil in the 1970s, which split Candomblé followers into two factions: one advocating the re-Africanisation of religious practice, following the Nigerian model, and the other favouring the 'desyncretisation' of the Bahia model, considered to be purer and more traditional.

During the same period in Cuba, the situation was quite different. The accession to power of the revolutionary government in 1959 marked a radical political, social and economic shift, and it was largely at a national level that practitioners of African religions focused their energies. With the establishment of the National Theatre of Cuba (TNC), five departments were set up, closely combining artistic and anthropological research: music, dance, drama, folklore, and publications and cultural exchanges.[13] With the support of UNESCO, the TNC Department for Folklore Studies aimed to preserve and disseminate 'Cuban folklore', a term which should be understood in the sense of a set of living practices that had previously been marginalised and in which the 'Afro-Cuban' dimension played a central role. For Argeliers León, adviser to the Centre and former pupil of Fernando Ortiz, it was a question of 'enabling us to become masters of our own culture'.[14] The Department began training around thirty young people, who learned 'on the job' how to collect ethnographic data and contributed both to the newly established journal *Actas del Folklore* and to the preparation of educational performances (for example, *Bembé*, *Abakuá*). It was the ethnographers' informants who were the stage performers, including those who had collaborated with Fernando Ortiz in previous decades, as well as their ritual associates and descendants. For its part, the Department of Dance and its National Modern Dance Group, directed by Ramiro Guerra, received an enthusiastic response from the public for its ballets that celebrated practices of African origin and showed dancers of all skin colours[15] (for example, *Mulato, Mambí*, and *Yoruba Suite*).

In December 1961, the TNC Department for Folklore Studies was dissolved and replaced by the Institute of Ethnology and Folklore (IEF), headed by Argeliers León. The Institute was to focus solely on academic research while the performance side was handed over in 1962 to the newly established National Folklore Ensemble (CFN) under the artistic direction of Rogelio Martínez Furé and the Mexican choreographer Rodolfo Reyes. León became the first Cuban ethnologist to set foot on African soil: in 1964 he made an ethnographic field trip to Ghana, Mali and Nigeria, where he collected objects that were subsequently added to the collection at the Casa de África museum, founded in 1986. León also represented Cuba in Dakar at the 1966 World Festival of Black Arts.

Enthusiasm for the role of Africa in the (re)construction of national identity was then at its height. In the journal *Présence Africaine*, the Haitian writer René Depestre, who had joined the Cuban Revolution, entered into a heated debate with Carlos Moore, a Cuban writer of Jamaican parentage and a political exile since 1963.[16] For Depestre, the prevalence of racism on the island was simply the legacy of previous segregatory structures, accompanying United States interference in Cuba after independence in 1902. Defending the revolutionary project inherited from the anti-racist thinking of José Martí, Depestre was already laying the foundations for his criticism of the concept of Négritude, a criticism that he would also defend at the 1969 Pan-African Festival in Algiers, which he attended as correspondent for the official Cuban newspaper *Granma*. At the 1968 Afro-American Studies Seminar organised in Havana by the Institute of Ethnology and Folklore, Depestre wrote:

> For the first time in the history of the Black Americas, the descendants of Africans are living in a community where they have no need to shun the dominant values, for these are values that unlock the power of imagination and knowledge of the Cuban people as a whole. We have no need to turn away from the Revolution, for it is we who are the revolution; it is our identity, our wealth of humanity, the new starting point for our culture; our cure, our remarkably good health in a history that Blacks, Whites and Mulattos alike can and must build together, in a society where we all recognise one another as standing together in the same endeavour – full liberation of the human condition.[17]

A fellow student of Depestre in Paris, the communist historian Walterio Carbonell, who came from a well-to-do 'coloured' family in eastern Cuba, contended that the religious practices of 'Cuban Africans' had acted as a unifying element in the Cuban working-class struggle, with African culture winning the dialectical struggle against the dominant European culture.[18] His essay was highly controversial, and for good reason, as the government's policy on religious practices was in fact ambiguous (as were the views of most ethnologists of the period). Those religious practices were extolled for their aesthetic, countercultural and identity-related qualities, but they continued to be strongly condemned for their 'obscurantism', which was deemed an insult to the social gains of the revolution.[19] Once the enthusiasm of the early years of the revolution had passed, the *santeros* and *abakuá* who had raised funds to support land reform or the national literacy campaign[20] were forced to return to semi-clandestinity, as did all the other religions present in the decidedly materialistic Cuba of the 1970s.[21]

While a new generation of Cuban anthropologists was being trained in the Soviet Union and mainly oriented towards large-scale national surveys such as the calendar of traditional festivals or the *Ethnographic Atlas of Cuba*, it was through the National Folklore Ensemble that those who practised Cuban religions of African origin found a degree of legitimacy and a place for applied research. Since its establishment in 1962, the Ensemble had included many artists familiar with Cuban religions of African origin who had collaborated with the TNC Department of Folklore. As the years passed, these artists and their ritual families gained a powerful position within the Ensemble,[22] whose work was extended beyond the initial aesthetic project of dramatising folklore.[23] As Lázaro Ros, one of the Ensemble's greatest solo singers (*akpwón*), put it:

> Sixty-two people were selected. That's how the Ensemble was formed. With working people – carpenters, builders, refuse collectors, street sweepers ... with the poor classes of people. It was the people that made the theatre, not the other way round: and that really transformed things. It was the people that were at the theatre, it was the people who expressed their feelings and it was the people who showed their roots.[24]

Thanks to its educational shows, the creation and glorification of a prestigious Afro-Cuban repertoire, the development of this repertoire through ethnomusicology research and stage performance, and the institutionalisation of the Ensemble as part of the national heritage, the religious practice itself spread among the Cuban population as a whole from the 1970s onwards, despite the discrimination it faced.[25] The proliferation of folklore ensembles inspired by this model reinforced this phenomenon: 'stories of the *orichas*[26] and Yoruba, Arará, Congo and Carabalí dances were taught throughout the island by hundreds of dance instructors. Unconsciously or otherwise, affirmative action of a cultural nature was taking place.'[27]

The careers of several figures associated with this institution are worthy of attention, but one in particular sheds light on the transatlantic dimension of the history that concerns us here: that of Rogelio Martínez Furé, a folklorist, dramatist, singer, poet, writer and one of the Ensemble's founders, whose work had a profound impact on the debate over how best to include African cultural heritage in the construction of a national Cuban revolutionary identity. Born in 1937 in the town of Matanzas into a family and district where several members and residents were *abakuá* or *santeros*, Martínez Furé defined himself as a *criollo rellollo*, that is to say, a descendant of ancestors of many ethnic origins (Amerindian, Mandingo, Lucumí, Iyesá, Spanish, Chinese, French and so on) over several generations: 'I am heir to all the world's cultures,' as he liked to say.[28] These words echo the prevailing view shared by Cuban citizens today, one that highlights, first and foremost, a Cuban identity, whatever one's skin colour or ancestry. On his arrival in Havana in 1956 to study law, Martínez Furé was shocked to find that the physical anthropology department was still teaching the theories inspired by Cesare Lombroso on the 'atavistic primitive' that had had such an impact on racism in Cuba.

When a training seminar on folklore was held in 1960 in the National Theatre, Martínez Furé enthusiastically signed up and, together with those whom he liked to define as 'living libraries', he began collecting songs, dances and oral literature from around the island, work that he continued throughout his life. A polyglot, he left no source unexplored, taking an interest in songs of Spanish origin, too. He was nevertheless deeply impressed by his reading of *Black Orpheus*, the first African literary journal in English, founded by the German writer and scholar Ulli Beier, some of whose articles he had translated for the TNC Folklore Department's new journal, *Actas del Folklore*. It was here that he discovered the works of Léopold Sédar Senghor. Asked at the time by a writer – whom he prefers not to name – whether there were poets in Africa, he replied: 'I will show those in Cuba who think like you that not only are there poets in Africa, but that African poetry is as old as the history of humanity.'[29] Martínez Furé thus embarked upon a masterpiece of compilation and translation of poetry from throughout the African continent, including the Maghreb, Libya and Egypt. Like many young artists of the period, he was also deeply influenced by the writings of Aimé Césaire and Frantz Fanon, whose work was brought to Cuba by Che Guevara:

> The young people were reading both Fanon and a bestseller of the time entitled *Now*, an anthology of writing and speeches on Black Power, compiled

> by Edmundo Desnoes . . .; the book was like a Bible for these young people along with other Caribbean and Pan-African literary, musical and theatrical successes, not forgetting the talks by Walterio Carbonell, exchanges with foreign intellectuals living in Cuba, like the Haitian René Depestre, North Americans Selma and Margaret Randall, or the young Congolese who arrived with the return of Che's group, Charlesson, Kasulé and others.[30] Added to this were the gatherings often organised by the Black Panthers who visited or lived in Havana at the time. Although this cultural mix had little influence on creative writing or television production, it did at least contribute to laying the cultural and ideological foundations of African presence and awareness that were beginning to supplant and share the then dominant role played by Eurocentric culture in the Cuban cultural field.[31]

Martínez Furé's artistic and literary output is too great to summarise here.[32] It should be emphasised that he never ceased to fight against racial prejudice[33] and to promote African culture in Cuba. But it was through the National Folklore Ensemble that his activism was able to take root in Africa, he himself acting as a bridge ('I've always dreamt of being a bridge', as he is fond of saying) between the

Figure 9.1: Ernesto 'Che' Guevara visiting the National Folklore Ensemble just before its first international tour in 1964. In the centre, Guevara; far left, Lázaro Ros; and far right, Rogelio Martínez Furé. Source: Archives of the Ministry of Culture, Cuba.

island of Cuba and the African continent. In 1964, during its first foreign tour,[34] the Ensemble accompanied Che Guevara to Algeria; and while, as previously noted, Argeliers León brought Yoruba musical instruments back to Cuba, 'as for us, we were the first to take *batá* drums back to Africa', he proudly proclaimed.

However, it was ten years[35] before the experience would be repeated when Martínez Furé returned to Algeria with the National Folklore Ensemble in 1973; thereafter he went to Ghana, Angola, Mozambique and Zambia in 1982; Angola again in 1986, 1987 and 1989; the People's Republic of the Congo in 1987; and Zaire, Benin and Nigeria, where he finally set foot on Yoruba soil in 1989 and met several religious dignitaries. In Brazil, to which he travelled on several occasions, he met Pierre Verger, with whom he exchanged information and documents. On each trip, he collected and brought back objects, texts and ideas that consolidated his encyclopedic knowledge of Cuban oral traditions of African origin and enabled him to add to, and sometimes 'correct', songs or chants that were 'mispronounced'. He explained these initiatives to the members of the Ensemble and to the well-informed audience of older initiates who attended and, with their presence, supported the weekly *Sábado de la rumba*, an educational show put on by the National Folklore Ensemble, which Martínez Furé had created and managed to introduce in 1982, despite neighbourhood protests, in the formerly well-to-do district of Vedado in Havana.

These emendations and innovations, which began to be incorporated into ritual practices in the 1980s,[36] also came from musicians who were initiates, several of whom belonged to different orchestras and art troupes who toured Africa, in particular Nigeria. For example, when the Danza Contemporánea de Cuba company performed at the Second World Black and African Festival of Arts and Culture (FESTAC) in Lagos in 1977, its *omó añá* percussionists, who included Jesús Pérez,[37] played the *batá* drums in Oyo at the Alafin's palace. This event, recounted with great emotion by the musicians themselves and by their ritual descendants, made a lasting impression: the members of the palace court expressed their astonishment, and then their joy and wonder, at 'rediscovering' ritual rhythms and praise for the *oricha* deity Changó, 'identical' but played 'in the old way' – testimony corroborated by my own interviews.[38] On their return, the musicians enjoyed huge prestige and continued to 'rectify' certain rhythms and chants, with the aim of bringing them more in line with what they saw as 'Yoruba tradition'. Martínez Furé gives a version of events that complements the previous one. In preparing for the Cuban delegation's participation in FESTAC, a Nigerian delegation visited the island and attended performances by the National Folklore Ensemble, where they discovered the similarities between the chants and rhythms of *santería* and their own repertoire: 'When they saw Changó (Alfredo O'Farill, with his traditional smooth elegant style), they went crazy!'[39] He explains: 'After some Nigerian officials came to Havana in the run-up to FESTAC 77, we began to correct the pronunciation of the word *Yoruba* through radio and TV programmes. Nowadays, the word is pronounced correctly throughout Cuba: *Yorubá* rather than Yoruba.'[40]

At first sight, pronunciation may seem of minor importance. However, in the system of signification involved in the practice of *santería,* this is a crucial issue. The rhythms beaten on the six skins of the three *batá* drums are intended to reproduce the exact melody of the sentences spoken: in Cuba, drums are said to 'speak', and it is the *aché* (vital energy) contained in this 'speech' that has the power to summon the *orichas* during the rituals. 'Correcting' the rhythms, chants and prayers is therefore not merely a question of prestige associated with liturgical knowledge. For the elderly *santeros* and *santeras* who took part in or watched the *Sábado de la rumba* in the 1980s, and who knew very little about the re-Africanisation process then under way in Brazil and the United States,[41] it was vital to recover the power of words in this way. One can therefore understand why, for Martínez Furé, sometimes described in Cuba as a *griot,*[42] the knowledge gained from ethnography or from encounters with various Pan-African artists and intellectuals always had to be passed on orally. 'Works now considered classics by authors such as Wande Abimbola, Olabiyi Yai, Juana Elbein and Descoredes dos Santos (Mestre Didi), and Pierre Verger, amongst others, show the way ahead. In their writing, high Yoruba African culture and its Afro-American offshoots are no longer simply *research subjects*; they have become *subjects that are self-explanatory* and reveal their truths from within.'[43]

REDISCOVERY OF THE PAST AND RITUAL RECONNECTION

'Away from home, I have arrived home.'
— Olubuse II[44]

While the issue of African contributions to Cuban cultural identity had perforce been abandoned by ethnographers and was espoused by the artistic and literary community at the cost of great struggle, it was taken up in the 1960s and 1970s by several Cuban historians, who adopted an approach that could be described as 'micro-historical' ahead of its time. For these historians, it was a question of radically revising Cuban history, rewriting it from the viewpoint of the margins of power, of ordinary people – including, therefore, the slave population. Juan Pérez de La Riva accordingly proceeded to unearth and publish in the *Journal of the José Martí National Library* documents that had never previously been made public in order to 'present, through specific cases, a comprehensive picture of the life and struggles of the Cuban people'.[45] In 1966, Manuel Moreno Fraginals wrote a famous text dedicated to Che Guevara,[46] in which he invited revolutionary historians to re-conduct research (*reinvestigar*), adopting innovative methodology and training the younger generations in this new historiographical approach.

Rodolfo Sarracino, a student of Moreno Fraginals, was among those who eagerly delved into the archives. Born in Matanzas in 1934 into a family of Catalan and Italian descent, he was a contemporary and friend of Rogelio Martínez Furé. He had studied in the United States and had a perfect command of English, which initially led him to join the Ministry of Foreign Affairs team that translated the speeches of Fidel Castro and Che Guevara. His older associate, Pedro Deschamps Chapeaux,[47] whose research focused on the class of 'free people of colour' in the nineteenth century, thought that Fernando Ortiz had been mistaken in attributing the mention of a return to Africa by some of these people to 'an error on the part of his poor informants'.[48] He himself had gathered similar information in Havana from elderly people of Lucumí origin.[49]

When Rodolfo Sarracino was appointed to the Cuban embassy in Nigeria in 1978 as a replacement for the economic and commercial counsellor, Deschamps Chapeaux encouraged him to investigate these issues: 'When he heard I was going, he said to me, "You're the one who must bring me this information." And I kept my promise to him.'[50] While organising an official visit by Juan Almeida,[51] and taking care not to offend Nigerian president Shehu Shagari, who was Muslim, Sarracino met a technician at the Lagos company where he was negotiating a cement deal who said that he was acquainted with descendants of Cubans. The man then simply took him to a well-known place called Campos Square, where a family home still stood, formerly assigned to house Cuban returnees, called Cuban Lodge. It would have been enough to 'look up a directory'[52] – but the research question still had to be formulated in the first place. This left the way open for further exploration, whenever his official duties left him the time, searching in the archives and gathering testimony from the descendants of these returnees, who explained that a number of them had gone back to Cuba:

> Finding them was a real discovery. And beyond this return to Africa, there was another very important idea, one that echoed with me immediately: the existence of an Atlantic community. For me, that was a remarkable and innovative notion: that irrespective of governments and politics,

> one population remained in contact with another. They wrote letters to each other, they wanted to learn about Cuba, they admired Cuba through their families without any kind of mediation on our part. One of the Cubans in our country, whose family was in Nigeria and whom I went to see in Matanzas, had been an internationalist volunteer in Africa.[53]

Another of Sarracino's Cuban-Nigerian contacts in Lagos dreamed of sending his son to study in Cuba. The Alafin of Oyo, whom he met during an official visit, described the emotion he had felt when the Cuban percussionists came to play. For Sarracino, 'behind these facts, underlying them, there is something more than the Cuban or Nigerian nations: there is a deep sense of a beloved Afro-Latin homeland'.[54] It is in this sense – Guevarist, Fidelist – that Sarracino believes Cuban missions to Africa should be understood: a means of paying off a debt to this 'brother continent',[55] in a constant common struggle to counter underdevelopment or the (neo) colonial enterprise in order to build a future 'Afro-Latin Atlantic community', whose uniting factor would be not the colour of one's skin but the idea of a shared destiny.[56]

While sending first-hand information to Martínez Furé, who also benefited from his friend's presence in Nigeria and his English-language skills,[57] Sarracino decided to supplement his research by reading the works of Nigerian historians and exploring the British, Nigerian and Cuban archives. This work culminated in the publication

Figure 9.2: Rogelio Martínez Furé next to the Alafin of Oyo during the tour of the National Folklore Ensemble in Nigeria in 1989. Source: Private archives of Rogelio Martínez Furé.

of a book entitled *Los que volvieron a Africa* (Those who returned to Africa) in 1988, which he presented at the Casa del Caribe in one of the early years of the Festival del Caribe in Santiago de Cuba. Several North American researchers in the audience bought copies of the book, but it had limited success in Cuban academic circles of the time. The book condemned a Cuban historiographical habit that was particularly limiting: 'writing about the African presence in Cuba at various stages of our national history without taking African history into account, and confining it solely to European history'.[58] However, Sarracino did not admit defeat and undertook to present the substance of his work to a wider audience: 'I set myself the task of going out into neighbourhoods and villages and talking to the poorest people there, who were mainly black or mulatto. This meant I had to be clear. I talked to them about the way I had gone about my research and received a wonderful response.'[59] Indeed, though unavailable in bookshops in the early 1990s, Sarracino's book was regularly cited by the *santeros* and given a prominent place in their library,[60] next to books by Lydia Cabrera and Fernando Ortiz, which were consulted and used at the time to establish the legitimacy of *santería* practices, then just beginning to be acquired.

Neither Sarracino nor his Cuban-Nigerian contacts were, however, *santeros* or *babalaos*: on the contrary, these families professed to be strictly Catholic, were proud of having built the Holy Cross Cathedral in Lagos, and seemed only to have anything to do with 'the religion of their ancestors' as a last resort, for example, if a loved one was suffering from an incurable disease.[61] The story could have ended there, but the paths already taken by their predecessors led other members of the Cuban diplomatic corps in the 1980s, including *babalaos*, as well as their Nigerian counterparts, to take up the search for kinship ties that were spiritual rather than biological. This was notably the case for the government official Heriberto Feraudy Espino, born in Guantánamo in 1940, a political science graduate and self-identified 'black', who was appointed ambassador to Nigeria in 1985. He had previously served as director of the Africa and Middle East division at the Cuban Institute of Friendship with the Peoples (ICAP), then as ambassador to Zambia and to Botswana. Feraudy Espino followed closely the research carried out by Sarracino. He consulted the extensive literature available in Nigeria on the history of the Yoruba peoples and met formally with a number of dignitaries linked to the Ifá religion, such as the Ooni of Ife, Alayeluwa Oba Okunade Sijuwade Olubuse II, whom he regarded and presented as the 'King of the Yoruba', the Ifá equivalent of the Pope in the Catholic religion.[62]

Feraudy Espino used these meetings and his reading as material for a book, published in Cuba in 1993, entitled *Yoruba: An Approach to Our Roots*. The book's stated objective was to explain to Cubans how the Yoruba religion was organised in Nigeria and to recount its history, which made it a great success among practitioners.[63] In simple, accessible language, he explained how the city of Ile-Ife – home today of a university – was a sacred city, cradle of the ancient Yoruba civilisation, 'a people capable of building kingdoms and empires long before coming into contact with any European'. He does not neglect to describe the wars fought by the various Yoruba peoples, not only against their Fon or Hausa neighbours but also among themselves. This leads him to remind us that not only was the slave trade conducted by these monarchs, but that a number of the slaves returned to Nigeria, where, in the nineteenth century, they played a vital part in creating a unified Yoruba culture. This reminder enables him from the outset to call the authority of the Nigerians into question when it comes to tradition: Cuba, in his view, had retained traditions that predated this 'artificial' unification. Nevertheless, taking up the arguments of the main interested party, he emphasised the supremacy of the Ooni of Ife over all the Yoruba kingdoms (including that of the Alafin of Oyo),[64] as the direct descendant of the deified founding ancestor Oduduwa. With old press clippings as supporting evidence, he added: 'Only the Ooni is authorised to confirm the right of Oba [kings] to wear the crown and to confer chieftaincy titles on members of the local population or on foreigners who have distinguished themselves with respect to Yoruba culture and traditions.'[65]

Feraudy Espino had in fact made arrangements with the Cuban Institute of Friendship with the Peoples for the Ooni to be invited to Cuba and to meet Fidel Castro in person. With the help of José Felipe Carneado, head of the Office of Religious Affairs, set up in 1985 by the Communist Party Central Committee, the official visit went ahead in Havana on 25 June 1987 in the presence of Jorge Risquet and Armando Hart.[66] In an article entitled 'Fidel Meets the Yoruba King', the official newspaper *Granma* described the encounter as a friendly, fraternal conversation on the development of the Yoruba people and the presence of their descendants in Cuban society and culture. The Ooni then paid tribute to the progress made in Cuba towards racial equality. Feraudy Espino himself recounts that when told of the drought the island was experiencing, the Ooni claimed to have 'brought the rain with him' and suggested holding the next Yoruba Congress in Cuba.[67] More importantly, the Ooni's visit also included a meeting with a fraternity of Cuban *babalaos* founded in 1976, who since 1985 had set out to revitalise the practice – one that had died out in Havana after 1959 – of issuing the Letter of the Year, the ruling divination sign that enabled predictions and recommendations to be made for the country as a whole, on 31 December each year. For the Ooni's visit, the fraternity held a 'drumming ceremony to Orula[68] for peace' with *batá* drums, and the Ooni presented its leader with a sceptre (*irofá*), a royal distinction and symbol of authority that instantly conferred great prestige on the *babalao* and his co-religionists.

At the time relations between the Cuban government and religious practitioners were rapidly changing. A rapprochement with Protestant and Catholic institutions had taken place,[69] and Fidel Castro himself was questioning the prevailing Marxist definition of religion as the 'opiate of the people'.[70] Furthermore, at the third congress of the Communist Party of Cuba (PCC) in 1986, the need to fight against racism had been reaffirmed.[71] The 1980s had seen a massive resurgence in turnout at annual pilgrimages in honour of the saints and virgins associated with the *orichas*. Not only did the folklore troupes, as described above, play a role in disseminating African religious practices beyond their original social environment, but a number of political leaders also seem to have made the connection between this religious revival (in the form of requests for miracles to the Catholic avatars of the *orichas*) and the dispatch of Cuban troops to Angola: 'How many internationalists do we have in Africa fighting for the defence of these populations? How many men and women are collaborating not only on defence but also in the health, education and other sectors on the African continent and in other countries? … Well, the families of each of these men and women want them to return to their homeland safe and sound.'[72]

More than just a factor in the expansion of Yoruba religious practice in Cuba in general, the meeting between the Ooni and these Cuban *babalaos* laid the foundation for the institutionalisation and official recognition of the Ifá religion on the island. Among the members of the *babalao* group was Omar Quevedo, an international economics graduate, State Security colonel, and political and economic counsellor at the Cuban embassy in Ghana (where he spent eleven years), in Congo (where he worked for six years), and later in Nigeria. Quevedo had been initiated into *santería* in 1966.[73] He had first met the Ooni in the context of trade and commercial exchange between Cuba and Nigeria in which the Ooni had financial interests,[74] and the two became friends when the Ooni 'recognised' him as a *babaaláwo*. He subsequently received various honours and distinctions from the Ooni and met his official spokesman, the philosopher Wande Abimbola, vice-chancellor of the University of Ile-Ife. One of Abimbola's sons came to study medicine in Cuba in 1997 and was co-founder of Ilé Tuntún, one of the most radical *babalao* groups in Cuba in terms of 'returning to African tradition', in the early 2000s.[75] With Abimbola, Quevedo set up academic and cultural exchanges between the two countries: 'It was necessary, as there are many believers in this philosophy in Cuba,' he explained, deliberately avoiding use of the word 'religion'. Quevedo was also co-founder (with other *babalaos* who had had contacts with the Ooni) of the controversial Yoruba Cultural Association of Cuba (ACYC), set up in December 1991 in a context of economic crisis – but also one of increasing religious freedom – at the beginning of the 'Special Period in Time of Peace'.

The history of the ACYC and its split into unofficial rival organisations, all of which developed direct links with Nigerian *babaaláwos* in the 1990s and 2000s, as well as with other African organisations,[76] is a fascinating one that has been the subject of much research.[77] These organisations were the first to reconnect Cuba with the transnational social field of the Orisha religion, in which Nigerian priests and dignitaries were already active, along with Brazilian *pais* and *mães de santo*,[78] Cuban *santeros and babalaos* resident in the United States, African American initiates,[79] and a growing number of Latin Americans[80] and even Europeans.[81] For the Ooni of Ife – as well as his own rivals – had begun his 'coronation' of initiates on the American continent from the beginning of the 1980s, and helped organise conferences and congresses that brought together a transatlantic network of practitioners with very different political interests.[82] For Cuba, the culmination of this transnational dynamic was undoubtedly the organisation of the 8th World Yoruba Congress in Havana in 2003, where Nigerian dignitaries from the Òrisha World Foundation recognised the island's status as the main propagator of Yoruba religion in the world. On that occasion, some of the delegates ended up abandoning English and speaking Russian with the Cuban *santeros* and *babalaos*, whose ancestry and skin colour varied considerably, after discovering that they had shared the experience of attending university in the Soviet Union.

For J.L. Matory, 'Yoruba religion and society in West Africa are as much the product of developments in the New World as of their own origins, and mutually transformative dialogue continues'.[83] It is to a chapter in the history of this 'transformative dialogue' between Cuba and Nigeria that I wanted to return here in an attempt to show, from the Cuban viewpoint, the relationship that exists between phenomena that are normally studied separately. Often analysed through the lens of political polarisation, which tends not to distinguish between individual initiatives, slight shifts in meaning, and the range of positions taken, the discussions that took place during the first thirty years of the Cuban Revolution on the issue of racism, the contribution made by African to Cuban culture, the role played by Cuban religious practices of African origin in the new society being constructed, and the sense of Cuba's internationalist commitment to Africa – all contributed to generating a unique dialogue between the two countries.

Beyond geographical confines, several worlds have met throughout these three decades. Links have been forged – tenuous at times, unique, exceptional and so all the more likely to strike the imagination – and these in turn have generated new dynamics on several levels. After the promising exuberance of the early 1960s, the 'Afro-Cuban' artistic, literary and anthropological field, which had reinforced the positive representation of a 'Yoruba tradition', superseding that of a barbarous and primitive Africa, seems to have been stifled. And yet it was on the perimeter of the folk-dance shows, which were real 'nerve centres' (to use Martínez Furé's term), that the practice of *santería* and corresponding membership of Lucumí spiritual lineages began to be shared by the majority of the population, irrespective of origin or phenotypic appearance. And it was in the wake of strictly official dance tours, or behind the scenes during diplomatic or trade exchanges, that 'reconnections' of great symbolic significance were made between Cuban and Nigerian practitioners.

Paradoxically, these developments did not necessarily give rise to any questioning of racial prejudices. On the contrary, such prejudices intensified in the Cuba of the 1990s.[84] Admittedly, it was thanks to the upward social mobility enjoyed by some of the actors in these exchanges as a result of the revolution that the connections could be made. Interacting within strict academic, political and economic frameworks but often going beyond their confines in their position as performers, they constructed 'their own truth', to quote Martínez Furé. In turn, they rewrote history, rectified the ritual, extended their kinship network, and created a transatlantic meeting place, the scene of intense power struggles, for want of the Afro-Latin community that Sarracino dreamt of. For the positions taken and initiatives described here were, or are, far from enjoying wide support, whether it be in Cuba or Nigeria, among religious practitioners, among activists (anti-racists, Pan-Africanists, internationalists, and so on) or even in the academic community. Various transnational senses of belonging[85] intersect, each leading to imaginary 'indigenous trans-nations'[86] that sometimes join forces but often clash: pan-Yoruba cultural nationalism, Guevarist anti-racist internationalism or Yoruba ecumenism,[87] which draws on transnational networks of *santería* ritual kinship.

Today, the entry of Nigerian *babaaláwos* into Cuban religious life has enabled the legitimacy of religious practice to be established nationally and confirmed the status of Cuban *santeros* and *babalaos* as internationally recognised tradition-bearers. However, it has also reinforced the conviction shared by most of its followers that only Cuban orthopraxis is valid, and that these 'Nigerians', who (re) initiate practitioners, are formidable – and unfair – competitors. Unlike African Americans, their religious involvement is not linked to a quest for their roots.[88] Instead it has become synonymous with 'Cubanness'. This is a Cubanness with multiple ethnic origins for each citizen, whatever their physical appearance, which enjoys a contemporaneous relationship with the African continent – relations that are all the more complex now that they are no longer indirect but concrete, tangible, fruitful and, inevitably, contentious.

NOTES

1 Juan Pérez de la Riva, 'Cuadro sinóptico de la esclavitud en Cuba,' *Actas del Folklore* 5, separate supplement (May 1961).

2 Respectively: initiates of the Orisha religion (called *santería* or *regla ocha* in Cuba), initiates of Ifá divination and initiates of *batá* ritual drumming. All three of these Cuban forms of religion have Yoruba origins.

3 See Rodolfo Sarracino, *Los que volvieron a África* (Havana: Editorial de Ciencias Sociales, 1988); David Brown, *Santería Enthroned: Art, Ritual, and Innovation in an Afro-Cuban Religion* (Chicago: University of Chicago Press, 2003). Juan Pérez de la Riva, encouraged by Pierre Verger, who was preparing his own landmark study on the same phenomenon in Brazil, had unearthed archives proving that several former Cuban slaves had left for Lagos in 1854 with the support of the British crown (see Juan Pérez de la Riva, 'Documentos para la historia de las gentes sin historia,' *Revista de la Biblioteca Nacional José Martí* 6, no. 1 (1964): 27–52; Pierre Verger, 'L'influence du Brésil au golfe du Bénin,' *Les Afro-Américains: Mémoires de l'IFAN* 27 (1953): 11–12; Pierre Verger, *Flux et reflux de la traite des nègres entre le golfe de Bénin et Bahia de todos os santos du dix-septième au dix-neuvième siècle* (Paris: Mouton/EPHE, 1968). Several Nigerian historians had in fact already investigated this phenomenon. See for example Jacob Festus Ade Ajayi, *Christian Missions in Nigeria, 1841–1891: The Making of a New Elite* (London: Longmans, 1965). But it was the two first-mentioned authors who clearly documented the existence of return journeys in the late nineteenth and early twentieth centuries as well as regular exchanges of letters between families on both sides of the Atlantic.

4 Fernando Ortiz, *Hampa afrocubana: Los negros brujos* (Havana: Editorial de Ciencias Sociales, 1995 [1906]).

5 Raimundo Nina Rodrigues, *L'animisme fétichiste des nègres de Bahia* (Bahia: Reis & Companhia, 1900 [1896]).

6 Robin Law, 'Early Yoruba Historiography,' *History in Africa* 3 (January 1976): 69–89; John D.Y. Peel, *Religious Encounter and the Making of the Yoruba* (Bloomington and Indianapolis: Indiana University Press, 2000).

7 Fernando Ortiz, *Los cabildos y la fiesta afrocubana del Día de Reyes* (Havana: Editorial de Ciencias Sociales, 1992 [1920, 1921]).

8 James Lorand Matory, 'El nuevo imperio yoruba: Textos, migración y el auge transatlántico de la nación lucumí,' in *Culturas encontradas: Cuba y los Estados Unidos*, ed. R. Hernandez and J.H. Coatsworth (Havana: CIDCC Juan Marinello and University of Harvard DRCLAS, 2001), 183–4.

9 Lydia Cabrera, *El monte* (Havana: Editorial Letras Cubanas, 1993 [1954]), 389–90.

10 Teodoro Díaz Fabelo, *Olorun* (Havana: Departamento de Folklore del Teatro Nacional de Cuba, 1960), 66. About this process in Brazil, see Stefania Capone, *La quête de l'Afrique dans le candomblé: Pouvoir et tradition au Brésil* (Paris: Karthala, 1999).

11 'Nombro las cosas y me apodero de su esencia al nombrarlas.' Rogelio Martínez Furé, *Cimarrón de palabras ('descargas')* (Havana: Editorial Letras Cubanas, 2010), 17.

12 Stefania Capone, 'Le voyage "initiatique": Déplacement spatial et accumulation de prestige,' *Cahiers du Brésil Contemporain* 35–6 (1998): 147–8; James Lorand Matory, 'The English Professors of Brazil: On the Diasporic Roots of the Yorùbá Nation,' *Comparative Studies in Society and History* 41, no. 1 (1999): 72–103.

[13] Salomé Roth, 'Quand les dieux entrent en scène: Pratiques rituelles afro-cubaines et performances scéniques à La Havane au lendemain de la Révolution,' PhD thesis in Hispano-American literature, Université Sorbonne Nouvelle , Paris 3, 2016, 174.

[14] Argeliers León, 'La expresión del pueblo en el Teatro Nacional Cubano,' *Actas del Folklore* 1 (1961): 6.

[15] For a detailed analysis of the performances staged and the contexts in which they were produced, see Roth, Quand les dieux entrent en scène, 194–211.

[16] See Carlos Moore, 'Le peuple noir a-t-il sa place dans la révolution cubaine?,' *Présence Africaine* 52 (1964): 177–230; René Depestre, 'Carta de Cuba sobre el imperialismo de la mala fe,' *Casa de las Américas* 6, no. 34 (1966): 33–57.

[17] René Depestre, 'Las metamorfosis de la negritud en América,' *Etnología y Folklore* 7 (1969): 53.

[18] Walterio Carbonell, *Crítica: Cómo surgió la cultura nacional* (Havana: EdicionesYaka, 1961), 108–12.

[19] This stance, still under discussion in 1961, gradually became the official position of the Communist Party of Cuba (PCC). See 'Ciencia y religión: La santería,' *El Militante Comunista* (October 1968): 82–90; 'Trabajo ideológico: La santería,' *Trabajo Político* 4, no 2 (1968): 48–58.

[20] See Rafael Leovigildo López Valdés, *Componentes africanos en el etnos cubano* (Havana: Editorial de Ciencias Sociales, 1985), 173; Tomás Fernández Robaina, *Hablen paleros y santeros* (Havana: Editorial de Ciencias Sociales, 1994), 6–7.

[21] The 1976 constitution, which has since been amended, stipulated: 'Every citizen is free to profess and practise his religious beliefs ... within the framework of respect for the law, public order, citizens' health and the norms of socialist morality' (*Tesis y resoluciones del primer Congreso del P.C.C.* (Havana: Editorial Ciencias Sociales, 1978), 316). For comparison, article 26 of the 1901 Constitution and article 35 of the 1940 Constitution refer to 'Christian morality'.

[22] Katherine J. Hagedorn, *Divine Utterances: The Performance of Afro-Cuban Santería* (Washington, DC, and London: Smithsonian Institution Press, 2001).

[23] Ramiro Guerra, *Teatralización del folklore* (Havana: Editorial Letras Cubanas, 1989).

[24] Mireille Mercier-Balaz and Daniel Pinos, *Osha Niwé, esclave de la musique*, documentary (26 min) (Paris: ATLZA/Planète, 1996).

[25] Kali Argyriadis, 'Les *batá* deux fois sacrés: La construction de la tradition musicale et chorégraphique afro-cubaine,' *Civilisations* 53, no. 1–2 (2005): 45–74.

[26] In this chapter, vernacular terms are spelt following the way they are used in their contexts. For example, in Cuba, *oricha*, Changó, *aché*, *babalao*; but in the USA, *orisha*, *babalawo*; and in Nigeria, *babaaláwo*.

[27] Tomás Fernández Robaina, *Identidad afrocubana, cultura y nacionalidad* (Santiago de Cuba: Editorial Oriente, 2009), 15.

[28] All quotations from this author are drawn from personal conversations held in 1992, 2004, 2015, 2016 and 2017, from the documentary *El aché de la palabra*, directed by Félix de la Nuez (ICAIC, 2012), from press interviews, or from his sung poetry recitals (*descargas*). Unless otherwise specified, they form the leitmotifs that run through Rogelio Martínez Furé's poetry and academic work.

[29] Félix, *El aché de la palabra*.

[30] See the chapter by Michel Luntumbue in this volume.

31 Roberto Zurbano Torres, '¿Un fantasma en el caribe? Muerte y resurrección de Frantz Fanon en cuarenta años de lecturas cubanas,' 2015, http://www.afrocubaweb.com/fantasma.html.

32 He expressed himself equally well through puppet theatre, song, radio, cinema, interactive children's theatre, poetry, lectures and academic articles.

33 In particular, through his membership of the Cuban Anti-Apartheid Committee from 1986.

34 As this tour included a stop in Paris, he also gave a lecture entitled 'African and Hispanic Influences in Cuba' at the Theatre of Nations Festival, attended by leading academics such as Germaine Dieterlen, Michel Leiris and Gilbert Rouget, as well as members of the Société africaine de culture, including Alioune Diop, Felix Tchicaya U Tam'si and Aimé Césaire.

35 During these years, he fell victim to the same ostracism suffered by other intellectuals of the time. In 1968, the puppets from his show *Ibeyí Añá* were burnt, accused of being 'propaganda for witchcraft' (see Dainerys Machado Vento, 'Rogelio Martínez Furé: Soy Agustín, soy mi infancia,' *La Gaceta de Cuba* (March–April 2013): 45). Martínez Furé prefers not to talk about this part of his career and emphasises the importance of forgetting, a tool that is just as important as memory for breaking free of the traumas of history.

36 In a conversation on 14 February 1992, where Rogelio Martínez Furé was commenting on my recordings of rituals, he informed me, for example, that one of the chants to Ochún performed at that time had been collected by him in 1962 from a very old man, then included in the National Folklore Ensemble repertoire broadcast on television, and in this way (re)popularised. In general, the chants that I was able to play to him then, recorded as part of my field research, included several Spanish expressions with a phonetic resemblance to the original chant in Yoruba (e.g. 'Ofé ni ti iyá' replaced by 'Oh felicidad'). At every *Sábado de la rumba*, he never failed to rectify these 'errors'. See also note 26. Argyriadis, 'Les *batás* deux fois sacrés', 63.

37 It should be noted that this renowned percussionist had also worked with Fernando Ortiz, been an accompanist for Mercedita Valdés and Celia Cruz, a founding member of the National Folklore Ensemble and an associate of Rogelio Martínez Furé.

38 Ivor Miller, 'Jesus Perez and the Transculturation of the Cuban Batá Drum,' *Diálogo* 7, no. 1 (2003): 71–2.

39 Interview with Rogelio Martínez Furé, Havana, 27 February 2016. By Changó, he means the interpretation of the role by the dancer mentioned.

40 Rogelio Martínez Furé, 'Descargas: Ritual y fiesta de la palabra,' *La Gaceta de Cuba* (January–February 2005): 30. In Spanish, when a word ends with a vowel, the stress falls on the penultimate syllable unless there is a diacritic mark on another syllable. This 'correction' therefore brings the pronunciation somewhat closer to the modern Yoruba language (which has three tones).

41 George Brandon, *Santería from Africa to the New World: The Dead Sell Memories* (Bloomington and Indianapolis: Indiana University Press, 1993); Stefania Capone, *La quête de l'Afrique dans le candomblé*; Stefania Capone, *Les Yoruba du nouveau monde: Religion, ethnicité et nationalisme noir aux États-Unis* (Paris: Karthala, 2005).

42 Nancy Morejón, *Rogelio Martínez Furé: ¿juglar o griot?* (Havana: Colección Sur, 2017).

43 Martínez Furé, 'Descargas', 29, emphasis in the original.

[44] 'He venido de mi casa y estoy en mi casa.' Words spoken by the Ooni of Ife on his arrival in Havana in June 1987 (quoted by Heriberto Feraudy Espino, 'El Ooni de Ifé,' *Cubarte* (29 September 2015)), http://www.cubarte.cult.cu/es/article/31323).

[45] Pérez de la Riva, 'Documentos para la historia de las gentes sin historia,' 27.

[46] Manuel Moreno Fraginals, 'La historia como arma,' *Casa de las Américas* 40 (January–February 1967): 20–8. As was the case with Walterio Carbonell, Moreno Fraginals's ideas had caused a great stir (Kate Quinn, 'Cuban Historiography in the 1960s: Revisionists, Revolutionaries and the Nationalist Past,' *Bulletin of Latin American Research* 26, no. 3 (2007): 386). But Che Guevara was a great admirer of his work, particularly his outstanding book on the plantation system in Cuba, *El ingenio: Complejo económico-social cubano del azúcar* (the first volume of which was published in 1964). This endorsement and the quality of his work meant that Moreno Fraginals enjoyed relative freedom of expression. After playing a key role, alongside historian José Luciano Franco, in the development of a research programme on 'Africa in Latin America' in collaboration with UNESCO, Moreno Fraginals finally went into exile in Miami in 1994.

[47] This chemist by training and self-taught historian from a modest Haitian background was one of the most representative figures in the new post-revolutionary approach to Cuban historiography. He wrote numerous works on the free and slave population 'of colour' in Cuba under the colonial regime. See Pedro Deschamps Chapeaux, *El negro en la economía habanera del siglo XIX* (Havana: UNEAC, 1971); Pedro Deschamps Chapeaux and Juan Pérez de la Riva, *Contribución a la historia de la gente sin historia* [compilation of texts published under this title in the *Revista de la Biblioteca Nacional José Martí* between 1963 and 1974] (Havana: Editorial de Ciencias Sociales, 1974). He received his doctorate in 1984.

[48] Interview with Rodolfo Sarracino, Havana, 23 February 2016, where he quotes Fernando Ortiz directly. See also Sarracino, *Los que volvieron a Africa*, 6.

[49] Pérez de la Riva, 'Documentos para la historia de las gentes sin historia,' 31.

[50] Interview with Rodolfo Sarracino, Havana, 25 February 2016.

[51] Born in 1927 into a poor family regarded as 'black,' Juan Almeida Bosque was a bricklayer, composer, member of the Politburo, vice-president of the Council of State, commander of the Revolution who fought in the very first hours of the uprising, was imprisoned with Fidel Castro on Isla de Pinos in 1953, and survived the Granma expedition. He was long considered to be the Cuban government's 'number three.'

[52] Sarracino, *Los que volvieron a Africa*, 12.

[53] Rodolfo Sarracino, 'Regreso a la tierra perdida' (interview with Luis Hernández Serrano). *Juventud Rebelde*, 25 December 2010, http://www.juventudrebelde.cu/cuba/2010-12-25/regreso-a-la-tierra-perdida-galeria-de-fotos/.

[54] Sarracino, *Los que volvieron a Africa*, 62.

[55] This feeling of having a 'debt' to pay to Africa was often expressed by Cubans on internationalist missions to the continent. It was taken up, for example, in an open letter to Afro-North American intellectuals and artists signed in 2009 by several leading Cuban figures, including Rogelio Martínez Furé and Heriberto Feraudy Espino (http://www.cubadebate.cu/noticias/2009/12/03/envian-desde-cuba-mensaje-a-los-intelectuales-y-artistas-afronorteamericanos/#.WXCqWFFpzcs).

[56] Rodolfo Sarracino, 'Premisas culturales para una comunidad atlántica latinoamericana: Cuba y Brasil,' *África* 18–19 (1997): 204, 212.

[57] Interview with Rogelio Martínez Furé, Havana, 11 May 2017.

58 Armando Entralgo, 'Prólogo,' in *Los que volvieron a África*, ed. R. Sarracino (Havana: Editorial de Ciencias Sociales, 1988), vii.

59 Interview with Rodolfo Sarracino, Havana, 25 February 2016.

60 This was how I myself became acquainted with the book when I began my field research in Havana in 1991.

61 Interview with Rodolfo Sarracino, Havana, 25 February 2016.

62 Feraudy Espino, 'El Ooni de Ifé.'

63 Since then, Heriberto Feraudy has written many works aimed at a wider audience as well as a number of Yoruba-inspired children's storybooks. He is best known as the first president of the Aponte Commission, set up in 2012 to commemorate the 200th anniversary of the death of José Antonio Aponte (see the Introduction to this volume). The Commission, which falls under the National Union of Cuban Artists and Writers, is responsible for combating racism and racial discrimination.

64 This supremacy is widely contested by Cuban *babalaos* living in Miami, such as Ernesto Pichardo, leader of the Church of the Lukumí Babalú Ayé. For more on these rivalries within both Cuba and the United States, see Kali Argyriadis and Stefania Capone, '*Cubanía* et *santería*: Les enjeux politiques de la transnationalisation religieuse (La Havane–Miami),' *Civilisations* 51, no. 1–2 (2004): 120.

65 Heriberto Feraudy Espino, *Yorubá: Un acercamiento a nuestras raíces* (Havana: Editora Política, 1993).

66 One month previously, Wole Soyinka had been invited to the Casa de las Américas as part of the International Theatre Institute Congress, where the National Folklore Ensemble was performing. For the Nigerian playwright, winner of the 1986 Nobel Prize for Literature and known for his criticism of the concept of Négritude, this visit came after a first stay in 1964 and was followed by several others, during which he received numerous prizes and honorary titles.

67 Feraudy Espino, 'El Ooni de Ifé.'

68 Orula is the *oricha* of divination.

69 Kali Argyriadis, *La religion à La Havane: Actualité des représentations et des pratiques cultuelles havanaises* (Paris: Éditions des Archives Contemporaines, 1999), 282–8.

70 Fidel Castro Ruz, *Fidel y la religion* (interview with Frei Betto) (Havana: Oficina de Publicaciones del Consejo de Estado, 1985), 333.

71 This was notably thanks to many open letters sent to the PCC by Walterio Carbonell, raising the need for greater 'black' representation in positions of power, and to a similar position taken by Rogelio Martínez Furé in the media (Fernández Robaina, *Identidad afrocubana, cultura y nacionalidad*, 19).

72 Carneado, quoted by Heriberto Feraudy Espino, *De la africanía en Cuba: El ifaísmo* (Havana: Editorial de Ciencias Sociales, 2005), 17–18.

73 Interview with Omar Quevedo, Havana, 25 September 2004. It should be noted that while he became an initiate of Changó in 1966, then a *babalao* in 1967, he had also been initiated into *palo-monte* (another form of Cuban religion that originated, among other places, between the kingdoms of Kongo and Luanda) in 1960. Omar Quevedo is considered to be 'black' in Cuba.

74 On motives of 'conquest' behind the Ooni's visit to Cuba, see also Stephan Palmié, *The Cooking of History: How Not to Study Afro-Cuban Religion* (Chicago: University of Chicago Press, 2013), 108–11. According to Bernard Müller (personal communication), the Ooni was a Christian businessman, educated in England who succeeded to the hereditary office in the context of his commitment to Yoruba federalism in Nigeria. For

activists in the Pan-Yoruba nationalist movement (whose genesis in the late nineteenth century went hand in hand with the emergence of independent African churches), Ile-Ife is the capital of a utopian community, seen as a real 'heavenly Jerusalem' (Bernard Müller, 'L'année prochaine à Ile-Ife! La ville idéale dans la construction de l'identité yoruba,' *Journal des Africanistes* 74, nos. 1–2 (2004): 159–79).

75 Argyriadis and Capone, '*Cubanía* et *santería*', 93–5; Alain Konen, *Rites divinatoires et initiatiques à La Havane: La main des dieux* (Paris: L'Harmattan, 2009), 329–40.

76 For example, for a long time the main rival group to the ACYC held its press conferences at the Angolan embassy in Havana, since several of its leaders had direct contact with the Angolan diplomatic staff. From 2004, however, the ACYC director and deputy director (Omar Quevedo) used their own diplomatic contacts to prevent them from meeting there. Despite this, after years of antagonism, the two groups – whose leaders are all ritually related – have now merged.

77 Argyriadis and Capone, '*Cubanía* et *santería*'; Emma Gobin, 'Du Nigeria à Cuba: Le second voyage d'Ifá: Récit d'une collaboration rituelle transatlantique.' In *Voyage à l'intérieur de la langue et de la culture yorùbá: En l'honneur de Michka Sachnine*, ed. G. Àlàó (Paris: Éditions des Archives Contemporaines, 2014), 57–78.

78 Capone, *La quête de l'Afrique dans le candomblé*; Matory, 'El nuevo imperio yoruba.'

79 See the chapter by Gonçalves in this volume and note 42. Brandon, *Santería from Africa to the New World*; Capone, *Les Yoruba du nouveau monde*; Stephan Palmié, 'Against Syncretism: "Africanizing" and "Cubanizing" Discourses in North American *Òrìsà* Worship,' in *Counterworks: Managing the Diversity of Knowledge*, ed. R. Fardon (London: Routledge, 1995), 73–104.

80 Ari Pedro Oro, *Axé Mercosul: As religiões afro-brasileiras nos paises do Prata* (Petrópolis: Editora Vozes, 1999); Nahayeilli Juárez Huet, *Un pedacito de Dios en casa: Circulación transnacional, relocalización y praxis de la santería en la Ciudad de México* (Mexico City: CIESAS, 2014).

81 Kali Argyriadis, 'Les Parisiens et la *santería*: De l'attraction esthétique à l'implication religieuse,' *Psychopathologie Africaine* 31, no 1 (2001–2): 17–43.

82 Argyriadis and Capone, '*Cubanía* et *santería*', 93–94; Nahayeilli Juárez Huet, 'De "negro brujo" a patrimonio cultural: Circulación transnacional de la tradición *orisha*,' *Desacatos* 53 (January–April 2017): 74–89.

83 Matory, 'El nuevo imperio yoruba,' 179.

84 Alejandro de la Fuente, 'Un debate necesario: Raza y cubanidad,' *La Gaceta de Cuba* 1 (January–February 2005): 62–4; Niurka Núñez González, Pablo Rodríguez Ruiz, María Pérez Álvarez and Odalys Buscarón Ochoa, *Las relaciones raciales en Cuba: Estudios contemporaneous* (Havana: Fundación Fernando Ortiz, 2011).

85 Peggy Levitt and Nina Glick-Schiller, 'Conceptualizing Simultaneity: A Transnational Social Field Perspective on Society,' *International Migration Review* 38, no. 3 (2004): 1010.

86 André Mary, 'Politiques de "re-conquête spirituelle" et imaginaires transnationaux,' in *Religions transnationales des Suds: Afrique, Europe, Amériques*, ed. K. Argyriadis, S. Capone, R. de la Torre and A. Mary (Leuven: Academia Bruylant/IRD CIESAS, 2012), 131–45, 138.

87 Stefania Capone and Alejandro Frigerio, 'Ifá reconquiert le monde ou les défis d'une "nation yoruba imaginée",' in *Religions transnationales des Suds: Afrique, Europe, Amériques*, ed. K. Argyriadis, S. Capone, R. de la Torre and A. Mary (Leuven: Academia Bruylant/IRD CIESAS, 2012), 171–91.

88 Capone, *Les Yoruba du nouveau monde*, 180–3.

REFERENCES

Ajayi, Jacob Festus Ade. *Christian Missions in Nigeria, 1841–1891: The Making of a New Elite*. London: Longmans, 1965.

Argyriadis, Kali. *La religion à La Havane: Actualité des représentations et des pratiques cultuelles havanaises*. Paris: Éditions des Archives Contemporaines, 1999.

Argyriadis, Kali. 'Les *batá* deux fois sacrés: La construction de la tradition musicale et chorégraphique afro-cubaine.' *Civilisations* 53, no. 1–2 (2005): 45–74.

Argyriadis, Kali. 'Les Parisiens et la *santería*: De l'attraction esthétique à l'implication religieuse.' *Psychopathologie Africaine* 31, no. 1 (2001–2): 17–43.

Argyriadis, Kali and Stefania Capone. '*Cubanía* et *santería*: Les enjeux politiques de la transnationalisation religieuse (La Havane–Miami).' *Civilisations* 51, no. 1–2 (2004): 81–137.

Argyriadis, Kali and Stefania Capone. *La religion des orisha: Un champ social transnational en pleine recomposition*. Paris: Hermann Editions, 2011.

Atlas etnográfico de Cuba: Cultura popular tradicional. Havana: CIDCC Juan Marinello/ Centro de Antropología/CEISIC, CD-ROM, 2000.

Brandon, George. *Santería from Africa to the New World: The Dead Sell Memories*. Bloomington: Indiana University Press, 1993.

Brown, David. *Santería Enthroned: Art, Ritual, and Innovation in an Afro-Cuban Religion*. Chicago: University of Chicago Press, 2003.

Cabrera, Lydia. *El monte*. Havana: Editorial Letras Cubanas, 1993 [1954].

Capone, Stefania. *La quête de l'Afrique dans le candomblé: Pouvoir et tradition au Brésil*. Paris: Karthala, 1999.

Capone, Stefania. 'Le voyage "initiatique": Déplacement spatial et accumulation de prestige.' *Cahiers du Brésil Contemporain* 35–6 (1998): 137–56.

Capone, Stefania. *Les Yoruba du nouveau monde: Religion, ethnicité et nationalisme noir aux États-Unis*. Paris: Karthala, 2005.

Capone, Stefania and Alejandro Frigerio. 'Ifá reconquiert le monde ou les défis d'une "nation yoruba imaginée".' In *Religions transnationales des Suds: Afrique, Europe, Amériques*, edited by K. Argyriadis, S. Capone, R. de la Torre and A. Mary, 171–91. Leuven: Academia Bruylant/IRD CIESAS, 2012.

Carbonell, Walterio. *Crítica: Cómo surgió la cultura nacional*. Havana: EdicionesYaka, 1961.

Castro Ruz, Fidel. *Fidel y la religion* (interview with Frei Betto). Havana: Oficina de Publicaciones del Consejo de Estado, 1985.

Césaire, Aimé. *Retorno al país natal*. Havana: Colección Sur, 2011 [first edition in Spanish, translated by Lydia Cabrera, 1943].

'Ciencia y religión: La santería.' *El Militante Comunista* (October 1968): 82–90.

Depestre, René. *Bonjour et adieu à la négritude*. Paris: Robert Laffont, 1980.

Depestre, René. 'Carta de Cuba sobre el imperialismo de la mala fe.' *Casa de las Américas* 6, no. 34 (1966): 33–57.

Depestre, René. 'Entrevista con Aimé Césaire.' *Casa de las Américas* 9, no. 49 (1968): 137–42.

Depestre, René. 'Las metamorfosis de la negritud en América.' *Etnología y Folklore* 7 (1969): 43–53.

Deschamps Chapeaux, Pedro. *El negro en la economía habanera del siglo XIX*. Havana: UNEAC, 1971.

Deschamps Chapeaux, Pedro and Juan Pérez de laRiva. *Contribución a la historia de la gente sin historia* [compilation of texts published under this title in the *Revista de la Biblioteca*

Nacional José Martí between 1963 and 1974]. Havana: Editorial de Ciencias Sociales, 1974.

Díaz Fabelo, Teodoro. *Olorun*. Havana: Departamento de Folklore del Teatro Nacional de Cuba, 1960.

Entralgo, Armando. 'Prólogo.' In *Los que volvieron a África*, ed. R. Sarracino, vii–x. Havana: Editorial de Ciencias Sociales, 1988.

Estrada Betancourt, José Luis. 'Siempre puente, nunca frontera.' *Juventud Rebelde*, 22 September 2012. http://www.juventudrebelde.cu/cultura/2012-09-22/siempre-puente-nunca-frontera.

Fanon, Frantz. *Los condenados de la tierra*. Mexico: Fondo de Cultura Económica, 1963.

Fanon, Frantz. *Piel negra, máscaras blancas*. Havana: Instituto Cubano del Libro, 1968.

Fanon, Frantz. *Por la revolución africana*. Mexico City and Buenos Aires: Fondo de Cultura Económica, 1965.

Feraudy Espino, Heriberto. *De la africanía en Cuba: El ifaísmo*. Havana: Editorial de Ciencias Sociales, 2005.

Feraudy Espino, Heriberto. 'El Ooni de Ifé.' *Cubarte*, 29 September 2015. http://www.cubarte.cult.cu/es/article/31323.

Feraudy Espino, Heriberto. *Yorubá: Un acercamiento a nuestras raíces*. Havana: Editora Política, 1993.

Fernández Robaina, Tomás. *Hablen paleros y santeros*. Havana: Editorial de Ciencias Sociales, 1994.

Fernández Robaina, Tomás. *Identidad afrocubana, cultura y nacionalidad*. Santiago de Cuba: Editorial Oriente, 2009.

Fuente, Alejandro de la. 'Un debate necesario: Raza y cubanidad.' *La Gaceta de Cuba* 1 (January–February 2005): 62–4.

Gobin, Emma. 'Du Nigeria à Cuba: Le second voyage d'Ifá: Récit d'une collaboration rituelle transatlantique.' In *Voyage à l'intérieur de la langue et de la culture yorùbá: En l'honneur de Michka Sachnine*, edited by G. Àlàó, 57–78. Paris: Éditions des Archives Contemporaines, 2014.

Guerra, Ramiro. *Teatralización del folklore*. Havana: Editorial Letras Cubanas, 1989.

Hagedorn, Katherine J. *Divine Utterances: The Performance of Afro-Cuban Santería*. Washington, DC, and London: Smithsonian Institution Press, 2001.

Juárez Huet, Nahayeilli. 'De "negro brujo" a patrimonio cultural: Circulación transnacional de la tradición *orisha*.' *Desacatos* 53 (January–April 2017): 74–89.

Juárez Huet, Nahayeilli. *Un pedacito de Dios en casa: Circulación transnacional, relocalización y praxis de la santería en la Ciudad de México*. Mexico City: CIESAS, 2014.

Konen, Alain. *Rites divinatoires et initiatiques à La Havane: La main des dieux*. Paris: L'Harmattan, 2009.

Law, Robin. 'Early Yoruba Historiography.' *History in Africa* 3 (January 1976): 69–89.

León, Argeliers. 'La expresión del pueblo en el Teatro Nacional Cubano.' *Actas del Folklore* 1 (1961): 5–7.

Levitt, Peggy and Nina Glick-Schiller. 'Conceptualizing Simultaneity: A Transnational Social Field Perspective on Society.' *International Migration Review* 38, no. 3 (2004): 1002–39.

López Valdés, Rafael Leovigildo. *Componentes africanos en el etnos cubano*. Havana: Editorial de Ciencias Sociales, 1985.

Machado Vento, Dainerys. 'Rogelio Martínez Furé: Soy Agustín, soy mi infancia.' *La Gaceta de Cuba* (March–April 2013): 44–7.

Martínez Furé, Rogelio. *Cimarrón de palabras ('descargas')*. Havana: Editorial Letras Cubanas, 2010.

Martínez Furé, Rogelio. 'Descargas: Ritual y fiesta de la palabra.' *La Gaceta de Cuba* (January–February 2005): 28–31.

Martínez Furé, Rogelio. *Diwán africano: Poetas de expresión francesa*. Havana: Editorial Arte y Literatura, 1988.

Martínez Furé, Rogelio. *Diwán africano: Poetas de expresión portuguesa*. Havana: Editorial Arte y Literatura, 2000.

Martínez Furé, Rogelio. *Diwán: Poetas de lenguas africanas*. Havana: Editorial Arte y Literatura, 1996.

Martínez Furé, Rogelio. *Pequeño Tarikh: Apuntes para un diccionario de poetas africanos*. Havana: Editorial Arte y Literatura, 2014.

Martínez Furé, Rogelio. *Poesía anónima africana*. Havana: Instituto del Libro, 1968 [expanded reprints in 1977, 1985 and 2010].

Martínez Furé, Rogelio. *Poesía yoruba*. Havana: Ediciones El Puente, 1963.

Mary, André. 'Politiques de "re-conquête spirituelle" et imaginaires transnationaux.' In *Religions transnationales des Suds: Afrique, Europe, Amériques*, edited by K. Argyriadis, S. Capone, R. de la Torre and A. Mary, 131–45. Leuven: Academia Bruylant/IRD CIESAS, 2012.

Matory, James Lorand. 'El nuevo imperio yoruba: Textos, migración y el auge transatlántico de la nación lucumí.' In *Culturas encontradas: Cuba y los Estados Unidos*, edited by R. Hernandez and J.H. Coatsworth, 167–88. Havana: CIDCC Juan Marinello and University of Harvard (DRCLAS), 2001.

Matory, James Lorand. 'The English Professors of Brazil: On the Diasporic Roots of the Yorùbá Nation.' *Comparative Studies in Society and History* 41, no. 1 (1999): 72–103.

Mercier-Balaz, Mireille and Daniel Pinos. *Osha Niwé, esclave de la musique*. Documentary (26 min). Paris: ATLZA/Planète, 1996.

Miller, Ivor. 'Jesus Perez and the Transculturation of the Cuban Batá Drum.' *Diálogo* 7, no. 1 (2003): 70–4.

Moore, Carlos. 'Le peuple noir a-t-il sa place dans la révolution cubaine?' *Présence Africaine* 52 (1964): 177–230.

Morejón, Nancy. *Rogelio Martínez Furé: ¿juglar o griot?* Havana: Colección Sur, 2017.

Morel, Géraldine. 'Afrocubanité, africanité et transnationalisation: Le cas de la société secrète abakuá (La Havane, Cuba).' In *Mobilité religieuse: Retours croisés des Afriques aux Amériques*, edited by P. Chanson, Y. Droz, Y.N. Gez and E. Soares, 115–29. Paris: Karthala, 2014.

Moreno Fraginals, Manuel. 'La historia como arma.' *Casa de las Américas* 40 (January–February 1967): 20–8.

Müller, Bernard. 'L'année prochaine à Ile-Ife! La ville idéale dans la construction de l'identité yoruba.' *Journal des Africanistes* 74, no. 1–2 (2004): 159–79.

Nina Rodrigues, Raimundo. *L'animisme fétichiste des nègres de Bahia*. Bahia: Reis & Companhia, 1900 [1896].

Nuez, Félix de la. *El aché de la palabra*, documentary (29 min). Havana: UNEAC/Centro de Desarrollo del Documental Octavio Cortázar, 2012.

Núñez González, Niurka, Pablo Rodríguez Ruiz, María Pérez Álvarez and Odalys Buscarón Ochoa. *Las relaciones raciales en Cuba: Estudios contemporaneous*. Havana: Fundación Fernando Ortiz, 2011.

Oro, Ari Pedro. *Axé Mercosul: As religiões afro-brasileiras nos paises do Prata*. Petrópolis: Editora Vozes, 1999.

Ortiz, Fernando. *Hampa afrocubana: Los negros brujos*. Havana: Editorial de Ciencias Sociales, 1995 [1906].

Ortiz, Fernando. 'Hampa afro-cubana: Los negros esclavos: Estudio sociológico y de derecho public.' *Revista Bimestre Cubana* VIII, no. 4 (1916).

Ortiz, Fernando. *Los cabildos y la fiesta afrocubana del Día de Reyes*. Havana: Editorial de Ciencias Sociales, 1992 [1920; 1921].

Palmié, Stephan. 'Against Syncretism: "Africanizing" and "Cubanizing" Discourses in North American Òrìsà Worship.' In *Counterworks: Managing the Diversity of Knowledge*, edited by R. Fardon, 73–104. London: Routledge, 1995.

Palmié, Stephan. *The Cooking of History: How Not to Study Afro-Cuban Religion*. Chicago: University of Chicago Press, 2013.

Peel, John D.Y. *Religious Encounter and the Making of the Yoruba*. Bloomington and Indianapolis: Indiana University Press, 2000.

Pérez de la Riva, Juan. 'Cuadro sinóptico de la esclavitud en Cuba.' *Actas del Folklore* 5, separate supplement (May 1961).

Pérez de la Riva, Juan. 'Documentos para la historia de las gentes sin historia.' *Revista de la Biblioteca Nacional José Martí* 6, no. 1 (1964): 27–52.

Quinn, Kate. 'Cuban Historiography in the 1960s: Revisionists, Revolutionaries and the Nationalist Past.' *Bulletin of Latin American Research* 26, no. 3 (2007): 378–98.

Roth, Salomé. 'Quand les dieux entrent en scène: Pratiques rituelles afro-cubaines et performances scéniques à La Havane au lendemain de la Révolution.' PhD thesis in Hispano-American literature, Université Sorbonne Nouvelle, Paris 3, 2016.

Sarracino, Rodolfo. *Los que volvieron a África*. Havana: Editorial de Ciencias Sociales, 1988.

Sarracino, Rodolfo. 'Premisas culturales para una comunidad atlántica latinoamericana: Cuba y Brasil.' *África* 18–19 (1997): 203–12.

Sarracino, Rodolfo. 'Regreso a la tierra perdida' (interview with Luis Hernández Serrano). *Juventud Rebelde*, 25 December 2010. http://www.juventudrebelde.cu/cuba/2010-12-25/regreso-a-la-tierra-perdida-galeria-de-fotos/.

Tesis y resoluciones del primer Congreso del P.C.C. Havana: Editorial de Ciencias Sociales. 1978.

'Trabajo ideológico: La santería.' *Trabajo Político* 4, no. 2 (1968): 48–58.

Verger, Pierre. *Flux et reflux de la traite des nègres entre le golfe de Bénin et Bahia de todos os santos du dix-septième au dix-neuvième siècle*. Paris: Mouton/EPHE, 1968.

Verger, Pierre. 'L'influence du Brésil au golfe du Bénin.' *Les Afro-Américains: Mémoires de l'IFAN* 27 (1953): 11–102.

Zurbano Torres, Roberto. '¿Un fantasma en el caribe? Muerte y resurrección de Frantz Fanon en cuarenta años de lecturas cubanas.' 2015. http://www.afrocubaweb.com/fantasma.html.

CHAPTER

10

The Island, the Peninsula, and the Continent: Cuban American engagements with Africa

João Felipe Gonçalves

In 1978, the Nigerian religious leader Ifá Yemí Elebuibon visited Miami for 42 days, having been invited by a Cuban American *babalao* (a priest in the Ifá religious tradition). Three years before, that Cuban American priest, José Miguel Gómez Barberas, had travelled to Elebuibon's Yoruba home town to obtain an *Olofin*, a precious ritual object that allowed him to legitimately initiate new *babalaos* and create his own ritual lineage. Gómez brought Elebuibon to Miami to make new *Olofins* for other Cuban American *babalaos*, and he would soon take three other Miami Cubans to Nigeria to be initiated. These transatlantic crossings were part of Gómez's efforts to break the dependency of Miami *babalaos* upon the *Olofins* produced by a powerful Havana-based *babalao*. To Gómez and other Miami Cubans, bypassing Cuba and going to Yorubaland enabled them to create an authoritative new line of religious descent and gave validity to their religious practices, imagined as authentically African.[1]

The same year in which Ifá Yemí visited Miami, other Cuban Americans were crossing the ocean to develop another sort of relationship with Africa. Nearly three hundred Cuban exiles, most of them veterans of the Bay of Pigs invasion, spent eight months of 1978 in war-torn Angola fighting the leftist government of the Popular Movement for the Liberation of Angola (MPLA) alongside local anti-communist guerrillas. This was a response to the heavy and growing military support of the MPLA by Cuba's socialist regime, and it gave the exiles the opportunity to engage directly with Cuban troops across the Atlantic. For several reasons this mission did not last long and Cuban Americans failed to be a major player in the Angolan war, but their endeavour indicates that Cuban exiles were then interested in Angola as a transatlantic space where they could confront the Cuban government and react to its widespread support for African leftist movements.[2]

One can only wonder what kind of relationship, if any, the Miami-based Cubans who met Ifá Yemí Elebuibon had with the Cuban Americans who fought in Angola. Yet, these snapshots from 1978 are quite revealing of broader and longer-lasting phenomena. In one case, Miami Cubans travelled to Angola as a way of opposing Cuban political leaders. In the other, a Nigerian priest travelled to Florida to help Miami Cubans break their dependency on a Cuban religious leader. These transatlantic movements illustrate two kinds of connections that Cuban Americans have had with Africa over several decades, each associated with one of two domains that modern Western thought likes to distinguish: the realm of 'politics' and the realm of 'culture'.[3] On the one hand, politically organised Cuban Americans have often engaged with African issues through a practice of reactive confrontation, taking positions contrary to those of the Cuban government and actively opposing its African allies. On the other hand, Cuban Americans have deepened and strengthened the Cuban tradition of searching in Africa for the original roots of several Cuban practices, especially in the religious sphere.

Both kinds of Cuban American engagement with Africa are based on a problematic relationship with Cuba, but, whereas in the first form Africa appears as a foreign ground on which the political struggle over Cuban sovereignty is reproduced, in the second form Africa is imagined as the original and authorising soil of Cuban cultural roots. To use Ferdinand de Saussure's classic terms, in the first case Africa appears in an associative relation to Cuba; in the second it has a syntagmatic relation to Cuba. In one case, the continent works as a political metaphor; in the other it works as a cultural metonym of the island.[4]

In this chapter I will focus mainly on the first kind of engagement – which, following John Borneman,[5] I call 'mirror-making' – and briefly and comparatively discuss the second kind of engagement – which I call 'root-searching'. A major complicating factor that I will also address here is race, since, when creating their own novel connections to Africa, US-based Cubans have had to deal with – in a rather uneasy way – Anglo-American racial representations and identifications. In order to approach these issues, I will examine more closely the military presence of Cuban exiles in Congo-Léopoldville in the 1960s, the relationship of Cuban Americans with Angola in the 1970s and 1980s, and the reaction of Cuban Miamians to Nelson Mandela's visit to their city in 1990. I will conclude by suggesting that the 1974 performance of the iconic Cuban American singer Celia Cruz in Kinshasa reveals a different kind of relationship with Africa that goes beyond mirror-making and root-searching.

The United States might seem a strange place to think about Cubans' relationship to Africa. Some might point out that the Cuban population in the United States is considerably 'whiter' than that of the island, and observe correctly that Cuban Americans are more oriented towards the Americas than to any other world region.[6] However, this orientation to the Americas is also true of the island dwellers. The former argument relies on a spurious racialist association between 'Africanness' and 'blackness' that is challenged by both the Cuban and Cuban American experiences. In contrast, the demographic relevance of the Cuban American population is undeniable: around two million people of Cuban descent live in the United States; there is around one Cuban-born person living in that country to every ten people living on the island; and Miami is the second-largest Cuban metropolis anywhere in the world.[7]

Most importantly, Cuban Americans have played a fundamental geopolitical, ideological and economic role in the island, without which one can hardly understand socialist Cuba. Since 1959 the staunch opposition of organised Cuban exiles has been fundamental for the self-legitimation of the Cuban government as the bastion of national sovereignty against US imperialism and against those it calls the 'worms' (*gusanos*) or 'scum' (*escoria*) who left the island. And, ironically, growing remittances from the United States have been fundamental for Cuba's economic survival after the fall of the Soviet Union and the East European socialist bloc.[8] As this chapter will make clear, the engagements of Cuban Americans with Africa are an important part of the relationships between Cubans and the continent, and their study adds new complexity to the understanding of those relationships.

CUBANS VS CUBANS IN THE CONGO

The first sustained political involvement of Cuban Americans in Africa was also the most violent. Between 1962 and 1967, around one hundred Cuban exiles fought leftist rebels in Congo-Léopoldville (hereafter, 'the Congo') and provided military support for the governments of presidents Joseph Kasa-Vubu and Joseph-Désiré Mobutu.[9] Secretly hired and trained by the US Central Intelligence Agency (CIA), those Cuban men fought on the ground as infantrymen, in boats on the waters of Lake Tanganyika, and in military aeroplanes flying over vast areas of the Congo.[10] Their actions were concentrated mainly in 1964 and 1965, when they helped crush the leftist Simba rebellion and defeat remaining rebel concentrations – one of which included Cuban troops sent by Fidel Castro and personally led by Ernesto 'Che' Guevara. Only in June 1965 did the exiled Cubans know with certainty that they were combating compatriots from the island, but from the beginning they had joined this enterprise enthusiastically – as one of them said – 'to accomplish in another country the mission I had imposed upon myself of fighting communists' and 'to confront the enemies of my country anywhere in the world'.[11] To this day, these soldiers express great pride in having helped to curb the Cuban government's plans for Central Africa and, more broadly, to stop the expansion of socialism on the continent.

The CIA first invited Cuban veteran pilots from the Bay of Pigs invasion to assist the Congolese government in 1962, in the aftermath of Patrice Lumumba's assassination and towards the end of the Katanga secession crisis. As the Cuban American Frank Villafaña convincingly argues in his history of the exiles' involvement in the Congo conflicts, the United States sought both to prevent the expansion of leftist governments in Africa and divert Cuban exiles from making filibuster raids against Cuba.[12] At that point the main mission of the pilots was to intimidate the opponents of the Congolese government, especially the remaining active Lumumbist groups. The Cubans' flights over Léopoldville and the countryside were indeed so intimidating that the local military gave them the nickname of Makasi (meaning 'strong and powerful' in Lingala) – a name the exiles gladly adopted and even painted on their aircraft. The pilots went to the Congo on a rotating basis and stayed there for different lengths of time, but their overall mission lasted for five years. Operating from 13 airports scattered throughout the country, and shooting at enemy troops, trains, boats, bridges, roads and villages, the Makasi terrified the Congolese rebels and their supporters until 1967.

When the Simba rebellion began in 1964 and took over a great part of the Congo, the Makasi became more active, fierce and relevant to official repression. In September that year, 18 newly hired Cuban exiled infantrymen arrived to assist in the conflict and, together with the Makasi, they participated in the takeover of the city of Stanleyville (today's Kisangani), where the Simbas had proclaimed an alternative government and taken nearly 2000 foreigners as hostages. The Cuban exiles fought in this takeover – the famous Red Dragon Operation, orchestrated by Belgium and the United States – alongside Belgian paratroopers and white mercenaries from several European and African countries. This operation received much criticism from Third World leaders, including Fidel Castro, but it managed to rescue the hostages and reduce the rebellion to a few remaining centres.

The exiled Cuban infantry left the Congo in February 1965, but four months later suspicions were confirmed that troops from Cuba were assisting rebels on the Congolese side of Lake Tanganyika, from across which they received Tanzanian assistance. The CIA organised a new group of Cuban exiles to join the Makasi – this time a small navy of 16 men who used two boats to patrol and attack rebels on the lake. Now fully aware that they were confronting Cubans from the socialist island, the exiles were again successful, and after a few long battles they managed to turn what Che Guevara once called the 'beautiful dream' of a socialist Congo into just that: a dream.[13] The Cuban troops from the island – around 200 men – fled the Congo in November 1965, but the Cuban exile navy stayed there until March 1966. The Makasi air force was dismantled only the following year, after helping Mobutu crush a revolt by foreign mercenaries on whom he had relied for several years.

The invaluable interviews given to the Miami-based Cuban journalist Pedro Corzo by the exiles who fought in the Congo focus mainly on their military operations and are full of real-life adventures worthy of the most imaginative Cold War novels and films: naval battles and friendly fire in the middle of the night, pilots using rivers as their only guide for orientation and getting lost in the jungle. Still, these interviews provide us also with a glimpse of the views of these Cuban Americans about Africans, which are twofold. On the one hand, their impressions of the people with whom they interacted directly and regularly are mostly positive: these Congolese appear as friendly, supportive, peaceful, and mostly happy about the Cuban American presence, although not particularly interested in or aware of political issues. A quite impressive story is told by a pilot who was helped by Zande villagers after a crash landing. He was not harmed in the accident, but his American companion was severely wounded and stayed to be treated in the village while he and three Zande men walked and canoed for days in the search of medical help. According to this narrative, not only was the American pilot successfully rescued, but, years later, American scientists came all the way from Texas to investigate the plants the Africans had used to heal his wounds.[14]

On the other hand, the same testimonies provide an exoticising portrait of Africans with whom the interviewees did not interact directly or regularly. When talking about an abstract African, the veterans repeatedly turned to two classic tropes of the Western primitivistic imagination of Africa: magic and cannibalism. Rumours about the eating of human flesh seem to have created much anxiety among the exiles, for the only thing they admit having feared in the Congo was being devoured by jungle dwellers. A Makasi reminisces about his reaction when he was approached by some Africans after an unscheduled landing in the country-side: 'I remember those guys had very sharp teeth, which I did not like, and I liked it even less when one of the mechanics that were accompanying us told me that we would be the food of those people.' This man ran away and obviously was not eaten. Another pilot explained their fear: 'some tribes in this region liked to take off the hearts and livers of their enemies and to eat them.' In contrast, when talking about the Africans' belief in war magic, the attitude of Cuban American veterans seems to have been not fright, but mostly condescension. They attribute that belief to superstition, ignorance and manipulation by ill-intentioned leaders: 'the witch of the tribe and the chief of the tribe were prepared by the communist instructors to tell the guerrillas that after drinking a magic beverage they could fight without fear of dying . . ., because the enemies' bullets would turn into water'.[15] The local belief in war magic was a widely popular topic among foreigners fighting in the Congo, and even inspired a special publication by the US Army on how to use it as a military strategy.[16] The Cuban Americans who went there were not immune from this fascination, which informed their primitivistic view of Africans.

However, Africa for the exiled Cubans was not a place to explore, but one in which to combat what they like to call 'international communism', a foreign territory in which to fight enemies that they could not fight at home. Some veterans describe theirs as a global humanitarian mission, or 'democratic internationalism', as one of them calls it in a clear response to the idea of 'socialist internationalism' deployed by the Cuban government. Another claims that he 'took part in the group of Cubans who went to the Congo to fight Castro-communism, this damned plague that scourges a great part of mankind, because we all have in our hearts the commitment to fight communism, because communism is the destruction of the world'. But all veterans recognise that this commitment stemmed from a nationalist attachment to their own country and the desire to attack Fidel Castro by defeating his overseas allies. More concretely, many veterans confess that they only went to the Congo because they were promised they would be given American support to invade Cuba – promises they bitterly denounce as outright lies. As the rumours of the presence of Cubans among the Congolese rebels grew, and especially after that presence was confirmed, the opportunity to fight troops from the island became a major motivation for these exiles to go to the Congo. A former Makasi states about his decision, 'at first I hesitated a little, but when I was told that Ernesto Guevara was in that country, my convictions gave me no choice'.[17]

And the Congo did see several direct confrontations between Cubans of the two sides. Frank Villafaña reports that as early as 1964, even before Guevara's troops reached the country, some Makasi pilots had a strange encounter with what they call 'communist Cubans'. Flying over the jungle, they spotted enemy troops on the ground and were ready to shoot at them, when someone in Cuban-accented

Spanish called them on the radio to say they should not attack those troops. Taken aback but confirming with other allies that the targets were not Cuban exiled infantrymen, they opened fire, after which 'the Cuban-accented voice [on the radio] said in Spanish: "Mercenaries, sons of bitches." We replied: "Asshole, stick up your head, and we'll take it off." There is no doubt these were Cuban soldiers, we believe stationed in Rwanda, who were making an incursion into Congo territory.'[18] The following year, an attack by Cuban exiles against a group of rebels confirmed that there were island troops in the Congo: one of the enemies they killed was carrying a diary and a passport that proved he had come from Cuba.[19] After that, several confrontations between the two Cuban sides happened on and around Lake Tanganyika, until the island troops left the Congo for good. Africa was the means for and the theatre of a combat among Cubans.

It is no surprise, thus, that the exiled veterans are one and all proud to have defeated their compatriot enemies on African soil and to have helped restrain Fidel Castro's plans for the expansion of socialism on the continent. A Makasi pilot puts it in more specific terms: 'we all had the desire to do something for our country and against communism. In reality we wanted to get revenge for what we had lived in the Bay of Pigs – in the end [it was] a revenge, if you want to call it that.'[20] Vengeful or not, the feeling of having inflicted a defeat upon the Cuban government animates current commemorations of these events in Miami – which include reunions of veterans, YouTube videos of exiles in the Congo, the production of a documentary, television reports, public talks by veterans, and even the interviews collected by Pedro Corzo that have made my analysis possible.[21] For decades the CIA's oath of secrecy kept most Miami Cubans in the dark about the events in the Congo, but they are now fully aware that the only significant military victory of exiled Cubans over their island adversaries took place in Africa.

MIRROR-MAKING IN ANGOLA

The conflict in the Congo was only the most dramatic and successful episode in a long-lasting pattern of engagement with Africa on the part of militant Cuban exiles in Miami. As is widely known, most of the politically organised Cuban migrants have adopted since 1959 an uncompromising and highly vocal oppositional standpoint regarding the Cuban regime, with the consequence that they have reacted to every international move of the adversary government by defending its foreign enemies and opposing its allies.[22] Most often this impetus has been directed towards Latin America, but for the three decades in which (as the other chapters of this volume show) the Cuban regime was deeply involved in African affairs, Miami-based Cuban groups, organisations and journalists have enthusiastically turned their eyes to the continent – be it to oppose socialism in Mozambique, criticise the Ethiopian Revolution, or denounce the Cuban presence in Sierra Leone. This interest continues to this day, and goes beyond cases of direct Cuban intervention in African conflicts, as is indicated by the enthusiasm that the 2011 ousting and assassination of Muammar Gaddafi – a friend and ally of Fidel Castro – generated in Cuban Miami. For six decades now, Africa has received much attention in Miami's public culture thanks to the presence of the socialist regime on the continent.[23]

I call this Cuban American reactive pattern 'mirror-making', a term I borrow from anthropologist John Borneman's analysis of the Cold War relationship between the Federal Republic of Germany and the German Democratic Republic – which is strikingly similar to the connections between the Cuban government and its exiled opponents. Borneman describes a mixture of conflict and mutual dependency, in which the two German states constantly responded to each other by taking opposite positions on various matters (currency reform, family planning, international alliances, and so on): 'in this process of mirror-making, the two states fabricated themselves as moieties in a dual organization'.[24] This German mirror-making was clearly asymmetric: most initiatives were taken by the Western side, while the poorer and smaller socialist state responded by taking the opposite direction. The Cuban mirror-making is also asymmetric, but here the political signs are inverted: most initiatives have been taken by the socialist state, and the organised exiles in Miami have responded vehemently against its actions and taken the opposite standpoint. And the asymmetry is much stronger here: instead of two states, as in the German case, the Cuban dual field opposes a highly militarised nation-state led by a charismatic leader to a myriad of small, weak and deeply divided migrant associations lacking any kind of centralised authority.[25] This asymmetry also prevailed in the engagement of the two Cuban sides with Africa.

In respect of the initiative for intervention, it may look as if the Congo case contradicts this point. The first exiles to go there were not aware that small isolated groups from the island were already operating in the country, and, by the time Fidel Castro sent a full-fledged guerrilla unit to support the Simbas, Cuban Americans had been there for three years. However, the exiles did not see their enterprise as specific to the Congo, but as a mission to Africa – a continent where they knew that the Cuban government had already been supporting leftist groups and governments in different capacities.[26] That is, it was the Cuban socialist regime that took the initiative to intervene in the continent as a whole. Moreover, the exiles knew there were Cuban troops in countries neighbouring the Congo and that Castro had close ties with Julius Nyerere's Tanzania, and so since the beginning it was clear to them that combating socialism in Central Africa was a way of attacking the Cuban regime. As I have shown, this reactive stance intensified when the exiles became aware that they would be directly fighting 'communist Cubans' who were personally headed by one of their most hated enemies. The Congo war was thus the first effort of mirror-making in Africa on the part of Cuban exiles.

But the Cuban American intervention in the Congo was in fact an exception in another crucial regard: its success. Overall, the asymmetry of resources meant that the presence in Africa of the small, fragmented exile organisations was far more modest and far less successful than that of the centralised Cuban government. As Piero Gleijeses, Christine Hatzky and several chapters in this volume have described it, Cuba's official engagement with Africa has been prolonged, widespread and largely successful in its goals of supporting different leftist regimes and movements, and garnering sympathy and support for the Cuban leadership on the continent.[27] In contrast, the interventions by Cuban Americans have been modest, sporadic and – aside from the case of the Congo – of limited success.

This is most evident in the case of the Cuban American relationship with the African country where the Cuban government has been most active: Angola. It was Cuba's massive military and civilian support of the leftist MPLA that sparked the interest of Cuban exiles in the former Portuguese colony.[28] In the late 1970s, as the post-independence war escalated in that country and rumours about the Cuban government's intervention started circulating in Miami, some veterans of the Bay of Pigs started raising funds and recruiting exiles to fight the MPLA and its allied Cuban troops. One of the organisers of the Angola mission explains their motivation: 'this was the opportunity to be able to directly confront Castro's forces and hit the ambitions of international communism'.[29]

Allegedly with no support from the US government, but funded by donations from Cuban American individuals, businesses, and associations these exiles formed the Comando Militar 2506 – a name inspired by the Brigada 2506, the armed group that had tried to invade Cuba through the Bay of Pigs in April 1961, of which most of the newly recruited fighters had been members. They made contact with the two major organisations fighting the MPLA – the National Front for the Liberation of Angola (FNLA) and the bigger and stronger National Union for the Total Independence of Angola (UNITA) – but for logistic reasons were unable to fight alongside the latter. According to Alvares Gimeno, the Comando asked for help from France, Britain and Israel, but all they obtained were some weapons from the French. Much more helpful were two Third World right-wing dictators, Anastasio

Somoza and Mobutu Sese Seko (the new name Joseph-Désiré Mobutu had given himself during his 'authenticity campaign'). The Nicaraguan president offered the Cuban exiles air transport and military installations to train for their mission, and Mobutu allowed them to reach Angola safely: they flew to Kinshasa (formerly Léopoldville), traversed Zaire (formerly the Congo) by land, and arrived in Angola by crossing the Congo River.

The first exiles to reach Angola signed a cooperation agreement with the leader of the FNLA, Holden Roberto, who occasionally visited the Cuban American camps. According to one of their leaders, around 280 Cuban exiles fought during eight months in Angola, each in two-month shifts. They commanded 300 Angolan troops and took part in several military operations, including an attack against Cuban troops in which six enemy aeroplanes were destroyed. However, their mission was not very successful, and they did not even get to the areas controlled by UNITA, as they had planned. The narratives of the former members of the Comando 2506 mission compiled by Pedro Corzo contrast starkly with those of the Congo veterans. They focus bitterly on problems such as language difficulties, food and water shortages, and even Holden Roberto's supposed lack of commitment to the war. Most importantly, they complain about the opposition they received from the US government, which they accuse of having interrupted the mission – in a way that the testimonies leave unclear. What is clear is that they returned to the United States with a strong sense of failure. If the Congo had given the exiles a sense of revenge for the Bay of Pigs fiasco, in Angola the Cuban government got its revenge for the Congo conflict.

Still, for several years Miami Cubans followed the war in Angola closely and anxiously from afar, protesting against Cuba's involvement in the conflict and cheering for FNLA and UNITA. In early 1979, shortly after Comando 2506 returned home, an issue of Miami's influential Cuban Catholic magazine, *Ideal*, published an interview with Angola's foremost anti-communist leader, UNITA's Jonas Savimbi. The cover of that issue (see Fig. 10.1) displayed big yellow letters declaring, 'Cuba and Angola: Two Peoples That Fight for Their Freedom', and a photograph of Savimbi with the Cuban American journalist that interviewed him, Tomás Regalado, who would later say that he contacted Savimbi hoping to help create 'a solid bridge between free Cubans and free Angolans'.[30] The correspondent of a major Cuban Miami radio station, Regalado covered for many years the wars in Mozambique and Angola and the anti-apartheid struggle – including the Soweto uprisings of 1976 – and would eventually enter formal politics, being elected mayor of the City of Miami in 2009. In this interview, given in Morocco, Savimbi repeatedly criticised the Cuban troops in Angola as imperialist aggressors who received privileges denied to most Angolans

Figure 10.1: Cover of Miami's Cuban Catholic magazine *Ideal* showing Tomás Regalado, a Cuban American journalist and later mayor of the City of Miami, with UNITA leader Jonas Savimbi. Source: https://villagranadillo.blogspot.com/2010/04/jonas-savimbi-un-rebelde-con-causa-por.html

and who spread violence gratuitously and indiscriminately. This, according to him, made Angolans of all political persuasions hate Cubans. The generalised use of the term 'Cubans' without the qualifier 'communist' must have displeased many exiled readers, but Savimbi's statements also gave them some reassurance: Fidel Castro was the only person responsible for the violence and hate, and, if given assistance from abroad, UNITA could easily defeat his troops.[31]

These hopes proved elusive, of course, but, until the last Cuban soldiers left Angola in 1991, the Cuban exiled press kept a close eye on that country, criticising Cuba's 'imperialist' intervention, denouncing the deaths of Cuban soldiers, documenting the Cuban troops' supposed loss of morale, criticising American peace negotiations with the MPLA, and reporting on desertions of Cuban officials.[32] Particularly revealing is the case of Radio Martí – the radio station owned by the US government, created in 1985 by the Reagan administration to broadcast to Cuba and express political views opposed to the Cuban government. Immediately after its creation, the Cubans who ran Radio Martí started informing the islanders about happenings in Angola, and in its very first month of operation Radio Martí broadcast a special six-part series about the country's civil war. The radio was keen on sending news that the Cuban government was slow and reluctant to share, especially about Cuban war casualties. The importance that the staff of Radio Martí gave to Africa was such that in 1987 they confronted the US federal government when it tried to prevent the station from sending reporters to Angola and Mozambique. The State Department was afraid that such activity would create problems for the US role in peace negotiations in those countries, but the Cuban leaders were adamant and protested against the restrictions on their journalistic activities. In a few weeks the problem was solved with a Cuban American victory over the State Department: the station was able to send its reporters to Africa and to keep informing islanders about the unfolding events on the continent.[33]

But fighters and journalists were not the only Miami-based Cubans to have been to Angola during the war. Also present was the Miami Medical Team, a Cuban American organisation of health professionals that promotes international solidarity with a conservative bent, providing medical aid mostly to refugees from leftist governments and to victims of natural disasters in right-wing-led countries. Thanks to Tomás Regalado's continuing friendly relationship with Jonas Savimbi, the Miami Medical Team was able to send humanitarian support to UNITA in 1987 and 1988, bringing them not only doctors and dentists, but also containers with medication, clinical equipment, and materials such as school desks and blackboards.[34] This short-lived intervention illustrates both the efforts that have taken Cuban Americans to Africa in opposition to the Cuban regime and the structural asymmetry of this mirror-making process. The Miami Medical Team is proud to have represented what it calls 'the Cuban people' in 24 countries (mostly in Latin America), but its actions obviously pale in comparison with the much longer and more effective medical and educational assistance that Cubans from the island have provided in Angola, the rest of Africa, and across the world.[35] Here again Angola clearly shows the asymmetry in the efforts of Cuban Americans to mirror the Cuban regime's presence in Africa – in humanitarian as well as in military actions.

MANDELA AND RACE IN MIAMI

However unsuccessful their adventures were in Angola, no engagement of Cuban exiles with Africa was as embarrassing in the long run as their demonstrations against the visit of Nelson Mandela to Miami in June 1990.[36] Unlike the events I discussed above, these protests have raised some scholarly attention from experts on Miami and the Cuban diaspora. For instance, two major books on those topics –

one by Alejandro Portes and Alex Stepick and the other by Guillermo Grenier and Lisandro Pérez – have analysed the 1990 demonstrations in relation to Miami's and American ethnic politics.[37] Here, in contrast, I approach these protests as a political and moral defeat that dramatically revealed the predicaments of the Cuban American mirror-making vis-à-vis the Cuban government's involvement in Africa.

Four months after being released from prison, Nelson Mandela made a tour of eight American cities, and was given a nearly universal and enthusiastic hero's welcome in all of them – except for Miami. A week before his arrival in town, in an interview on American television, the anti-apartheid leader professed his friendship with Fidel Castro, Muammar Gaddafi and Yasser Arafat, and thanked and praised them for the support they had given him and the African National Congress for decades. Not surprisingly, Miami Cubans felt deeply offended by these comments and responded fiercely. By this time, Cuban Americans had become Greater Miami's politically and economically dominant ethnic group. As several analysts have shown,[38] they had entered formal American politics for at least a decade: thousands had obtained US citizenship, and several had been elected to political office. This gave them much power when reacting to Mandela's visit. The Cuban-controlled Miami City Commission rescinded the resolution that it had prepared in honour of Mandela, and refused to grant him any kind of welcome. The mayors of the City of Miami and four other municipalities in Miami-Dade County – all of them Cuban – issued a joint declaration that proclaimed, 'We, Cuban Americans, find it beyond reasonable comprehension that Mr. Nelson Mandela, a victim of oppression by his own government, not only fails to condemn the Cuban government for its human rights violations, but rather praises virtues of the tyrannical Castro regime.'[39]

This was basically the message of the hundreds of public statements and letters of protests issued by Cuban Miamians in those days: they complimented Mandela for his admirable history of struggle, but found it incompatible with his defence of Fidel Castro, which they abhorred. Most suggested that Mandela must have been very misinformed or confused about the Cuban regime, which a Cuban journalist called 'a political apartheid'. Popular reactions in Cuban Miami were less cautious and more furious. Some Cuban Americans called live Spanish-language radio programmes to say things such as 'Mandela, go home!' and 'Out with Mandela, we have enough communists here!' Some press reports mention even less politically correct reactions: many people called Mandela a terrorist; one man said Mandela 'did not learn anything in the last 27 years'; and some argued that apartheid was a lesser evil compared to the plight of black-ruled countries.[40]

Mandela went to Miami to deliver a speech at the convention of the American Federation of State, County and Municipal Employees (AFSCME) – a union that had actively participated in the US campaign against apartheid. Cuban American associations called for demonstrations outside the Miami Beach Convention Center, where Mandela would give the speech, and 300 Cubans are estimated to have arrived, joined by some Israel-supporting Jews who were not pleased with Mandela's praise of Arafat. But ten times more people – mostly black – came to support Mandela, and the two groups were separated by fences placed by the police. On one side, people played drums, wore African-style clothing and T-shirts with Mandela's face, carried placards supporting him, and shouted his name enthusiastically. On the other, Cubans chanted 'Mandela, communist and terrorist, go back to Africa!' and displayed posters with sayings like 'Freedom from apartheid and communist tyranny' and 'Human rights for blacks and Cubans too'. The two groups made obscene gestures and yelled at each other. Some Mandela supporters shouted, 'Go back to Cuba,' and a short fight took place when a few blacks crossed the fences. All the time two aeroplanes flew over the crowd carrying enormous banners with the words, 'ANC – Mandela – partners in communism' and 'Kadafi [*sic*] Arafat and Castro are pigs'. Indicating that not all Cubans shared the predominant view, a third aeroplane sponsored by a Cuban American labour union flew a banner that read, 'Welcome Nelson Mandela – Cubans of Miami'. On the ground, only ten Cubans reportedly joined the Mandela supporters, whereas the former Black Panther activist Tony Bryant – who had spent eleven years in prison in Cuba – was on the Cuban side. Inside the Convention Center, before a euphoric audience, Mandela gave a speech that thanked his American supporters and asked for more international pressure against the South African government – but made no comment about the dispute going on outside.[41]

Most non-Cubans in Miami and beyond framed this confrontation as a racial question. They saw the protests against Mandela as a racist insult and, unsurprisingly, the outrage was strongest among black Miamians. A Mandela supporter outside the Convention Center wore a T-shirt that said, 'Racism is an illness and Miami is sick,' and a New York-based black man said, 'This is racism. I was born in Miami Beach and now I come back and I see nothing but racism.' Many black Miamians painfully remembered the relatively recent days of segregation in their city and most took the offence to Mandela personally. Several activists demanded that the City of Miami offer Mandela the key of the city and proclaim a Nelson Mandela Day, threatening an electoral backlash against city officials. An African American civil rights leader called the attack on Mandela 'a slap in the face' of Miami's blacks, because 'to reject Mandela is to reject us. He is our brother. If they say he's not welcome, they're saying we're not welcome, too.'[42]

As Marvin Dunn and Portes and Stepick show,[43] the relationship between Cubans and non-Cuban blacks in Miami had been problematic since the first waves of massive migration from the island to the city. For three decades Miami blacks had realised that these newcomers were quickly gaining power and privileges in their home town while they remained subordinated, impoverished and discriminated against. They had rioted three times in the 1980s because of tensions with Cubans and other Latinos, and the controversies around Mandela's visit culminated in a new riot one week afterwards. Several powerful black and civil rights associations successfully called for a black boycott of Greater Miami, which was nicknamed 'the quiet riot' and caused the area to lose millions of tourism dollars. The boycott only ended in 1993, after the mayor of the City of Miami had declared a Nelson Mandela Day and several political groups and associations negotiated a compromise. Still, only in 2003 did Alex Penelas, another Cuban American mayor, offer an official apology to Nelson Mandela for the snub the City of Miami had given him.[44]

The events of June 1990 say much about racial relations in the United States, but for my purposes here what matters is the clash they revealed between two ways of imagining Africa in Miami. By framing Africa mainly in an associative or metaphoric way, militant Miami Cubans got into serious trouble with neighbours who defined themselves by a syntagmatic or metonymic relationship to Africa. These neighbours called themselves African Americans precisely because they claimed a biological genealogical link with the continent – which made them see Mandela literally as their kin. In contrast, most organised Cuban exiles saw Africa not as a place of origin – cultural or racial – but as a place like any other where they could and should fight the Cuban government. Since 1959, politically mobilised Cubans based in Miami have been evaluating any political situation according to one foremost standard: the relationship of the events and characters in question to Fidel Castro's regime. Moreover, as Portes and Stepick argue, 'as the Cuban community gained political power it imposed a monolithic outlook on the city, often with little regard for the concerns and interests of other segments of the population.'[45] With this nearly exclusive focus, they ignored or overlooked the different meanings that Africa had for other Miamians, and thus became trapped in a typical US pattern of racial relations and imaginations, based on open antagonisms between clearly bounded groups claiming biological origins in different continents.

I agree with Portes and Stepick's point that, in Mandela's visit as in less visible cases, 'Cuban discrimination [in Miami] operated more by neglect than by deliberate action. Preoccupied with their own economic progress and with the political struggle with Castro, Cubans had little time for the complaints of Blacks.'[46] Their attack on Mandela was not a demonstration of racial hate, but a fierce display of exclusive concern with one single political issue and of insensitivity towards the plight of other groups. This, of course, is not to deny the existence of racism in (overwhelmingly white) Cuban Miami.[47] Albeit seldom overtly expressed in public, racism has been rampant there, and its victims include black Cuban Americans. Alan Aja argues that white Cubans in Miami have imposed a 'white wall' onto their black compatriots, which drove many to move to the city's less Cuban areas and to other American cities.[48] However, scholars have shown that in Cuba too, despite the remarkable achievements of the first years of socialism, racial discrimination and inequalities have persisted since then and have deepened in the last three decades. There are several reasons for this, including the official silencing of the racial question, the exoticisation of Afro-Cuban culture, continuing racialised residential patterns, and racially unequal access to tourism jobs and remittances from abroad.[49]

What has indeed differentiated the leadership of the island and that of the exiles is the level to which they have linked racial issues to their engagements with Africa. Since 1959 the Cuban regime has rhetorically externalised racism by denouncing racism abroad – especially in the United States and South Africa – and expressing solidarity with the colonised and the exploited in Africa and the African diaspora.[50] This has meant framing some official interventions in Africa in racial terms. For allegedly military strategic reasons, nearly all Cuban guerrillas sent by the government to the Congo were black, and, according to a prominent (white) member of the mission, careful phenotypical criteria were applied to select 'the ones that looked more like Congolese'.[51] The Cuban troops sent to Angola had a more even racial distribution (50 per cent black), but were still disproportionally black.[52] Also, the name of the Cuban military intervention in Angola tried to create a transatlantic historical connection between the struggles of enslaved and colonised blacks: it was called Operation Carlota in honour of the slave who had started a rebellion in the Cuban province of Matanzas in 1843, roughly on the same date as the intervention was launched.[53] This connection was reaffirmed on the 40th anniversary of the beginning of the intervention in Angola, when the sugar mill where that slave rebellion had broken out became a museum with permanent exhibits on two topics: the history of slavery and Operation Carlota.[54] Because apartheid South Africa supported the opponents of the MPLA and was among Cuba's most powerful enemies on the continent,[55] the Cuban regime was able to portray its operation in Angola also as a struggle against, among other things, racial oppression – a belief that many non-Cubans still cherish, despite the obvious fact that it was mostly black people and organisations that Cubans combated in Angola and countries like Ethiopia and Somalia. And Fidel Castro was, among global leaders, one of the earliest and most outspoken supporters of the anti-apartheid struggle – which again explicitly gave a racial character to the involvement of his regime with African issues.

In contrast, Cuban Americans rarely, if ever, framed their engagements with Africa as anti-racist, or in any racial terms. With the apparent exception of one single black man – Eulogio Amado Reyes Morales – only white Cuban exiles fought in Africa, which embarrassingly made of the battles among Cubans in the Congo a confrontation between white and black Cubans. In the testimonies compiled by Pedro Corzo, racial issues appear only in one anecdote, in which a Congolese woman proposed to Reyes once she realised he was a foreigner – a story that those who told it, including Reyes himself, found amusing.[56] Surprisingly, only occasionally did Cuban Miami journalists accuse Cuba's interventions in Africa of being racist, as in a 1991 piece according to which 'it was clear to a good part of [Cuba's] black population that Castro's strategy had become a racist mechanism ... In one moment of the "African decade" practically all Cuban ambassadors in Africa were black; however, in the rest of the world, with the exception of the Caribbean, they were white. The troops sent to the continent were also disproportionally black. So were the dead.'[57]

The mirror-making character of Cuban exiles' political engagements with Africa has meant that their link to the continent was mainly a metaphoric one, in which Africa was the theatre of a global struggle against 'Castro-communism'. This colour-blind reactive pattern has contributed to the deterioration of relations between Cubans and African Americans in Miami, for the wounds of the dispute over Mandela's visit last to this day. This episode is painfully brought back to light in any moment of tension, as in the wave of police violence against blacks in the City of Miami in the 2010s – the worst since the 1980s. It is no small irony that this wave came about precisely during the municipal administration of one of the Cuban exiles most committed to African issues – Tomás Regalado. Miami's foremost black historian, Marvin Dunn, guarantees that 'there's not a racist bone in [Regalado's] body', but black discontent with his mayoral mandate suggests that exile leaders who were once committed to Africa as a political ground might not be equally committed to racial justice at home.[58]

Needless to say, this is certainly true of the Cuban regime as well. But, as Mark Sawyer notes about the 1970s and 1980s, 'the opening created [by Cuba's involvement in Africa] for domestic racial progress was not insignificant' and allowed for greater black participation in official positions, timid affirmative action initiatives, and the recording of ethnic data in the census.[59] As Sawyer himself shows, this opening did not last long, and since the 1990s racial disparities and discrimination in Cuba have only grown.[60] Still, the island's government was able, at least abroad, to present some of its African interventions as partly an anti-racist odyssey. This, coupled with their demographic profile, left the exiles with no choice but to deracialise their reaction to those interventions and their engagement with Africa. Given the global hegemonic racialised imagination of Africa,[61] this situation put Cuban Americans in a considerably weaker moral position when trying to mirror their island compatriots in Africa. In this way, global racial imaginations complicated the predicament of asymmetry in Cuban American mirror-making.

BACK TO THE ROOTS AND BEYOND

Although politically mobilised Cuban exiles got into trouble for their colour-blind and exclusively metaphoric relationship to Africa, in other domains Miami Cubans also related to Africa in a syntagmatic way. Here the imagined historical genealogies were not biological – as in the case of African Americans – but mainly spiritual and cultural.[62] Even before the Cuban Revolution, the first Cuban adepts of Afro-Cuban religions who migrated to the United States had brought with them the Cuban tradition of africanía, that is, of locating in Africa the roots of their practices. But this only led to a real new connection with the continent in the 1970s, when Miguel Febles Padrón, a powerful Havana-based *babalao*, refused to provide the Miami-based *babalao* José Miguel Gómez Barberas with an *Olofin* – a ritual object required for the initiation of new *babalaos*. According to David Brown, 'Olofin may be read as the embodiment of accumulated spiritual and social investments, a kind of fetish or storehouse of "symbolic capital"', and since the 1950s Febles had 'gained for himself the power to select Olofin's recipients – most often those who could pay a premium price – and "block" the receiving of an Olofin from other sources, particularly those to whom he had already given an Olofin'.[63] Such control extended beyond Cuba itself, and by the 1970s dozens of *babalaos* had been initiated in Miami thanks to *Olofins* made by Miguel Febles Padrón. After being continuously prevented by Febles from receiving an *Olofin*, the émigré José Miguel Gómez Barberas, in an act of rebellion, asked for help from one of the greatest specialists in Afro-Cuban religions, the Cuban anthropologist Lydia Cabrera, also living in Miami then. In turn, Cabrera contacted another major specialist and agent in transatlantic Yoruba matters, the Franco-Brazilian Pierre Verger, then a professor at the University of Ile-Ife. Verger arranged contacts that not only allowed Gómez to receive the consecration he needed in Nigeria, in 1975, but ended up strengthening and multiplying the direct links between Miami and Yorubaland. In 1978 – as I anticipated in the opening of this chapter – Gómez brought to Miami Ifá Yemí Elebuibon, the Nigerian *babalao* who gave him his *Olofin* and who then started initiating several other Cuban Miamians, both in Florida and in Nigeria.

My narrative of these events summarises those of two excellent books, David Brown's *Santería Enthroned* and Stephan Palmié's *The Cooking of History*. Here I follow especially Palmié's argument, according to which what Gómez did in Miami was 'to reactivate "Africa" as a viable chronotope of primordial authenticity and legitimacy'.[64] By creating a direct link between his new home and the continent, Gómez bypassed the island in its very tradition of africanía. He and his allies on both sides of the Atlantic forged Miami's own new africanía, producing, in Brown's words, 'a fresh rebirth of the African homeland in a second Diaspora, in suburban Miami'.[65] These practitioners of Afro-Cuban traditions in Miami were indeed leaders in a 'secondary religious diaspora', to use Alejandro Frigerio's helpful term.[66] But they were also innovatively creating a new *primary* metonymic connection to the homeland of the African diaspora, and claiming greater African religious authenticity.

This syntagmatic relationship was, of course, fundamentally different from the metaphoric relationship of the Miami Cubans who participated in the conflicts I have described previously. But in the case of cultural metonyms too, Cuban Americans have encountered tensions with Anglo-American racial patterns, for American blacks also brought Yoruba traditions from Cuba to the United States and later bypassed Cuba to claim direct Yoruba religious roots – and did so on their own terms. This was most clearly the case of the American Yoruba Movement, also known as the Yoruba Reversionist Movement. Created in the 1960s by a Detroit-born African American who was initiated into Ifá first in Cuba and later in Africa, this movement intended to create a Yoruba religion devoid of anything non-African and to make it the exclusive heritage of those who may claim a biological relationship to the continent.[67] The Yoruba Reversionists, therefore, have racialised the African traditions they first got to know in Cuba by reinterpreting them according to what Stephan Palmié has aptly described as 'a North American experience of racial corporatism', based on 'distinctively North American conceptions of the *necessary* coincidence between "Africanity" and "blackness"'.[68]

Such conceptions are fundamentally different from the africanía imagined by Cuban practitioners of Ifá on the island and in Miami, which supposes no necessary connection between African roots and blackness. Their religious practice is not seen as the exclusive prerogative of any specific group based on biological descent, for the Yoruba deities can and do interpellate people of any phenotype or genotype into their cult. In fact, white Cubans were key actors in the formation of the Afro-Cuban religious forms of *santería* and *abakuá*, and, according to the Cuban phenotypical classification, José Miguel Gómez Barberas himself was white. As such, Cuban and Cuban American claims to African *cultural* authenticity are not necessarily claims to *racial* authenticity. As Stephan Palmié has carefully shown, the difference between the view of Cuban American Ifá practitioners and that of the racialised American Reversionist Movement has not prevented strategic alliances between the two groups, though it has caused conflicts between them and threatened the image of Cuban Americans as the legitimate keepers of Yoruba religious traditions in the United States.[69] Here again, Anglo-American conceptions of race somehow destabilised the engagements of Cuban Americans with the African continent.

But at least on one occasion Cuban Americans have taken advantage of US racialised views of Africa to create a new encounter with the continent. It was a memorable encounter, which went beyond patterns of both mirror-making and root-searching. The occasion was a three-day-long music festival held in 1974 in Kinshasa, in which great names of African and American music – like Miriam Makeba, B.B. King and James Brown – performed for an estimated 80,000 people. Conceived by the South African musician Hugh Masekela and the American musical producer Stewart Levine, Zaire '74 – as the event was called – was held in Kinshasa so as to coincide with a major fight that was then being sponsored by Mobutu, between African American boxers Muhammad Ali and George Foreman. The intertitles of the festival's official film, *Soul Power*, explain that the 'dream' of the organisers was to 'bring together the most renowned African-American and African musicians in their common homeland'. This view – clearly based on the idea of a connection between Africa and blackness, as described by Palmié – appears throughout the film in the voices of several Americans involved in the event. Muhammad Ali, for instance, articulated a discourse of racial solidarity and return to primordial origins, saying of Africa, 'this is our homeland, this is our civilization'. North American singer and songwriter Bill Withers expressed a similar view by explaining that 'what we are coming back here with is what we left here with, plus the influences that we picked up from living where we've lived for the last three, four hundred years'. Withers's use of the first person plural performatively reproduced the idea of a single racialised collective subject whose life spans both the centuries and the ocean.[70]

This American concern with racial origins is what allowed Kinshasa to see in person the greatest Cuban American artistic icon: Celia Cruz. Her performance with the famous New York salsa group Fania All-Stars was one of the biggest successes of Zaire '74. Two documentaries – *Soul Power* and *Fania All-Stars Live in Africa* – show a delighted crowd dancing in frenzy at the stadium while Celia

Cruz sings 'Guantanamera' and 'Quimbara'.[71] But this unique encounter of a Cuban American celebrity with Africa to a large extent uncoupled race and culture, and subverted the racialised views that underlay the holding of the festival. Given the wide variation of phenotypes among its members, the band with which Celia Cruz performed might as well have been called Fania All-Colours. Besides its Dominican founder, Johnny Pacheco, the group's mix included Cuban, Puerto Rican, Nuyorican and Jewish members of various phenotypes, most of whom had travelled and lived widely throughout the United States and the Caribbean. Like salsa itself – the dance music to which it helped give visibility and popularity in the 1970s – the Fania All-Stars presented a Caribbean hybridity that mixed elements of already hybrid styles and broke any possible association between biological and cultural heritages.

To better understand this point, we can use a little help from the founder of Afro-Cuban studies, Fernando Ortiz, who argued in 1940 that the most apt metaphor to describe Cuban culture was the *ajiaco*, a stew made of a wide variety of ingredients that never stops being cooked. For Ortiz, Cuban culture is 'a heterogeneous conglomerate of diverse races and cultures, of many meats and crops, that stir up, mix with each other, and disintegrate into one single social bubbling'.[72] One of the most valuable implications of Ortiz's metaphor is that, just as anyone can choose which ingredients to pick from the *ajiaco* to eat with its broth, any Cuban can choose what Cuban cultural elements he or she wants to enjoy and cherish. This is actually how Ortiz understood africanía: the conscious and affective attachment to the African components of the ajiaco. Most importantly, such a choice for him has nothing to do with supposed biological origins or appearances, for the very cooking of the ajiaco is a ceaseless process of exchange that dissociates its cultural elements from the human groups which brought them to the mix.

If one applies Ortiz's metaphor to other Caribbean islands, one sees that what Celia Cruz and Fania All-Stars offered Zairians was New York's own meta-ajiaco, an ajiaco made up of several ajiacos, where people of mixed origins brought together already-mixed cultural elements to the point of making cultural and racial boundaries disappear altogether. As Stephan Palmié puts it, 'once we choose the ajiaco as a metaphor circumscribing our perspective, the world of clearcut units is lost to us. Inside the *olla cubana* [Cuban pot], Africa, America and Europe can no longer be disentangled. There are, at best, unstable gradations by which one mutates into the other, and this process of refraction, decomposition, and its corresponding movement of recomposition and autopoiesis generates a potentially infinite series of possible perceptions of difference'.[73] The same can be said of the New York ajiaco being performed in Kinshasa: Cuban and African markers could be noted, felt, appreciated and praised there, but there was no more space for purity and clear boundaries, cultural or racial – or even political, if one considers that the musical icon of the Cuban exile was then sharing the stage with musical icons of the anti-apartheid struggle. The city that a few years before had seen military aeroplanes flown by Cuban American pilots now watched a Cuban American woman not making mirrors, not looking for roots, but performing cosmopolitanism and bringing to Africa the salsa of the ajiaco.

NOTES

1 David Brown, *Santería Enthroned: Art, Ritual, and Innovation in an Afro-Cuban Religion* (Chicago: University of Chicago Press, 2003), 92–7; and Stephan Palmié, *The Cooking of History: How Not to Study Afro-Cuban Religion* (Chicago: University of Chicago Press, 2013), 68–72. Throughout this chapter, I use the term 'Miami' to refer to the metropolitan area of Miami, which I here consider coextensive with Miami-Dade County, composed of 34 municipalities and several unincorporated areas. When I use 'City of Miami' I am referring specifically to the municipality that bears this name, the most populous of these 34 municipalities.

2 Pedro Corzo, *Cubanos combatiendo el castrocomunismo en África* (Miami: Instituto de la Memoria Histórica Cubana contra el Totalitarismo, 2014), 142–58; and René González Barrios, 'Girón: La lección,' *Iberoamericanskie Tetradi / Cuadernos Iberoamericanos* 4, no. 10 (2015): 27–34. Throughout this chapter, I use the term 'Cuban American' broadly to refer to Cubans and people of Cuban descent permanently living in the United States after 1959 – regardless of citizenship status, time of arrival, place of birth, or political involvement. I use the term 'exile' to refer to Cuban Americans who are actively opposed to the Cuban government, claim to live abroad for political reasons, and tend to reject the label of 'immigrants'. I made these terminological choices for the specific purposes of this chapter. For alternative uses and discussions of this terminology, compare María Cristina García, *Havana, USA: Cuban Exiles and Cuban Americans in South Florida, 1959–1994* (Berkeley: University of California Press, 1996); Guillermo Grenier and Lisandro Pérez, *The Legacy of Exile: Cubans in the United States* (Boston: Allyn and Bacon, 2003); Silvia Pedraza, *Political Disaffection in Cuba's Revolution and Exodus* (Cambridge: Cambridge University Press, 2007); Susan Eckstein, *The Immigrant Divide: How Cuban Americans Changed the US and Their Homeland* (New York: Routledge, 2009).

3 Of course, these realms are not really separate in practice. My distinction here is not a general analytical assumption, but a specific empirical observation: practices *imagined* by those involved as 'religious' and 'political' appear differently in the Cuban American engagements with Africa I analyse in this chapter. For illuminating analyses of the relationship between politics and Afro-Cuban religious practices, see Kali Argyriadis and Stefania Capone, '*Cubanía* et *santería*: Les enjeux politiques de la transnationalisation religieuse (La Havane – Miami),' *Civilisations* 51 (2004): 81–137; Kenneth Routon, *Hidden Powers of the State in the Cuban Imagination* (Gainesville: University Press of Florida, 2012).

4 Ferdinand de Saussure, *Course in General Linguistics* (Peru, IL: Open Court, 1986).

5 John Borneman, *Belonging in the Two Berlins: Kin, State, Nation* (Cambridge: Cambridge University Press, 1992), 17.

6 In the 2010 US census, 85.4 per cent of Cuban Americans declared themselves 'white' and 4.6 per cent of them declared themselves 'black'. In contrast, the 2012 Cuban census recorded on the island 64.5 per cent self-declared 'whites' and 9.3 per cent self-declared 'blacks'. (Sharon R. Ennis, Merarys Ríos-Vargas and Nora G. Albert, *The Hispanic Population 2010*, 2010 Census Briefs (Washington, DC: United States Census Bureau, 2011), 14; Oficina Nacional de Estadística e Información, *Informe Nacional: Censo de población y viviendas: Cuba 2012* (Havana, 2014), 81.) In both sets of statistics, 'race' or 'colour' appears as a self-description.

7 According to the Pew Research Center, an estimated 1 986 000 people of Cuban descent lived in the United States in 2013, out of which an estimated 1 135 000 were born in Cuba (Gustavo López, *Hispanics of Cuban Origins in the United States: Statistical Profile* (Washington, DC: Pew Research Center, 2015), 1). According to the 2012 Cuban census, 11 167 325 people lived in Cuba in that year (Oficina Nacional de Estadística e Información, *Informe nacional*, 69). The 2000 US census recorded that 525 841 people *born* in Cuba lived in Miami-Dade County in that year, whereas twelve years later Santiago de Cuba, the island's second-largest city, had a population of 506 037 (Miami-Dade County Department of Planning and Zoning, *Miami-Dade County Facts* (Miami, 2009), 26; Oficina Nacional de Estadística e Información, *Informe nacional*, 111).

8 Marifeli Pérez-Stable, *The Cuban Revolution: Origins, Course and Legacy* (Oxford and New York: Oxford University Press, 1993); Susan Eckstein, *Back from the Future: Cuba under Castro* (London: Routledge, 2003); Argyariadis and Capone, '*Cubanía* et *santería*'; Silvia Pedraza, *Political Disaffection*.

9 Kasa-Vubu was the president of the Republic of Congo between its independence in 1960 and 1965. Mobutu was the head of the army between 1961 and 1965, when he became the president through a coup d'état. He ruled the country in a ruthless one-party dictatorship until 1997. The country was officially renamed the Democratic Republic of the Congo in 1965, the Republic of Zaire in 1971, and again the Democratic Republic of the Congo in 1997.

10 Frank R. Villafaña, *Cold War in the Congo: The Confrontation of Cuban Military Forces, 1960–1967* (New Brunswick: Transaction Publishers, 2012); Corzo, *Cubanos combatiendo*. These two books have provided nearly all the data I present here on the conflicts in the Congo. Villafaña is a Cuban-American engineer and public historian, and his book is a detailed historical account of the Cuban-American involvement in the Congo during in the 1960s. Corzo is an exiled Cuban journalist and activist, and his book is an invaluable compilation of personal testimonies given by Cuban exiles who fought in the Congo and in Angola.

11 'Para cumplir en otro país la misión que me había impuesto de luchar contra los comunistas'; 'confrontar los enemigos de mi país en cualquier parte del mundo.' Roberto Pichardo, quoted in Corzo, *Cubanos combatiendo*, 71. Unless otherwise noted, all translations are my own.

12 Villafaña, *Cold War in the Congo*, 33–51.

13 Ernesto Che Guevara, *Pasajes de la guerra revolucionaria: Congo* (Milan: Mondadori, 2005), 87.

14 Juan Carlos Perón, quoted in Corzo, *Cubanos combatiendo*, 130–2.

15 'Yo recuerdo que aquellos tipos tenían los dientes muy afilados, cosa que no me gustó y me gustó mucho menos cuando uno de los mecánicos que nos acompañaba me dijo que la comida de esa gente íbamos a ser nosotros.' Federico Flaquer, quoted in Corzo, *Cubanos combatiendo*, 118. 'Algunas [*sic*] tribus de esa región les gustaba sacarles el

corazón y el hígado a sus enemigos y comérselos.' Ignacio Rojas, *Cubanos combatiendo*, 93. 'El brujo de la tribu y el jefe de la tribu, [*sic*] eran preparados por los instructores comunistas para que le [*sic*] dijeran a los guerrilleros que después que bebieran un brebaje mágico ellos podían combatir sin miedo a morir …, porque las balas de los enemigos se convertirían en agua.' Generoso Bringas, *Cubanos combatiendo*, 65.

16 Villafaña, *Cold War in the Congo*, 84. In his Congo diaries, Guevara relates that he saw his African soldiers' adamant belief in war magic as a major strategic problem (*Pasajes*, 23–4).

17 'Internacionalismo democrático.' Félix Toledo, quoted in Corzo, *Cubanos combatiendo*, 68. 'Integré el grupo de cubanos que fue al Congo a luchar contra el castro comunismo [sic], contra esa plaga maldita que azota a gran parte de la humanidad, porque el compromiso de luchar contra el comunismo lo llevamos todos nosotros en nuestros corazones, porque el comunismo es la destrucción del mundo.' Generoso Bringas, *Cubanos combatiendo*, 59. 'Al principio vacilé un poco, pero cuando me dijeron que Ernesto Guevara estaba en ese país, mis convicciones no me dieron otra opción.' Armando Cantillo, *Cubanos combatiendo*, 95.

18 Reginaldo Blanco, quoted in Villafaña, *Cold War in the Congo*, 95 (translation in the original).

19 Villafaña, *Cold War in the Congo*, 146.

20 'Todos teníamos deseos de hacer algo por nuestro país y en contra del comunismo. En realidad queríamos vengarnos por lo que habíamos vivido en Bahía de Cochinos, en fin una revancha si le quieren llamar así.' Federico Flaquer, quoted in Corzo, *Cubanos combatiendo*, 115.

21 See, for instance, https://www.youtube.com/watch?v=XEU401OdG1M; https://www.youtube.com/watch?v=uZd3bBQxpKc; https://www.youtube.com/watch?v=sOM9GHTiKbQ; https://www.youtube.com/watch?v=u5XhG8CEHu0;https://www.youtube.com/watch?v= dKSK3yOU7tA;https://www.facebook.com/asecretlegacy/; https://www.youtube.com/watch?v=UMNxarY3eBE&t=5s; and https://www.youtube.com/watch?v=uZd3bBQxpKc&spfreload=10(all accessed on 3 June 2017).

22 See García, *Havana, USA*; Grenier and Pérez, *Legacy of Exile*; João Felipe Gonçalves, 'The Hero's Many Bodies: Monuments, Nationalism, and Power in Havana and Miami,' PhD diss., University of Chicago, 2012; and Gonçalves, 'Martí versus Martí: Nacionalismo e hegemonia em Havana e Miami,' *Novos Estudos Cebrap* 102 (2014): 73–91.

23 For the concept of public culture, see Akhil Gupta, 'Blurred Boundaries: The Discourse of Corruption, the Culture of Politics, and the Imagined State,' *American Ethnologist* 22, no. 2 (1995): 375–402.

24 Borneman, *Belonging in the Two Berlins*, 17.

25 See García, *Havana, USA*; Grenier and Pérez, *Legacy of Exile*; Pedraza, *Political Disaffection*; Eckstein, *Immigrant Divide*.

26 See Piero Gleijeses, *Conflicting Missions: Havana, Washington, and Africa, 1959–1976* (Chapel Hill, NC: University of North Carolina Press, 2002). See also the Introduction to this volume.

27 Piero Gleijeses, *Conflicting Missions*; Gleijeses, *Visions of Freedom: Havana, Washington, Pretoria, and the Struggle for Southern Africa, 1976–1991* (Chapel Hill, NC: University of North Carolina Press, 2013); and Christine Hatzky, *Cubans in Angola: South–South Cooperation and Transfer of Knowledge, 1976–1991* (Madison: University of Wisconsin Press, 2015).

28 The unique importance of the Cuban presence in Angola is reflected in its recurrence as a topic in this volume (see chapters by Kiriakou and André, and Hatzky in this volume).

[29] 'Era la oportunidad de poder enfrentar directamente a las fuerzas castristas y golpear las ambiciones del comunismo internacional.' Miguel Alvares Gimeno, quoted in Corzo, *Cubanos combatiendo*, 115. My discussion of the Cuban-American military intervention in Angola is based mainly on the testimonies of its participants compiled by Pedro Corzo in this book.

[30] 'Un sólido puente entre cubanos libres y angoleños libres.' Tomás Regalado, 'Al doblar la esquina,' *El Nuevo Herald*, 11 August 1985.

[31] Jonas Savimbi, interview by Tomás Regalado, *Ideal* 8 (1979): 90.

[32] See, for instance, 'Donde mueren los cubanos,' editorial, *El Nuevo Herald*, 12 January 1983; 'La aventura africana de Castro,' editorial, *El Nuevo Herald*, 13 February 1983; Tomás Regalado, 'Angola: La otra versión,' *El Nuevo Herald*, 25 November 1984; Tomás Regalado, 'Al doblar la esquina'; Iván Román, 'Llegan a Miami 26 desertores cubanos,' *El Nuevo Herald*, 10 February 1991.

[33] Alfonso Chardy, 'Radio Martí impedirá que escondan la verdad,' *El Nuevo Herald*, 14 May 1984; Lourdes Meluza, 'Locutores de Miami dicen que su fuerza es la verdad,' *El Nuevo Herald*, 26 May 1985; Andrés Vigliucci, 'Un nuevo estilo de hablar a Cuba,' *El Nuevo Herald*, 26 May 1985; Lourdes Meluza, 'Radio Martí vence interferencia oficial para cubrir papel de Cuba en África,' *El Nuevo Herald*, 10 July 1987.

[34] Miami Medical Team Foundation, *Boletín* (Miami: Miami Medical Team Foundation, November 1990).

[35] Eckstein, *Back from the Future*; Hatzky, *Cubans in Angola*; chs. 4 and 5.

[36] Regarding the 1990 visit of Nelson Mandela to Algiers, see Alcaraz in this volume.

[37] Alejandro Portes and Alex Stepick, *City on the Edge: The Transformation of Miami* (Berkeley: University of California Press, 1996), 140–1, 176–8; Grenier and Pérez, *Legacy of Exile*, 79–80.

[38] See Portes and Stepick, *City on the Edge*; Grenier and Pérez, *Legacy of Exile*; Pedraza, *Political Disaffection*; Eckstein, *Immigrant Divide*.

[39] Quoted in Sandra Dibble and Carl Goldfarb, 'Suárez, 4 Others Denounce Mandela,' *Miami Herald*, 26 June 1990. See also Kimberly Crockett, 'Aumenta polémica por visita de Nelson Mandela a Miami,' *El Nuevo Herald*, 24 June 1990; Carl Goldfarb, 'Mandela Backers, Critics Brace for Momentous Visit,' *Miami Herald*, 28 June 1990.

[40] 'Castro gobierna mediante un apartheid político,' quoted in Andrés Hernández Allende, 'Mandela y sus amigos,' *El Nuevo Herald*, 26 June 1990. '¡Vete a Casa, Mandela!'; 'Fuera, Mandela, aquí tenemos suficientes comunistas,' quoted in Crockett, 'Aumenta polémica.' 'No aprendió nada en los últimos 27 años,' quoted in '¿Qué opina de Mandela?,' *El Nuevo Herald*, 28 June 1990. See also Goldfarb, 'Mandela Backers, Critics'; Ana E. Santiago, 'Grupos de exilio cubano envían cartas a Mandela,' *El Nuevo Herald*, 28 June 1990; 'Mensaje a Mandela,' *El Nuevo Herald*, 28 June 1990; and Ramón Mestre, 'Mandela entre la moral y la política,' *El Nuevo Herald*, 29 June 1990.

[41] Corzo, 'Exilio cubano prepara una protesta,' *El Nuevo Herald*, 26 June 1990; Kimberly Crockett and Elinor Burkett, 'Mandela's Arrival in Miami Low Key,' *Miami Herald*, 28 June 1990; Kimberly Crockett, Elinor Burkett and Karen Branch, 'Grass-Roots Welcome Counters Official Snubs,' *Miami Herald*, 29 June 1990; and Gladys Nieves and Iván Román, 'Expresiones de apoyo y rechazo recibieron al líder sudafricano,' *El Nuevo Herald*, 29 June 1990; Howard French, 'Mandela Travels to Miami amid Protests over Castro,' *New York Times*, 29 June 1990; Carl Goldfarb, 'Mandela's Visit Prompts Rerun of Old Ethnic Battles,' *Miami Herald*, 1 July 1990.

[42] Goldfarb, 'Mandela's Visit Prompts Rerun of Old Ethnic Battles'; Nieves and Román, 'Expresiones de apoyo y rechazo'; Dibble and Goldfarb, 'Suárez, 4 Others'; Goldfarb, 'Blacks Reject Suárez's Olive Branch on Mandela,' *Miami Herald*, 27 June 1990; Carl Goldfarb and David Hancock, 'Presionan a la alcaldía líderes negros,' *El Nuevo Herald*, 27 June 1990; 'Refusal to Honor Mandela Outrages Blacks in Florida,' *Los Angeles Times*, 27 June 1990; and Charles White, 'Mandela Slap Is Self-Serving and Insensitive,' *Miami Herald*, 28 June 1990.

[43] Marvin Dunn, *Black Miami in the Twentieth Century* (Gainesville: University Press of Florida, 1997); Portes and Stepick, *City on the Edge*.

[44] Tony Pugh, 'A Biracial Blueprint for Change: Boycott Ends with Pact,' *Miami Herald*, 13 May 1993; Gail Epstein, 'Smith: Mandela Snub Convenient "Hook" for Boycott,' *Miami Herald*, 13 June 1993; Andrea Robinson, 'Mandela to Receive a Belated Apology,' *Miami Herald*, 8 July 2003; Jim DeFede, 'Penelas' Apology Too Little, Too Late,' *Miami Herald*, 15 July 2003; and Charles Rabin, 'Mandela Visit to Miami Beach Sparked Black Boycott, Caused Change,' *Miami Herald*, 5 December 2013.

[45] Portes and Stepick, *City on the Edge*, 138.

[46] Portes and Stepick, *City on the Edge*, 199.

[47] See note 6.

[48] Alan A. Aja, *Miami's Forgotten Cubans: Race, Racialization, and the Miami Afro-Cuban Experience* (New York: Palgrave Macmillan, 2016).

[49] See, for instance, Alejandro de la Fuente, *A Nation for All: Race, Inequality, and Politics in Twentieth-Century Cuba* (Chapel Hill, NC: University of North Carolina Press, 2001); Mark Sawyer, *Racial Politics in Post-Revolutionary Cuba* (Cambridge: Cambridge University Press, 2006); Pablo Rodríguez Ruiz et al., *Las relaciones raciales en Cuba* (Havana: Fundación Fernando Ortiz, 2010); and Kristina Wirtz, *Performing Afro-Cuba: Image, Voice, Spectacle in the Making of Race and History* (Chicago: University of Chicago Press, 2014).

[50] See Fuente, *A Nation for All*; Eckstein, *Back from the Future*; and Sawyer, *Racial Politics*. See also Introduction, and the chapter by Tsafack in this volume.

[51] Dariel Alarcón Ramírez (aka Benigno), quoted in Villafaña, *Cold War*, 124. This phenotypical selection was not devoid of ironies: it was a white Argentinian who commanded these troops, and the Simbas apparently refused to take orders from black Cubans (Gleijeses, *Conflicting Missions*, 145).

[52] Jorge Domínguez, *Cuba: Order and Revolution* (Cambridge, MA: Harvard University Press, 1978), 354.

[53] See Gleijeses, *Conflicting Missions*; Gabriel García Márquez, *Operación Carlota* (Lima: Mosca Azul Editores, 1977). See also Introduction and the chapter by Hatzky in this volume.

[54] Field visit by the author, January 2016; and Ventura de Jesús, 'El legado de Triunvirato,' *Granma*, 4 November 2015.

[55] See Gleijeses, *Conflicting Missions* and *Visions of Freedom*.

[56] Corzo, *Cubanos combatiendo*, 66, 77.

[57] 'Era claro para un buen grupo de la población negra que la estrategia de Castro había derivado en un mecanismo racista . . . En un momento de la 'década africana' prácticamente todos los embajadores de Cuba en África eran negros; sin embargo, los asignados en el resto del mundo a excepción del Caribe eran blancos: Las tropas enviadas al continente eran desproporcionadamente negras; los muertos, también.' Eduardo Ulibarri, 'El derrumbe del afrocastrismo,' *El Nuevo Herald*, 7 June 1991.

[58] Tim Elfrink, 'Recall Tomás Regalado,' *Miami New Times*, 28 July 2011.

[59] Sawyer, *Racial Politics*, 61.
[60] See Fuente, *A Nation for All*; and Rodríguez Ruiz et al., *Relaciones raciales.*
[61] See Kwame Anthony Appiah, *In My Father's House: Africa in the Philosophy of Culture* (New York: Oxford University Press, 1992) and V.Y. Mudimbe, *The Idea of Africa* (Bloomington: Indiana University Press, 1994).
[62] The same sort of claim is analysed, for Cubans based in the island, in the chapter by Argyriadis in this volume. I thank Kali Argyriadis deeply for her insightful and useful comments about this section of my chapter.
[63] Brown, *Santería Enthroned*, 89.
[64] Palmié, *Cooking of History*, 71.
[65] Brown, *Santería Enthroned*, 94.
[66] Alejandro Frigerio, 'Re-Africanization in Secondary Religious Diasporas: Constructing a World Religion,' *Civilisations* 51 (2004): 39–60.
[67] Palmié, *Cooking of History*, 21, 114–15.
[68] Palmié, *Cooking of History*, 64, emphasis in the original.
[69] Palmié, *Cooking of History*, 133–4.
[70] Jeff Levy-Hinte, *Soul Power* (New York: Antidote Films, 2008), film.
[71] Levy-Hinte, *Soul Power*; Leon Gast, *The Fania All-Stars Live in Africa* (New York: Fania Records, 2012), DVD.
[72] Fernando Ortiz, 'The Human Factors of Cubanidad,' trans. João Felipe Gonçalves and Gregory Duff Morton, *Hau: Journal of Ethnographic Theory* 4, no. 3 (2014): 462.
[73] Palmié, *Cooking of History*, 101.

REFERENCES

Aja, Alan A. *Miami's Forgotten Cubans: Race, Racialization, and the Miami Afro-Cuban Experience*. New York: Palgrave Macmillan, 2016.

Appiah, Kwame Anthony. *In My Father's House: Africa in the Philosophy of Culture*. New York: Oxford University Press, 1992.

Argyriadis, Kali and Stefania Capone. '*Cubanía* et *santería*: Les enjeux politiques de la transnationalisation religieuse (La Havane–Miami).' *Civilisations* 51 (2004): 81–137.

Borneman, John. *Belonging in the Two Berlins: Kin, State, Nation*. Cambridge: Cambridge University Press, 1992.

Brown, David. *Santería Enthroned: Art, Ritual, and Innovation in an Afro-Cuban Religion*. Chicago: University of Chicago Press, 2003.

Corzo, Pedro. *Cubanos combatiendo el castrocomunismo en África*. Miami: Instituto de la Memoria Histórica Cubana contra el Totalitarismo, 2014.

Domínguez, Jorge. *Cuba: Order and Revolution*. Cambridge, MA: Harvard University Press, 1978.

Dunn, Marvin. *Black Miami in the Twentieth Century*. Gainesville: University Press of Florida, 1997.

Eckstein, Susan. *Back from the Future: Cuba under Castro*. London: Routledge, 2003.

Eckstein, Susan. *The Immigrant Divide: How Cuban Americans Changed the US and Their Homeland*. New York: Routledge, 2009.

Frigerio, Alejandro. 'Re-Africanization in Secondary Religious Diasporas: Constructing a World Religion.' *Civilisations* 51 (2004): 39–60.

Fuente, Alejandro de la. *A Nation for All: Race, Inequality, and Politics in Twentieth-Century Cuba*. Chapel Hill, NC: University of North Carolina Press, 2001.

García, María Cristina. *Havana, USA: Cuban Exiles and Cuban Americans in South Florida, 1959–1994*. Berkeley: University of California Press, 1996.

García Márquez, Gabriel. *Operación Carlota.*Lima: Mosca Azul Editores, 1977.

Gast, Leon. *The Fania All-Stars Live in Africa*. New York: Fania Records, 2012, DVD.

Gleijeses, Piero. *Conflicting Missions: Havana, Washington, and Africa, 1959–1976*. Chapel Hill, NC: University of North Carolina Press, 2002.

Gleijeses, Piero. *Visions of Freedom: Havana, Washington, Pretoria, and the Struggle for Southern Africa, 1976–1991*. Chapel Hill, NC: University of North Carolina Press, 2013.

Gonçalves, João Felipe. 'Martí versus Martí: Nacionalismo e hegemonia em Havana e Miami.' *Novos Estudos Cebrap* 102 (2014): 73–91.

Gonçalves, João Felipe. 'The Hero's Many Bodies: Monuments, Nationalism, and Power in Havana and Miami.' PhD diss., University of Chicago, 2012.

González Barrios, René. 'Girón: La lección.' *Iberoamericanskie Tetradi / Cuadernos Iberoamericanos* 4, no. 10 (2015): 27–34.

Grenier, Guillermo and Lisandro Pérez. *The Legacy of Exile: Cubans in the United States*. Boston: Allyn and Bacon, 2003.

Grenier, Guillermo and Alex Stepick, eds. *Miami Now! Immigration, Ethnicity and Social Change*. Gainesville: University of Florida Press, 1992.

Guevara, Ernesto Che. *Pasajes de la guerra revolucionaria: Congo*. Milan: Mondadori, 2005.

Gupta, Akhil. 'Blurred Boundaries: The Discourse of Corruption, the Culture of Politics, and the Imagined State.' *American Ethnologist* 22, no. 2 (1995): 375–402.

Hatzky, Christine. *Cubans in Angola: South–South Cooperation and Transfer of Knowledge, 1976–1991.*Madison: University of Wisconsin Press, 2015.

Levy-Hinte, Jeff. *Soul Power*. New York: Antidote Films, 2008, film.

Mudimbe, V. Y. *The Idea of Africa*. Bloomington: Indiana University Press, 1994.

Ortiz, Fernando. 'The Human Factors of Cubanidad.' Translated by João Felipe Gonçalves and Gregory Duff Morton. *Hau: Journal of Ethnographic Theory* 4, no. 3 (2014): 445–80.

Palmié, Stephan. *The Cooking of History: How Not to Study Afro-Cuban Religion*. Chicago: University of Chicago Press, 2013.

Pedraza, Silvia. *Political Disaffection in Cuba's Revolution and Exodus*. Cambridge: Cambridge University Press, 2007.

Pérez-Stable, Marifeli. *The Cuban Revolution: Origins, Course and Legacy*. Oxford and New York: Oxford University Press, 1993.

Portes, Alejandro and Alex Stepick. *City on the Edge: The Transformation of Miami*. Berkeley: University of California Press, 1996.

Rodríguez Ruiz, Pablo, LázaraY. Carrazana Fuentes, Rodrigo Espina Prieto, Ana Julia García Dally, Estrella González Noriega, Niurka Núñez González, María Magdalena Pérez Álvarez, Hernán Tirado Toirac and Odalys Buscarón Ochoa. *Las relaciones raciales en Cuba*. Havana: Fundación Fernando Ortiz, 2010.

Routon, Kenneth. *Hidden Powers of the State in the Cuban Imagination*. Gainesville: University Press of Florida, 2012.

Saussure, Ferdinand de. *Course in General Linguistics*. Peru, IL: Open Court, 1986.

Sawyer, Mark. *Racial Politics in Post-Revolutionary Cuba*. Cambridge: Cambridge University Press, 2006.

Villafaña, Frank R. *Cold War in the Congo: The Confrontation of Cuban Military Forces, 1960–1967*. New Brunswick: Transaction Publishers, 2012.

Wirtz, Kristina. *Performing Afro-Cuba: Image, Voice, Spectacle in the Making of Race and History*. Chicago: University of Chicago Press, 2014.

CONTRIBUTORS

Emmanuel Alcaraz is a historian and an associate researcher at University Paris X Nanterre and at the Research Centre on Contemporary Maghreb in Tunis. He has authored numerous articles on memory and patrimonialisation in Maghreb, and on sites of memory related to the war of independence in Algeria. He has published as well several works about Libyan migrants in Tunisia, transitional justice after the Tunisian revolution in 2011, and the workers' movement in this country. His book, *Les lieux de mémoire de la guerre d'indépendance algérienne*, was published by Karthala in 2017. He is writing a new book about engagement and distance regarding the Algerian war of independence and its memories.

Bernardo J. Capamba André is completing a PhD in history at Sorbonne University. His dissertation focuses on the relations between Angola and Cuba between 1961 and 1991, under the supervision of Professor Luiz Felipe de Alencastro. Bernardo participated in the organising committee of the Third Meeting of Young Researchers in African Studies (JCEA) held in Paris in January 2016. He was a scientific co-editor of the special issue of *Afriche e Orienti* on 'International Solidarities and the Liberation of the Portuguese Colonies', published in 2017.

Kali Argyriadis is an anthropologist, a researcher at the Institute of Research for Development (IRD) and holds a position at URMIS at University Paris Diderot. She holds a PhD (1997) from the École des hautes études en sciences sociales (Paris), for which she conducted two years of ethnographic research in Havana. She carried out extensive research in Cuba and Mexico, focusing on the study of Cuban religious and artistic practices, their patrimonialisation, and their transnationalisation and relocalisation in Veracruz State. She was the coordinator of the research project 'Transnacionalización religiosa de los Sures: entre etnicización y universalización' (www.ird.fr/relitrans). She is currently focusing on the epistemology of Afro-Cuban studies, and is the coordinator of the research programme 'Epistemología comparada de la disciplina antropológica a partir de Cuba y Haití' (http://meso.hypotheses.org/159). She has published numerous books and papers, including *La religión à La Havane: Actualité des représentations et des pratiques cultuelles havanaises* (1999); and, with S. Capone, R. de la Torre and A. Mary, *En sentido contrario: Transnacionalización de religiones africanas y latinoamericanas* (2012).

Giulia Bonacci is a historian, a researcher at the Institute of Research for Development (IRD) and holds a position at URMIS at the University of Côte d'Azur. She has a PhD (2007) from the École des hautes études en sciences sociales (Paris), and an MA from the School of Oriental and African Studies (London). She studies historical and contemporary relations between the Caribbean and Africa. Her book *Exodus! Heirs and Pioneers, Rastafari Return to Ethiopia* was published by the University of the West Indies Press (2015) and received the IndieFab Book of the Year Award in 2015 and the Choice Outstanding Academic Title in 2017. Her research is based on archival, print and oral sources, and is regularly published in academic journals as well as in the cultural press, in French and English.

Adrien Delmas holds a PhD (2010) in history from the École des hautes études en sciences sociales in Paris. He is currently director of the Centre Jacques Berque, Rabat (USR 3136) and an associate researcher at the Institut des mondes africains, Paris (CNRS UMR 8171). From 2012 to 2016, he was the scientific director of the French Institute of South Africa. He has published on travel writing in the early modern world, including *Written Culture in a Colonial Context: Africa and the Americas 1500–1900* (Brill, 2012) and *Les voyages de l'écrit: Culture écrite et expansion européenne à l'époque moderne* (Honoré Champion, 2013). He is also the principal researcher at Globafrica, a research programme on African medieval history (eleventh to seventeenth centuries).

Elina Djebbari is a postdoctoral research associate at King's College London for the ERC-funded project 'Modern Moves' led by Prof. Ananya Jahanara Kabir. Her research project investigates the 'return' of Caribbean music and dance practices in Africa. Her PhD in ethnomusicology from the École des hautes études en sciences sociales in Paris dealt with the national cultural policies and the heritage process, using traditional music dance performances in Mali, in the National Ballet, private dance companies and the state-sponsored festival Biennale artistique et culturelle.

João Felipe Gonçalves is assistant professor in the Department of Anthropology at the University of São Paulo. He holds a PhD in anthropology from the University of Chicago, and has conducted archival and ethnographic research in Havana and Miami for over 15 years. He is currently working on a book on monuments and Cuban nationalism in Havana and Miami. His research interests include nationalism, urban space, state socialism, diasporas, and historical representations.

Charlotte Grabli holds a PhD (2019) in history from the École des hautes études en sciences sociales in Paris, and she is at present conducting postdoctoral research in the ERC-funded project 'MUSICOL' coordinated by the École normale supérieure (ENS). Her research focuses on Afro-Atlantic musical circulations, and on the sound and musical cultures of various African metropolises, mainly Johannesburg, Léopoldville (now Kinshasa), and Brazzaville during the late colonial context (1930–60). She is the author of the chapter 'The Listeners' City: Radio, African Urbanity and the Appropriation of Space in the Colonial Town of Léopoldville during the 1950s' in K. Balogun et al. (eds), *Everyday Life on the African Continent: Fun, Leisure, and Expressivity*, forthcoming from Ohio University Press.

Christine Hatzky is professor of Latin American and Caribbean history at Leibniz University in Hanover, Germany. She is director of the Centre for Atlantic and Global Studies (CAGS) and regional director of the Centre for Advanced Latin American Studies (CALAS) in Guadalajara, Mexico. Her specialty in research is the social and political history of Mexico and Central America, Cuba and the Caribbean as well as the history of Africa, especially the Portuguese-speaking countries. She has written a biography of the Cuban student leader Julio A. Mella, entitled *Julio A. Mella: Una biografía (1903–1929)* (2008). Her latest book, *Cubans in Angola: South–South Cooperation and Transfer of Knowledge 1976–1991* (2015), deals with the transnational phenomenon of internationalist solidarity and civil cooperation between Cuba and Angola. This publication was awarded the Luciano Tomassini Prize of the Latin American Studies Association (LASA) in 2016. Her current research deals with the role of civil society in peace and transition processes in Central American countries after the civil wars of the 1980s.

Héloïse Kiriakou holds a PhD in history from the Institut des mondes africains (IMAF) at the University of Paris 1 (Panthéon-Sorbonne). Her dissertation is entitled 'Brazzaville: Laboratory of the Congolese Revolution (1963–1968)'. Using a micro-local approach, she analyses the involvement of youth activists and their influence on the political process. On this subject, she has also written (with M. Swagler) a chapter, 'Autonomous Youth Organizations' Conquest of Political Power in Congo-Brazzaville, 1963–1968' in F. Blum et al. (eds), *Etudiants africains en mouvements: Contribution à une histoire des années 1968* (2017). Her work is part of a renewal of studies of African socialisms. She has participated in several symposiums on this topic in Paris (2016), Dakar (2017), New York (2018) and Brazzaville (2019), and she is a scientific co-editor of the book *African Socialisms / Socialisms in Africa* (forthcoming 2020). Currently she is working from a comparative perspective on the constitution of the first single-party regimes, using as examples Congo-Brazzaville, Benin and Angola.

Michel Luntumbue has a degree in political science and international relations from the Université Libre Bruxelles (ULB). He is passionate about Cuba's history. He devoted his graduate work to the study of citizenship and ethnicity under the first Cuban Republic (1902–40). He is the author of various studies of development issues, North–South relations, and the dynamics of social movements in Southern countries. After a career in the field of cooperation, where he has supervised development projects in West Africa, Central Africa and Latin America including Cuba, he is currently a researcher and political analyst in the field of conflict prevention and peace-building.

Pablo Rodríguez Ruiz is a social anthropologist, a senior researcher, and director of the Department of Ethnology at the Instituto Cubano de Antropología (Cuban Institute of Anthropology, ICAN) in Havana. Following his fieldwork in Angola, he published a book, *Los Nhaneca-Humbi de Angola, procesos etnosociales* (1996). He is a specialist in race relations, marginality and systems of resourcefulness in Cuba. He is the author of numerous works, including *Los marginales de las Alturas del Mirador: Un estudio de caso*; and *Las relaciones raciales en Cuba: Estudios contemporaneos* with N. Núñez González Gonzales, M. Perez Alvarez and O. Buscaron Ochoa, both published in Havana by Fundación Fernando Ortiz in 2011.

Delmas Tsafack holds a PhD in the history of international relations from the University of Dschang in Cameroon. He is now serving as political and economic affairs officer at the Embassy of the Kingdom of Belgium in Yaoundé, Cameroon. He has been programme officer at the Muntu Institute, Yaoundé, and a researcher at the Administrative, Social and Political Research Group (GRAPS) of the University of Yaoundé 2. His research interests include the history and regional policy of Equatorial Guinea, the foreign policy of small states, regional integration, and international relations theories. He has published various articles on Equatorial Guinea. He has participated in a dozen international conferences and is a member of several scientific organisations such as the Council for the Development of Social Science Research in Africa (CODESRIA), the Cameroon History Society (CHS) and the International Political Science Association (IPSA).

INDEX

Page numbers in *italics* indicate photos, maps or tables.

B

S

CPSIA information can be obtained
at www.ICGtesting.com
Printed in the USA
JSHW020748020122
21716JS00001B/36